A HISTORY OF MODERN INDONE

Although Indonesia has the fourth largest population in the world, its history is still relatively unfamiliar and understudied. Adrian Vickers takes the reader on a journey across the social and political landscape of modern Indonesia, starting with the country's origins under the Dutch in the early twentieth century, and the subsequent anti-colonial revolution which led to independence in 1949. Thereafter the spotlight is on the 1950s, a crucial period in the formation of Indonesia as a new nation, which was followed by the Sukarno years, and the anti-Communist massacres of the 1960s when General Suharto took over as president. The concluding chapters chart the fall of Suharto's New Order after thirty-two years in power, and the subsequent political and religious turmoil which culminated in the Bali bombings in 2002. Drawing on insights from literature, art and anthropology, Vickers portrays a complex and resilient people struggling out of a troubled past.

ADRIAN VICKERS is Professor of Asian Studies at the University of Wollongong. He is author of the acclaimed *Bali: a Paradise Created* (1989), as well as many other scholarly and popular works on Indonesia.

A HISTORY OF MODERN INDONESIA

ADRIAN VICKERS

University of Wollongong

CAMBRIDGE UNIVERSITY PRESS
Cambridge, New York, Melbourne, Madrid, Cape Town, Singapore, São Paulo

CAMBRIDGE UNIVERSITY PRESS
The Edinburgh Building, Cambridge CB2 2RU, UK

Published in the United States of America by Cambridge University Press, New York

www.cambridge.org
Information on this title: www.cambridge.org/9780521834933

First published 2005

Printed in the United Kingdom at the University Press, Cambridge

A catalogue record for this book is available from the British Library

Library of Congress Cataloguing in Publication data

ISBN-13 978-0-521-83493-3 hardback
ISBN-10 0-521-83493-7 hardback
ISBN-13 978-0-521-54262-3 paperback
ISBN-10 0-521-54262-6 paperback

Contents

Figures

Maps

Acknowledgements

This book is the product of over thirty years of conversations with hundreds of Indonesians – at times I have not listened as attentively as I might, and for that I ask forgiveness, *sampunayang titiang yening wenten kirang langkung.*

Footnotes cannot do justice to my debt to all the people who have influenced me. My mentors and colleagues at Sydney University played the strongest role in shaping my understanding of Indonesia, in particular Peter Worsley and the late Boy Joseph, along with Jenny Alexander, Paul Alexander, Richard Chauvel, Linda Connor, Tony Day, Rudy de Ionge, Helen Jarvis, Michael van Langenberg, Thea van Lennep, Jennifer Lindsay, Doug Miles, George Quinn, David Reeve, Kathy Robinson, Raechelle Rubinstein and Jon Sumaryono. Thanks particularly to Max Lane for his insights into Pramoedya's thinking.

In Bali the late A. A. Kompiang Gede and his family, and the late Gusti Ngurah Bagus gave me a different view of Indonesian modernity, as did my friends in Kamasan and Batuan villages. In more recent years Sutjaja and Ari, Nyoman Darma Putra, Dr Djelantik, Putu Suasta, Ngurah Kariadi, Agus Waworunto, Janggo Paramartha and Gus Surya helped me in many ways, as did particularly the *Latitudes* gang, Degung Santikarma, Lesley Dwyer, Gung Alit and Hani. In Jakarta the Appono family, Tatap Loebis, Chusnul Mariyah, Reni and Alex Winata; in Yogya Syafri Sairin, Abdul Haris, Irwan Abdullah, Bambang Purwanto and many others at UGM showed me different sides of Indonesia, and I still remember fondly the hospitality of the late Umar Kayam.

In other places Geroge Aditjondro, Jan Breman, Howard Dick, Anthony Forge, Herb Feith, Hildred Geertz, Kunang Helmi, Mark Hobart, John Ingleson, David Jenkins, Ward Keeler, Philip Kitley, John Legge, Ben Maddison, Jamie Mackie, Hamish McDonald, Henk Maier, Lyn Parker, Michel Picard, Ratna Saptari, Tony Reid, Henk Schulte Nordholt, Hersri Setiawan, Paul Stange, Heather Sutherland, Esther

Velthoen, Carol Warren, Andrew Wells and a number of others, particularly through collaboration at the Centre for Asia Pacific Social Transformation Studies at Wollongong University, provided me with support, advice and/or comments that have found their way into this book. Equally important have been the discussions, sharing of information and ideas of my students, namely all those who have experienced this book as HIST379 at Wollongong University, and my PhD students, especially Adriana Elisabeth, Anandita Axioma, Jo Coghlan, Vicki Crinis, Stephen Fitzpatrick, Michele Ford, Rob Goodfellow, Charles Hawksley, Marianne Hulsbosch, Phil King, M. Dwi Marianto, Julia Martinez and Susanna Rizzo.

As well as contributing to my general world-view, the following people have made important direct contributions to this book: Bob Elson in first putting my name forward to write it, and for his other encouragement and support over the years. Robert Cribb, Jan Elliott, Keith Foulcher, Bill Frederick, Elsbeth Locher-Scholten, Anton Lucas, Indriati Kurniana, Ari Poespodiharjo and Nyoman Wijaya all commented on chapters, but bear no responsibility for my views or errors. Safrina Thristiawati provided me with crucial materials from the 1950s and 1960s and useful comments and advice. Leo Haks kindly provided many of the illustrations.

The home editorial team, Hazel, Emma, and particularly Fran Moloney, have helped this book make sense. My parents first encouraged my interest in Indonesia in the early 1970s when they supported me to go to Indonesia. Sadly my mother did not live to see this book's completion.

A note on spelling, pronunciation and names

Indonesian has gone through several different spelling systems, and there is generally great inconsistency between public uses of these systems. For the sake of simplicity I have generally used the spelling system introduced in 1972, although Pramoedya prefers the Dutch-era 'oe' instead of 'u' in the spelling of his name, likewise Dr Djelantik prefers the pre-1972 'dj' instead of 'j'.

Syllables in Indonesian words are generally pronounced with even weight; 'a' is pronounced like the English 'u' in 'up'; 'e' is usually pronounced like English 'step' or 'a' in 'day'; 'i' is pronounced as in 'hid'; 'u' is pronounced like 'o' in 'do'; 'c' is pronounced like English 'ch'; 'sy' is pronounced 'sh'. Javanese is transcribed variably in the sources used, the 'a' is more like Danish 'å', and so is usually rendered as 'o', but inconsistently (e.g. 'Ronggowarsito').

Although many Indonesians have adopted the use of family names or surnames, there is a great deal of variation in personal names in Indonesia. Some people have only one name, such as Suharto and Sukarno. Many names also incorporate titles, such as the Sumatran aristocratic title Sutan in Sutan Syahrir's name. It is quite common to change names at different stages in life, as when Suwardi Suryaningrat changed his name to Ki Hajar Dewantoro at the age of forty. Many people are known by abbreviated names for simplicity, as with Abdurrahman Wahid, know as 'Gus Dur', which combines a Javanese familiar title, 'Gus' (short for Gusti but sometimes Agus or Bagus), and an abbreviation of his main name.

Chronology

1870	Beginning of a 'Liberal Policy' of deregulated exploitation of the Netherlands East Indies
1873	Beginning of the Aceh War
1888	Founding of the packet steam-ship line *KPM*
1890	World depression
1894	Lombok War
1898	General van Heutsz becomes chief-of-staff of Aceh campaign
	Wilhelmina becomes queen of the Netherlands
1901	Ethical Policy proclaimed
1903	Aceh declared conquered
1904	Van Heutsz made Governor General
1907	Raden Mas Tirto Adhi Suryo founds civil servants' association *Sarekat Priyayi*
1908	Budi Utomo proclaimed as first official nationalist movement
	Last Balinese rulers to resist Dutch rule wiped out in battle to the death
1911	Founding by Tirto Adhi Suryo of the Islamic Traders' League
1912	Islamic League (*Sarekat Islam*) becomes first mass-based nationalist party
1914	World War One, the Netherlands is a neutral country in the war
1917	East Indies trade with Europe cut off by the war
	Russian Revolution
1918	Death of Tirto Adhi Suryo
1920	Founding of the Communist Party of the Indies (*PKI*)
	Economic downturn
1925	Birth of Pramoedya Ananta Toer
	Sharp rise in world commodity prices brings prosperity to the Indies
1929	Great Depression

1930	Sukarno's famous nationalist speech, 'Indonesia Accuses', given as defence in his political trial
1940	Germany invades the Netherlands
1941	8 December, US naval base at Pearl Harbor bombed by Japanese
1942	Japan invades the Netherlands East Indies
1945	15 August, Japan surrenders
	17 August, Sukarno and Hatta proclaim Indonesia's independence, signalling the beginning of the Indonesian Revolution
	10 November, Battle of Surabaya
1946	Social revolutions, including Three Regions (*Tiga Daerah*) Revolt
	Republican capital established in Yogyakarta
	Federal states set up by Dutch in outer islands
1947	25 March, Linggajati agreement, first ceasefire
	20 July, first Police Action
1948	Abdication of Queen Wilhelmina
	19 January, Renville Agreement, Van Mook line established between Republican and Dutch territories
	August, fall of Amir Syarifuddin government
	18 September, Madiun Affair
	December, second police action, fall of Yogyakarta to the Dutch, execution of Amir Syarifuddin by Republicans
1949	February, execution of Tan Malaka by Republican Army
	1 August, official ceasefire
	December, Dutch forced to take part in Round Table Agreement
	27 December, Indonesia achieves full sovereignty
1950	Federal states dissolve and Indonesia becomes a unitary Republic
	Korean War brings high prices for rubber and other Indonesian commodities
1955	First national elections
1957	State of war and siege declared, beginning of Guided Democracy
	Dutch enterprises nationalised
1962–3	Irian Jaya (West New Guinea) campaign
1963–5	Confrontation with Malaysia
1965	'30th September Movement' 'Coup' (*Gestapu*) leads to the death of 500,000–1 million people identified as Communists

1966	Sukarno hands over power to Suharto through the 11 March Declaration (*Supersemar*), beginning of the New Order regime
1969	'Act of Free Choice' legitimises Indonesia's control over Irian Jaya
1970	Death of Sukarno
1971	First New Order election
1974	15 January upheavals (*Malari*) end the New Order's 'honeymoon' period
	Pertamina Affair
1975	Invasion of East Timor
1977	National election
	'Normalisation' of university campuses programme
1982	National election
1983	Mysterious killings (*Petrus*)
1984	Tanjung Priok Affair involving killings of Muslims in Jakarta
	Clamp-down on Islamic political leaders
1987	National election
1989	'Openness' campaign announced
	Establishment of Indonesian Muslim Intellectuals' Association, *ICMI*
1992	National election
1994	Press bans end 'Openness'
1996	Death of Tien Suharto
	Attack on Megawati's faction of the *PDI*
	Bre-X or Busang gold mine scandal
1997	Asian financial crisis and drought
	National election
1998	21 May, fall of Suharto, replaced by B. J. Habibie
1999	Legislation to create regional autonomy
	National election
	Referendum leads to political violence and the independence of East Timor
	Abdurrahman Wahid (Gus Dur) becomes president
2001	Abdurrahman Wahid resigns
	Megawati Sukarnoputri becomes president
2004	National election followed by first direct presidential election
	Susilo Bambang Yudhoyono (SBY) becomes president
	26 December, tsunami

Introduction

Indonesia is the fourth largest country in the world, with a population its government estimates at 220 million. It consists of 19,000 islands strung across the equator, some of these no more than sand spits, others like Java and Sumatra, large and densely populated. Two of the world's largest islands, Borneo and New Guinea are partly within Indonesia: Kalimantan is the Indonesian name for its part of Borneo, while Indonesia's half of New Guinea is now called Papua – formerly Irian Jaya. As a country joined by water, Indonesia covers an area as wide as Europe or the United States.

There are over 200 major cultural and language groups on the islands. Java is the most populous island, with over 100 million people packed together on its 132,000 sq. km. Jakarta, the national capital with a population of 15 million, is located on the island of Java. Javanese culture dominates the other cultures of Indonesia, but the main language of the nation is a form of Malay called Bahasa Indonesia or Indonesian.

Indonesia is generally featured in the world's media for political violence and involvement in international terrorism. It has rated at the top of international corruption watch lists, and its president between 1967 and 1998, Suharto, has been named as the head of state who extorted the most personal wealth from his country.

Such negative images do not do justice to the country. It may have the largest Islamic population in the world, with 90 per cent of the population identifying themselves as Muslims, but no more than a few hundred would want to be associated with the fanatical violence of terrorism. Indonesia is not an Islamic state, but rather has a long history of religious tolerance. Before many parts converted to Islam in the fifteenth century, Hinduism and Buddhism were the majority religions, and there are still significant minorities who adhere to these faiths. Chinese temples can be found throughout the archipelago, as well as Protestant and Catholic churches, and even synagogues. There are still many Indonesians who practise ancient forms of ancestor worship or animism, and these earlier spiritual beliefs pervade the observances of the larger religions.

The many religions of Indonesia are part of the cultural richness of this diverse country. Indonesia's famous shadow puppet theatre, the *wayang*, is an ancient art that combines Indian epic tales with indigenous mythology. Indonesia also developed some of the richest textile traditions in the world, the best known of which is *batik*, the art of wax-resist dyeing. Each part of Indonesia has its own wealth of music and theatre, the visual arts, poetry and literature. This diversity and depth of Indonesian culture is a product of openness to new ideas and practices that have come to the islands via millennia of trade with India, China and the rest of the world, the same kind of openness that has embraced shopping malls, mobile phones and DVDs.

In political terms, Indonesia has turned, slowly and hesitatingly, towards democracy, as shown by the mass demonstrations that brought Suharto down. After more than thirty years of military-dominated dictatorship, Indonesians have entered the twenty-first century with a desire to clean up government and make it representative of the people. Indonesia has had far fewer political assassinations than the United States or India – no president has ever been killed. It is safer to walk the streets of major Indonesian cities at night than to walk through some of the inner parts of Sydney or Los Angeles.

Indonesia's historical experience explains its diversity, and why it is a country of paradoxes. Although in earlier times there were kingdoms that embraced large parts of the Indonesian archipelago, Indonesia did not come into existence as a country until the middle of the twentieth century. The physical boundaries of Indonesia were established by the Netherlands when they took over the many islands and made them into a single colony: the Netherlands East Indies. Some parts of Indonesia were ruled by the Dutch for 300 years, others for less than thirty. Dutch rule explains many aspects of Indonesia, because it provided administrative and economic foundations for the modern state. Legal systems, labour relations, urban development and many other aspects of present-day Indonesia were stamped by the Dutch.

Under the Dutch, Indonesians began to conceive of themselves as a nation. After the Japanese invaded Indonesia in 1942, a small group of Indonesians developed that notion of nationalism into a struggle for independence: the Indonesian Revolution of 1945 to 1949, led by Sukarno, Indonesia's first president. When sovereignty was transferred from Dutch to Indonesian hands at the end of the Revolution, Indonesia became one of the new nations of the era of decolonisation. As a new nation it has struggled to balance the interests of different groups and maintain coherence against both the pressures of its own diversity and tensions created by international politics. The present state of Indonesia is as much a product of struggle and the use of force for political ends as it is the realisation of national identity.

Telling the history of modern Indonesia is difficult because a country as huge and heterogeneous as this does not have a single narrative. Most historical accounts have been concerned with the activities of a small group of political leaders, those who created the nationalist movement under the Dutch, led the country to independence, and who have fought amongst themselves to control it ever since. There have been official histories, which play up nationalism and unity in ways that paper over the cracks in the national edifice. These are usually histories of state heroes and big events, and do not say much about the experiences of ordinary Indonesians.

One of the few Indonesians with a coherent and developed vision of the nation's history is the country's most famous novelist, Pramoedya Ananta Toer. Of the 220 million individual stories that could be told about Indonesia, Pramoedya's links the world of politics with everyday life. Pramoedya was born in a small town in Java during the colonial era. His father and mother gave him a strong sense of nationalism and its importance, and in his writings he has wrestled with the problems of Indonesia's national identity. Amongst those writings is a series of four novels about the formation of nationalism, *This Earth of Mankind*, and a series of semi-autobiographical stories about growing up on Java and experiencing Dutch rule, the Japanese invasion and the Indonesian Revolution.

The novels that make up *This Earth of Mankind* provide insights into how Dutch colonial society was riven with contradictions, especially between the desire to control Indonesians and the desire to bring them progress. In these books Pramoedya gives insights into the feeling that developed amongst Indonesians of becoming modern people, desiring emancipation, leading to the need to be an independent nation. What Pramoedya's writings show is that ideas of progress, the modern, and the nation, are contested by different social groups, mirroring the physical struggles of Indonesian history.

The Earth of Mankind begins with the volume of the same name, and portrays a naïve young man, Minke. This character is based on the historical figure of Tirto Adhi Suryo, one of Indonesia's first nationalists. In this novel Minke struggles to rebel against his aristocratic Javanese traditions and come to terms with the wonders of technology and enlightenment promised by the West. An important aspect of modernity brought out in Pramoedya's writings is that tradition becomes a self-conscious process of identifying the older facets of identity and emphasising them. Pramoedya, like other nationalists of his generation, rejects what they call 'feudalism' in tradition, the emphasis on hierarchy that links birth to power.

Pramoedya's novel presents Minke's growing awareness of living in a colonial culture of subjugation. Over this and the next two volumes, readers see through Minke's eyes the processes by which the Dutch took over the islands of Indonesia and exploited them economically, and the developments through which Filipinos, Chinese and other Asians came to form their own senses of national identity. The important elements these novels identify are the growing gulf between different ethnic and class groups in Indonesian society, and the ways this gulf is emphasised by the colonial state; and the awareness of a need for emancipation that grows out of the frustrations of colonialism, emancipation that includes the struggle of women for recognition. Pramoedya gives a detailed impression of urban life and its relations to colonial modernity, and in the last novel gives a detailed portrayal of how Indonesians became their own torturers under the colonial system, shown through the figure of an Indonesian spy for the Dutch who is responsible for the death of Minke. These facets of the experience of colonial rule are examined in the first three chapters of my book through focusing on Pramoedya's identification with Tirto's life.

Pramoedya wrote his novels to convey how his parents' generation grew to become nationalists. His father, a nationalist teacher, was born in the same year as the fictional Minke, and through Minke, Pramoedya examines his father's frustrations as a nationalist left powerless by the efficiency of the Dutch suppression of indigenous politicians, a powerlessness that led him to gambling as an outlet for his stymied political desires.

Pramoedya moved to the city, and worked as a journalist during the Japanese period. He was gaoled by the Dutch for supporting Indonesia's struggle for independence, then gaoled during the regime of President Sukarno for being outspoken in support of Indonesia's Chinese minority. He has described life in Indonesia's capital, Jakarta, in a way that no other author has, by taking his readers into the backstreets and slums. As someone active in left-wing cultural politics, he was caught up in Indonesia's major upheaval, the purge of Communists that began in 1965, and led to the killing of at least 500,000 people. It was this purge that brought Sukarno's successor, Suharto, to power. Pramoedya was one of hundreds of thousands gaoled by Suharto's military-led government in the aftermath of the purge, and he spent fourteen years in prison, most of those in the harsh conditions on the remote prison-island of Buru, in eastern Indonesia. There, when eventually given paper by his gaolers, he wrote *This Earth of Mankind*. Returning to Jakarta in 1979, he spent almost twenty more years under house arrest, his books banned. When Suharto fell Pramoedya was free to become a public commentator and publish again.

Other key prison writings by Pramoedya give detailed insights into his personal experiences and the ways that they have been incorporated into his writings. His prison letters and articles, published as *A Mute's Soliloquy*, give a moving insight into what it was like to live through the colonial period, the Japanese occupation of Indonesia and the Revolution. He tells how he used his personal experiences as the basis of his early fiction – accounts of life in the countryside and the city which convey the sense of a struggle for survival in the face of unbearable suffering. Pramoedya's many novellas and short stories on the Revolution give more detailed guides to his formative experience of this struggle, and chapters 4 and 5 of this book draw on them to connect the personal to the larger scheme of political and economic changes of these periods.

Pramoedya's writings echo his bitter life experiences, showing what so many millions of Indonesians went through as Indonesia turned from a parliamentary democracy, to a semi-dictatorship under Sukarno, and then an authoritarian regime Suharto called his New Order. They evidence the cynicism that many Indonesians still feel about the promises of political leaders, beginning with the disillusion of the national revolution of 1945–9 that did not bring the bright new world of prosperity that many people had hoped for. In his writings from the 1940s and 1950s he conveyed the experience of daily life for people who live in grinding poverty at the whims of politicians. Fictional and non-fictional accounts merge in the clear realism of his prose. Chapters 5 and 6 trace this process, up to the beginning of Pramoedya's long imprisonment. The experiences of imprisonment form a counterpoint to the prosperity that Suharto brought about in the nation, changes discussed in chapters 7 and 8.

Pramoedya's life and writings are a guide to understanding modern Indonesian history, an epic and highly serious vision of the story of Indonesia as a nationalist tragedy that began at the turn of the twentieth century, and was betrayed by Suharto's New Order. Any history writing involves leaving out most of 'what happened', and by selecting a series of themes about culture and society, Pramoedya's writings provide an alternative historical agenda, one concerned with power and everyday experience. They are also writings that are jaundiced, partial and partisan, elevating nationalism to the centre of Indonesian life, arguing that nationalism should be rooted in the people, and that it should be a modern nationalism, for which most aspects of traditional culture are irrelevant. In this they differ from the works of some of his contemporaries, for example the novelists Umar Kayam (1932–2002) and Father W. S. Mangunwijaya (1929–99). Kayam was an author, actor, film-maker and academic who explored tradition as the basis of modern Indonesian culture, and in particular used the so-called 'feudal' traditions of Central Java to find elements of value for Indonesians as a new people. One of the great contradictions of Indonesia is its dependence on ancient characteristics – temples such as Borobudur, or royal traditions – to define a distinctive modern national personality. Mangunwijaya, a Javanese Catholic priest, engineer and writer, combined the *wayang* shadow play with a James Joyce-style of modernism to criticise the moral corruption and materialism of his country.

Mangunwijaya wrote his novel *Durga Umayi* as a reply to *This Earth of Mankind*, depicting the country as the product of the tail-end of colonial rule, and of a struggle so full of contradiction that it is almost farcical. Mangunwijaya took on the ancient Javanese characterisation of the world as part of a mad age, where survival depends on coming to terms with contradiction.

Still, Pramoedya's descriptions of life in the slums of Jakarta or in the prison camps on Buru are written in hope, a faith in humanity's struggle for a better life. In his fiction he tries to move outside himself to illuminate the lives of ordinary people under tragic circumstances. While he was still banned, Indonesians and foreigners alike savoured Pramoedya's writings as forbidden fruit, as his writings were part of continuing dissent against the Suharto regime, dissent that ultimately contributed to the disintegration of that rule.

His works have also been immensely influential in the writing of foreign histories of Indonesia because they have provided an Indonesian perception of historical experience that is an alternative to the official view. During the Suharto era the discipline of history was heavily repressed, and starved of its basic resources – access to archives and critical debate. In the post-Suharto era there has been a flood of books and articles in Indonesia that challenge earlier accepted histories, but most of these have been little more than attempts to counter New Order propaganda. The republication of Pramoedya's works has been one wave of this flood, contributing to a new kind of public debate which promises to revivify public history. The fall of Suharto has had the paradoxical effect of allowing Pramoedya to return to being a major public intellectual, as he was in the 1950s and early 1960s, but at the same time creating new political agendas for Islam and ethnic struggle that are outside Pramoedya's vision of Indonesia. The waters have still to settle.

Indonesia is a place of tragedy and farce, of tradition and modernity. Umar Kayam's emphasis on traditional roots for a new nation answers the need for depth in a country uneasy with the modern. He and Mangunwijaya are both much more in touch than Pramoedya with the spiritual and religious interpretations that most Indonesians employ to make sense of their lives. The tragedy of Indonesian history is its continued pattern of exploitation, lives lost and opportunities squandered. The farce is of the surreal aspects in a disjointed nation, but mixed with these is an enduring optimism that has enabled Indonesians to salvage a sense of shared purpose out of their existence in a state created under foreign rule.

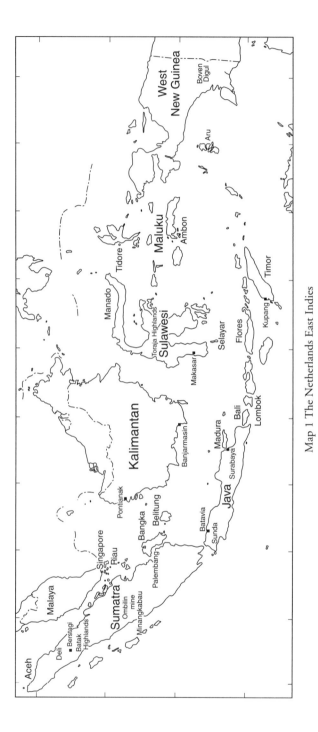

Map 1 The Netherlands East Indies

CHAPTER I

Our colonial soil

> Having spent myself the greatest and the best part of my life in the
> Dutch colonial service and having pawned my heart to the welfare of
> the Dutch East Indies and the people over there ...
> (former Governor General Jonkheer Mr A. C. D. de Graeff)[1]

Before 1945 there was no Indonesia, but rather a collection of islands spread
across the Equator that the Dutch made into the Netherlands East Indies.
In 1898 a new queen, Wilhelmina, ascended the throne of the Kingdom of
the Netherlands. Wilhelmina's tropical empire, known simply as the
Indies, numbered more than 28 million subjects on the prime island of
Java, and some 7 million others on what were referred to as the Outer
Islands, although not all of these as yet were under Dutch rule.[2] Although
she ruled for the rest of the colonial period, Wilhelmina never visited her
colony. She never experienced the sudden monsoonal downpours, the
green landscapes dominated by volcanoes, or the spicy heat, but every
year her birthday was celebrated there, with night markets and festive
arches.

What was it like for the Dutch, ruling that vast archipelago of Indonesia?
The Dutch made up a special, upper social class of the Indies – soldiers,
administrators, managers, teachers, pioneers. They lived linked to, and yet
separate from, their native subjects. From 1900 to 1942 these colonial rulers
worked to make the islands into a single, prosperous colony, and for that
they expected gratitude. In 1945 when the Pacific War ended and the Dutch
attempted to reassert their control over the islands of Indonesia, they were
genuinely shocked that some of the peoples of their islands would fight
to the death to keep them out. There was a vast gap between Dutch
perceptions of their rule, and the views of their Indonesian subjects, but
it is important to understand Dutch views, because they have shaped
modern Indonesia.

CONQUERING THE INDIES

To create a modern colony Wilhelmina's loyal subjects had to complete a takeover begun when their ancestors founded the port city of Batavia – now Jakarta – on the north-west coast of the island of Java in 1619. It was significant for Indonesia's creation as an unplanned colony that it was founded on business, not Dutch national expansionism. These seventeenth-century Dutchmen set up this colony as investors in the world's first great multinational company, the United East Indies Company. Batavia became the centre of its Asian trading network.

Over the next 200 years, the Company acquired additional ports as trading bases, and safeguarded their interests by gradually taking over surrounding territory. By 1800 the Company had been wound down, but the Dutch had achieved control over most of Java, parts of the larger island of Sumatra, the fabled eastern spice islands of Maluku (the Moluccas), and the hinterlands of various ports where they had established bases for themselves, such as Makasar on the island of Sulawesi (Celebes) and Kupang on the island of Timor.

By the end of the nineteenth century steam-ships and the new Suez Canal made for shorter journey times from Europe, and new attitudes towards expansion. Tiny Holland, nostalgic for its seventeenth-century greatness as a world trading power, joined in the competition for empire that had overtaken the mentality of Europe. Despite claims that the Dutch government had no policy of aggression, only one of 'reluctant imperialism',[3] from the 1870s onwards the Dutch fought a series of wars to enlarge and consolidate their possessions.

The Dutch venture into full-blown empire-building began with the strong and independent Muslim sultanate of Aceh. Aceh, on the vast and promising island of Sumatra, is known today as a centre of bitter conflict and rebellion. Its name also dripped blood in the nineteenth century. The French, British and Dutch were all trying to consolidate their holdings in Southeast Asia, and were interested in the natural wealth that Aceh had to offer, particularly pepper and oil. In 1873 the Dutch invaded Aceh, little realising that it would take thirty years to complete the takeover.

For a Dutch soldier watching the lush green shore-line as he sailed towards Aceh it must have seemed as though the pending task was going to be very easy. Standing with him on the ship were troops from all over Europe whom the Dutch had signed up, men down on their luck or getting away from their pasts. In separate quarters on board were local soldiers from Java and from Ambon, in the spice islands of Maluku. The colonial army had the latest repeating rifles and heavy artillery, while the Acehnese merely had spears and knives.

Despite the confidence of the Dutch invasion, the Acehnese almost won. Indies warfare was a nightmare. The Dutch were faced with resistance from local guerrilla fighters whom they could not distinguish from the rest of the Acehnese population. Acehnese guerrilla tactics involved traps and ambushes, surprise attacks near the barracks on soldiers who wandered off on their own. Every village harboured potential death. The ordinary European soldiers lived in fear and hatred, and they were reduced to levelling villages and killing women and children in an attempt to undermine an invisible enemy.

The generals running the campaign were heavily criticised by the Dutch public – the war was going on too long, was costing too much, and stories leaked about the execution of prisoners and innocent civilians alike. Forced labour, torture and sadism were commonplace Dutch tactics. Photographs from the war showed colonial troops, dressed in black, standing over scenes of villages where the Acehnese corpses formed a tightly packed, bloody carpet on the ground, interrupted only by a single surviving child, crying. Dutch political cartoonists picked up this theme, commenting on the blind and immoral adherence to the colonial policy of successive political leaders (figure 1.1). The Dutch government hid behind official denials and the fog of war propaganda.

A victory in the battle for public support came in 1894. On Lombok, the island to the east of Bali, reports emerged that Lombok's Hindu Balinese rulers were oppressing the local Muslim Sasak people. Sasak leaders appealed to the Dutch for help. The Dutch army moved in and, with relative ease, killed or captured most of the Balinese rulers, allowing the campaign to be presented to the public as a success. Lombok showed politicians and critics that there would be no repeat of the débâcle that had almost seen the Dutch defeated in Aceh. The resulting enthusiasm for conflict was echoed in one of the soldiers' songs:

> And to Lombok off we go
> And we are bored with peace
> So we'll shoot with powder and lead
> Those Balinesers dead.

However, the long-term results were not so good for the Sasaks. The Dutch forced the exportation of their rice, while taxing them heavily. After a few decades of Dutch rule, Lombok went from being a wealthy rice-bowl to an impoverished and semi-desert island.[4]

Figure 1.1 'East Indies Blind'. Minister [of the colonies] Fock: 'I have no time for all these newspapers and private correspondence. My officials report that we act humanely, and I'll stick to that.' *The Nutcracker*, volume 1, 16 November 1907, commenting on the Aceh situation.

The warrior General J. B. van Heutsz (1851–1924) finally solved the problem of Aceh. During a frustrating tour of duty there he met Christiaan Snouck Hurgronje (1857–1936), an academic who made a career of studying Islam. A man who radiated presence and authority, Snouck's first major colonial assignment had been to get inside information on the activities of Muslims from the Indies who lived in the Middle East or travelled there to undertake the pilgrimage to Mecca. When his investigations revealed that Aceh was becoming an international rallying-point for Muslims opposed to European colonialism, Snouck's response was to try to understand the social basis of Acehnese resistance. He discovered that the religious leaders played the key role in heading the Acehnese struggle, and that there was a growing tension between these Muslim heads and the traditional Acehnese aristocracy. Snouck correctly advised on the need to capitalise on this divergence by doing more to win over the Acehnese nobles.

Appointed chief-of-staff in Aceh in 1898, van Heutsz followed Snouck's advice: 'when one wishes to rule a country, to have one's will respected there, then one must establish oneself in that country.'[5] In this approach, respect was won by separating the Acehnese resistance from their bases in the countryside, and by strengthening the authority of the Acehnese rulers. At the suggestion of an Acehnese aristocrat, van Heutsz adopted some of the guerrilla tactics of the enemy by creating highly mobile units in the Dutch army. He combined their use with the superior firepower that came from using the new repeating carbines until he had created a deadly scorched earth policy that saw 10,000 Acehnese flee to Malaya. As a result, the resistance lost its local supplies and support, and van Heutsz was made governor of an Aceh declared pacified in 1903. To give the appearance of peace, the European troops were kept to a minimal level of 12,000, but continuing popular resistance meant that 23,000 Indonesian soldiers, mainly from Java, Ambon and Manado in Sulawesi, over half the entire colonial army, had to be in Aceh. The total cost of the war was ƒ400 million (US$160 million, equivalent to over US$10 billion in present-day terms), 37,000 troops killed on the Dutch side, and 60,000–70,000 Acehnese lives lost.

General van Heutsz's success in Aceh made him a popular hero of expansion, and his supporters were able to silence the voices of doubt and criticism in the Dutch parliament and newspapers. Van Heutsz's achievement was further recognised in 1904 by his elevation as Wilhelmina's Governor General in the Indies. Monuments were later erected to him in Aceh, Batavia and Amsterdam in the 1920s and 1930s, and a boulevard in Batavia was named after him.

The politicians and military leaders were able to claim they had a moral duty to free common people from oppression or backwardness. They said they had to punish or modernise independent indigenous rulers who practised slavery, ruled unjustly, and did not respect international law.

So the colonial army rolled through sultanates and small kingdoms in Sumatra, Maluku, Borneo, the Southeast Islands and Sulawesi between 1901 and 1910. Some rulers, such as the Sultans of Tidore (Maluku), Pontianak (Kalimantan) and Palembang (Sumatra), wisely asked for Dutch protection from independent neighbours to avoid military conquest. By doing this they could negotiate better rights and conditions when they came within the colonial system.

Two expeditions were sent to conquer the rulers of South Bali. When one of the South Balinese kings let his subjects claim the contents of a ship wrecked on his shores, the Dutch argued that international shipping rights had not been protected and consequently launched an invasion in 1906. The justification for a second action in 1908 was that Bali had become a major centre of opium smuggling. In both cases the results were spectacular but appalling. Rather than surrender their independence, the Balinese kings, queens, princes, princesses and their followers armed themselves with swords and spears to face the Dutch forces. Dressed in ceremonial white, they marched into a barrage of Dutch bullets and cannons where death was bloody, brutal and certain. A total of over 1,300 of the ruling class and their servants died in these actions that the Balinese still speak about today.

By 1909 the Dutch had established an integrated territory. Many areas of the Indies were placed initially under military rule, which often amounted to establishing what one contemporary critic called dictatorships.[6] The final tidying up of the map occurred in the 1920s when the Dutch took full control over part of the island of New Guinea against the threat of expanding Australian interests.

ADMINISTERING THE EMPIRE

Local lords who survived the takeovers served well as the vehicles for a policy known as indirect rule. Under this system, the Dutch saw themselves as preserving tradition by providing a layer of wise administration above the natural native leaders of the people. Traditional rulers became regents, the indigenous aristocracy became an indigenous civil service. They were placed under the hierarchy of Dutch officials: the Residents, Assistant Residents, and the District Officers. This indirect rule would not disturb the traditional life of the peasantry, and besides, it was cheap, since the

Dutch did not have to recreate a state from the bottom up. In 1900 Queen Wilhelmina needed only 250 European and 1,500 indigenous civil servants, and of course her army, to rule 35 million colonial subjects.

Snouck Hurgronje's earlier successes as a colonial adviser on native affairs meant that he was able to influence the administration. He and his followers saw expert knowledge as the best way of providing 'vigorous but righteous colonial government'.[7] Snouck supported the development of Dutch bureaucrats expert in language, culture and local law, who, like him, would have special insights into the cultural motivations of local populations. After he left the Indies he went back to Leiden University, the colonial training centre, where he himself had been educated. Now, as a professor, he could lead the way in training his successors.

In the system Snouck supported, civil servants had to pass examinations, and fewer were promoted on the basis of family connections. Efficiency based on merit would make government run like a machine, for the purpose of social engineering. Whereas colonial officials had once all come from the aristocracy, by the early twentieth century their numbers were increasingly from the upper bourgeoisie, and eventually from the middle and even working classes. During van Heutsz's period as Governor General the first female colonial civil servant, Laura Ellinger, took her examination, although she never achieved high rank. The bureaucrats took their duty very seriously. They wanted to act on behalf of the peoples of the Indies, to protect them from the worst effects of modern life, but in contradictory fashion, to develop the Indies at the same time into a modern state.[8]

'Peace and order' was the stated aim of the administration, but it was an order obsessed with files and memos. Even Dutch observers thought this bureaucratic attitude extreme. One critic was the Netherlands' major novelist at the turn of the century, the flamboyant Louis Couperus (1863–1923). In his novel of colonial life, *The Hidden Force*, he used a fictional civil servant to satirise the fussy bureaucracy of the colonial period, while at the same time unconsciously highlighting the concepts of race that underpinned colonialism: 'The Secretary, Onno Eldersma, was a busy man. The daily mail brought an average of two hundred letters and documents to the residency office ...' Eldersma 'worked morning, noon, and night. He allowed himself no siesta. He took a hurried lunch at four o'clock and then rested a little ...' Europeans were better suited to this work than natives: 'he needed all his blood, all his muscles, all his nerves, for his work'. Whether it was worth the effort or not, men like him left impressive sets of statistics through which to understand the Indies.

As they professionalised themselves, Dutch officials moved to an uneasy relationship with the indigenous regents. In Dutch accounts the latter were strange and corrupt, but fascinating, despots. The ambivalent relationship between Dutch and indigenous rulers was a legacy of the nineteenth century, when Dutch administrators felt that they should adopt local customs such as large entourages of servants, including one to carry a gold-painted ceremonial umbrella of office. Governor General van Heutsz had attempted reform in 1904 by banning the Dutch from using symbols like the umbrellas, but until the 1940s Dutch high officials encouraged regents to hold elaborate rituals, at the centre of which both parties to government would sit, with their wives and servants, on gold-painted chairs, as their subjects turned out to pay obeisance.[9]

ETHICAL PROGRESS

Queen Wilhelmina reigned in a time of new attitudes, of which a disposition towards bureaucracy was one. Aged only eighteen when made Queen, she inherited a realm that was in poor economic shape. Her coronation came at the end of what had been the greatest economic depression in the modern world. In the late 1880s and early 1890s the commodity prices on which the colony had previously depended had collapsed. Wilhelmina sought advice from her parliamentarians in The Hague on how to manage the colony for the greatest good of all her subjects.

Throughout the nineteenth century a colonial surplus had been extracted each year as a payment into the Dutch treasury. Thanks in part to this payment, the Netherlands had modernised and built a thriving bourgeois society. Prior to the Depression the Liberal Party had been the dominant voice in policy-making and politics in the Netherlands. Believing in the free market above all else, it instituted policies to expand the plantations in the Indies, not only causing an increase in agricultural production for export, but also focusing the colony's economy on the Netherlands. Liberals had promised that, as the economy expanded, the life of the natives would be improved because local opportunities would increase as prosperity trickled down. The Depression exposed this as an illusion. It became apparent to journalists and civil servants on the ground that the majority of the population of the Indies were as badly off under liberalism as under the regulated economy that had preceded it. While a few Dutch profited, tens of thousands of colonial subjects starved.

The worst results of the policy were clearest on the Outer Islands, the islands outside of Java, Madura and Bali, where frontier plantations of tobacco and rubber pushed back the jungle. Coolies from China, India and later Java, who were imported in tens of thousands to work these plantations, were controlled by regular floggings and a regime that resulted in high death rates. Dutch who attempted to document abuses usually found themselves discredited and demoted when plantation company executives back home complained to friends in parliament, who in turn complained to their friends administering the Indies. Negative reports were buried in archives.[10]

One campaigner against the inequities of the colonial system was Piet Brooshooft (1845–1921), a plump crusading journalist with a walrus moustache. From the time of his arrival in the Indies he began to write about the moral duty of the Dutch to give the Indies what the Indies was due. Brooshooft, encouraged by a small group of socialists and concerned middle-class Dutch in the colonies, campaigned against the colonial surplus as an unjust imposition on the Indies. In his view the 'childlike' peoples of the Indies needed assistance, not oppression.

As editor of the largest and liveliest of the Dutch-language Indies' newspapers, *The Locomotive*, Brooshooft published works by Snouck Hurgronje about how to understand the natives, and sent reporters out into all parts of the colony to dig into local developments. In the twenty-first century it is hard to remember how important newspapers were, but as the main medium of communication, they were the thoughts and voice of the Indies, particularly in the absence of any bodies that allowed for political representation in the colony, or of the colony in the Dutch parliament. Brooshooft drew attention to the uncomfortable issues of colonialism, particularly what was euphemistically called 'declining Native welfare' – the grinding poverty, crop failure, famine and epidemics evident in 1900.[11]

People of like-mind gathered to Brooshooft because of the impact of his writings. They included lawyers and supportive politicians who were able to get the Queen's ear. They turned Brooshooft's campaign into the notion that the Netherlands owed the peoples of the Indies a 'debt of honour'. Bad conscience was translated into a noble policy of improving their lives. The young Queen Wilhelmina, under advice from her prime minister of the Christian Anti-Revolutionary Party, proclaimed the new policy for the new century when in 1901 she formally inaugurated a benevolent 'Ethical Policy', intended to bring progress and prosperity to the natives, including the provision of education and other opportunities.

Because this aim was so vague, it could be interpreted in many different ways: as economic progress with which the liberals could identify; as welfare for the peasantry that the socialists advocated; as Christianity for the religious parties; or as a more general guidance to ease the local people into the modern world. Whatever form 'progress' took, the basis of the colony was still profit: 'the Liberals entered "Love for the Javanese" in their published accounts, but did not let it touch their pockets; and when the Ethical [Policy] leaders hauled down the Jolly Roger and hoisted the Cross, they did not change the sailing orders.'[12]

The Ethical Policy period actually depended on the concurrent military takeover, because only when the Indies were a single entity could the Policy's stated aim of modernisation be achieved. That is why, ironically, Governor General van Heutsz was one of the Policy's strongest supporters. Under the rule of this 'unifier of the Indies' railways were expanded over Java and Sumatra, ancient monuments such as the temple of Borobudur restored, and educational opportunities were expanded with great vigour.

A type of progress did occur under the Ethical Policy as the economy improved. Commodity prices recovered from the Depression and resumed their upward climb, leading to substantial capital investment in the colony. The old standards of Indies trade had been sugar, tin, copra, and the coffee Americans identified with Java. In the early decades of the twentieth century these were joined by rubber, tobacco, tea and oil as the principal exports of the Indies. Big multinationals came on to the scene: the British Billiton Tin Company moved into mining, Standard Oil from the US was attracted to oil-rich areas such as Aceh, while Royal Dutch Shell was established as a joint venture.

The plantations of the Outer Islands, especially the former Sultanate of Deli, part of the East Coast of Sumatra Residency, required a tough approach. Planters were an alienated foreign legion from all over Europe. These people, often escaping dubious pasts, endured the malarial conditions of the 'burning forest ... the vibrating sky above the motionless smoke' and the smell of the rubber processing factory – 'like rotten eggs combined with lysol' – in the hope of one day returning home with vast wealth. Some did, considering that during the boom time for rubber around 1925, supervisors earned bonuses of ƒ140,000 (US$56,000, equivalent to millions of dollars in present-day terms) per year. They saw themselves as hard-working, although the job consisted mainly of walking around giving orders to coolies, a monotonous existence broken by the excesses of weekly drinking bouts, creating the masculine camaraderie of a football club. Dutch, German, English, French and others built grand fantasy houses for themselves in attempts to create an imposing style of life.[13]

As one management manual of the time observed, industrial knowledge was not the major qualification for running a tobacco plantation:

'A man . . . might know everything on how to cultivate tobacco and care for it, but he will be useless in Deli if he does not know how to exact obedience.' These Europeans lived in an atmosphere of constant menace, regarding the coolie workers as less than human and liable to run amok. The threat of violence would be met by violence, and these labourers, simultaneously perceived as lazy and treacherous, would be forced to carry out their arduous work.

A typical incident was cited by Dutch authorities in support of a request for state-sanctioned force to be used in the area. An assistant, 'Heer O., when making his way at 5 in the morning to his work, encountered a group of coolies who assumed an unwilling posture.' Workers were expected to show subservience, but instead 'While he was speaking to the men and giving them orders, he suddenly was dealt a hard blow with the shaft of a hoe, whereupon he fell into a ditch.' Luckily he was armed, 'and he shot his fierce opponent smack dead. Instead of being deterred, the rest of the band assumed such a threatening stance that the assaulted assistant was forced to make use of his weapon again with the result that a second assailant lost his life and a third was seriously wounded.' The rest fled. Workers and managers were caught up in this cycle of antagonism and violence.

A manager had to be able to manipulate the coolie foremen through a combination of economic incentives and claims to represent legal authority in order to avoid such rebellion. Distance from the natives was all-important, even for Europeans lower in the hierarchy: 'the European employees . . . seldom spoke to them in anything other than a snarl in bad Malay, which is said to be necessary for their prestige!' Maintaining white status also meant that local people saw only what was an ideal white society – poor whites, let alone the disabled, should be invisible in the colony, and were usually repatriated.[14]

The Dutch population in the Indies saw a rise in their general standard of living between 1902 and 1913. The Netherlands remained neutral in World War One, and initially Dutch investors at home and in the colony did well out of supplying raw materials for both sides. However, when the Germans employed submarines to attack shipping in 1917, trade between the Indies and Europe was cut off. Those Dutch businessmen who were able to hold on became rich after the Great War from speculating against internationally inflated prices for the kinds of raw materials the Indies supplied.

Despite an economic downturn in the early 1920s, a partnership was developing between the Dutch political and business leadership to inject cash into the Indies. The partnership was instrumental in making the Indies a single economic unit.

Supporting the unification of the colonial economy was the new shipping line, the KPM or *Koninklijke Paketvaart Maatschappij*, founded in 1888. In this instance, government and industry worked together to push other shipping lines out of the Indies, although they were not entirely successful. Still, the KPM served to integrate a whole range of economic activities under Dutch domination, by setting up a network of ports that was centred on Tanjung Priok, Batavia's new harbour. Islands that had previously been linked to Singapore or the Malay peninsula now focused their economic activities on Java. Thus, through the KPM the centre of political power became the centre of the colony's economy. When Batavia became Jakarta in 1950 that central role was passed over to independent Indonesia.[15]

Even with sharp fluctuations, the growth rate of the colonial era averaged 2 per cent per annum between 1901 and 1929, and although plantations took a leading role in this expansion, manufacturing, construction, transport, wholesale and retail trade and the government sector all increased rapidly. By 1929 capital investment had grown to US$1,600 million (over $50 billion in present-day terms). The government provided infrastructure for business such as the laying of 7,425 kilometres of rail and tram tracks by 1930. In turn business invested heavily in the latest technology, for example installing 6,472 boilers in plantation factories in 1930. Although they were dependent on the British for big capital, the politicians did everything they could to encourage Dutch-owned or jointly owned business, so that, for example, the majority of the colony's US$76 million worth of petroleum exports in 1930 belonged to Royal Dutch Shell. The sign of the success of government and business was that in 1929 the value of exports was in excess of US$433 million. At the peak of its trade in the 1930s the Indies produced 37 per cent of world rubber, 86 per cent of the smaller trade in pepper and was a significant player in markets such as sugar and copra.

The Great Depression that transpired at the end of 1929 was a major setback to business, and many of those who had profited earlier went bankrupt. The Dutch government had done almost nothing to encourage the development of the colony's economic independence, and provided only minimal protection for local manufacturing through the introduction of tariffs in 1933. Dutch politicians were not interested in allowing the Indies to stand on its own feet. Profits went to big business rather than being invested in the colony. Between 1935 and 1939 – even after the impact of the Great Depression – the Indies still provided 14 to 17 per cent of the Netherlands' national income.[16]

CONTRADICTIONS OF EMPIRE

Because Dutch politicians did not want to lose control, the Indies remained an appendage of the Netherlands throughout the colonial period. However, government advisers from Snouck onwards argued that there should be greater autonomy for the colony, and won a concession to autonomy in the form of a policy of decentralisation, initiated in 1903. But this resulted in separation in appearance only.

Decentralisation led to increased local authority through the establishment of city and regency councils. In 1918, a People's Council was set up for the whole colony, a progressive move compared to other colonial regimes. This body had been a long time in planning, but its establishment was hastened by the growth of Communism in both the Netherlands and the Indies. However, the potential for democracy through these institutions was undermined by a combination of Dutch fascination with indigenous aristocracy, and an unwillingness to give up real power.

Setting up the regency councils strengthened the aristocracy. In Bali, as in a number of other areas, heads of royal families previously exiled because they had stood up to Dutch invasions, were now reinstated and made into regents heading councils in each of the island's former kingdoms.

In the slightly more democratic city councils, suffrage was severely limited. Dutch positions were guaranteed, and the highest roles (such as mayor) were always appointments, as was the case in the Netherlands itself. The prerequisites for franchise on city councils were that one was literate, and paid tax of more than ƒ300 per annum (US$120). While a Dutch Resident earned what was considered a modest sum by the standards of his equivalents in other colonial systems – ƒ13,500 p.a. (US$5,400) – the highest-paid coolies would have needed to work day-and-night for a year to earn ƒ300 in total, let alone pay tax on it. More than 80 per cent of the taxpayers of Java and Madura earned less than this. In theory the vote was given to women after a long struggle, but through official stalling they never actually got to exercise that right, mainly because they did not pay tax. However, they were allowed to stand for office, and in the 1930s four Javanese women were members of municipal councils, mainly by direct appointment.

Government policies placed great emphasis on education as the path to native progress, at the same time trying to keep the native population from assuming too great a role in the colony. Colonial adviser Snouck Hurgronje expounded the view that 'our rule will have to justify itself on the basis of lifting the natives up to a higher level of civilization in line with

their innate capacities.' This was the basis of Snouck's policy of 'association', since it was association with Europeans that would 'lift up' the
natives. Snouck's test of the theory was to see if an elite of educated natives
could absorb Western knowledge to the point where it improved their
'inner character'. If this occurred, they could be elevated to 'help' to govern
the Indies, a view that was controversial amongst colonials who refused to
believe there could be equality between rulers and ruled. In pursuing his
theory, Snouck became the patron of a carefully selected group of
Sumatran and Javanese aristocrats, collaborators who could be paraded as
examples of success in colonial policy.[17]

For some Dutch advocates, educational expansion was the opportunity to
open up the Outer Islands for missionary activities. It was a way of bringing
the Light without the government making major investments in building
schools and providing teachers, providing only subsidies as they did to
church schools in the Netherlands. So areas with existing Christian populations, such as Ambon (Maluku), Manado (North Sulawesi) and Flores, were
joined by new mission fields in the Toraja highlands of Central Sulawesi, the
Batak highlands of Sumatra, and West New Guinea. The missionaries,
arriving in remote mountain regions after weeks of arduous trekking, needed
the strongest of faiths to persevere. They had to spend years learning the local
languages, and were continually worried that their converts might slip back
into local spiritualism or animism.

While religious politicians were all in favour of expanding missionary
activities, rationalist planners, including Snouck, saw such moves as an
unhelpful provocation to Islam. The planners succeeded in curbing the
missions, and banning them entirely from some areas.

Some Dutch took to heart Snouck's views on improving the natives.
Socialist and Communist teachers helped the peoples of the Indies by
bringing them notions of freedom and equality. A group of these teachers
set up an Indies Party, and spread the idea that the natives should do more
than just help to rule. These radicals called for an Indies ruled by a coalition
of Dutch born in the Indies, those of mixed descent, and, most shockingly,
natives. A teacher of German in a Surabaya high school inspired one young
native man to read Karl Marx, and introduced him to politicians who
treated their native friends as equals. This was an important lesson that the
student, Sukarno, was to carry into his career as political leader and
Indonesia's first president. When identified, subversive teachers were
expelled from the colony.[18]

In 1927 a reform of the People's Council saw the number of elected
members (thirty-eight) outweigh appointments (twenty-two), and by 1929

thirty of the sixty members were natives, mainly from the aristocracy. The number of native seats mattered little, however, since this body never had real legislative power. The Council's only gesture towards voicing the desire for an independent Indies was a mild petition to the Queen requesting a conference to discuss self-government. This resulted in a furious exchange of letters between Dutch officials. The Governor General at the time was embarrassed, and his recommendation to the Minister for the Colonies was a masterpiece of bureaucratic stonewalling that dismissed the petition as unconstitutional and undesirable.[19]

Dutch contemporaries, such as the acerbic novelist, Louis Couperus, knew that at the heart of administration was an attitude meant to impress other Westerners: 'the European ... rules arrogantly ... amidst all the intricate machinery of his authority .... [which] he slips into gear with the certainty of clockwork, controlling its every movement.' This was a system of rule that appeared as 'a masterpiece, a world created'.[20]

Part of the creation of this 'masterpiece' had been the establishment in 1916 of a body to spy on the population, the Political Intelligence Service (PID). PID spies were recruited from all levels of indigenous society, since the pay was good, and there were many opportunities to prove one's loyalty and avenge one's enemies. The reports that PID members compiled emphasised the strength of Communists and other subversives, mostly in order to justify continued employment. The secret police magnified government paranoia that the natives were getting too much education without showing due appreciation of Dutch benevolence.[21]

Peace and order often meant arbitrary rule amounting to dictatorial power. On PID advice, the Governor General and those immediately below him could gaol, or exile to remote islands, those deemed to be a political threat, without having to provide detailed justification. The PID's major effect was to undermine local trust in government, so that its spy networks corrupted social relationships. The almost simultaneous establishment of a People's Council with its opposite, a secretive security body, is an indication of the impossible contradictions that tore the Ethical Policy to shreds.

PUBLIC WELFARE

The social results of the Ethical Policy and decentralisation were best seen in the new neat public space of cities. In the first three decades of the twentieth century the Department of Public Works sponsored major public buildings and introduced city planning, embodied in the work of the Indies' leading architect and town planner, Thomas Karsten (1884–1945). He developed predecessors' ideas of incorporating indigenous elements – the spirit of the Indies – into a rational European structure. On arrival in the Indies in 1914, Karsten started working in Java's third major city, Semarang. He was later involved in urban extension and rebuilding in almost every city in Sumatra and Java. For leading Dutch citizens he designed solidly monumental two-storey houses, the roofs of which were in the high-pitched colonial style; for royalty new pavilions that were simultaneously modern European and traditional Javanese; to organise the small traders of the central Javanese cities of Yogyakarta and Surakarta he planned public market buildings; for major firms splendid headquarters; and for the new suburbs in Batavia he produced master plans, including of the central square of the city. Still, in 1930 the cities were for Europeans. The majority of natives (over 90 per cent) lived in the country, while the majority of Europeans (over 75 per cent) lived in the cities.[22]

The basis of Karsten's cities was order, and bringing hygiene to native quarters was an important part of that. Besides expertise in language, law and culture, the Dutch promoted new kinds of knowledge of medicine and public health. In the nineteenth century there had been a government preoccupation with venereal disease amongst soldiers. By the twentieth century concern about sexual health was extended to the general population, which meant government officials spent much of their time attempting to monitor prostitutes.

In the nineteenth century Dutch officials had also been concerned about smallpox, and large-scale vaccination programmes were well underway by the 1850s. This concern was extended to examining the sources of other diseases, especially plague, which arrived in Sumatra in 1905 and Java around 1910. Dysentery remained a major killer during the Dutch period, and it was not until the advent of antibiotics in the second half of the twentieth century that many of the intestinal diseases could be brought under control.

Public health programmes, promoting clean water and better living conditions, were the only measures that could be used to control many diseases. By the 1930s, public health was being taught in the Indies by people such as J. H. de Haas. Dr de Haas was a pioneer of infant nutrition, and a radical socialist who, distressed by infant mortality rates of up to 300 per 1,000, tried to ensure basic nutrition. He supervised programmes in which condensed and evaporated milk, as well as sour milk, were dispensed to mothers, and he and his colleagues introduced the innovation of soya milk as an alternative source of vitamins.

Malaria remained a problem for Dutch and natives alike, although quinine brought a major breakthrough in the battle against it. Programmes to clean up native housing areas aimed at getting rid of the breeding grounds for mosquitoes in order to reduce malaria and dengue fever. Other programmes also attempted to get rid of the rats that were major disease carriers, but with little success – rats that would outweigh cats are still a familiar sight in Indonesian cities. Government efforts to get involved in all aspects of daily life for the good health of the natives were not that successful. The native sections of the cities remained wild areas resistant to official campaigns.

De Haas was unusual in the health bureaucracy, which saw its aims as researching health issues and making policy, not actually treating the sick. Health expenditure was never more than 5 per cent of the budget for the Indies, sometimes as low as 2.5 per cent, half what was spent on education, one-fifth to one-ninth of what was spent on the military.[23]

MAINTAINING DUTCH SOCIETY

When Wilhelmina became Queen only 76,000 Eruopeans were living in the Indies. Policing and policy could only do so much in enabling a small foreign group to rule over a massive population. The colonial rulers needed to be able to keep social groups apart, keep them from conceiving of a common interest, and make the European presence seem somehow natural. The main mechanism by which the Dutch achieved this was through institutionalising the concepts of race that were common throughout all colonial societies at the time. These ideas produced a version of what would later be referred to in South Africa as apartheid.

Colonial race-based societies are hierarchical – whiteness puts you at the top. In the Netherlands East Indies this was never straightforward, however, since the boundaries and definition of who was white were contested. As colonial authorities attempted to legislate boundaries, contradictions became apparent. In particular there was a split between the groups Dutch referred to respectively as 'stayers' and 'pures'.

'Stayers' were the successors of the original employees of the United East India Company. Company colonialism created a culture in the Indies quite different from that of the constrained Protestant society of the Netherlands. The Company's legacy produced sarong-and-sandal-wearing Dutch men who ate rice, spoke a version of Malay and took local women as concubines. Their twentieth-century successors were often born in the Indies, and strove to create something that tied them to the place.

Figure 1.2 Dutch cartoonist Menno: a Dutchman in the East: newly arrived, and thirty
years later, from *Herinneringen aan Java* (Soerabaja: Nijland, 1915).

They wanted to live in an Indies society that was a 'higher synthesis
between east and west'. One of them, Rob Nieuwenhuys, looking back,
expressed it as: 'culturally I am a European ... but emotionally many parts
of my person lie in Indonesia.' Being brought up by a Javanese maid, living
in the colony for the formative years of his life made the Indies part of his
character (figure 1.2).[24]

The stayers were cosmopolitan. They imported English, French and
German magazines from neighbouring colonies, rather than Dutch magazines from the Netherlands. Their language was smattered with indigenous
words, mostly for communication with servants or workers – *nasi goreng*
(fried rice), *babu* (maid), *tong-tong* (the time bell on a plantation). Writers
contributed to the sense of an Indies society of 'stayers' with its own
distinctive cultural identity, and established new local publications on
everything from tourism to literature. Artists' organisations – Art Circles –
were established by 'stayers' in all the major cities of the colony. Painters
from these circles depicted an Indies of palm trees and peasants in paddy
fields, a peaceful green world.[25]

The distinctive cultural identity of 'stayers' was passed on through subsequent generations. For many Dutch the Indies meant family mementoes such as pieces of *batik* textiles or *wayang* puppet figures, or even 'buffalo horns, a wild panther hide' hanging on their walls back home. Looking back at the end of the twentieth century, the Netherlands' leading novelist, Hella Haasse, herself one of those who lived in the Indies, evokes the colonial emotional pull in her semi-factual book *Lords of the Tea*. For her main character, the founder of tea estates in Sunda (West Java), 'Java was a constant in the life of his family. His parents had themselves previously resided there for two years, since in the passage of two decades many relatives had gone before them.' From trips with his grandfather he acquired an interest in 'colonists': 'They looked up to the viewer in the Netherlands from photographs in prominently displayed albums, posed against the background of a veranda with white pillars, or of avenues surrounded by exotic trees ... '[26] These distant family members were constantly recalled at gatherings, their long letters home creating a desire for the warm tropical promise of the Indies far away from the cold, wintry Netherlands.

By the end of the nineteenth century the second group of Dutch, the 'pures', had risen in number to become the dominant group. They usually had little or no emotional attachment to the Indies, and were just there to make money and go 'home' as soon as possible. As Europeans started to assert imperial ambitions, their sense of being European increased. Cartoonists produced satirical images of the stayer as fat, gin-sodden and self-important. If the Dutch become 'too Indies' they were in danger of 'disappearing into the *kampung* [native quarter]' – the term for going native.

The Dutchman's whiteness started to solidify. Many who grew up in the cities of the early twentieth-century Indies remember having very little indigenous contact; those who were 'too Indies' received lesser wages. 'Pures' started to keep 'stayers' out, as one woman recalled of her 'stayer' father in Sumatra. Even though he was on a Dutch soccer team, when playing away he had to sleep in downmarket hotels apart from his teammates. Whiteness even had to be worn, in the form of the white colonial suit (sometimes complete with pith helmet), an import from neighbouring British colonies. In colonial images the Dutch civil servant or plantation manager in his glaring white outfit stands out above the crouching coolies or peasants.[27]

The push for separateness was a consequence of the fact that many Dutch leaders considered Snouck's association policy to have failed, since rather than producing pro-Dutch intellectuals, it produced Indonesian nationalists. Thus the advocates of 'whiteness' become more actively political. A Fatherland Club was established by 'pures' in 1929 as a way of ensuring that patriotism was centred on the Netherlands. Its ideology was fostered by conservative elements at home and in the colonies, and by the late 1930s had merged into a form of National Socialism – the Netherlands had proportionally one of the largest Nazi parties in Europe. In 1935 the head of the Dutch National Socialist (Nazi) Party visited the Indies and was twice received by the Governor General. J. B. van Heutsz Junior, son of the great Governor General, was an officer in the German Army, the *Waffen-SS*.[28]

Institutionally, separateness was most apparent in law, as with other colonial systems. Law was a matter of race, race a matter of separate law, separate taxation, and separate ways of being treated by state authorities. European law overrode all other forms. Native law was religious or traditional law. Chinese and others not classified as Native (known generally as Foreign Orientals) occupied an intermediate position. This did not mean that the Chinese were well regarded – Dutch accounts portray them as sneaky and inscrutable. Proposals made in the early twentieth century to give Chinese equal status to Europeans were strongly resisted on all sides. Those called Indos (Eurasians) could be reclassified, living some parts of their lives as Dutch, and other parts as native. Their status depended mainly on whether their fathers recognised them in law. The government operated on the principle that 'racial consciousness is the lifeblood of colonial society'. All aspects of life were racially distinguished, from train tickets to toilets.[29]

Men dominated the public image of the Indies, women occupied difficult positions on the faultlines of Dutch–Indonesian relations. More and more white women arrived in the colony once transport became quicker – by 1930, 113,000 of the 240,000 Europeans were women. They had to manage complicated households, maintain as European a lifestyle as possible, and be symbols of their husbands' status. This was never going to be easy. Ice chests struggled to keep the beer cold, and the cheese and butter from going off. On arrival women found that they already had servants, at the minimum a houseboy (who could be a man older than the new lady of the house), gardener, cook, and for the children, a nursemaid-cum-housemaid. A woman had to have a seamstress, who unlike the others did not live in the Dutch compound. A driver and a washerwoman made up the set of servants, and the size of one's household indicated one's status in the Dutch pecking order. To be poor was to have only one servant. Houseboys and drivers were dressed in special livery selected by the lady of the house.[30]

To teach colonial hierarchy, ladies' manuals for the Indies, books of etiquette, were produced in the early twentieth century. A Colonial School for Girls and Women, teaching domestic science and other practical things, was set up in The Hague in 1920. In 1930 an Association for Housewives in the Indies was established in Batavia, and then expanded to teach indigenous servants how to prepare proper European food. The Dutch were getting sick of eating the array of local dishes served up at the feasts called 'rice table'.[31]

The arrival of the Dutch women increased anxiety about the results of the proximity of Dutch men and Indonesian women, since men had come to regard the servants as sexual property. The reverse situation – liaisons between Dutch women and native men – were regarded as scandalous, even when the men involved were princes, as happened on a number of occasions.

By the Great Depression, the Dutch had shifted their social patterns towards a life lived in enclaves. The 'stayers' expressed pangs of regret, but the 'pures' were keen to take advantage of new ways of organising their lives. Dutch modernity, in the forms of electricity, piped water and sewerage, enabled the building of estates designed by top architects, as in the case of the Comal sugar estate near Java's north coast, designed by the famous Karsten. The Comal estate included a major symbol of separation, a 'hygienic' whites-only swimming pool. Its lawns and herbaceous borders and special clubhouse were all set away from the native quarters. The clubhouse was the ultimate 'pure' institution, the acme of clubs being the Harmonie in Batavia. Dutch social activities, such as jazz dancing and tennis at the club, could not include natives.[32]

Even after the Great Depression of the 1930s, many Europeans in the Indies could still maintain a luxurious lifestyle. Besides the soldiers, civil servants, businessmen and planters, the idyll of the Indies attracted those in search of an artistic lifestyle: painters, photographers, beachcombers. The cooler hill stations of Java, such as Garut, were principal destinations. The lifestyles of those days were beautifully captured by the growing number of professional photographers who have left a splendid record of ideal life as seen through Dutch eyes. Their work was already material for colonial nostalgia before colonialism ended.

A network of hotels grew up, Batavia's Hotel des Indies premier among them, along with a new tourism industry. The novelist Louis Couperus was one of those who enjoyed the colonial lifestyle of the Indies. He might have given a jaundiced view of the Indies in his novel *The Hidden Force*, but when commissioned to write a travel book encouraging tourists from the Netherlands, Europe and America, Couperus was lavish in his praise for the cool hill stations, the delights of the ancient Borobudur and Prambanan temples of Central Java, and new opportunities to view the temples and rituals on the island of Bali.

The idea that colonial life was some kind of Eden was undermined at the end of Dutch rule. As war loomed at the end of 1938, the Dutch attempted to assert their moral supremacy in the Indies. The rawest example of the sexual exploitation that had been an undercurrent of Dutch rule was an aggressive sex industry that had flourished by selling young men and boys. Suddenly it became the subject of police raids and intense public scrutiny. In 1938 and 1939, 223 men from all over the Indies, European, Eurasians, Chinese and Indonesians, were prosecuted for having sex with boys below the age of consent. At least seventy were convicted; two committed suicide. The sexual partners of many of those convicted were often between sixteen and twenty, but some cases involved children as young as nine. Artists, school principals, district officers, linguists, journalists and retired planters all found themselves subject to the same colonial law, and in the same gaols, but the heaviest penalties, up to three years' imprisonment, went to Indonesians, Chinese and an Armenian, despite the fact that the majority of those convicted were Dutch.[33]

The paedophilia scandal was forgotten as World War Two cut off contact between colony and home country, and there was a brief period of enforced autonomy. In 1942 the Dutch surrendered to the advancing Japanese with a rapidity that shocked their subjects. For most of the Dutch who lived under Japanese rule, the main memory is of privation and suffering in internment camps, women and children in places like Ambarawa on Java, men on the Burma Railway. The architect, Thomas Karsten, and the nutritionist, J. H. de Haas, were imprisoned together at Cimalin concentration camp near Bandung, where Karsten died in 1945.

Some of those Dutch who survived the war later moved to Australia rather than go back to the Netherlands. Those who chose to remain in the Indies at the end of the war faced a hostile reception from Indonesian nationalists who wanted independence. Typical of the reversal of roles experienced by the Dutch was a miserable encounter of one former prisoner-of-war, forced to let her one-time gardener sexually molest her in return for a supply of rice for her children, payback for his life of subservience. Those who chose to stay in the colony now lived in fear of rape and murder from Indonesian freedom fighters.[34]

In 1948, her jubilee year, Queen Wilhelmina abdicated in favour of her daughter, Juliana, just over a year before Indonesia gained its full independence. A small number of Dutch became Indonesian citizens, but most of those who stayed beyond the period of the Revolution and Indonesian independence were eventually expelled when the new Republic of Indonesia nationalised Dutch assets in 1957 and 1958. Such experiences made the time before 1939 seem doubly golden in Dutch memories.

The conflicts brought out by World War Two were symptomatic of the deep unease within colonialism. The Dutch felt disquiet about how to rule, and how to relate to those whom they ruled. The image of control was always an illusion, but one to which the Dutch held strongly. The wartime prime minister of the Netherlands, looking back on the colonial period, saw it in the patronising terms shared by so many colonialists, as a period in which natives happily paid tribute to the Dutch, who in turn devoted themselves selflessly to native welfare: 'the Netherlands Indies was a Free State, an evolutionary product of history, attached by indissoluble political and economic bonds to the Netherlands. Whites and coloured lived in harmony beneath a cloak which sheltered all, to the most humble.' This devotion to native welfare was what enabled former Governor General de Graeff to say that he had 'pawned his heart' to the natives of the Indies. However, Louis Couperus, in his great novel of the Indies, saw the project of colonialism as an exercise in futility:

The mysticism of concrete things on that island of mystery called Java . . . Outwardly, a docile colony with a subject race . . . But, down in its soul, it had never been conquered, though smiling in proud contemptuous resignation and bowing submissively beneath its fate . . . it lived in freedom its own mysterious life, hidden from Western eyes, however these might seek to fathom the secret . . . deep within itself divinely certain of its own views and so far removed from all its rulers' ideals of civilization that no fraternization between master and servant will ever take place, because the difference that ferments in soul and blood remains insuperable.[35]

Despite creating the institutional and economic bases on which a state could be built, the Indies was still a colonial extension of the Netherlands. It was not an entity that was entirely known, let alone completely governed, by the Dutch. Attempts to create an 'Indies' society were always going to founder against the need to be separate in order to rule. Couperus showed how some Dutch realised that there was something rotten underpinning colonial rule. To understand how those who would become Indonesians viewed that rule, we have to turn to their experiences of modern life in the early part of the twentieth century.

Pramoedya Ananta Toer, looking back on the colonial era in which he was born, attempted in his novels dealing with that period to understand the effect of Dutch attitudes on his fellow Indonesians. When he wrote the series of novels *This Earth of Mankind*, he used the model of one young Javanese man, Raden Tirto Adhi Suryo, to understand the lure of the modern world that Western rule promised, and the contradictions between these attractions of modernity and the deep discrimination and suffering that resulted from colonialism. Pramoedya must also have been thinking about the experiences of his father, who was born just before Wilhelmina ascended the Dutch throne, and used his father's experiences of life in the little Javanese town of Blora, the same town from which Tirto came, to reflect on the wider colonial picture.

CHAPTER 2

Cultures of the countryside

Blora, in the teak forests of northern Central Java, is an undistinguished country town located in a regency of the same name. It lies on the Lusi river, and besides teak, is known for its limestone cliffs. The dusty streets are lined with mainly typical Javanese houses, small wooden dwellings with a welcoming veranda leading on to a front room, where there are chairs ready to receive visitors. Generations in Blora have studied the Koran and other holy works of Islam, woven striped cloth, performed puppet theatre, danced, grown rice or gone off to the sugar mills to find work. The Dutch did not leave much there, a post office – later destroyed in the war – a pillar commemorating forty years of Queen Wilhelmina's rule, and the railway.

Yet despite its ordinariness Blora has had more than its share of fame and upheaval. In 1925, Pramoedya Ananta Toer, Indonesia's most famous novelist, was born there and before him, Raden Mas Tirto Adhi Suryo (1880–1918), an aristocrat who was to become the father of Indonesia's modern press, founder of the nationalist movement and hero of Pramoedya's novels describing colonial society. In Blora Regency is the grave of Indonesia's foremost feminist, Raden Ajeng Kartini, another member of the aristocracy.

Blora exemplifies the cultural and social diversity found throughout the islands of Indonesia. In this one town were local lords and commoners, strict and liberal Muslims, peasants who adhered to local spiritualism, farmers fixed to their land and labourers forced by poverty to travel thousands of kilometres to find work. Just as there was a massive gulf between the Dutch and those they called natives, so Dutch rule magnified the differences between future Indonesians.

THE STRUGGLE OF THE ARISTOCRACY

The aristocrats who made up the thin upper social layer of places like Blora were members of family networks that covered the whole island of

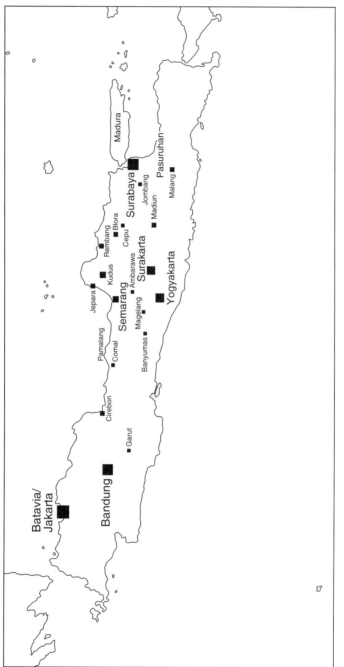

Map 2 Java

Java and its small neighbour, Madura. They had equivalents, rajas, sultans or chiefs, in each of the islands of the archipelago. Tirto Adhi Suryo was part of those networks through his grandfather, one of the regents of Blora. While Tirto developed his nationalist sentiments from ideals of nobility espoused by the traditional aristocracy, he was unusual because he rejected aristocratic hierarchy. Most Javanese regents and their relatives imitated the elaborate ceremonial life of their relatives in the palaces of Central Java – the four courts of the cities of Yogyakarta and Surakarta. Blora's nobility, like the other Javanese aristocrats, regarded itself as younger brothers and sisters of the royal families of the two cities.[1]

When Wilhelmina came to the Dutch throne, one of the Central Javanese rulers was Hamengkubuwono VII ('He Who Holds the World in His Lap'), Sultan of Yogyakarta, Regulator of Religion, born in 1839. In 1898 he had reigned for twenty-one years. Every morning a troop of servants came to bathe him, and then carried the water out to distribute to the populace as holy water that could cure illnesses and bring good fortune. Everywhere he went he was escorted by a troop of bodyguards who were also trained dancers. His status was shown by the size of the retinue that accompanied him, one to carry the gold umbrella of state over his head, others to carry the gold and silver equipment for chewing betel nut, and traditional weapons such as the wavy-bladed *kris* daggers. These were all heirlooms that connected the Sultan with his ancestors, the ultimate the source of his power.

He had many wives, one of whom was the designated queen. Her children were the heirs to the sultanate, but there were dozens of other children besides them. The contending wives of the palace were major players in royal politics, particularly when they were able to have their children married into one of the three other main royal families of Central Java. All of these families were part of a clan descended from the kings who had ruled Java before the Dutch arrived.

The Sultan had grown up with a strong sense of being the head of a warrior caste, a descendant of the epic heroes whose adventures were depicted in the *wayang* shadow theatre. His imagination was also fired by his more immediate ancestors, the ancient rulers he knew about from the Javanese chronicles preserved in his vast palace library.

The Sultan sponsored major festivals, especially *Lebaran*, the celebration at the end of the Muslim fasting month, and also annual parades, celebrations of the birthday of the Prophet, the Great Feast commemorating Abraham's sacrifice of Isaac, and other Javanese holy days. Such celebrations involved fireworks, huge parades, massive offerings, feasts and general distribution of largesse.

Like his ancestors, he was a patron of the arts. In 1899, he held a four-day spectacular in which the Javanese dance-opera, *wayang wong*, was watched by between 23,000 and 36,000 people each day, at a cost of ƒ30,000, equivalent to over US$400,000 in present-day terms. This dance, like the music of the *gamelan* ensembles, the making of *batik* cloth, and the performance of the *wayang* shadow theatre, had been developed within his palace to the highest point of refinement.

The palace, a network of open courtyards with pavilions and sleeping quarters, was the centre of the universe for Javanese. It was approached from the north by a huge open square, flanked on either side by two massive sacred banyan trees. As well as the army of servants, bodyguards, relatives and hangers-on, the Sultan brought together the great artists of Java, and all kinds of unusual people including dwarfs and albinos. He also had an extensive zoo.

The close relations between Dutch administrators and Javanese rulers created a new version of royal culture. The Dutch admired the splendour of these courts, although they were suspicious of the kings and regents who headed this and the other palaces. They worked to keep royalty at the top of a hierarchy so they could be vehicles of indirect rule, so the Dutch supervised the awarding of titles, and vetted marriages between Central Javanese royalty and the families of the outlying regents. The Dutch very clearly conveyed the message to the nobility that they should be 'feudal'.

The Dutch policy of indirect rule turned the kings, regents and other aristocrats into civil servants, albeit ones who retained all the titles and outward signs of ceremonial hierarchy (figure 2.1). Under this policy one single term, *priyayi*, was used for 'native civil servant' and 'aristocrat'. This blurring of identities distorted notions of nobility, at the same time warping understandings of the role of a civil service. The most important result of the transformation caused by the policy was to distance the aristocracy from the rest of the population. The regents were meant to be lesser versions of the Central Javanese kings, but subordinates of the Dutch state at the same time. The rulers from the islands outside Java were also placed in this same difficult situation.

In the early decades of the twentieth century, the Dutch worked to break the systems of land control that enabled rulers and regents to collect taxes and make their subjects work for free as a form of tribute to their lords (corvée labour). This wave of attempted reform followed nineteenth-century efforts to change conditions, but the twentieth-century policies also tightened state control. Dutch officials found the systems of land ownership and rights to corvée labour confusing, and struggled to turn

Figure 2.1 The regent of Pasuruhan. Photo by Eurasian photographer Tassilo Adam, in an album owned by Mas Pirngadi, one of Java's first modern artists.

them into rational modern institutions in which taxation and labour were obligations to the state. The regents and their extended families now received government salaries instead of corvée and the products of the land, which more closely aligned land rights with Western notions of property. In this new system the peasants were meant to become owners of the land they worked, but it rarely turned out that way, as more and more peasants simply became sharecroppers, working the land of others for a percentage of the harvest. To compound already-complex problems of land tenure, the Dutch favoured the interests of the sugar estates present throughout the countryside, giving them greater control over the best farming land.[2]

When the Dutch changed the sultans, kings and nobles into civil servants, they did not leave them enough to live off. The regents and the Central Javanese monarchs tried to maintain themselves, their extended families and their retinues in style by putting pressure on those below them in the social structure. Complex manoeuvres by rulers and regents allowed them to keep some of the income from their land, even when the land had been formally taken away from them. By convincing village heads and peasants to remain loyal to traditional leaders, not abstract notions like 'the state', the regents were able to continue extracting corvée from their subjects. They backed up their pressure on the peasants by employing spies and thugs to show them what their obligations were.

The rulers and regents had already worked out arrangements with sugar estates and their equivalents on other islands, to ensure that when land was taken over by them the payments often went to royalty, rather than the peasants who depended on that land. To add insult to injury for the peasants, the sugar estates often demanded corvée labour from them as well.

The Dutch saw royal resistance to changes in land ownership as corruption. Examples came to light in a series of cases documented in 1905 by Dutch civil servant Snouck Hurgronje as the Chief Adviser on Native Affairs, where one Central Javanese regent was found to have extorted money from village heads, made false loans to traders, and appropriated the mosque treasury, but still owed a Dutch printer and a Chinese opium farmer ƒ10,000 (US$4,000) in loans. Similar stories of exploitation were unearthed when the Dutch investigated the traditional rulers of the Outer Islands. For example, in 1903, Daeng (the local aristocratic title) Remba of the island of Selayar, near Sulawesi, was investigated by the Dutch after forty of his followers murdered a rival and all his household and looted the family treasures. The subsequent reports revealed that Remba had been misappropriating coconut palms, the local source of income, through manipulation of the religious courts, as well as forcing peasants to cultivate land, and to hand over their daughters for 'marriage'. Even after they removed Remba from power in 1907 the Dutch had to replace him with members of his extended family.[3]

Soon after the Javanese case was prosecuted, Snouck was involved in a power struggle to demote and disgrace another regent, Raden Mas Adipati Brotodiningrat ('Esteemed Golden Lord Who Performs the Most Noble Meditation in the World'), regent of Madiun. The Brotodiningrat Affair had been sparked by the theft of a curtain from the home of a Dutch resident, the highest form of colonial regional official. The curtain was used to maintain the privacy of the resident's sitting room and therefore was seen as a symbol of his authority. The proud regent Brotodiningrat was known to be a man who looked down on the Dutch, and this had niggled at the resident. The overwrought resident saw the theft as the last straw in a campaign to undermine him, and instigated detailed investigations that implicated Brotodiningrat in the theft. The resident claimed the action was yet another way that the regent continued to defy Dutch authority. As a result of these machinations, the regent was forced to resign. Brotodiningrat fought back through a drawn-out sequence of court cases in which Snouck worked behind the scenes first to reach a compromise, and then stalled the regent's last libel suit against his accuser, which, if successful, would have damaged the power of the Dutch administration.

Even though the regent was not successful, his daring act of taking on the Dutch administration inspired other members of the aristocracy. No longer able to take up arms against the Dutch, they found new weapons in the arena of public opinion. Brotodiningrat's cousin, Tirto of Blora, was already making a name for himself as a rebel when he became involved in publicising his cousin's case. Setting up his own newspaper and a civil servants' association, Tirto used the case to politicise the aristocracy-cum-civil service.[4]

Tirto also heavily criticised those civil servants who were corrupt and self-serving. He picked up on the general view from within the ranks of the nobility that the old systems of loyalty, and the noble obligation to rule justly, were falling apart. Members of the aristocracy could all recite a famous poem to this effect, 'The Poem of the Time of Darkness', written in the 1860s by the last great court poet of Central Java, Ronggowarsito. Ronggowarsito composed this piece when Hamengkubuwono VII, the future Sultan, was still a young man. Hamengkubuwono must have felt the impact of its words.

> Now the glory of the realm
> Is seen to be faded,
> Rules' regulation in ruin
> For lack of examples.
> . . .

What worth, being leader?
So are sown the seeds of error
Sprinkled with water of unawareness,
They sprout into flowers of failure.

This poem describes the colonial period as an 'age of madness'. It was a despairing cry for the nobility of Java to return to a moral life, to live up to the duty of being members of the warrior caste.

Some tried. In 1920 Sultan Hamengkubuwono VII abdicated, officially because of his age, but in fact because he was worn down by pressure from Dutch administrators to reform land holdings and cut back on his expenditure, especially to drop family members from the royal payroll. Publicly he expressed all this as concern about the decline in respect for tradition shown by other Javanese. His son, the next Sultan, worked to revive the arts as the outward signs of such tradition, but could do little about political rights. That was a struggle that Tirto and others were to take up in the arena of the mass media and new kinds of organisation, using the Western education brought by the Dutch.[5]

EDUCATION AND EMANCIPATION

Western education was only being opened up to the indigenous inhabitants of the Indies at the beginning of the twentieth century. In 1900, a mere 1,500 of those classified as natives went to European schools, along with 13,000 Europeans. It was hard work getting the natives there. The Dutch interpreted reluctance to attend school as meaning that 'the natives are not lazy, but they are very careless and thoughtless about the future. The main reason for this is that they do not use their brains, because they have not been taught to do so'. By 1928, almost 75,000 Indonesians had completed Western primary education, and nearly 6,500 secondary school, still a very small portion of the total population. In a town like Blora, with its population of around 15,000 when Pramoedya Ananta Toer was born there, there was only one European school and one Dutch native school, besides the independent school in which Pramoedya's father taught.[6]

The aristocracy were the first to get access to Western education. Some were grateful, looking to the Dutch as examples of all that was modern. Others felt that they were being patronised. Raden Ajeng Kartini, Indonesia's founding feminist, buried in the teak forests of Blora, was one aristocrat whose Dutch education provided her with personal enlightenment and a desire to do more for her people. Kartini was one of the daughters of the regent of Jepara, a centre of intricate wood-carving not far from Blora. As a noble's daughter she had to go into seclusion on reaching puberty, around the age of twelve: 'be put into the "box" . . . totally separated from the outside world to which I could not return unless it was at the side of a husband, a complete stranger chosen for us by our parents'.

While in her 'box' Kartini made *batik* and took up other Javanese pursuits, but she also developed the language skills and education that allowed her to become what she craved to be: 'a modern girl'. Her father, despite being a mediocre regent of little ambition, had joined with his brothers in being among the first Javanese leaders to advocate wider education, catching the attention of the followers of the Ethical Policy, notably the director of the Department of Education and Public Worship. This director worked energetically to expand educational opportunities, opening up the primary school system for broader participation, and creating new high school and tertiary opportunities, albeit limited ones. Most Indonesians were seen to need only vocational education, but a small number were able to study in the Netherlands.

Through the director's official patronage, Kartini became a close friend of his wife, Rosa Abendanon-Mandri. At the age of twenty-one, Kartini entered into effusive and sharp-witted correspondence in Dutch with Rosa, a Spanish–Puerto Rican-born feminist. The year before they began to write to each other, Kartini had also begun writing to a Dutch feminist, Stella Zeehandelaar. She subsequently met and received encouragement from other Dutch women.

Kartini's remarkable correspondence with Rosa and Stella combined turn-of-the-century sentimentalism with a clinical analysis of the situation faced by Javanese women and the steps that were needed to liberate them. In writing to Rosa she recognised the importance of the Ethical Policy's progressive move of allowing girls to be educated along with boys: 'It will be a giant step forwards!' But she also knew the limits of this: 'But . . . but what use will it be for the girls to be so educated if sooner or later they will still have to return to the traditional society, if there is only one avenue available for them to exist on this earth: marriage!' Her solution: 'Accompany it with vocational training and then, the education intended as a blessing would truly be a blessing instead of a torture which it now is for many girls.'

Kartini was a realist: 'Ideals, we Javanese girls cannot have ideals.' She saw that a combination of tradition and Dutch government policies kept women constrained. Not only did she recognise the need for more radical action, she knew that this must be combined with shattering aristocratic privilege amongst the Javanese: 'the nobility must earn the reverence of the people, be worthy of it.' Women must be independent and 'of use to our fellow human beings'. Kartini challenged polygamy and established a school system for women that departed from the Dutch one, a system that was radically egalitarian in its outlook.

Her Dutch male patrons struggled to cultivate her as an example of their good work. A leading socialist parliamentarian created an opportunity for her to go and study in the Netherlands, but the director of Education and her father decided it was not in her best interests to go. After denying her an education in the Netherlands, her family pushed her into an arranged marriage to the regent of Rembang. She died in childbirth on 17 September 1904, aged just twenty-five. Stella wrote to Kartini's parliamentary patron that it was 'so utterly painful to think that this beautiful and promising life was sacrificed to selfish interests ... sacrificed to the interests of the Netherlands Indies Government'.[7] It was left to her three sisters to continue her work in setting up schools for girls.

Kartini's brief life inspired others from the aristocracy, and her school network spread. Consequently, Tirto Adhi Suryo began his career as a journalist and political organiser in her shadow, and one of his newspapers, *Daughters of the Indies* (supported by a fund created by Princess Emma, the mother of Queen Wilhelmina), was organised in collaboration with a woman who set up Kartini Schools in the West Javanese city of Bandung. This type of school spread to other islands, forming the basis of a small but significant feminist movement. The Dutch continued their recognition of Kartini's work.

Kartini and Tirto both recognised that if the whole colonial system were to be challenged, the first step would be to reform the indigenous aristocracy. Kartini and Tirto also wanted to extend their campaigns down into improving the lives of all peoples of the Indies, but for the ordinary peasants of Blora, aristocrats were the problem, not the source of hope for a better life.

PEASANTS AGAINST THE COLONIAL STATE

At the same time as the Dutch were attempting to take over royal lands and curtail regents like Brotodiningrat, they received reports of strange mystical movements that defied the colonial order. In encountering these movements, officials had to deal with ways of thinking and acting that were alien to their rational modern state. The Dutch were also finding out that the indigenous aristocrats, who were meant to be instruments of colonial rule, were alienated from the peasant world.

When indigenous officials came to collect taxes on forestry lands from the villagers in Blora, they encountered people who spoke to them insolently. Javanese is a hierarchical language with high and low forms. Correct behaviour means speaking to another using a language level appropriate to that person's standing in society. High-ranking people spoke the low form to commoners, and in return expected to be addressed in high language. The tax collectors expected High Javanese as their due, and were unimpressed by peasants speaking down to them with implied defiance. There was no direct refusal to carry out orders to perform their corvée service, but instead a series of oblique Javanese puns that added up to acts of passive resistance. These peasants were followers of Samin (b. 1859), an influential local spiritual teacher.

For Saminists, there was no colonial law, only 'laws of action, speech and necessity', which included 'not doing evil, not arguing, fighting, being jealous, coveting or stealing ... not telling lies or slandering ...'. It was impossible for officials to reason with them, because to any question or command to carry out service to the state a Saminist man would just point to his genitals and say 'I am in service, my work is sex with my wife.' In a society where polygamy was the norm, the Saminists were monogamous. When asked what they believed in, Saminists replied that they were followers of the religion of Adam, and did not believe in heaven and hell, only the realities of daily life and attachment to the land. This was interpreted as a rejection of orthodox Islam as well as bureaucratic authority. Saminists avoided money wherever possible and repudiated trade. They refused schooling, passing on their knowledge orally and by example, which they called 'writing without a blackboard, a blackboard inside the written'.

The Saminists were radical egalitarians who thought of their leader as a messiah, and they spread his practices to neighbouring regions. Despite the fact that they never numbered more than around 3,000 families, and that their movement showed no violence, Dutch frustration was such that Samin himself was exiled to Sumatra, where he died in 1914. The movement has continued to the present day. In 1997, fourth-generation Saminists held a mass wedding in Kudus, north-west of Blora.[8]

'Have you ever been to Blora, friend? It's a social convention there that all live in poverty. Those who buy meat once a week, friend, are no longer commoners but "lords"', writes Pramoedya Ananta Toer of his home town. Pramoedya grew up in poor surroundings. His father, 'a farm boy with an athletic build', had moved there as a teacher, along with his young bride from a relatively well-off family, and their learning and origins led the other people of Blora to regard them as aristocrats.[9] Already poor because

Blora has unproductive soil, the people of Blora found at the beginning of the twentieth century that their struggles to survive were compounded by new demands. These were the deteriorating conditions of life that produced Saminism.

The majority of people in Blora, as elsewhere in the archipelago, farmed at subsistence level. They usually lived in earth-floor houses made of bamboo, with woven palm leaf or rattan walls and thatched roofs, and could afford little in the way of possessions. What little income they had was usually shared on a family basis, and priority went to buying animals that could provide meat or support farming. Tasks were divided on gender lines, but women usually did over 60 per cent of the work of rice farming. Their daughters could not be hidden away like the aristocratic Kartini was: they were needed for work.

Javanese peasant life had for centuries been oriented around the staple crop, rice. On Java the majority of the population farmed rice using an intensive 'wet' system, one in which the fields were flooded. Blora's landscape resembled that of other parts of the archipelago outside Java because much of its rice was grown on rotating 'dry' fields. Incomes were supplemented by working for others during harvest time, and growing secondary crops in the dry season, as well as by harvesting coconuts for oil, tapping palm trees for sugar, and weaving locally grown cotton.

Typically, peasants rose before dawn to look after their houses, sweeping the yards before going off to work in the rice fields where they hoed, planted, weeded and eventually harvested. Their children worked in the fields with them. Lunch was a hasty meal grabbed in the middle of the day, before resting through the hottest hours. After siesta it was time to tend the fowl and perhaps buffalo and goats (or pigs in non-Muslim areas), before an evening meal and sleep.

Rice was the basis of every meal, but in times of poverty it was replaced with cassava. Peasants rarely ate meat, they mostly had spiced vegetables, such as different forms of beans or peas, water spinach, and chillies, cooked with a paste made from the essence of fermented seafood – a salty black flavouring known as *terasi*. In Java soybeans were made into cakes called *tempé* that were sliced thinly and fried in coconut oil. Salt was manufactured by the thousands of poor fishermen from coastal villages who supplemented their meagre incomes by evaporating seawater. One of the only things that peasants and sultans had in common was an addiction to chewing the mildly narcotic betel, made up of peppery leaves from the betel vine, areca palm nuts and a pinch of lime, and usually supplemented by chewing tobacco or in some cases marijuana.

The government had a monopoly on salt that kept the prices high. There was a single rate of capitation tax that most people had to pay up until 1927, irrespective of their incomes, then taxes to slaughter animals, wealth taxes, taxes for trade, firearms tax, and many others, but the main imposition was land tax, called 'land rent' by the government. To pay all these taxes, and to meet the basic necessities of life, many farmers frequently pawned their crops in advance of the harvest to buy the seed for the next crop. On other islands it was the same story, whether the crop was maize or coconuts to produce copra. Chinese shops and roving traders provided the ubiquitous money lenders that thrived throughout the archipelago. Resources that had once been regarded as common property, such as the teak forests and forest lands, were no longer accessible to the people of Blora, even for activities such as collecting firewood. Forestry officers attempted to husband the teak as a state resource and keep people from using the land and harvesting the trees. Attacks on these officials were common.

Between late 1899 and the beginning of 1903, the Indies had gone through a period of El Niño drought. Its worst year, 1902, saw the second lowest rainfall on record. Cholera was rampant and food prices soared, the animals essential for working the rice-fields and providing food were dying of rinderpest, so starvation was everywhere, with people dying in 'unburiable' numbers. The rate of population increase for the Indies was halved in that year. This starvation attracted Dutch protests and became the catalyst for the Ethical Policy. The government was forced to spend millions on relief programmes. They instituted a commission that concluded it had been a mistake to think of a peasant as someone able 'to understand his own interest' and therefore more government intervention in local administration would be needed.[10]

The results were mixed. Although there were few repetitions of the drastic famines, wholesale changes in land ownership, taxation and labour conditions that followed from this intervention widened the gap between rich and poor, particularly on Java. This widening resulted in part from the reduction in the amount of land owned communally, which was turned into individual holdings, a process similar in nature and effect to enclosure in Britain at the beginning of the Industrial Revolution. By the 1930s, 83 per cent of all land was individually owned, an increase of nearly 20 per cent from the situation at the beginning of the century, holdings were consolidated into fewer hands, and the number of landless was increasing. Village headmen ended up the biggest land owners because they were able to manipulate the changes, particularly as Dutch policies created a more tightly circumscribed definition of what constituted a village.

Compounding the land problem was rapid population growth, which outstripped any increases in the amount of land available for farming. Forests were rapidly turned into rice-fields or plantations, but the population of Java and Madura, which had jumped in size in the nineteenth century, kept increasing until it reached 45 million by the end of Dutch rule, with an even more rapid rise in the Outer Islands.

Anti-colonial revolts similar to Saminism erupted throughout the Indies. In 1905, hundreds of farmers in Central Java downed tools and marched to the palace of Yogyakarta, where they sat silently in front of the palace as a way of asking their sultan to relieve them of their burdens. On the cane-fields of East Java protest took a devastating form for the sugar industry. Those who resented the low wages, harsh conditions, and the industry's drain on farming resources, waited until the cane was almost ready to harvest, then torched the crops. In 1911, at the high point of this protest, there were 1,383 cane burnings in the Pasuruhan region of East Java. In 1917, East Java, Bali and neighbouring islands experienced a series of severe volcanic eruptions and earthquakes. In 1918 the Spanish influenza pandemic took 2 million lives in the Indies, and devastated production, just ahead of another drought in 1919. The reaction to these events was a series of large-scale strikes, involving up to 20,000 people, that spread throughout the sugar estates in 1919 and 1920.

These 'incidents', as the Dutch called them, were not confined to Java. In 1907 there was an attack on Dutch soldiers in a revolt in Central Sulawesi, and in subsequent years revolts against corvée in Bali that were put down with violence. In a 1915 revolt in East Kalimantan supporters of a deposed sultan combined with political activists and indigenous Dayak people to start a movement that accentuated the myths and ceremonies of the latter. In the Batak highlands of Sumatra between 1915 and 1918, a local teacher proclaimed that 'white eyes' should be expelled, the legendary king of the Bataks returned, and tax and corvée abolished. This movement, which mixed Christian elements with indigenous practices, spread with a speed that alarmed the Dutch. The Dutch were always anxious that every riot, demonstration or peasant strike might escalate into an anti-colonial uprising, but in most cases those who took part in such actions were thinking of the short term, refusing to do work that was beneath them, struggling to get an advantage over fellow villagers, or despairing of having to pay yet more tax.[11]

PEASANT SPIRITUALITY

Peasant leader Samin's status as a messiah was not unusual in the Indies. Many movements featured messiah-figures who proclaimed the end of the millennium and the coming of a golden age, one in which the land would be returned to how it was before the foreigners came. Occasionally such movements developed into armed revolts, as with the 1904 uprising where hundreds of Javanese proclaimed a wealthy peasant as the Mahdi, the Islamic messiah. Other movements took on aspects of the Hindu or Buddhist beliefs that pre-dated Islam in Indonesia, or took on characteristics of an indigenous spirituality older than any religion.

The rebellions exaggerated aspects of everyday spiritual practice. Finding ways to control external forces has always been important for those otherwise at the mercy of fate. Indigenous spiritualism aimed to make fate more manageable. It involved sets of ceremonies, the most important of which were the ritual feasts called Blessings. Eating together promoted solidarity and an ethos of helping each other, especially important since farmers needed their neighbours to help maintain water systems and during harvest. Male heads of household held feasts at important times, to celebrate births and marriages, to ward off pests or diseases, at harvest time, or to mourn the dead. These were times in which people could escape the pressures of everyday life, and watch the troupes of dancers that would come, or cock-fights and other games of chance where a farmer's lot could be improved. Ceremonies were meant to restore balance to the world. They were a way of coping with the extremes of existence. Feasts were also a mechanism to redistribute wealth: the feast-holder poured his worldly goods into a meal shared with the community. In places such as the Toraja highlands of Sulawesi, rituals were regarded as the defining moments of local culture, the real 'work' of life, and people dated the important events of their lives around them.

Throughout Indonesia there were strong beliefs, still current, that significant life events necessitated the giving of gifts. People ran heavily into debt rather than avoid this social duty. Weddings were one of the key forms of gift-giving ceremonies because they linked families into wider kin groups. These family ties were maintained by elaborate dowries and bride-prices, usually consisting of beautiful textiles and buffaloes, as well as cash. Throughout Indonesia, death rites were another important way to maintain connections with ancestors, who were believed to remain active forces in the community, influencing fate. Death rites involved exchanges of offerings with the world of the spirits. These practices and beliefs strengthened communal identity because they increased both the material and spiritual ties amongst villagers.

Related to beliefs that the dead were linked to the fate of the living, was the concept that there are other kinds of spiritual force active in the material world, and that some people have the power to manipulate these forces. Influential forces included many types of ghosts, familiars and invisible beings likely to be encountered in forests, graveyards or other special places. The influence of these spirits could be seen in people's lives. For example, if a man suddenly became extremely wealthy, his neighbours would know that he had probably acquired a spirit familiar, which had directed his luck. One could acquire a spirit, or influence invisible forces, by various means including help from a shaman or spiritual teacher.

In keeping with a view of the world where mundane powers and invisible spiritual forces were equally appreciated, peoples throughout Indonesia used ceremonies and ancient stories and songs to describe their environment. Pearl divers on the island of Aru, for example, had to take gifts to their 'undersea wives', conceived of as real women who, if appeased, provided access to pearls, and if angry brought poverty and death.

Meditation was another way to influence the spiritual world: if one fasted and meditated in a certain place for a set period, usually to fulfil a vow, then the resulting inner strength brought outward rewards. Spiritual power was concentrated in special places such as caves, mountain-tops, beaches or graves of village founders and saints. Kudus, north-west of Blora, for example, was a place to visit on pilgrimage because one of the saints who founded Islam on Java is buried there. A pilgrimage to his grave, the making of offerings, the acquisition of a magic talisman or learning a secret formula were all ways to improve one's lot in life. People have been reputed to meditate for years at a grave like this, needing neither food nor drink to sustain them, such is the grave's power. Another holy grave in Java was visited by women wanting to become pregnant, while a thief's grave in Pemalang was the site of pilgrimage for the power to steal. Similar beliefs and practices are still almost universal in Indonesia.[12]

Spiritual leaders, healers, shamans, teachers and shadow puppet performers who helped to explain the world for peasants were, as a consequence, important people in the Javanese countryside. They mediated fate, and could help others with their special knowledge. Leaders like Samin were regarded as people who had acquired great spiritual power, and when proclaimed as messiahs, or Just Kings, they acted as alternatives to the traditional rulers who had failed the peasantry. Even modern politicians who were active amongst the peasantry could be declared Just Kings.

Another type of spiritually powerful individual important to village life, and another symptom of the imbalanced nature of colonial society, was a figure who was spy, police, thief, stand-over man, pimp, Robin Hood, Mafioso and protector of the mosque. These men were known as Fighting

Cocks, and they were experts in esoteric knowledge (which included magically inserting bits of metal under the skin for strength and invulnerability), incantations (so that people would not wake up when you were burgling them) and powers of invisibility. They also practised forms of the martial arts, along with poaching, gambling and drinking. In some parts of the countryside, for example in the area close to the Comal sugar estate on the north coast of Java, there were whole villages of Fighting Cocks.

To maintain control and keep watch on those under them, headmen and officials would employ these travelling toughs to spy on villagers and provide muscle to keep them in line – an indication of how alienated village heads had become from their fellow villagers. The Fighting Cocks were supposed to act as local police, but just as often they were the thieves and robbers for whom police were needed. At the same time they could be defenders of the people, robbing landlords in order to provide food for the starving. Equivalents to Fighting Cocks were also found outside of Java, notably in Minangkabau, West Sumatra. The Dutch knew about the thuggery and worse, but turned a blind eye in the interests of peace and order. The dramatic changes to social institutions brought about by Dutch policies undermining existing social structures had given rise to the Fighting Cocks in the first place.[13]

A MOBILE WORKFORCE

Despite the orientation to the land evident in examples of Javanese spirituality such as Saminism, mobility was also a trait of Javanese life. In the early twentieth century those who had no land to farm joined a labour force that moved about the countryside. The new railway system expanded the possibilities. Hundreds of thousands of people travelled 'goat class' seeking economic opportunities. Some worked as share-croppers, some moved from place to place to find seasonal work, travelling to the cane-fields and factories, and the tea and coffee plantations. Ideally a man could plant rice, leave his wife and children to work the fields, and then return at harvest time.

On the cane-fields and in the sugar factories work was harsh. Workers typically toiled in twelve-hour shifts. In 1929 there were 180 sugar factories employing 60,000 permanent hands, most of whom lived near the plantations and worked in the factories or in transporting cane. Many of those workers were the same people who had been extorted into renting their rice land to the mills. Another 700,000 temporary hands came to cut the cane or perform the other seasonal tasks.

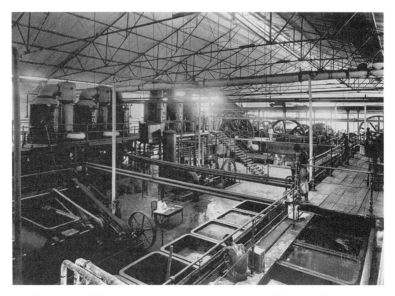

Figure 2.2 Mills and damping stations, sugar factory. Photo by Kurdjian,
the Armenian master photographer from Surabaya.

The village heads were important in helping the sugar factories control
the best local land. They also played a role in supplying workers to the
plantations and their factories: in order to guarantee a supply of casual field
workers, the factories paid advances to the labourers, but the village headmen were paid a bonus of 10 per cent on these advances.[14]

The sugar industry's vast capital investment materialised in the form of
huge shiny machines that filled the cavernous factories (figure 2.2).
Workers with metal-working skills readily adapted to working on these
impressive imports, ensuring that the vast wheels kept turning to mill
the raw cane. Because they were reputed to have better powers of concentration, women worked the centrifugal machines. The worst work was
stoking the cane waste into the furnaces that drove the steam engines.
Contemporary photographs showed the workers bowed semi-naked in
the stuffy sheds before the giant European machine-monsters, while the
white-clad Dutch managers presided over the momentous tasks of crushing
and milling the cane. Those workers lived on the cutting edge of the
modern age.

In 1929, sugar, the king of Indies' industries, collapsed and never
recovered. When sugar prices dropped to almost one-third of the pre-
Depression level, the industry dismissed first the casual, then the permanent

workers. All those who had shared in the prosperity of the industry, including petty entrepreneurs, also shared in the suffering, as the population at large turned to subsistence farming to survive.

Once the Great Depression was in full swing, the average yearly income per person on Java and Madura declined from *f*47.60 to *f*20.30 (US$19.04 to $8.12 or $1,750 to $750 in present-day terms), with an even greater rate of decline for the rest of Indonesia. What this meant for those who worked the sugar plantations in East Java, was that daily wages declined from 46c per day for men and 35c for women in 1926, to 27c and 22c respectively in 1934.

A survey of Javanese workers on and off plantations at the end of the Dutch period found that those with steady work were better off than peasants whose labour was regarded as free, although there were huge discrepancies between areas. The best-off plantation coolies were estimated to have had a daily individual caloric intake of 2,535, the worst-off only 652, while local peasants consumed between 2,267 and 894 calories. The minimum necessary to maintain heart beat and internal organ function is 1,200 calories per day. Little wonder that the peasants of Java lived short lives, had high infant mortality rates, and were constantly in ill-health and in debt.[15]

The poorest of Javanese sold themselves to join the coolie labour force of 360,000 working in Deli or other Outer Islands. In 1931, nearly 50 per cent of this force were Javanese 'contract coolies', but when the workers put their mark on the indenture papers they were not fully aware of the horrific terms to which they were agreeing. These contracts had clauses about ideal working conditions, but since most of the coolies could not read, they did not know what the employers' side of the bargain was. All the workers knew was that they were being advanced *f*10 to go off to work in a place they had never heard of.

On the rubber plantations coolies had to get up before dawn to cut the bark of the havea trees, drain off the sap that was to become rubber, carry the heavy pails to the foul-smelling factories, weed and clear land for more trees to be planted. If they were too slow they were beaten. If they stood up to the foreman they were beaten. If they broke any clause of the contract-they-could-not-understand they were liable to penal sanctions, that is, criminal conviction and canings or gaol. The one benefit coolies did receive was medical attention in the plantations' private hospitals, which meant that they suffered less than their contemporaries from cholera, beri-beri and other debilitating diseases. After all, sick workers were not productive workers.

The foremen who kept the coolies in line also supplied them with prostitutes and opportunities for gambling. The high cost of both activities ensured that the coolies were not able to pay off their original indenture, and so at the end of one contract (a year and a half to three years) they had to re-sign for another period. Everyone on the plantations knew that 'if you were a contract coolie ... then you were no longer the owner of your body.' Following decades of protest some reforms were instituted in the early 1930s. The system of penal sanctions was phased out, largely as a result of pressure from international trading partners, and despite loud complaints from the planters.[16]

Other coolies worked either in the coal mines, or in the tin mines of Bangka and Belitung Islands. In the large Sumatran mine at Ombilin, conditions were extremely harsh, with a high proportion of convict labour having to be imported. Death from fighting and suicide was a weekly occurrence. Only a few Javanese coolies ever made their way home, their fate typified by a beggar found on the road near Yogyakarta in 1931, who had returned only to find that his family had died, no one remembered him, and his property was all gone.

Despite the awful nature of the plantations, they did provide local benefits, and for small-holders there was the possibility of joining a small but growing indigenous middle class. Large plantations stimulated the development of local cash economies and the growth of petty trade. This was most evident in the highlands above Deli. There, particularly around the hill station of Berastagi, the local Karo Batak people became involved in growing and marketing vegetables, trying out new crops such as potatoes, until the region became a thriving market centre. More and more Bataks gained an appreciation of cash money, something that was still foreign. Taxation pushed the Batak people into greater use of cash, but money acquired a special role all of its own within the local status system. Batak culture did not encourage the development of Western-style capitalism, however, since the status system and local solidarity meant that most wealth would be ploughed into ritual gift-giving and gambling.

Some economic indicators point to a growth in general prosperity for the peoples of the Indies in the latter stages of Dutch rule: rice became more available and cloth imports picked up, while the number of Indonesians able to make the pilgrimage to Mecca – obligatory for all Muslims who can afford it – increased. At the height of local prosperity, before the Great Depression, the number of pilgrims to Mecca reached 40,000 per year. These mainly consisted of traders and those who had made their money by growing export crops on small-holdings. They came from the most mobile of ethnic groups, the Minangkabau who had long traditions of economic migration, and the seafaring Bugis and Makasar peoples of Sulawesi.

Indigenous small-holdings had always been more efficient than the big European estates. During the spike in rubber prices around 1925, there occurred what the people themselves called a 'rain of gold' – export farmers of Sumatra and Kalimantan briefly became wealthy, as shown by sharp rises in imports of cars, bicycles and sewing machines in cities such as Banjarmasin (Kalimantan) and Palembang (Sumatra) where these farmers were concentrated. They were badly hit by the Depression, especially since the Dutch government introduced new taxes that took 95 per cent of their incomes, again as a way of protecting the European plantations. The government also took until 1935 to devalue the currency in order to restore markets. Overall the Dutch government increased the tax burden on the indigenous population so that by 1940 it was 250 per cent of its 1928 level. In the years from 1938 onwards the plight of people in the countryside was compounded by another series of droughts.[17]

The novelist Pramoedya Ananta Toer, like most of the inhabitants of Blora, was born into a world dominated by Islam. His maternal grandfather had been a Haji: someone who had gone on the pilgrimage to Mecca. In his novels on the colonial period Pramoedya recognised the importance of Islam as the main vehicle for popular opposition to the Dutch, even if in more personal works he rejected those who deny critical thinking in the name of religion.

As a Haji, Pramoedya's grandfather – 'a tall lean man with a straight nose and sallow complexion, probably because of some Arab or Indian blood' – was both wealthy and one of the most important people in the community. Hajis were looked upon as people of great knowledge and experience. He was someone who could afford to take more than one wife, even though he divorced Pramoedya's grandmother soon after a daughter was born, consigning Pramoedya's grandmother, then just fourteen, to a life of hard work. Some of Pramoedya's negativity towards the pious comes from his resentment of his grandfather. Hajis were rarer in Blora than other parts of Central Java, testimony to the dominance of Javanese spiritualism in the area. We know little else about his grandfather's life, but more detailed information on the complexities of Islam in Java emerges through the lives of other quite different pilgrims, one rural, Kiai Haji Hasyim Asy'ari (1871–1947), and the other urban, Kiai Haji Ahmad Dahlan (1868–1923).[18]

Both of these men came, like Pramoedya's grandfather, from trading families, and this trade gave them the wealth to travel to Mecca. We do not know much about Hasyim's entrepreneurial activities, although one of the products of the area from which he came was indigo, used to make blue fabric dye. Ahmad Dahlan came from a group of entrepreneurs who made up the embryo of an indigenous middle class, the *batik* merchants of Java. These came mainly from the two Central Javanese cities of Yogyakarta and Surakarta, but travelled extensively throughout Java and overseas. Ahmad Dahlan's family traded in the beautiful wax-resist dyed cloths of Java. The women who made the cloths developed an immense range of regional styles and designs, but the prestige of the palaces ensured that the twin royal cities remained the epitome of the dyer's art. Yogyakarta and Surakarta had been boosted by nineteenth- and twentieth-century developments in production. New methods of using metal stamps to produce designs had replaced laborious hand-waxing, artificial dyes were introduced, and cheaper machine-made cloth replaced local cotton. With these changes, Java began to export *batik* in bulk to other islands in the first part of the twentieth century.

Hasyim came from the small town of Jombang in East Java, and claimed descent from ancient kings of Java, his family migrating from Central Java to Jombang several generations before he was born. Dahlan was born in the city of Yogyakarta, in the Muslim quarter, a set of narrow streets entered through gateways, situated behind the Sultan's Great Mosque. He was the son of the chanter of Arabic prayers for the mosque, and learned that language from his father. Although Muslims believe that one can only know the holy Koran in its original Arabic, few Indonesians were fluent in the language, so the prayer-chanter was a man of great learning. Islam has no priesthood, all men are believed to be equal under God, but there are seven stages of closeness to God. Teachers, pilgrims, prayer leaders and experts in Islamic law are closer to becoming the Perfect Man, someone full of God's knowledge. The Javanese title 'Kiai' was thus bestowed on teachers of superior knowledge, as both of these men were. The term *ulama* ('mullah' in its anglicised form) is also used of such leaders of the congregation.

Rulers were also supposed to be at a higher stage on the ladder, exemplary 'Regulators of Religion', as the Sultans' title had it. Many religious leaders looked at royalty during the colonial period and found them wanting as paragons of Islam, particularly since these supposedly exemplary men were under the command of heathen foreigners, the Dutch.

Both of these future religious leaders travelled extensively to study Islam. Dahlan was sent from the city to the country to deepen his religious knowledge through study in a special religious boarding school, called *pesantren*, found throughout the countryside of Sumatra, Kalimantan and Java. Hasyim's family ran one of their own *pesantren*, but in accordance with tradition he was sent to live in others from the age of fourteen, and for seven years he moved from one *pesantren* to another through East Java and Madura.

Pesantren have played a major role as social institutions in Indonesia over the centuries, emphasising core values of sincerity, simplicity, individual autonomy, solidarity and self-control. In them young men were separated from their families, contributing to a sense of individual commitment to the faith and close bonding to a teacher. These schools aimed to deepen knowledge of the Koran, particularly through learning Arabic grammar, traditions of exegesis, the Sayings of the Prophet, law and logic. In the nineteenth and early twentieth centuries many still included study of the Hindu-Buddhist stories found in *wayang* shadow theatre, apocryphal stories about heroes from the Middle East associated with the early history of Islam, and a wide range of Javanese mystical texts.

Muslims viewed faith as a struggle between daily life and Islam, one that was not always a success. Muhamad Rajab, who had been a young man in a Minangkabau village on Sumatra in the colonial era, recalled the agony of being forced to give up his beloved soccer in order to study religion. His first lesson was full of obscure pronouncements and meaningless chanting led by an unappealing teacher: 'after reciting for some two hours, listening to his murky explanations, which repeated themselves and twisted and turned like a snake's armpit, half in Arabic, half in Indonesian, I was still totally confused. So were my friends.'

In the Indonesian context, there is no clear line between orthodoxy and heresy in Islam. It is a religion that has been adapted and maintained in a variety of ways since it came from India to Indonesia in the twelfth century. The founders of Islam on Java brought the religion peacefully, through trade. The early teachers of Islam in Indonesia were mystics who travelled around passing on knowledge from teacher to pupil. They taught inner awareness, something already present in Javanese mysticism. Some forms of Indonesian Islam incorporated pre-existing indigenous forms, as in the Hindu influences on the 'Three Times Praying' Sasak people of Lombok. Newer twentieth-century movements also departed from religious purity, as with the Muhdi Akbar cult of Selayar island, which proclaimed that it was not necessary to pray five times a day, and that meditation and chanting could lead to direct unity with God.[19]

Hasyim Asy'ari and Ahmad Dahlan went on the pilgrimage to Mecca because it was one of the five obligations of the faith, the others being the confession of faith ('There is no other God but Allah and Muhammad is his Prophet'), giving alms to the poor, fasting during the lunar month of *Ramadan*, and praying five times a day. These obligations entail living a clean life and avoiding drugs, gambling, other immorality, and unclean animals such as pigs and dogs.

The two did not meet in Mecca. Dahlan returned to Java around 1888 and Hasyim went to Mecca four years later, but they both studied under the same teacher, a famous expert on religious knowledge from Minangkabau in Sumatra. The profound experience of the pilgrimage included meeting with Muslims from all over the Indies, and the greater international community of believers. They learned of growing anti-colonial movements throughout Africa and the Middle East. Fellow Indies pilgrims from Sulawesi, West Java, Minangkabau, Aceh and other areas regarded as centres of strong belief, helped them conceive of a common interest against the Dutch. For some who had been on the pilgrimage, the need for a crusade to purify and renew Islam was developing.

Both became major community leaders on return from Mecca. Hasyim Asy'ari founded his own *pesantren* in a village outside of Jombang that was known for its brothels and drinking, determined to reform the community as a first step to reforming society as a whole. Dahlan married the daughter of the head of the Great Mosque in Yogyakarta. He argued with his in-laws about theology, about where the pulpit should be placed, and on which day to start the fasting month. As one of a growing group who regarded themselves as modernists, Haji Dahlan worried about the many Javanese practices that were not justified by scripture. He looked to return to the basics in order to create a renewed Islam that was better able to cope with the modern world. As a means of realising this ideal, he formed an educational organisation with these aims, called *Muhammadiyah*, in 1912. The movement was quickly taken up by traders and craftsmen, and spread to the Outer Islands, establishing a strong base in Sulawesi only a decade after it was founded. This organisation has become the second largest Muslim organisation in Indonesia, today numbering some 20 million followers.

Kiai Haji Hasyim Asy'ari found himself on the other side of the fence, in the group labelled by Dahlan's followers as 'the Old People'. Even though Hasyim's *pesantren* was innovative, having reformed the structure of religious teaching, he still held strongly to the need to maintain what was now coming to be defined as tradition: the different streams of religious law, the rituals of worship at holy graves and other practices that had grown up over the centuries in Java that were now under threat from the modernists. This threat became stronger when hardline purists, the founders of the Saudi state, took over Mecca in 1924. These purists wanted to demolish holy graves and get rid of traditions of Islamic law. Hasyim and other country leaders got together in Surabaya in 1926 to form an Association of Religious Scholars, called *Nahdlatul Ulama*, which would give them a political voice. The organisation's initial aim was to counter the work of the modernists of *Muhammadiyah*, but their group also realised that they needed to be active in politics to survive. *Nahdlatul Ulama* grew to be the largest Muslim body. At the end of the twentieth century it had 30 million members. Its leader, Hasyim Asy'ari's grandson, Kiai Haji Abdurrahman Wahid, became Indonesia's fourth president.

Muhammadiyah's sense of its own modernity marked a departure in Javanese thinking, a rejection of tradition. As one of the leaders of the movement put it, it aimed to liberate people from their fear of the immaterial and the material: 'people here ... were afraid of the powers of the living as well as the dead.' He elaborated that the former were the Dutch, the Sultan, the regent and other officials, and the latter an ancient king buried in his village, as well as 'certain trees, graves, stones, old houses, and even such a man-made thing as a bronze statue in front of the Governor's Residence'. This fear of 'ghosts' was countered with 'true Islamic teachings', which 'tell us that no one should be afraid of anything or anybody except Allah, the Almighty'.[20] Islam has always had strong roots amongst Javanese royalty, but these views show that with the coming of modernism, aristocratic authority was no longer automatically linked to religion.

Muhammadiyah and *Nahdlatul Ulama* were two of many organisations founded in the first three decades of the twentieth century. A key figure in establishing such organisations had been Tirto Adhi Suryo, using the medium of print to publicise opposition to the Dutch, as in the Brotodiningrat curtain affair. Journalism gave the colonial power struggle an entirely new form and directed it towards a new aim. It was becoming a struggle for emancipation that Tirto, supporter of the Kartini Schools, knew had to be fought for gender as well as racial and social equality. At the end of the struggle, the Netherlands East Indies was made into Indonesia. But the struggle could not be fought in the countryside: the peasants, fishermen and coolies of the archipelago were too divided and diverse. Both of these new religious organisations for expressing and defending belief were founded in cities. Blora was not a place from which to launch a revolution.

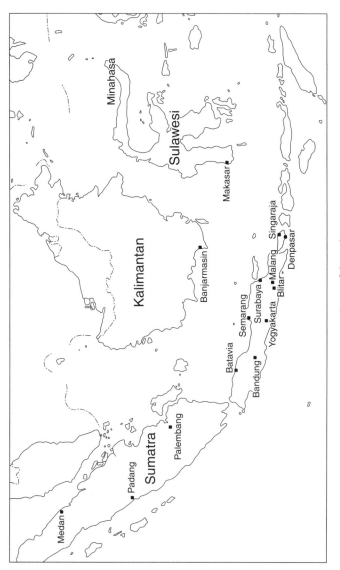

Map 3 Cities of the Indies

CHAPTER 3

'*To assail the colonial machine*'[1]

Travelling to cities broadens the mind, or it did in the Netherlands East Indies. One Balinese prince, Anak Agung Made Djelantik, can recall the experience in 1931 of being sent to junior high school in the town of Malang, in East Java, leaving behind his primary school days of Bali's largest town, Denpasar. Djelantik had grown up in East Bali, in a palace that was an extended set of houseyards, around which were clustered some of the dwellings of his father's subjects. His early life was the life of a village where society was rigidly hierarchical, and life revolved around farming. For his preliminary schooling he had to travel five hours from his family palace, to Denpasar, then a town of 15,000 people, just over a hundred of whom were Europeans.

In 1931, after a six-hour drive to Singaraja in North Bali, the young Djelantik caught a KPM steamer en route from Ambon and Makasar, for an exciting journey to Surabaya. From Surabaya he took another car 80 km south to Malang – population 87,000 – where he met not only local Javanese, but people from all over the Indies. He boarded with a Dutch teacher's family, where he learned new kinds of behaviour. He had to learn to wear pyjamas, say '*wel te resten*' (sleep well) and turn off the lights at night, to eat breakfast of chocolate granules sprinkled on bread spread with Palm Tree brand margarine, to do the opposite of Balinese politeness and comment on a meal, as well as conversing during it, and to like cheese, cauliflower and brussels sprouts.[2]

Djelantik's journey was similar to the experiences of a small but crucial group of young men and a few women who came from the Batak highlands of Sumatra, the forests of Kalimantan, the remote and rain-deprived South-east islands, and the orchid-shaped island of Sulawesi, to continue their education in Java, a process which helped make Java the centre of the Indies. Javanese also moved from villages and towns to big cities for education. Few from the Outer Islands would have been able to travel first class, or to live in the style Djelantik did. His father paid *f*100 per month for him to live with a Dutch family because of the high status and special access to Dutch knowledge this provided. His school-mates who boarded with Javanese families only paid *f*15 per month. Even for those who did not have close contact with the Dutch, coming to a city like Malang meant encountering modern lifestyles at a crucial stage in their personal development. Although Djelantik did not go to the biggest cities, his experience expanded beyond the world of kings, priests and peasants in which he had grown up.

By the 1930s, only 5 per cent of the Indies' population lived in cities, but their influence was out of proportion to their size. Cities played a key role in creating a sense of Indonesia for those the Dutch called natives. This was not only because cities were centres of education and work and meeting places, but also because cities represented all that was modern, both good and bad. A sense of the modern, especially the need for progress, was important in forging nationalism amongst Indonesians.

The major cities of the Indies were ports: Surabaya, Batavia, Semarang on Java, Medan and Palembang on Sumatra, Makasar on Sulawesi. Some of them were old, pre-dating the United East India Company's mercantile ventures. Batavia had been founded by the Company, and like the other port cities had a deeply cosmopolitan nature, expressing the maritime nature of Indonesia's history. Because Indonesia is a set of islands linked through trade, it has always thrived on exchange, not only of goods, but of ideas, cultures and languages. The coming of European industries intensi-fied the experience of exchange, which is why the most important cities were those on Java. Port cities had quarters of other Indies' ethnic groups – the Malay, Bugis and Balinese quarters – and also Chinese, Arabs, Bengalis, Armenians and Jews. The great trade cities such as Makasar and Batavia looked outward to the wider world. By the early twentieth century none of the cities of the Outer Islands could match Java's in size.

THE MODERNNESS OF CITIES

By the time of Djelantik's voyage to Java, the cosmopolitan urban experi-ence was being opened up to more and more Indonesians, and in the next decade more people from less-well-off circumstances, including Pramoedya Ananta Toer, moved into the modern Indonesia of the cities. To better understand urbanisation's significance in forming new ways of seeing the world, however, it is important to look at the experiences of the early twentieth-century pioneers of migration to the cities. They included some of the founders of nationalism, an idea that could only develop in the urban context. The first modern nationalists made up only a small proportion of the new urban societies – many like Djelantik had no interest in the idea – but the nationalists created Indonesia.

One of the first modern nationalists, Pramoedya's hero Tirto Adhi Suryo, had made the journey from the little town of Blora to the big city three decades before Djelantik. Tirto first travelled to larger towns such as Madiun for education, but wanting to study medicine at the new tertiary institutions for natives, he had to continue on to Batavia. When Tirto lived there in the first decade of the twentieth century, Batavia's population was around 139,000, making it the second largest city in the Indies after Surabaya's 150,000. Batavia's population was to grow to 533,000 by 1930.[3]

Tirto passed the tests that allowed him to learn Dutch, a talent he used to write some early pieces subsequently published in newspapers. In being able to interact freely in Dutch, Tirto was both part of an elite close to the Dutch, and a rebel against the colonial order. At the beginning of the twentieth century Dutch officials had made their language exclusive, refusing to allow Javanese to speak to them in it, even those who could speak Dutch fluently. Javanese had to use respectful High Javanese, and to show the Dutch all the feudal gestures of obeisance: the prayer-like hand-gesture and the squatting pose that had also to be used when addressing indigenous rulers. Although there had been attempts to reform this attitude under Governor General van Heutsz, it was so entrenched that younger aristocrats like Tirto, rather than comply, totally rejected the whole relationship between the Dutch and the indigenous aristocracy. In the coastal cities, away from the courts and influence of the regents, Tirto and his fellow students could act in a democratic social manner.

Tirto served an apprenticeship on one of the many Dutch-language newspapers, where he quickly rose to the rank of editor, and became well known throughout the colony. Successful enough to drop out of medical school, Tirto became the first Indonesian newspaper owner on Java. He joined with editors and writers from Minahasa (North Sulawesi), Sumatra and Central Java in creating a new consciousness of the issues of daily life in the Indies.[4]

Through his newspapers Tirto campaigned against corruption by the Dutch, the regents and other members of the civil service, attempting to create awareness amongst the junior civil servants and the traders of the city of their duty towards the poor, 'the little people'. To achieve his aim he turned to the language of the city, Malay, since Eurasians and ethnic Chinese were producing newspapers in that language. When he wrote in Malay, he knew that only a small proportion of the urban population could read in Latin script, but he also knew that newspapers and other publications in Malay were frequently read aloud in communal groups.

As well as newspapers, there was a growing demand for popular novels, and so Tirto wrote in the 'dime novel' style of the day popularised by Chinese-Indonesian writers. There had been lending libraries in cities such as Palembang and Batavia going back at least to the nineteenth century, and with the advent of more locally printed books these libraries became widespread throughout other major cities. As well as local tales, translations of English-language detective stories, such as Nick Carter and Sherlock Holmes, were very popular.[5]

By publishing in Malay, Tirto and his colleagues helped make it the dominant language of the archipelago. The language itself probably originated in the eastern part of Kalimantan, and was the mother tongue of coastal peoples there, on the Riau, Bangka and Belitung islands off Sumatra, in some of the coastal sultanates of Sumatra, and the British-ruled Malay peninsula. In its more common forms it was a language of trade from South China to the Middle East. The Ambonese and Manadonese developed their own Malay dialects, as did the acculturated Chinese of the cities, but native speakers of Malay were a small part of the total population in 1900.

The Dutch supported the use of Malay primarily because they considered it easier to learn than their own language. Although there were 200 other major languages in the archipelago, few of those would have been suitable. Javanese had the largest number of speakers, but was both hard to learn and difficult to use in administrative communications and record keeping. In promoting Malay the Dutch had to standardise it, choosing the court Malay of the Riau islands as the model form, rejecting the everyday urban Malay used by Tirto. The Dutch attempted to counter the growth of popular writing in ordinary Malay and promote what they regarded as literary standards in the high form of the language by setting up an official publishing house in 1908.[6] Newspapers and fiction in common Malay produced by Tirto and his colleagues were automatically radical, just by their language. Tirto's fellow rebels would later call their new language 'Indonesian'.

When it came to content, Tirto and the other Malay writers struggled to make sense of a new world for their readers, and so they promoted the concept of a new, modern, age. Tirto's racy popular novella of 1909, *The Story of Nyai Ratna (Or How a Faithful Wife Did Wrong. A Story that Really Happened in West Java)*, conveyed the newness and complexity of Batavia. The things in it that seem ordinary by twenty-first-century standards were shockingly new at the beginning of the twentieth century.

Figure 3.1 An Indo family relax at home.

In Tirto's story the main character was a concubine called Ratna. Women who were concubines of Europeans and Chinese formed the mainstay of urban society, linking the different social groups. They did not marry the European men, but lived as financial dependants until their men died, left the country, or chose another woman. These women had some influence behind the scenes of public life. They were the conduits of knowledge between the separate societies: European, Chinese and those who lived in the various native quarters.

Many children of the concubines, Eurasians – referred to by everyone as Indos – lived in the native quarters. There they were often seen as intruders, so that in cities such as Surabaya, Indo and native youths formed gangs who were at war with each other. As the people in between Dutch and natives, the Indos could join the ranks of either civil service. Their role in the indigenous civil service helped to transform it, because they usurped the aristocrats' exclusive access to bureaucratic office. In the early twentieth century the growth of a non-aristocratic civil service in the cities created a special new middle class, which in his novella Tirto depicts in its early stages of development.[7]

In Tirto's story, Ratna met a young aristocrat, but not in ordinary circumstances. They met in the heart of Batavia, during the Queen's coronation celebrations, when the city was decorated with arches, fountains, 'and a number of electric lamps, with bulbs of various colours. There were red, blue, green ones.' Electricity was one of those modern things that

Tirto described as a source of great wonder. Tirto also described the main buildings, the General Secretariat – centre of government – as well as the Harmonie Club, the Concordia Club belonging to the military, and 'the shops EigenHulp, Versteg, Houpt, Van Arken', which along with the other buildings beside the Noordwijk canal, were all decorated. Who could doubt that this was a Dutch city?

However, other city dwellers were also enthusiastic about the coronation. A sign in Chinese style at New Market declared in Dutch: 'Hail to Her Majesty, Queen Wilhelmina, Empress of The East Indies', while the house of the mayor of the Chinese was decorated with arches and flags. The celebration went on for over a week.

Into this bright and beautiful scene came Ratna, described as a girl from the boondocks, standing at the second arch of New Market, 'wearing a long-sleeved top of white lace, a sarong from Banyumas [to the west of Yogyakarta] with a *batik* pattern on a white background, black lacquered close-toed slippers [*pantoffel*], flowery dark red silk stockings, a velvet cape, and her hair in the type of bun Dutch women wear'. Such was high fashion in 1909. The very modern top, a *kebaya*, has now become conventionalised and classed as traditional national dress for all Indonesians.

She espied a neat, handsome, young man in a horse-drawn sulky (*sado*), 'Wearing a sarong in the *batik* design of the broken cliffs [a royal Central Javanese design], black shoes with black socks, a smoking jacket of white linen, a new shirt just purchased from the shop, stand-up collar with a little black tie, a head-cloth fringed with batik, black cap' – part of an elaborate head-dress that showed that he was a medical student. He also carried eye-glasses, and had a moustache, all things that set him apart as a modern man. She was so impressed she hired a taxi to pursue him. Few besides Europeans wore shoes in the early years of the twentieth century, and the European authorities disapproved of natives who were too European in their dress. There were literally government dress codes. Only high-ranking civil servants, or members of those indigenous ethnic groups who had special status because they were considered pro-Dutch, notably the Ambonese and Manadonese, were allowed to approximate European dress, and even then the Dutch commented on them with sniggers. In spite of Dutch disapproval, more and more Indonesians bought Singer sewing machines, setting up in businesses as seamstresses and tailors and adapting designs from the West to produce distinctive new styles. The machines themselves were a sign of modernity, with their sleek black streamlined bodies and cast-iron treadle frames. In the following decades the most radical young men swapped their sarongs for trousers and cut their hair short.

In his book Tirto painted an extraordinary picture. The audience would probably have been used to the plain striped or plaid sarongs of the country-side, usually worn with very little else, but these were the most modern clothes, so splendid that the aristocrat mistook Ratna for a Dutch woman.

When he convinced her to leave her master and run away, they did so in modern fashion: 'The two lovers left for Sukabumi on the morning train, they were accompanied by a manservant and a maid. There they rented a fully-furnished house.' Servants accompany all noble heroes and heroines in traditional literature and theatre, but the idea of renting a house for a week, with its furnishings, was startling. The rest of their journey contin-ued this sense of newness: 'A week later they went to Central Java. In Maos they lodged at a Chinese restaurant.' They then went on a tour – something Europeans were only just starting to do – to Yogyakarta to see the animals in the palace zoo, to Magelang to see the ancient temples of Borobudur and Mendut, to Solo to buy *batik*, then to Surabaya, Tosari, Semarang, Cirebon and then Bandung, before returning to Sukabumi.

In the story we meet members of new professions to which Indonesians were just gaining access, including doctors and engineers, who were to develop into a new class. These new people of the cities also learned new activities, such as dealing with paper money, working in offices, getting involved in legal cases, reading newspapers, having photographs taken, wearing Eau de Chinin perfume and hair oil, buying shares, and smoking El Chombata cigarettes.[8]

Ratna was not just a passive victim of colonialism. She actively made her choices, seeking economic security, although in the end these turned out to be bad ones, eventually leading her to poison a later master. Although a flawed and tragic tale of gender relations based on conservative morality, Tirto's novella showed its audience new possibilities of free action in the cities.

CITY LIFESTYLES

Moving to the cities meant becoming a new kind of person through taking part in urban activities. As the novelist Pramoedya Ananta Toer recalls, 'When I moved to Surabaya I picked up two new habits . . . smoking *kretek* and wearing shoes.' Pramoedya's first shoes were brown, made by Bata.[9] If wearing shoes made you equal to the Dutch, then the new sensation of smoking Indonesia's unique clove cigarettes marked you as someone who had city sophistication. Modern people gave up old-fashioned habits of chewing betel nut.

Kretek were originally the cigarettes of the poor from Kudus, near the north coast of Central Java. A Haji was first credited with the idea of impregnating tobacco with cloves and other spices in the 1880s, but they did not become manufactured items until a Javanese entrepreneur, Nitisemito, met a woman street seller who taught him to package and sell them in 1906. Paper partly replaced the old corn-husk wrappings. Nitisemito's company, Three Balls, under the direction of his son-in-law, then mass-marketed *kretek* through stalls at fairs, employing travelling theatre groups to spread the word, and offering amazing promotional prizes, bicycles and even cars. Three Balls was one of the largest indigenous businesses that thrived during the colonial period. At its height it employed 15,000 people. Its success demonstrated how cities provided a new commercial reality, although the company eventually suffered from a series of family feuds.

The colonial system encouraged natives to go into the civil service, be coolies or peasants. Only a few such as Tirto and Nitisemito tried other options. Mobile ethnic groups like the Minangkabau people of West Sumatra often fitted well into middle-level business activities in the cities. They opened restaurants offering their unique Padang style of food, which became universal through the archipelago from the 1920s onwards. *Batik* merchants were amongst the other successful entrepreneurs, the wealthiest of these coming from the Kauman of Yogyakarta and the Lawéan quarter of Surakarta.[10]

Because they had always run village markets, women adapted well to petty trade in cities, but most of the big-time entrepreneurs were men. In the male-dominated world of Islamic trade, the Hajis, with their international connections, kept women out of larger ventures. Equally, so did male domination in the trade of Europeans and Chinese, as well as the restrictive nature of Dutch law that gave women few property rights.

Even successful indigenous-run businesses such as Three Balls tended to be eclipsed by those of Chinese merchants, who came to dominate the *kretek* and *batik* industries, since the economic and political system created by the Dutch encouraged the Chinese to fulfil the role of a merchant middle class. In the case of *batik*, Chinese and Arab merchants controlled the import of new manufactured textiles on which the patterns were dyed.

Chinese migration had grown during the time of the East India Company, which initially imported Chinese workers to create a labour force for Batavia. Later, in the nineteenth century, indentured coolies were brought in from southern China. Some Chinese remained low-paid workers or small shopkeepers, others pioneered plantation industries such as coffee and sugar, or took advantage of licensing opportunities opened up by the Dutch for opium farming and the outsourcing of tax collection. Both of these systems were phased out at the end of the nineteenth century, but a few Chinese families that had done well out of them deployed their capital into other areas.

The most successful early twentieth-century Chinese families came from Semarang on Java's north coast. One, the clan led by Oei Tiong Ham (c.1866–1924), created a large conglomerate on the back of the sugar trade and opium farming licences. Oei Tiong Ham moved into banking and manufacture, as well as dealing in all other kinds of export crops, shipping goods out of both Semarang and Singapore. When the Dutch cut out opium use, Oei's conglomerate was well positioned to develop its other activities because it had established a network of personal and business ties that stretched throughout the Asian Pacific. Oei was highly respected from Japan to Thailand. He married into Chinese-Javanese families, had his children taught English (by an Australian tutor) as well as the Malay and Hokkien that he spoke. He was personally progressive – he gained permission from the Dutch to wear coat, tie and trousers in public in 1889, and cut off his Manchu hair braid in 1900, urging others to follow. Companies like his imported the latest technology, and he made major social and financial contributions to the progress of the city of Semarang.[11]

Oei was one of the acculturated Chinese-Javanese who had taken on a lifestyle that was distinctive to South-east Asia. Other more recently migrated Chinese families used their own networks to launch successful trading ventures. In most cities Chinese were a sizeable minority, almost twice as large a proportion of the urban population as Europeans. They constituted between 6 and 20 per cent of the population of the six major cities, the majority being acculturated Chinese. Even in conservative cities such as Yogyakarta, they were respected landlords, shop owners and traders, or owners of factories that produced such things as ice, tiles, coffee and biscuits.

The progressive civic face of Chinese entrepreneurial activities did not prevent strong prejudice against them being common in Java, despite the fact that it was European companies that dominated the Indies' economy. Anti-Chinese views were encouraged by the fact that most money lenders were Chinese, mainly recent migrants. Such money lenders took advantage of the need for cash created by Dutch taxation and the increasingly marginal levels of income from agriculture. The term for those in this line of business was *lintah darat*, 'leeches of the land', which gives some sense of the feelings aroused. Dutch attitudes and policies fostered anti-Chinese racism, so it is no coincidence that times of unrest in Java have been marked by anti-Chinese riots. In early twentieth-century Batavia there were violent actions against exploitative Chinese landlords and employers.

Despite the prejudice of many, one or two modernising intellectuals such as Tirto appreciated the role that the Chinese played in advancing the Indies. As well as their economic contribution and influence on popular literature, the Chinese contributed to all aspects of the arts, not only *batik*, but also traditional *gamelan* music and the theatre.

CULTURAL LIFE

In theatre, Chinese culture mixed with a host of others to contribute to modern new urban styles. In the early twentieth century, Comedy Stambul (from 'Istanbul') was *the* style. Workers watched it avidly, but the modernising intellectuals thought it low-brow.

Stambul developed as a mélange of old and new theatre forms. The once-numerous Chinese opera companies of South-east Asia were immensely popular amongst all ethnic groups, and their influence in Stambul was obvious in its performance of Chinese tales such as those of the lovers, Sam Pek and Eng Tai. From the English colonies came a new mixture of Indian and Malay styles which gave Stambul its South Asian effect. Other indigenous theatre forms and stories contributed to making Stambul a fascinating combination of local and trans-Asian arts, where Indonesian stories of the romantic prince Pañji appeared alongside *The Merchant of Venice, Ali Baba* and stories of the concubines of Batavia. Scripts from Stambul performances were published in Malay newspapers, and the growing modern Malay literature drew on the performances for dialogue and plot structures.

The staging of Stambul reflected its modern dreams of cosmopolitan Asian city life. European-style backdrops and curtains were popular innovations, and costumes incorporated fantasy versions of Arab, Indian and Chinese clothing, European stockings and football shorts, and lavish traditional jewellery. This strange mixture of elements was a rejection of the formalised and highly conventional nature of indigenous theatre in favour of novelty and exoticism. Like the changes in everyday clothing that were occurring, Stambul was a way of adapting new ideas in material form, and its subject matter also encouraged new ways of thinking and acting. This description of a performance in Bali gives a sense of its craziness:

we were introduced to a Javanese student, spectacled, shod, hatted, in a European suit and with a voice so refined that it could not be heard, who had been wrecked on the coast of New Guinea on his way to study in Germany; a Papuan chief in football stockings and Inverness cape, also spectacled, but wearing an American Indian headdress of white feathers, Papuans of low birth with whitened faces.

This description, by a disapproving European, also notes the new kind of content of the plays, which reflected themes of modernity versus tradition: 'the Javanese student appeals in Malay to the humanity of the king! "All men are brothers." He is overpowered and carried off to be drowned ... while the Papuan chief still moralizes in a low, unemphatic voice.'[12] The use of Malay, and the idea of egalitarianism, would have been remarkable to audiences that had grown up with the shadow puppet theatre's tales of gods and demons.

Three Balls *kretek* company's use of a Stambul group to sell cigarettes shows how much this was an art form for the masses. Stambul gave its audiences the impression of a connection across Asia. It asked them to think about all the different locations of Asia and Europe as part of the modern world. They could even contemplate belonging to an Indies which included the most remote and exotic of locations, New Guinea. Thus while indigenous intellectuals were reading Western literature and getting to know Dutch culture first hand, through Stambul the broader urban population were also getting their own picture of the world as a diverse place in which they too could participate.

The music that accompanied Stambul performances often incorporated local styles, but with Western instruments such as accordions and guitars. Its evolution was closely related to the development of the music called *kroncong*. Halfway between Portuguese and Hawaiian music, *kroncong*'s main feature was the combination of guitar and violin in smooth, melodious singing. As the Portuguese element suggests, it grew out of the Eurasian community of Batavia that had strong Portuguese roots. In the early twentieth century *kroncong* was performed at open air events like the Queen's Birthday 'night markets', which also featured industry stalls, circuses and other popular entertainment. By the late colonial era *kroncong* was thoroughly Indonesian; it had gone from being low-class entertainment to the form favoured by a broad segment of the urban population. The greatest of its songs, written in sentimental praise of Central Java's main river, 'Bengawan Solo', was composed in 1940 by Gesang, a Javanese singer. Both Stambul and *kroncong* were enjoyed because they spoke of the vitality of the city. People like Pramoedya remember *kroncong* then as having the buzz of modern life.[13]

The other modern passion of the cities was soccer, enjoyed by young people throughout the Indies. Exciting matches, such as those between Surabayans and their rivals from Malang, resulted in broken legs on field and riots on the side-lines. Football madness was one of the few things that people of the different ethnic groups had in common, but the organisation of the sport was along ethnic lines. Colonial authorities would not let native soccer teams play all-Dutch ones, for fear of loss of prestige.[14]

Cinema and radio came quickly to the Indies, where they met Stambul and *kroncong*. Cheap cinemas had become mass entertainment on a par with Stambul by the mid-1920s, although ticket prices were still high: the cheapest seats costing one-third of a coolie's daily wages. Films came from Europe and China as well as Hollywood. When Charlie Chaplin came to Bali in the 1930s everybody knew who he was and followed him through the streets. Just as the Chinese had inaugurated Indonesian print culture at the turn of the century, around 1929 Chinese companies started an indigenous film industry. Sound came to the cinema of the Indies two years later. In 1941 thirty-two films were made on Java, ten times the number in 1936, and there were 240 cinemas in Java.

Only a small number of Indonesians could afford a radio – 1,500 licence holders in 1935 (compared to 8,469 Dutch). In three years that number had increased almost ten times, and *kroncong* singers had become standard fare of radio formats. Broadcasts on anything to do with politics or other controversial subjects were not allowed.[15]

WORKERS' CITIES

When Tirto established his newspapers he attracted bright young people to work for him. The brightest of them was a commoner, Mas Marco Kartodikromo (c.1890–1932), the son of a lower-level government employee from the oil-producing area of Cepu, thirty kilometres to the east of Blora. He went on to publish his own newspapers, which presented stories of the city by Marco and his friends. Like Tirto's stories, these tales were serialised in the newspapers for popular consumption, and formed the model for later writers like Pramoedya.

Stories in Marco's newspaper about the port cities of Semarang and Surabaya paint a much less glowing picture than Tirto's *Nyai Ratna*. One story of Surabaya from 1924–5, for example, was called 'The corrupted life of a big city'. Surabaya, 'Indonesia's premier trading city', was described as a place that was busy day and night, in contrast to sleepy villages. '[A]t midnight the workers of Surabaya were crowding about . . . The tooting of horns was almost deafening.' As in Tirto's story, gas and electric lighting were sources of fascination, but by now trams and motorcars also filled the cities.

This story focused on the workers, who made up a large proportion of the urban population, even though they were 'too poor to afford to live in the city, close to the theatres and cinemas owned by the capitalists'. The term 'city' technically meant the Dutch centre, not the village clusters or quarters, called *kampung*, that made up the real population centres. In 1925, 30 per cent of the populations of towns and cities were labourers of some kind, the majority of them dock and railway workers, or employees of the municipality. Approximately 20 per cent of those in the cities were artisans and small traders, a similar percentage blue- and white-collar workers in European and Chinese enterprises, with only 11 per cent civil servants. The majority of coolies were casual workers, lining up every day to seek work. By the end of the Dutch period, large factories in the Indies employed 350,000 people. But all the men who drove horse carts, the women who sold food in little street stalls, the children who sold newspapers and the others of the city were not included in the statistics. So when the Depression came and urban workers lost their jobs, there was no way to document how many were pushed into deeper poverty.

'The corrupted life of a big city' described how after workers had paid to go to the cinema or theatre, they could only afford the cheap 4 cent tram fare back to the main workers' quarters, Wonokromo and Kampung Tembok (at that time the average annual income of a city worker was ƒ51.90). On the streets people slept in doorways, the rich drank champagne at the Dutch Simpang Club, while prostitutes plied their trade with sailors. A tale of Semarang, published in the same newspaper, tells how a clerk was lured by a prostitute into a life of extravagance, and, finding himself with venereal disease and huge debts, had to sign a coolie contract to work in the Sumatran plantations of Deli.[16]

The workers of the city lived poorly. Many of them were servants. In 1930, there were an estimated 350,000 servants in the colony working as cooks, cleaners and nursemaids for the Dutch and the rich, but many more were servants of other Indonesians. The majority of servants of the Dutch worked in cities, and over 60 per cent were women. They were given pitifully small rooms attached to their employers' houses, and women who had been in service recall their time as one of tedium and hard work. Those employed by the Dutch lived under constant suspicion, and complained about the awful way the Europeans smelt because of their milk-based diet.

Wages and conditions for urban coolies and servants were never good. In a 1937 government study on workers in Batavia, over half of those surveyed earned less than 30 cents a day, with food costing them just over 60 per cent of their incomes, and housing another 15 per cent. The range of city wages was huge, the lowest paid received only 10 cents per day, the highest *f*2.50. This study did not capture the full extent of living conditions. The houses of the poor were often single rooms with an earth floor, bamboo supports, and woven matting for walls. Less than one-eighth of houses had latrines – and those were just pits. Most families lived from pay to pay on credit, their food intake amounting to only 1,581 calories each per day.

The indigenous quarters of the cities were built around rivers, because, as in villages, these supplied water for bathing and drinking, as well as toilets and garbage disposals. Dutch-made canals and drains along the streets served the same roles. As population density increased, disease and death became rife. In the absence of major infrastructure investment, Dutch health authorities' attempts to intervene in the *kampungs* were only resented as bureaucratic interference.

The 1937 study was another attempt to measure basic welfare at a time when the government was trying to create new employment possibilities to remedy the Depression, after devaluating the Indies guilder and introducing protective tariffs. An incipient textile manufacturing industry was established in Bandung, with branches in Surabaya and other cities. Dutch and major international investors came to set up shop. Unilever bought into the new margarine industry based on the palm oil of the Indies. Goodyear manufactured tyres in West Java. A branch of Proctor and Gamble invested in coconut oil and soap manufacture in Surabaya. There were also new kinds of small businesses. In 1936 rickshaw tricycles to carry passengers, called *becak*, appeared in Batavia. These were to become ubiquitous in all big cities in the following decades.[17]

THE MOVEMENT

The segment of the intelligentsia to which Marco and his colleagues belonged diagnosed the problems of the workers as arising from one source: capital. Others argued that there were different causes and presented different solutions. Many nationalists, especially progressives from an aristocratic background, saw ignorance as the problem, and education as the solution to a better life. Conservative aristocrats wanted to return to tradition and improve cultural life, religious leaders sought moral reform, others saw the development of indigenous enterprise as a major goal and others campaigned for better wages and healthier conditions for workers, to ban prostitution, or to eliminate child marriage and polygamy.

'The corrupted life of a big city' tells us about people who were interested in the workers' lives. While the cinema and theatre provided major social activities for many urban dwellers, a small group was participating in a new activity, holding political meetings. These meetings were often associated with study groups or debates, where a sense of injustice was expressed. From this sense of injustice came a new movement, nationalism, which Tirto did much to start, and which Marco supported during its most radical phase in the 1920s.

The first modern political and social organisations set up in the Indies along Western lines were limited in their aims. Around 1900, societies of the nobility were social bodies, and Tirto's first organisation used these as a model. However, Tirto looked at what the Chinese were doing at that time in establishing their own groups with broader aims to reform society. He found a particularly inspiring example in the Indies' branches of the revolutionary nationalist movement that had just started in China. Tirto and others realised that the new idea being advocated in China, nationalism, expressed the needs of the intellectuals of the Indies. He and some of his fellow journalists set about creating a nationalist agenda. Some of the resulting organisations had cultural and educational aims, such as the aristocrat-dominated 'Highest Endeavour', whose establishment in 1908 is celebrated in Indonesia as the moment of 'national awakening'. Its aim of progress for the Javanese was the first time that the Dutch ethical ideal had been taken over by natives.

Indonesia's nationalist movement was much slower in its development than that of other countries because the colony had been unified by the Dutch only recently. The newness of 'the Indies' meant that until the early nineteenth century there was no ground on which a nationalist spirit could take roots, no strong links, even including the common enemy of the Dutch, to enable people to conceive of themselves as a nation.

Tirto's Civil Servants' League, set up in 1906, did not last long, but he also set up an Islamic Traders' League just afterwards, which in 1912 was taken over by others and became the Islamic League. Of the dozens of different organisations that developed in the first four decades of the twentieth century, this was the most important, growing to more than a million members. Tirto himself faded into the background as he was caught up in personal lawsuits, political censorship by the Dutch, and a series of business failures, but many other leaders sprang up from the cities to replace him.

The Islamic League initially found support in Central Java as an anti-Chinese movement – it presented itself as uniting *batik* merchants and other indigenous traders against Chinese businesses. The League soon took on a much broader agenda of linking up with the other different political

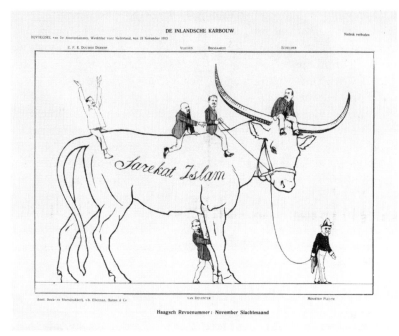

Figure 3.2 The Dutch government struggle to come to terms with the Islamic League, symbolised by a water buffalo being led by the minister of colonies, with Ethical Policy formulator van Deventer holding one leg, other Ethical Policy defenders riding at the front, and E. F. E. Douwes Dekker, leader of the socialist Indies Party and advocate of Indies autonomy, celebrating at the back. The caption at the bottom reads 'Hague Review Issue: November, Slaughter month (23 November 1913)'.

groupings, and through this means it achieved a mass following (figure 3.2). At first the Dutch looked on the League as a promising outcome of colonial adviser Snouck Hurgronje's policies, and the Governor General gave it his blessing. Some of those Snouck saw as examples of the new kinds of leadership of the Indies were members.

One Snouck favourite in the League was Haji Agus Salim (1884–1954), of Minangkabau ethnicity. The feminist Kartini had lobbied on Salim's behalf for him to study medicine in the Netherlands, but Snouck convinced him to enter the civil service, where he was made an honorary European, and trained in the Dutch consulate in Jeddah. Back in the Indies, Salim had many jobs, one of which was as a translator for the government publishing house. Despite his impeccable Islamic credentials, Salim also liked a drink, and so was known as 'Haji Bottle'. He initially joined the Islamic League to spy on it, but soon became close to the chairman, Raden Umar Said Cokroaminoto (1883–1934), and enthusiastic about the aims of the League. In 1917, Salim set up the Young Sumatrans' Alliance, which was typical of the kind of organisation being established as part of the movement.

Marco found many like-minded people in the movement. One was the Yogyakartan aristocrat, Suwardi Suryaningrat (1889–1959), who in 1913 had written a satirical article, 'If I were ever a Dutchman'. 1913 was the year that the Netherlands celebrated the centenary of its liberation from Napoleon's rule, and Suwardi enjoyed the irony: 'What a joy, what a pleasure it would be to be able to commemorate such a very great day . . . ' Musing on how it must feel to be liberated, Suwardi noted that some people who were not so free might feel upset at the celebrations: 'but I would not want the natives of this country to participate in this commemoration . . . I would even close off the area where the festivities took place so that no native could see our elation at the commemoration of our day of Independence.' The Dutch are usually known for their own dry humour, but these stinging comments on Dutch hypocrisy earned Suwardi six years of exile to the Netherlands, where he could see how Dutchmen lived at home.

Marco started a newspaper in 1914, at the beginning of World War One, called *World in Motion* – the Malay words for 'motion' and 'movement' being the same. Such motion was the opposite to the Dutch aim of 'peace and order'. Marco's writings gave the movement a sense of how it could shake up the world on behalf of 'the little person' or 'the masses'.

When Marco was first gaoled in 1915 under the repressive Dutch censorship that governed 'Press Offences', he and Suwardi exchanged open letters. Marco praised Suwardi as a true warrior, a proper son of the aristocracy, not like the civil servants. A sense of the disdain Marco and the other radicals felt about those aristocratic bureaucrats who worked for the Dutch is conveyed by a later newspaper advertisement in the paper *Light of the Indies*:

Wanted,
by the editor of *Light of the Indies*, people of the refined class, aristocrats or Javanese warriors, competent in
a) flattery
b) selfish politics
c) corruption
Information to be sent to: Samsi, Chief Editor.[18]

Members of the movement who were inspired by the new mood took up the term 'youth' as the way of describing themselves, even if they meant young in spirit rather than age. People in the Indies felt this was the right word to describe those with a new outlook for the new modern age.

One of the most prodigious of these young people was Semaun (1899–1971). Unlike Tirto, Salim or Cokro, he did not come from an aristocratic background, his father was a poorly paid railway employee from East Java, and Semaun had only a basic education. Nevertheless he got his first job as a clerk in the railways in Surabaya, becoming a member of the Islamic League at the age of fifteen. At that time, left-wing Dutchmen, as well as Eurasians campaigning for Indies independence, were members of the movement. One of these Dutchmen set up an Indies branch of the Dutch Workers' Social Democratic Party, and took Semaun on as an apprentice. Semaun learned quickly about unionism, and became an activist in the Tram Workers' Union in Semarang, where in 1917, aged eighteen, he became the local head of the Islamic League.

In 1917 people in the Indies found out what revolution was. The Russian Revolution was quickly translated into local terms, as Semaun and his friends spread talk of the overthrow of emperors, and Dutch soldiers and sailors briefly set up a revolutionary Soviet in Surabaya. This was too much for the Dutch authorities, who gaoled anyone who spread dissent. Despite Cokro's protestations of loyalty to the government, the Dutch spy bureau had the movement in their sights. Semaun's Dutch patron was expelled from the Indies in 1918, not long before Tirto Adhi Suryo died in poverty in Manggadua, a suburb of Batavia. Tirto's biographer, Pramoedya, suggests (without much evidence) that he was poisoned by the Dutch.

Semaun and his friends taught a new word to the people, 'strike', and both through their unions and then as activists they attempted to spread strikes throughout the countryside, beginning with railways and pawn-shops, spreading to plantation workers in Java and Sumatra. They set up People's Leagues for this end, and tried to create a new sense amongst workers of being a proletariat. Marco and the other journalists articulated what strikes meant. From his prison cell Marco wrote his most famous poem, 'Solidarity and equality' (*Sama rasa sama rata*), the title of which became a battle cry for the left for another fifty years. Of the tens of thousands of workers who went on strike, however, most were interested in better pay and conditions rather than nationalism and revolution.

In 1919 Semaun had his first period in prison for writing seditious articles, and made use of his four months there to write a novel, *The Story of Kadirun*, which described the ideas and actions of revolutionary youth. The story was first serialised in newspapers and then published as a book. It protested against the sugar factories' appropriation of indigenous land, against money lenders who charged rates of up to 350 per cent, against the Press Infringement Law and the operations of capital, and provided a solution in the establishment of Leninist workers' and peasants' councils.[19] Once he was out of prison, in 1920, Semaun founded the first Communist party in the Asia-Pacific, the Communist Party of the Indies, the PKI. The PKI worked within the Islamic League to further its aims of total emancipation from Dutch rule and from the rule of capital.

Others worked for different ends. Haji Salim's aim was the establishment of an independent Islamic state. His Islamic wing opposed the Communists, and made use of a weapon that became a constant in Indonesian politics: mob outrage. The League's first use of this weapon was in anti-Chinese riots that occurred in Surakarta and Kudus in 1911, 1912 and 1918. In 1918, League leaders got together with members of the Arab community and created a Committee for the Army of the Prophet Muhammad to protest against a newspaper that had claimed the Prophet had smoked opium and drank gin. The violent agitation was actually a way for the central leadership of the League to discredit a member of an opposing power bloc, Abdul Muis (1890–1959), because he was on the editorial board of the offending newspaper. Orthodox Muslims were mobilised again seven years later to attack another newspaper that had published an anti-Islamic Javanese poem. Again in 1937, there were angry protests and death threats against a female journalist who had written a story that questioned the Prophet's sexual morality and argued that he would have supported anti-polygamy laws then being promoted by feminists.[20]

The various parts of the movement garnered support through youth groups, which were seen as vehicles for recruitment and would also instil a sense of discipline in potential nationalists. The model for these groups was the international Scouting Movement, with its aims of healthy minds and healthy bodies, and its quasi-military character. Discipline was emphasised through uniforms, parades and training in traditional forms of martial arts, which made the Scouts popular. Almost every political and educational group formed its own Scouts, and these native Scouting groups broke away from the Dutch Scouting Movement. Right-wing, pro-Dutch, Scout groups also existed in the Indies.

Along with Scouting came a sense of ordering life, including training people to tell the time. In villages there were no clear markers of time, but public clocks and new personal watches provided a structure to city life. Semaun, in his novel, took pains to describe the daily life of the ideal modern person: he got up at 5 a.m. to do exercises and clean up, went to work at 7 a.m., came home for lunch after 1 p.m., took an afternoon nap at 2.30 p.m., cleaned up with his wife at 4 p.m., went for a walk with his wife from 5 until 6 p.m., studied until dinner at 8 p.m., the wife studied 8.30–9.30 p.m. while the husband read the papers, and they went to sleep at 10 p.m. Saturday nights were for going to the movies, Sundays for gardening. Ordered people like this were monogamous, and wives took their husbands' names. These were all astonishing ideas for the majority of people in the Indies, ideas with which the new civil servant class of the cities were experimenting, but Semaun specifically wanted to direct this sense of discipline towards socialism, in a way that reconciled the new life with the old. At the same time as his novel presented a prescription for a new lifestyle, he depicted the true path of integrity as being Islam's search for inner truth. A person could be a good Muslim and a revolutionary at the same time.

Before 1919, the Islamic League's all-embracing nature was its strength. Semaun estimated, probably exaggerating, that the League achieved 2,000,000 members, of whom 27,000 were in the Communist Party and 35,000 were members of the progressive women's movement. The League had branches on almost all islands, and was involved in local politics in ways that worried the Dutch.

Cokro and his faction struggled for a middle road in the movement so that the League could continue as its principal vehicle, but the differences in aims and backgrounds between the various nationalist groups made this path increasingly difficult to follow. As part of the middle road, Cokro and a number of others had joined the new Dutch-sponsored People's Council in 1918, much to the left's disdain. Semaun's newspaper, *The Light of the Indies*, attacked the candidates for the People's Council: 'Bosscha, Tea Capitalist . . . Mr Dr Schumann, said to be kind to the Natives . . . R. M. T. A. Koesoemo Oetojo, Regent of Jepara [a relative of Kartini], has obtained a high level of education, but has never felt for himself the hard life of the little man. Of the leaders of the League the paper was even more sarcastic: 'Abdoel Moeis, Deputy Chair of the Central Islamic League . . . who doesn't like it if the people fight hard for their needs . . .' and of another leader, 'has spent a long time in Holland, used to be a very clever journalist, but isn't so well known now, because he can be said to be "bored" with mixing with the little man'. For another twenty years nationalists argued about whether cooperation or non-cooperation with bodies like the People's Council was the best means to achieve independence.[21]

Such inflammatory language as Semaun's and Marco's, especially when accompanied by violent agitation, ultimately split the League in 1919. Two incidents signalled the end of League unity. The first came after a visit by

Abdul Muis to Central Sulawesi, when a strike against corvée, allegedly inspired by him, led to the murder of a Dutch district officer. The second happened near the pleasant hill station of Garut, West Java, where, after shooting a local Haji and his family dead for resisting forced rice appropriations, the Dutch police found documents proving that there was a secret group of violent subversives in the League. These documents discredited the League in moderate eyes, and led Haji Salim to stage a walkout of the Islamic right. Despite this rift, members of the left remained firmly committed to uniting Islam and Communism.[22]

THE PARTIES

Political leaders of the 1920s used strikes and revolutionary language to challenge Dutch rule, but they did not have a strong enough organisational vehicle to spread their actions. Once the split in the League occurred there was no longer a sense that one was able to move in and out of various groups and bodies. People had to give their exclusive loyalties as members of parties. The consequence of this was a splintering of the nationalist effort.

By 1920, the most intriguing of words appeared in the parties' vocabulary: 'Indonesia'. Originally coined by a nineteenth-century English naturalist to classify the distinctive ethnic and geographical identity of the archipelago, this was a word that could be adapted to new ends. Previously the Youth Alliances had talked about a separate Balinese nation, Javanese nation, Sumatran nation and so on, now 'Indonesia' spoke of a single people. The term had first been used for such nationalist ends by students in the Netherlands, and it was taken up by Semaun, who changed the name of his party to the Communist Party of Indonesia. Marco aimed to popularise the term in his articles and stories.

In 1923, there was an attempt on the life of the Governor General, so the government came down hard on the nationalists. For his agitation and for leading a huge railway strike, Semaun was forced to leave the Indies in that year. He travelled around Asia as an agent of the Soviet-based international organisation, the Comintern, before taking up a career as a translator and language teacher in the Soviet Union. He was only to return to a free Indonesia in 1957, but by then the Communist Party had passed him by. Throughout the 1920s, the government weakened all the nationalist groups by arresting leaders and suppressing publications.

In 1926, a council of Communist unions, fearing that they were losing ground too quickly, declared the need to start the Revolution. More sensible

Party members thought this precipitate, but Communist uprisings went ahead. They broke out in uncoordinated ways in Batavia and Central Java at the end of 1926 and the beginning of 1927, with the largest support coming in the strongly Muslim areas of West Sumatra and West Java. Some joined because they believed in modern revolution, some because they wanted to wage a holy war against the Dutch, some because they thought that the Just King of messianic tradition was coming. Lacking cohesion and effective communications, and with leading members of the Party withdrawing their support, the revolts were easily suppressed. After the uprisings 18,000 people were arrested – a number were executed as terrorists – and 4,500 were imprisoned, of whom 1,308 were sent to the remote Boven Digul camps in West New Guinea. Marco was one of those, and he died in the malarial conditions there in 1932.

The Dutch government's spying mechanisms were very effective in identifying potential leaders and monitoring meetings, but the momentum amongst the nationalists was unstoppable. The various political groups came together in a Youth Congress held in 1928, providing a key moment for the advancement of nationalism. While a young journalist played a tune he had just written, 'Indonesia the Great' – the future National Anthem – the Congress declared that they had one homeland, Indonesia, were one people, the Indonesian nation, and strove for one language, the version of Malay they now called Indonesian.

One young man who attempted to recapture the lost unity of the Islamic League was an engineering student educated in Surabaya and then Bandung, named Sukarno. In Surabaya he apprenticed himself to Cokroaminoto, whose daughter became the first of Sukarno's many wives. From Cokro he learned the power of making speeches, and of trying to find a message that would unite the disparate elements of Indonesian society into a single struggle with a single direction. Thus Sukarno wrote of the need to unite the different parts of the movement, beginning with Islam – 'Muslims must not forget that capitalism, the enemy of Marxism, is also the enemy of Islam!' He reconciled religion, socialism and the nation: 'Marxism, which was previously so violently anti-nationalist and anti-religious, has now altered its tactics, especially in Asia, so that its previous bitter opposition has turned into comradeship and support.'[23]

Sukarno, who was to become the first president of a free Indonesia, wanted to blend all the different aspects of nationalism along the lines promulgated by the other movement leaders, many of whom he had met in Cokro's house. The Theosophy movement, originally established in the US in 1875 to connect the spirituality of the East with the development of modern society, was important to his aim of creating a synthesis between widely variant views. The Theosophists' central belief that Eastern spiritual knowledge could be superior to Western technology held a powerful grip on the nationalists. It gave a modern, cosmopolitan form to the Javanese and Balinese spiritualism Sukarno inherited from his father and mother respectively, and allowed for his mixing of Islam, other religions and Marxism.[24]

Sukarno's father had been a teacher, and he realised that a new nation could only be created through education. Inspiring him in his belief were leading nationalist radicals Cipto Mangunkusumo (1885–1943) and Suwardi Suryaningrat, the latter who, on returning from the Netherlands and changing his name to Ki Hajar Dewantoro, diverted his energies into the cause of education, the same cause that Kartini had advocated and Haji Dahlan had promulgated through his Islamic modernist movement. Suwardi's school movement, the 'Garden of Pupils', incorporated the ideas of Theosophy in its aim of creating a whole people, Indonesians, who were aware both spiritually and intellectually. They believed they could take the best of Western education and adapt it, although these nationalists had a fundamentally ambivalent attitude towards the Dutch, who were both sources of knowledge and of oppression. The Dutch for their part regarded the nationalist schools with justifiable suspicion, but were not able to suppress them as easily as they suppressed the political leaders because these schools were too widespread and their teachers were willing to work for a pittance.

Throughout the 1930s, more and more nationalist schools were set up. The Dutch called these 'wild schools'. The teachers in the 'wild schools' were the ones remembered by those who grew up in the quarters of the cities and in small towns as the inspiring, uncompromising voices for this new idea of nationalism. Pramoedya Ananta Toer's father was one of those men, whom he remembered in Sukarno-like terms, 'a powerful speaker, a lion at the rostrum' who dropped the government school curriculum for his own nationalist one. 'No longer were history lessons straight out of *The History of the Netherlands* or *The History of the Netherlands East Indies*. Now they focused on the history of the people of Indonesia. He had his brother ... paint life-size portraits of historical figures whom he considered to be heroes in the struggle against the Dutch. He also wrote songs about these people and taught them to his students.'[25] This was the most effective way to spread the idea of an independent Indonesia.

Typical of the experience of the new generation of 1930s nationalists was a group of young Balinese teenagers. In the same year that Prince Djelantik went to Malang, twenty-five young women from Bali and Lombok were sent by the government to study at a special school for girls in Blitar, East Java. There they mixed with others from Kalimantan and Madura, and learned modern things, such as eating with cutlery rather than their hands. They were taken into the care of Sukarno's parents, although they missed their one chance of meeting the great man as he travelled from prison to exile because they were under a curfew. When these girls returned to Bali a group of them, including Gusti Ayu Rapeg (from an aristocratic family) and Ni Made Catri (a commoner) began their own school for girls, as well as starting a Balinese branch of the 'Women Aware' movement, in which they campaigned against polygamy and for the rights of women.[26]

New parties continued to be formed and then crushed, with another wave of repression coming in 1933. These new parties still had the main aims of the earlier movement – progress for the people, which should be realised as *merdeka*, freedom – but they continued to differ on how these aims should be achieved. The Indonesian public was presented with a confusing welter of abbreviations and acronyms for the new political bodies that developed in the decades after the Communist uprisings: PI, PNI, PSII, PPPKI, Partindo, Parindra, Pari, Gerindo, GAPI. None of these was ever able to replicate the mass membership of the Islamic League. Sukarno's National Party (PNI) had the potential to do this, but the Dutch were able to stifle it.

Sukarno, like many others, was arrested and exiled for refusing to cooperate with the Dutch authorities. His speech at his 1930 political trial, 'Indonesia Accuses', one of the great works of anti-colonial rhetoric, was widely circulated and inspired many younger Indonesians. He spent most of the colonial period in Flores, one of the south-eastern islands, and Bengkulu on Sumatra, places where there was no one to hear his powerful speeches. Another emerging political leader who was to be imprisoned by the Dutch was Sutan Syahrir (1909–66), who was sent to Boven Digul detention centre in West New Guinea, and later Banda island in Maluku. During his exile he compounded his defiance of Dutch authority by marrying a Dutch Marxist, Maria Duchateau (who was also divorced, something shocking in Dutch society at the time). She was not allowed to join him.

In exile Syahrir analysed the problems of the Indies as lying in the warped social relations of colonialism, expressing his deep hatred of the 'nonsensical relationships and … psychopathic inhabitants' of the colonial world, a world full of 'sadists' and megalomaniacs on the one hand, and 'souls that are distorted by inferiority-complexes' on the other.[27] His personal experiences provided a basis for a broader analysis of the psychology of Dutch rule, but he and the other intellectuals struggled to find a way to define Indonesian nationalism and spread its message.

In the end, all meetings of more than four people were banned by the Dutch. The Communist Party had gone so deeply underground that it was invisible, working through small cells whose members could not contact others for fear of spies. Some of the nationalists did agree to compromise, but many, such as Pramoedya's father, became disillusioned with the lack of progress. Pramoedya records the bitterness this period raised, the arguments over whether or not to cooperate with the authorities, and the resulting ambivalence he felt towards his father.

A few of the nationalists found an outlet in cultural activities. Former Islamic League activist Abdul Muis laid out the path that others like Pramoedya were to follow by writing a novel that became one of the classics of Indonesian literature, *A Wrong Upbringing*, published by the government publishing house in 1928. This book, like other important works to follow, described the struggle between modernity and tradition as a moral dilemma for Indonesian youth. It began with a tennis game, usually an exclusively European sport, and portrayed the problems of a young Minangkabau man who had fallen in love with a modern Indo girl.

In the same vein, young painters challenged the Dutch images of the Indies as islands of peaceful peasants by creating their own modern styles of art. On Bali, peasants who had no direct experience of Western education encountered the modern world through meeting Western artists, and from their commercial interactions with them created a unique style of modern art.

Nationalist organisations had emerged through the diversity and sense of modernity that the cities fostered. The nationalists conceptualised a new force in Indies society, the masses, but the aristocratic and middle-class lifestyles of the nationalists made it difficult for them to communicate the ideals of nation and freedom to these masses. Most of the population of the Indies might have 'feared and disliked' the Dutch, but they could do little about such feelings. Throughout the colonial period, the majority of the population simply avoided the Dutch, with members of the aristocracy content to collaborate. The modern movement against colonial rule was maintained by the passion and commitment of a few remarkable men and women.[28]

The people who were eventually to overthrow the Dutch order also had links to the cities of the Indies during the 1920s and 1930s. The Japanese had gradually spread throughout Asia; the first to do so were women who had been shipped in as prostitutes, *Karayuki San*. After them came businessmen – many Indonesian towns had Japanese photographic studios, barbers and salesmen. As one Balinese who was impressed by the Japanese ability to gather intelligence put it, 'they became barbers because, the ear is closest to the mouth, eh?' Around the time of the Depression the number of Japanese department stores in cities like Yogyakarta had almost trebled. Major Japanese firms such as Suzuki and Mitsubishi became involved in the sugar trade.

When Japan began its aggression into Manchuria and China, Chinese people in the Indies became increasingly anxious, setting up funds to support the anti-Japanese effort after 1937. The Dutch government turned their intelligence observation to the growing numbers of Japanese. Some Japanese had in fact been sent by their government to establish links with the nationalists, particularly the Muslim parties. Some Indonesians identified for their anti-Dutch sentiments were sponsored to visit Japan. The Japanese plan was to expand Indonesian nationalism into a broader sense of 'Asia for the Asians'. In 1942, when the Japanese Imperial Forces chased the Dutch out and made Indonesia part of their Greater East Asian Co-Prosperity Sphere, some of the Indonesians who lined the streets to cheer their liberators might have recognised Japanese friends, returning in military uniform.[29]

CHAPTER 4

The Revolution

People died or lived, just like pebbles that got caught in a sieve.
And I was like a grain of sand that escaped.
Javanese former forced labourer Damin, aka Mbah Ubi[1]

For Indonesians World War Two and their subsequent national Revolution started optimistically, kicked off by the enthusiasm of being liberated from the Dutch by the Japanese. Pramoedya Ananta Toer recalled the arrival of the Emperor's forces in Blora in 1942. The Japanese had swept rapidly through the Indies early in March, and people came to meet their army, waving flags and shouting their support for the liberators from the Dutch. 'With the arrival of the Japanese just about everyone in town was full of hope, except for those who had worked in the service of the Dutch.'[2]

But looking back on his experience as a teenager witnessing the arrival of the Japanese, Pramoedya added, with acrimony arising from his subsequent experiences, 'there was a bad smell about the whole thing, a stench that rose from the bodies of the Japanese soldiers.' The shouts of 'Japan is our older brother' and '*banzai Dai Nippon*' would soon be replaced by bitterness. Tens of thousands of Indonesians were to starve, work as slave labourers, be forced from their homes, and die in brutal hand-to-hand conflict before Indonesian sovereignty could be achieved. It took more than four years from when Independence was proclaimed in 1945 for the Dutch to transfer sovereignty to the Indonesians, and even then many Indonesians like Pramoedya were not satisfied with the result.

Given the success that the Dutch had in suppressing the small nationalist movement in Indonesia, the country would not have come into being without Japan's intervention. The Japanese encouraged and spread nationalist sentiments, created new institutions such as local neighbourhood organisations, and put political leaders like Sukarno in place. Equally they destroyed much of what the Dutch had built. The combination of nationalism and destruction were essential ingredients for the Revolution that followed the end of World War Two.

THE ARRIVAL OF THE JAPANESE

There was much anticipation about the arrival of the Japanese. While the Dutch and some Indonesians hid their apprehension and disbelief behind bravado, for some Muslim and other nationalist leaders the landing of the Emperor's troops was the fulfilment of a dream.

Japan had spread the word that it was the 'Light of Asia'. It was the Asian nation that had successfully made the transition to a modern, technological society at the end of the nineteenth century. Japan had remained independent where most other Asian nations, with the exception of Siam, had fallen under European or American power, and in 1905 Japan had beaten a European country, Russia, in war. Militarism came to dominate the Japanese state during the 1930s, leading up to Japanese expansion into China. As they turned their attention to South-east Asia the Japanese spread the message that other Asians could be part of a 'Greater East Asian Co-Prosperity Sphere', a kind of trade zone, under Japanese leadership. Pramoedya gives an impression of the efficacy of Japanese propaganda in his fictional figure of the head of a family in Blora, based on his ambivalent view of his own father:

Father was a man of strong feelings. He thirsted for social improvement, he hated the Dutch oppression (and was not yet aware of how oppressive the Japanese could be) ... He studied Japanese night and day and was foremost in two districts on the subject.

Before the Japanese landed he had studied by correspondence from the Bushido College in Bandung. The lessons stopped when the world political situation became tense.[3]

The Japanese promise for Indonesians was an end to the racially based Dutch system, but for the Chinese in Indonesia, Japanese rule in China gave them no reason to be sanguine. The Indonesian Communist underground were equally concerned. They followed the international policy of a popular united front against fascism promulgated by the Soviet Union, until Hitler and Stalin signed a non-aggression pact in 1939.

A socialist lawyer from Medan, Amir Syarifuddin (1907–48), had been one of those to caution against the danger of fascism. From Sumatran aristocracy, Amir's outstanding intellectual abilities and wealthy background meant that he was able to enter the highest elite schools and be educated in Haarlem and Leiden before gaining his law degree in Batavia. There Amir, a convert to Christianity, attended lectures on Eastern and Western philosophy organised by the Theosophical Society. He had headed political parties and known Sukarno during the Dutch period, and by 1940 Dutch intelligence suspected him of being linked to the Communist underground. His groups urged boycotts against Japan, since the Netherlands Indies was a major exporter of raw materials such as oil, tin and rubber to East Asia until the invasion of the Netherlands by Japan's ally, Germany, in May 1940. It was probably his prominence in campaigns for the boycott that led the head of Dutch intelligence to give Amir funds in March 1942 to organise a resistance movement, just before the top Dutch military leadership fled to Australia.[4]

As Pramoedya recalls it: 'The landing of the Japanese army made the young men more dynamic. They were in awe of the Japanese. The Japanese had severely dented the glory of the white man's realm both in mainland Asia and throughout the archipelago.' Japan's lightning push south from China was already underway when they launched the pre-emptive strike that ripped the heart out of the United States' navy at Pearl Harbor in December 1941, and then took the US colony of the Philippines. Helped by quasi-neutral governments in Indo-China and Siam (Thailand), the Japanese quickly marched into Malaya and Singapore, and parts of Sulawesi and Kalimantan were under their control by January 1942. By February 1942 the Japanese had landed on Sumatra, where they had already encouraged the Acehnese to rebel against the Dutch. The Allied navy's last efforts to contain Japan were swept aside in the Battle of the Java Sea, and the Dutch army crumpled under the Japanese onslaught.

On 9 March 1942, after some confusion about who was in charge of the Indies, the Dutch commander surrendered, along with the aristocratic Governor General Jonkheer A. W. L. Tjarda van Starkenborgh Stachouwer. The Governor General and his wife, like most of the Dutch, had refused to leave 'their' people, the natives. They expected that Dutch administrators would be kept on by the Japanese to run the colony. Instead the Dutch became prisoners. Tjarda and his wife were put under house arrest, and over 100,000 other civilians (including some Chinese) were put in detention camps on Java, while a further 80,000 military from the Dutch, British, Australian and US Allied forces ended up in prisoner-of-war camps. The death rates in those camps ranged from 13 to 30 per cent. Strangely, since they did not send away many of their own people, the Dutch took the trouble to evacuate the Indonesian Communists and other nationalists who were imprisoned in Boven Digul, in West New Guinea. These political prisoners were sent to Australia, where the Dutch intended to have them interned along with Japanese prisoners. When this plan was discovered by members of an Australian Communist union, the Waterside Workers' Federation, the Australian government was pressured into releasing the Indonesians.[5]

A few Australian and other Allied soldiers took a brave but futile stand in places such as Ambon, for which they earned local admiration. Those locals who might have witnessed the subsequent beheadings of over 200 Australian prisoners by the victorious Japanese learned that their new masters were not as benevolent as Dai Nippon's propaganda had led them to believe.

EXPERIENCES OF JAPANESE RULE

The Netherlands East Indies was no more. The basis of Indonesia had come into existence – but not as an independent state. Instead it consisted of three Japanese military commands: Sumatra (along with Malaya) under the 25th Army, Java under the 16th Army, and the eastern islands, including Kalimantan, under the Navy. All reported to Singapore, which in turn reported to Saigon, which in turn reported to Tokyo. A 'new order' was proclaimed, Java switched to Tokyo time and the Japanese calendar. Indonesians could now call themselves Indonesians in public, Java's capital changed its name from Batavia to Jakarta, and signs of Dutch rule, like their street names, disappeared. But Indonesians were not yet in the positions of real power.

The reason that the Navy took over the eastern islands was that it wanted direct control of the oilfields in places like Balikpapan, on Kalimantan. The east was administered from Sulawesi island's capital of Makasar, since that was the most central city for that part of the archipelago. As well as taking harsh action against military captives, the Navy command encouraged nationalists and quickly stamped out any potential opposition, a policy which translated into large-scale massacres of Chinese, local aristocrats, Dutch and anyone else regarded as pro-Dutch on Kalimantan.

E. U. Pupella of Ambon was one of the nationalists suddenly thrust into a position of authority. Pupella, a Christian, had led the nationalist Ambonese League since 1938. Educated on Java in one of nationalist Suwardi Suryaningrat's 'Garden of Pupils' schools, he had returned to Maluku to work for independence through education. The Japanese chose him to head Ambon island, rather than any of the members of the Dutch administration. In this he was typical of the new nationalist class for whom the Japanese period provided their chance to gain access to power, although not all of his colleagues in the other islands were as fortunate: on Java, for example, the Japanese reproduced the structure of the Dutch civil service, adding only a new layer of neighbourhood associations.

Ambonese in general were regarded with great suspicion because the Christians amongst them were a resolutely pro-Dutch indigenous military elite. Pupella was also chosen above the traditional kings who had served the same ruling role for the Dutch as the aristocracy did on Java. The reluctant Pupella had no administrative experience at all, and had to quickly read up on Dutch reports to understand how things were done. He did have great credibility with the Muslim community because his nationalist organisation had crossed religious lines, and that was probably one of the main reasons the Japanese selected him.

Pupella's tasks included balancing relations with the Muslim community, attempting to limit the powers of the kings and moderating Japanese demands for supplies and appropriation of local women. The Islamic leaders were pleased with the way the Japanese supported them over the Christian community, but not so happy when the Japanese demanded that the fasting month not be observed because the Japanese war was a Holy War that overrode other concerns. Pupella had to convince the Muslim heads to forgo the fast, arguing that all communities were making sacrifices so that Greater East Asia could conquer the heathen Allies. It was particularly frustrating for nationalists that the Japanese did not deliver on their suggestions of independence. Had those hints been a cynical ploy by the Japanese high command to guarantee resources?

Feeding the population was the most difficult task. At the end of the Dutch period the Netherlands Indies as whole was self-sufficient in rice, but Eastern Indonesia was not, and had always depended on importing rice from Java, Burma and Thailand. The Ambonese experienced Japanese rule as a period of extreme food shortage, and also a shortage of other basic necessities, particularly cloth. The Japanese launched programmes to promote the growing of vegetables, the making of soap, and home weaving, saying that Ambonese were too used to the 'easy life'. Despite importing looms, the Japanese were not able to get a textile industry going in the short time they were in Indonesia. Barter and black-market activities became the mainstays of the local economy, and even those who had previously been pro-Japanese resented the rationing.[6]

Men were drafted by the Japanese as labourers, smaller numbers of women to provide 'comfort'. Pramoedya remembers the fate of one of these 'comfort women'. During his imprisonment on the remote eastern island of Buru, near Ambon, a fellow prisoner was working in the fields when this man met up with a middle-aged women who spoke to him in High Javanese. She had been 'the daughter of a deputy village chief from Wonogiri', Central Java. In 1943 the occupying forces sent her away from

Java, aged fourteen, with the promise that she was to be educated. Shipped to Ambon, and then to the remoter island of Seram, she found herself in a dormitory with other young women where, 'their real duties began: they were the Japanese officers' sexual toys.' She had tried to return home after the war, but got no further than Buru, where she stayed for another three decades. Women were taken from all over Asia to work in the barracks brothels, and Dutch and Allied prisoners were also forced to work there. A few, such as the woman on Buru, were recruited by trickery, most were raped and brutalised. There have been no estimates of how many Indonesians suffered this way, but there were tens of thousands of 'comfort women' throughout the Japanese empire. Many have had to live out their lives with the disgrace of their experiences, despised by their communities if they returned, as with Suharti from Java, who fifty years later was still suffering a double blow, 'That burden they call "dignity" is so heavy to carry ... It was Japanese officers who abused me – but my honour was destroyed by my own people.'[7]

When the Dutch had left Sumatra, they had attempted a scorched earth policy, setting alight oilfields and refineries. Japanese civilian governor Yano Kenzo's duty in the Minangkabau area of the island was to restore oil production, but despite forcing Indonesians to work on fixing Dutch refineries, production levels never attained their pre-war volume. As the war effort became more difficult through 1943 and 1944, Governor Yano had to deal with the effects on the population. He complained about government policies of printing more money to subsidise the war, since this just resulted in high levels of inflation, and he avoided some of the policies of forced labour that were being implemented elsewhere in the Indies. Under his administration, the local women's movement success-fully protested against the recruitment of Minangkabaus as comfort women, and demanded that all brothels be closed.

After Yano resigned in 1944 his successor drafted villagers to work on construction projects, which included building a railway from Pekanbaru in the highlands to the coast to transport oil. Sumatra could not supply all the labour for this project needed, so Javanese and some 6,500 prisoners-of-war made up the labour force of perhaps 100,000. Pekanbaru railway is not as infamous as the Thai–Burma railway, which claimed perhaps 80,000 lives, but conditions were just as much like hell.

Corvée labour under the Dutch was nothing like the Japanese approach to labour recruitment. The Japanese drafted as many able-bodied men as possible to increase war production, the majority coming from Java. The teak forests around Blora were depleted as workers were forced to build boats for transport. Those sent on a fortnightly basis for local construction tasks were relatively lucky; up to half the working population of Java and Madura was affected in this way. The numbers sent overseas are estimated to have been between 160,000 and 200,000, of whom 50,000 were sent as military support. Amongst these were ordinary Javanese like Sarman Praptowidjojo, who were forced to slave on the Burma railway. Originally from Surakarta, he had been a railway worker in Surabaya before being sent to Singapore and then on to Thailand to work on the railway, where he witnessed the destruction of the bridge on the River Kwai. He and his fellow Javanese workers saw those around them dying initially at the rate of three a day, then five, then ten. Sarman survived, but he was one of thousands who did not return to Java, preferring to marry and live in Bangkok.[8]

Sarman was fortunate not to have been among the forced labourers involved in what may have been a botched Japanese biological warfare experiment in 1944. Between 5,000 and 10,000 men from a group of forced labourers held on the outskirts of Jakarta, awaiting shipment outside Java, died writhing in agony from injections of tetanus. Japanese scientists had prepared the lethal vaccines to see what their effects would be, but an Indonesian scapegoat was found after a number of physicians were tortured by the *Kenpeitai*, the feared secret police. The scapegoat's punishment – he was beheaded, his body crushed by a steamroller and then dumped in a mass grave – was presented as 'relatively light' in official accounts.[9]

Despite planning extensively for the occupation, the Japanese resources were too stretched for them to be able to run their empire effectively and fight a war at the same time. Initially the Japanese were faced by a situation of chaos, as Pramoedya depicts in one of his stories of Blora:

Each day the people revenged themselves by violating the laws of the newly-deceased Netherlands East Indies. Obvious looting filled the first week of the Japanese army's arrival. The town was flooded with people who came thronging in from the forest edges and the mountain foothills to witness the death of the history of Dutch greatness in our land. And others came to pillage the shops, offices and school buildings.
It was a time when men no longer understood order and government.

There were spontaneous attacks on Dutch officials, indigenous civil servants, and on Chinese, with murders and atrocities such as forced circumcisions of Chinese carried out by Muslims from the traditionalist *Nahdlatul Ulama* movement in East Java. Farmers took back their land from plantations, the Japanese took over all the foreign businesses, and with most of the Dutch imprisoned, the top layer of management suddenly disappeared. This was a revolutionary situation where the whole economic, as well as the political order, had been overthrown.[10]

The Japanese used harsh military discipline to restore order, and even Japanese soldiers who violated laws were dealt with summarily. Indonesians from this time remember how they were made to bow to Japanese officers, and how physical violence was inflicted on a regular basis. Since Indonesians regard the head as the most respected part of a person's body, the slaps in the face meted out by Japanese were more than physical hurt. The *Kenpeitai* were particularly feared for their use of arbitrary arrest, torture and execution.

One aspect of restoring order that was unpopular on Java was the elevation of village heads and local officials to new positions of power. Many throughout the countryside had grown to hate these collaborators for the way they grew rich from the Dutch system. Now they were the agents of the Japanese, which in the eyes of people in the villages was even worse. Village heads were notorious for abusing the rice requisition and rationing systems, although some were scrupulously honest and risked their lives to protect their fellow villagers.

On Java, extensive famines were not the result of an overall lack of food, just an inability to organise distribution. Since petrol was requisitioned and the trains taken over, Javanese could not travel to market, so their everyday economies became more restricted. Rice was commandeered by the Japanese, who ordered that stockpiles be created for a long war, but without due regard to what the people needed to live. When the drought that had been scorching the Asia Pacific region intensified at the end of 1944, the effects were felt all over the Indies. Pramoedya, making his way back home to Blora from Jakarta, saw the effects of Japanese policy in action: 'I had seen people wearing clothes made from burlap and thin sheets of rubber.' Pramoedya saw people who had starved to death by the side of the road; like many people he only had one bowl of rice porridge with leaves to eat each day. Possibly as many as 2.4 million Javanese died of starvation in these years.[11]

International trade had collapsed, and while the Japanese had plans to rebuild it within their Co-Prosperity Sphere, that would take time. For Indonesians survival depended on improvisation – *becak*s, the tricycle transport, came into their own, *batik* makers on the north coast of Java made their designs more and more intricate in order to compensate for the fact that there was not enough cloth to work on. The Japanese brought their own imports – soy sauce, soft drinks and eating utensils all became local manufactures. Having to be self-sufficient was to be an unintended preparation for the struggle for independence.[12]

MOBILISING THE POPULATION

Under Dutch 'peace and order' Indonesians were meant to be passive, but the Japanese mobilised the whole population for the war effort. This was total war. Sukarno, along with other nationalists, was elevated by the Japanese in order to unite the Japanese and Indonesian causes. It briefly became legal, if not encouraged, to sing 'Indonesia the Great', to raise the red and white flag of the independence movement, to hold rallies. While the Japanese military authorities were wary of giving the Indonesians too much licence, they recognised that they could not maintain their position by force alone.

Sukarno was allowed to travel the countryside giving speeches with nationalist messages, as long as those speeches made it clear that supporting Indonesia was a way to support the war effort. His work involved recruiting forced labour. Other Indonesian politicians were drafted into leading roles on Java, where nationalists mixed with regents in 'advisory bodies'. Indonesians were not allowed to have their own political organisations, but they could participate in Japanese-sponsored ones.

Pramoedya got a glimpse into the world of politics and government through the Japanese propaganda machine. He joined the 250,000 Indonesians who moved from the countryside to Jakarta looking for opportunities, and found work in the Japanese newsagency as a stenographer and researcher. Artists, performers of traditional theatre, writers and ideologues were all recruited for the war effort, producing plays, films and newspaper articles. The Japanese supervising these activities had clear ideas about what should or should not be portrayed. For example, films were not allowed to reproduce Western values by showing 'stories of a petit bourgeois character, those which describe the happiness of individual persons only, scenes of a woman smoking, café scenes ... and frivolous and flippant behaviour'. Rather films should encourage patriotism, 'Japanese values, such as self-sacrifice, motherly love ... modesty of women, diligence, and loyalty' and emphasise a work ethic that would increase production. Under the Japanese, radio came into its own as a popular medium. During the Dutch era few Indonesians could afford radio, so the Japanese set up public loudspeakers to spread radio broadcasts, so that everybody could hear popular *kroncong* music and the message of the Emperor.[13]

Japanese propaganda proclaimed a new age. In this new era women were expected to maintain femininity, but were simultaneously part of the mobilisation of the general population. They were conscripted into work groups where they wore pants, and even into a military training body, named after a heroine of the *wayang* theatre who dressed as a man to join in battle.[14]

Most of all the Japanese new age promoted military values. The Japanese had the most modern technology, but presented themselves in the ancient tradition of the Samurai warriors. Indonesians were trained in *Bushido* discipline as an introduction to a new kind of martial modernity, one in which young men could move up to higher social levels without needing an aristocratic background.

The Japanese provided new opportunities for military training for large numbers of officers and soldiers. Few Indonesians had been given officer training by the Dutch, and they were always under Dutch commanders. The Japanese set up various kinds of militias, such as the Hizbullah troops recruited from the various Muslim groups and ready to sacrifice themselves for God against Westerners. The most important of the military groups was the Defenders of the Homeland, which recruited 37,500 members, even though only about half of them had rifles. The main weapon provided for Indonesians was the bamboo spear. The Defenders was not entirely loyal and in 1945 two separate rebellions or mutinies against the Japanese occurred.[15]

When Pramoedya was in Jakarta he benefited from the education that the Japanese set up. He attended lectures by Sukarno in the former hall of the Dutch People's Council on the topic of politics, and Sukarno's deputy, the highly efficient ethnic Minangkabau, Muhammad Hatta (1902–80), provided training in economics. Hatta's lectures were mainly on his favourite topic of cooperatives, an experiment that nationalists had tried in the early 1940s, and of which the Japanese approved. The most promising Indonesians received special training in Youth Hostels in Jakarta. Here was instruction for the future leadership of Indonesia, men such as the Sumatran D. N. Aidit (1923–65), then just entering his twenties, who was part of the most radical grouping in a Dutch-style hotel at Menteng 31, on a main street leading into Jakarta's garden suburb.

Aidit had been a member of the socialist idealist Amir Syarifuddin's organisation before the Japanese invasion. Aidit's leftist background indicates that the Japanese leadership did not have a unified policy about which Indonesians should receive political training. Sukarno had been supported, but his careful deputy Hatta had been regarded with suspicion by the *Kenpeitai*, who had planned to assassinate him. The Japanese used the surviving archives of Dutch intelligence to hunt down and imprison or kill Communists, and Amir, who was jailed, was only saved from execution by the intervention of his friend Sukarno. Not too far from Menteng 31, at the Medical Faculty's boarding house, Prapatan 10, was a group of intellectuals who had formed a position of non-cooperation with the Japanese, under the leadership of another Sumatran intellectual, the rationalist Sutan Syahrir. They seem to have been able to hold their discussions without Japanese interference.

By 1943 Japan was losing the war, but the nationalist leadership in Jakarta could do little to take advantage of this because they had limited contact with the rest of Indonesia, where political developments followed different trajectories. A major popular alternative to the Jakarta leadership was one of Indonesia's leading left-wingers from the old movement, the romantic hero Tan Malaka (1897–1949). He had been an early member of the Communist Party, but was regarded as a Trotskyite by its leadership because he had opposed the 1926–7 uprising and was against Stalin's policies. He had been in exile since 1922, during which time his reputation had assumed legendary proportions because of his involvement in spreading Communism throughout South-east and East Asia. By 1942 he was back in Indonesia, witnessing the suffering of forced labourers in the coal mines of West Java, and attempted to organise for independence.[16]

Although news leaked out in August 1945 that the Allies had dropped a huge bomb that could destroy cities, the Japanese were reluctant to admit that they had surrendered. Sukarno, Hatta and the other older leadership were hesitant, but had their hands forced by the younger members of the new elite, who believed that 'the youth' had the duty to push for revolution. A group associated with Menteng 31 kidnapped Sukarno and Hatta to force them to agree to proclaim independence, which they did two days after the Japanese surrender, making their statement at Sukarno's house, Pegangsaan Timur 56, Jakarta, on 17 August 1945.

Since this was the moment that formally ended what Sukarno called, with great exaggeration, 350 years of Dutch rule, and which launched one of the largest national revolutions of the twentieth century, the Proclamation could have been expected to be one of grand rhetoric. Instead Indonesia's new leaders simply announced that they were declaring independence, and would work out the details later. The substance was less important than the act.

INDEPENDENCE

The situation at the end of the war was confusing for all involved. Once the US-led Southwest Pacific Command had reconquered islands taken by the

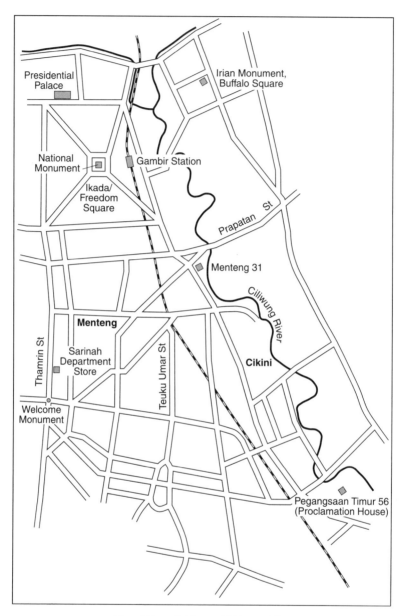

Map 4 Central Jakarta, 1940s to 1960s

Japanese in the Pacific and established a base on the Malukan island of Morotai, US and Australian forces could successfully beat back the Japanese. The Australians took control in the East. The British-led South-east Asia Command was charged with restoring order in Java. Although the leadership of the Command had a progressive outlook, its main role was restoring civilian government, which the Dutch took to mean pre-war colonialism. Because the Dutch government-in-exile in London had been allied to the British, they expected the return of their colony. The Japanese and members of the Allied Forces reluctantly fulfilled this promise.

According to the terms of the surrender, the Japanese were supposed to maintain order in the period up until the Allied forces under Lord Louis Mountbatten could take control. This meant that the first blows of the Indonesian Revolution had to be struck against Japanese, in attacks to secure control of cities and take arms. These attacks mainly occurred as a result of Allied orders that the Japanese should disarm the Indonesian troops, which many militia leaders, and a few Japanese, had no intention of letting happen. In places like Bandung open conflict broke out, and the first heroes of the Revolution fell.

The Indonesian leadership struggled to come to terms with popular sentiment. Some wanted to lead the rising passion for struggle, others preferred a more reasoned approach. In Jakarta Tan Malaka linked up with the leaders of the Menteng 31 group to launch mass demonstrations, which Sukarno and Hatta immediately attempted to quell. Tan Malaka and those on his side spread the idea that this was a revolution led by the youth of Indonesia, a revolution that would win freedom by a spirit of struggle. Sukarno and Hatta were more interested in planning out a government and setting up new institutions to achieve independence through diplomacy.

The struggle message had spread rapidly across Java and on to the other islands almost the day independence was proclaimed, through the use of radio and telegram, and by word of mouth. In southern Kalimantan it was actually Australian Communist soldiers who spread the word of the Declaration of Independence and who helped the nationalists to organise.[17] Everywhere struggle groups set up their own radio stations and newspapers. Graffiti proclaimed the nationalist message: even General van Heutsz's monument in Jakarta was daubed with signs in English announcing the end of Dutch rule. On most of the islands struggle committees and militia were set up. The British-led forces arrived in the middle of the struggle for control, and attempted to restore Jakarta to the Dutch.

It was unfortunate that the British were at the receiving end of the worst fighting of the Revolution. By September 1945, those who had proclaimed themselves to be the 'youth' who were ready to die for '100 percent Freedom' were getting impatient. They had been told this was the 'getting ready period', but the question was, 'getting ready for what?': 'What Comrade Sukarno has said we must do, we must gouge out the British (*linggis Ingris*) and iron out the Americans (*seterika Amerika*) ... but ... why haven't we started fighting?' During this period there were frequent attacks on Dutch, Eurasians and Chinese and anyone suspected of being a spy; in some instances these amounted to organised massacres, particularly of women and children. Such atrocities continued throughout the Revolution.[18]

Late in September the situation got out of hand in the steamy port city of Surabaya, where revolutionaries were not prepared to countenance the return of the Dutch. After a series of incidents involving pro-Dutch Eurasians, and in which atrocities were committed against Dutch prisoners, the spirit of Revolution arose in all its passionate ugliness. 'The liberated were drunk with victory. They could do anything and dream of everything. Courage rose like a snake in the grass. Self-confidence and nationalism welled up like froth in beer.' As the writer Idrus remembered it, the Indonesian freedom fighters acted as if they were in a Hollywood western. 'The cowboys stood in the middle of the road with revolvers on their hips and knives in their belts.' The revolutionary hero, a young man with long hair, dressed in coolie trousers made of sacking, bandana on his head, samurai sword at his waist, was born.[19]

In Surabaya a British brigadier-general died in a confused incident, shot either by the revolutionaries or by 'friendly fire'. The British response was swift and angry. Throughout November they bombed and shelled this city of 600,000, fighting the Indonesians hand-to-hand, house-to-house, street-to-street. Sukarno came and went on the scene, but he wiped his hands of the struggle forces, leaving them to fight, flee or be killed. On the Allied side fourteen were killed, but there was no way to determine the total number of Indonesian freedom fighters dead; estimates vary between 6,300 and 15,000. The latter number probably includes civilian casualties, including at least 1,000 Chinese, and probably a similar number of Dutch and Eurasians, killed by Indonesians. The long columns of refugees winding out of Surabaya might not have known it as they were strafed by British planes, but they were part of an event showing the world that the Revolution was serious. Indonesia was a cause worth dying for.

The British assisted the Dutch to land their own Netherlands Indies Civil Administration (NICA) forces in Jakarta and a number of other key centres. The fight to take Jakarta was reported by the revolutionary side as resulting in 8,000 Indonesian deaths up to the beginning of January 1946. Jakarta could not be held, so the leadership of the newly created Indonesian Republic moved to the royal Javanese capital of Yogyakarta, where the new Sultan, Hamengkubuwono IX, quickly realised the importance of throwing his weight behind the Republican cause. The Dutch were able to capture only major cities on Java and Sumatra, but were more successful in taking the Outer Islands (including Bali), where they set up autonomous states, the largest of which covered most of Eastern Indonesia and was centred on Makasar. Republican strategists called on revolutionaries from the other islands to join the struggle on Java. Some men and women remained in jungles on Bali, Sulawesi and other islands, and many later told stories of being protected by mystical powers, claiming that if they led pure lives they would be kept from death.

Lord Mountbatten, the head of the British-led South-east Asia Command, had immediate tasks such as repatriating 300,000 Japanese still in the archipelago and restoring the freedom of prisoners-of-war. He was not prepared to commit his troops to a long struggle for the Dutch cause. His mainly Indian troops were keen to have independence in their own country, his British troops just wanted to get back home after years of vicious jungle warfare, and he had already come to respect South-east Asian desires for independence through experiences in Burma.

During the course of the Revolution the Dutch refused to acknowledge Indonesian independence, calling their two major offensives against the Republic 'police actions'. The first of these took place between 21 July and 4 August 1947. This action was launched in violation of an agreement between the Republic and the Dutch, who were attempting to set up puppet states to create an Indonesian Federation. At the end of the fighting the Dutch had succeeded in reducing the Republic to smaller areas of Sumatra and Java, divided by Dutch zones.

More Indonesians than the fighters felt the impact of the Revolution. Indonesians, often armed only with bamboo spears and mystical powers of invulnerability bestowed by teachers and talismans, died in much greater numbers than their enemies. The total number of British and Dutch troops killed over the whole period from 1945 to the end of 1949 was 700, the majority of whom was British. More Japanese were killed. In heavy fighting in cities such as Bandung, 1,057 of the Emperor's men died, only just over half in actual combat, the others murdered in rampages by the Indonesians.

Figure 4.1 Poster from the Revolution: 'Women, if necessity demands,
be ready to help the Youth'.

There has been no accurate count of the number of Indonesians who died
over the course of the Revolution, but those who died in fighting could be
anywhere between 45,000 and 100,000. Six thousand Indonesians were
estimated to have been executed as part of ruthless Dutch counter-insurgency
tactics in Sulawesi in late 1946 and early 1947 (the Republicans claimed
the real number was 40,000). Civilian casualties overall exceeded 25,000,
and could have been as high as 100,000. Over 7 million people were displaced
on Java and Sumatra. Tens of thousands of Chinese and Eurasians were killed

or left homeless, mostly at the hands of Indonesians, despite the fact that many Chinese supported the Revolution.[20]

The social impacts of the Revolution went beyond the numbers of dead, wounded or homeless. Economic life was also threatened by the continuing shortages of clothing and food. Indonesia was not a unified economy as it had been under the Dutch; instead the Dutch were trying to re-establish all that they had lost while the Republic was seeking markets for the goods produced in the areas under its control. The Republic had to set up all the necessities of life, everything from postage stamps to army badges to train tickets. The Republic printed its own money and attempted to fix exchange rates, but this was in competition with new Dutch money, and Japanese money also remained in circulation for the first few years of the Revolution. As each new type of money was introduced or attempts made to change currencies, there were inflationary surges that made life impossible for ordinary people. As one Balinese dancer recalls it: 'Independence (*Merdeka*), at that time money changed many times. Now it was like this, now like that, now it was yellow, then white, then red, then black; that's how money always changed, what could you do?' The only response was to try to get on with whatever you could, in her case by teaching dance: 'I'd get a little, just so much per month, twenty-five *ketip* [a bundle of Chinese coins] that's what I was paid ... so I used to work as a trader as well.'[21]

Eurasian Marguerite Schenkuizen, who had been born and grown up in East Java and who lived in an area under Indonesian control for part of the Revolution, saw a difference between what she called 'the extremists', who threatened the lives of anyone not on the side of the Revolution, and the regular Indonesian military. She describes the countryside of East Java as being either 'extremist' or Republican Army zones.[22] Her simplistic view of the complex forces that made up the Revolution missed the fact that while there were certainly many who desired a total overthrow of the old social order through social revolutions, there were equally leftist elements present in the Indonesian military, and more conservative forces amongst the Republic's civilian leadership.

SOCIAL REVOLUTIONS

The social revolutions following the Proclamation were a re-run of the upheavals that had occurred when the Japanese first landed: that is, they were challenges to the social order established by the Dutch, with an added element of resentment engendered by the Japanese policies. All over the archipelago, people rose up against traditional aristocrats and village heads, and attempted to assert popular ownership of land and other resources.

For Pramoedya, a young man committed to the Revolution, the violence of Indonesians against Indonesians that was conjured up in the early stages of the struggle was a surreal mystery. In his early short stories and novels he struggled to come to terms with the combination of youthful bravado, boredom, chaos and unfettered emotions that made up the struggle. In one story, 'Revenge', he evoked the terrible passions of a mob who had identified a Muslim trader as a spy. The violence of the attack on the Muslim, a Haji, went on interminably in this narrative, as it was transformed into a mystical battle between the Haji's strange powers of invulnerability and the determination of those who made him the object of all their desires for revenge against the English, the Dutch and any other enemies. The main character describing the execution realised with horror that he was no longer a bystander, but had been dragged into a cycle of killing and risking death. The culture of violence so acutely observed here had its roots in the deep conflicts that split the countryside under Dutch rule, and would erupt again with awful regularity in the second half of the twentieth century.[23]

Most of the social revolutions ended quickly and very badly, their challenges to the social order put down. In the ethnic Malay sultanates along the coasts of Sumatra and Kalimantan, as soon as Japanese authority disappeared there were attacks on sultans and others whose authority had been boosted by the Dutch. One of the many lessons learned from the Japanese was the use of violence, as crystallised in the potent symbol of the samurai sword. Those identified as 'feudal', whether kings, regents, or just rich, were attacked, and sometimes beheaded. Rape became a weapon against 'feudal' women. The local lords of Aceh, who had been the backbone of Dutch policy, were executed or otherwise deposed, and Aceh remained a firm Republican stronghold throughout the Revolution, unlike most of the sultanates, which fell back into Dutch hands as the surviving rulers struggled to regain their pre-war power. In other areas even regents and royals who had been known to support Independence were murdered, or simply disappeared.

The social revolutions combined attempts by the left to organise real revolution and a wanton use of violence to achieve revenge, express resentment, or to assert power on a small scale. Nowhere was this combination more apparent than on the north coast of Java, in the regencies known as the Three Regions: Tegal, Brebes and Pemalang. These were areas that had been destabilised by the sugar plantations (Comal was one of these plantations in Pemalang), had suffered greatly under the Japanese, and where there were both well-organised members of the left and highly coordinated gangs of toughs, the Fighting Cocks. In the Three Regions a coalition was formed between a local tough with his own militia, and members of the underground Communist Party. The regents and other officials were attacked and publicly humiliated, founding feminist Kartini's sister amongst them. Village heads who had hoarded rice under the Japanese were stripped and made to peck seeds and husks in front of villagers. Eurasians and others suspected of being pro-Dutch were murdered. Chinese shop-owners were saved if they agreed to keep prices low and to support the Revolution. A Communist government was proclaimed. It was in power for less than a week before it was destroyed and the leaders were captured and tried, with the main tough sentenced to death (although this sentence was not carried out until 1951). But it was the new army of the Republic of Indonesia, not the Dutch, that had ended the Three Regions Revolt.

Despite the limitations of the social revolutions, the sentiments underpinning them spread throughout the archipelago, shown by the spread of the language of struggle. In the highlands of Sumatra place names came to reflect ideals of freedom – for example, 'the fields of the king' became 'the love of the people'. 'Freedom' and 'the people' took over everything. The proponents of social revolution wanted to express their wildness through the names they used, calling themselves 'Tigers' or 'Buffalo'. Hatred for Dutch colonialism was a uniting passion.

Building on the seizure of land from plantations during the early days of the Japanese occupation, unions organised the seizure of plantations in Java and Sumatra, and there was even a brief, and rather limited, attempt to set up a people's economy for the whole of the Republic, using 1920s radical journalist Marco's cry of 'equality and solidarity'. Given the starvation and misery inherited from the later years of Japanese rule, the popular desire for enough food, land and jobs expressed in this slogan could never be fulfilled.

When the Dutch returned to the plantation area of the former sultanate of Deli, in East Sumatra, after the settlement following the First Police Action, 173 estates were 'recovered'. The main problem for the owners was that they could not recover their workforce, as perhaps a million people had fled from Dutch to Republican territory throughout Sumatra. For once, coolie labour was expensive, and strikes and walk-outs became potent weapons, along with attacks on foremen and managers.[24]

Most Indonesians lived in fear and uncertainty, even when the social revolutions had settled – the popular revolutionary cry of 'Freedom or

Figure 4.2 Dutch troops take the Javanese city of Malang on the morning of
31 July 1947, at the beginning of the First Police Action. Dutch soldiers supervise
the movement of Chinese.

Death' could mean death at the hands of those who had assumed the
authority of the Revolution. A large proportion of the Indonesian
population still supported the Dutch, or at least remained under Dutch
control.

On the fringes of a city such as Jakarta, Dutch and Republican zones
met. If you were in a Dutch controlled area, you could not show any of the
symbols of the Red and White, the Republican flag. If you were in a
Republican area and happened to be wearing the Dutch flag's colours, red,
white and blue, you could be killed. The heart of a Dutch-controlled city
like Jakarta was not safe from bombings or other acts designed to undermine colonial confidence. Traders were pressured by Republicans to
boycott all sales to the Dutch, but Dutch police were equally ruthless in
tracking down smugglers who were trying to keep the Republican economy
running. In some areas the term for 'exercising the sovereignty of the
people' became a synonym for robbery and extortion. Anyone who identified himself as a 'soldier' considered that he had an automatic entitlement
to free food in the markets and free rides on the trains. What Pramoedya
describes in one novel as the 'half thug half military' uniform became the
style of the Revolution – black, deep pillbox-style cap, baggy coolie trousers
or shorts, khaki or dark shirt, gun belts worn at an angle from shoulders to
hips, boots if you could find them.[25]

FORMING A MILITARY AND A STATE

At the beginning of the Revolution, being part of a struggle group was a matter of pride for many young Indonesians, resulting in the formation of many militias. One of the Republican government's many problems was turning these into a single unified army, as they endeavoured to channel their violence.

The militias represented a wide range of groups who considered themselves part of the youth movement, and therefore epitomes of the romantic spirit of the Revolution. Some militias grew out of Japanese-sponsored bodies, for example the women's fighting units and the Islamic militias. Others were new. Some militias were rebranded versions of criminal gangs, the only real local authority that many people had left. Radical leaders among the youth saw the popular support of local Fighting Cocks as an advantage, and tried to link up with whoever looked sufficiently patriotic, as was the case in the Three Regions Affair. For some criminals this was an opportunity to acquire legitimacy, while others were simply mercenaries, changing sides when the money was better.

Typical of the militias was the Wild Tiger Brigade of the Batak highlands, a group of peasants and labourers commanded by men who had been trained by a captain of the Japanese secret police to see themselves as the basis of a new society. Their leader characterised them as uneducated boys led by illiterates (himself included): 'You have to understand what our troops were like. They had no experience with military discipline. In the military, if your commander says, do this, you have to obey immediately without thinking. But our troops would ask, "Why?" They wanted to know what was going on.'[26]

The Indonesian army started as a government-run competitor with the many militias. The Republic's political leaders used Dutch- and Japanese-trained officers as the foundation of their army, in the form of a People's Security Body. This was the first stage in the creation of state apparatuses. The Independence Planning Body, the initial vehicle by which Sukarno, Hatta, Syahrir and Amir Syarifuddin set up the Republic, debated how to organise the army as a crucial step in setting up the Indonesian state.

By the time of the Battle of Surabaya in November 1945 the People's Security Body had become the People's Security Army. Since the army was a coalition of different groups, its formation involved difficult negotiations over who should have power. On 18 December 1945 these negotiations were resolved when the leadership elected the popular teacher, Sudirman (1915?–50), as general. Sudirman was viewed by his followers as committed to a path of uncompromising struggle; other military leaders saw him as a man of charisma and fixity of purpose. A slight figure in a huge greatcoat, wearing traditional Javanese head-gear, he remained free of the abuse of uniform that was common, and partly because of this he became a symbol of the purity of the Revolution. Sudirman did not necessarily get on with the political leaders. His appeal, and the fact that he died of tuberculosis soon after the end of the Revolution, meant that the high regard in which he was held has endured, making him one of the great mythical heroes of the Revolution. The army was merged with various struggle organisations and renamed the National Army of Indonesia.

Those under Sukarno organised successive cabinets as they attempted to weld together the different forces that could make up the nation and its state. Sukarno and Hatta were president and vice-president, jointly sharing powers and responsibilities. Sukarno, the most charismatic of all these appealing leaders, continually toured the Republican territories, his speeches maintaining enthusiasm for the cause. Syahrir was most often in the role of prime minister. Amir, 'a man even his political adversaries found it difficult to hate',[27] played a key role as minister of defence in different cabinets, and briefly became prime minister himself.

These political leaders claimed to be dedicated to a strategy of diplomacy, but had to deal with an alternative political leadership that emphasised struggle. The Marxist Tan Malaka was the latter's most prominent figurehead, and the army leadership and the more radical youth gathered around him and his associates. The Sukarno leadership recognised this group as a threat to their power, and were able to hold them at bay by gaoling Tan Malaka for an alleged coup attempt. Amir and Hatta supported a hard-nosed Batak officer, Abdul Haris Nasution (1918–2000) in the section of the army operating in Sunda, West Java, and quickly elevated him because they recognised that here was a brilliant strategist and someone who understood discipline and unifying authority.

The political leadership abandoned Sukarno's initial idea of having a one-party state. Syahrir believed the opposite: 'we must never forget that we are creating a *democratic revolution.* Our *national revolution* is simply the "tail end" of our *democratic revolution.* Top priority must be given … to democracy, even though it may seem easier to arouse the masses by encouraging their xenophobia.' Nor did he think the leadership of the struggle should be military.[28]

Good in theory, Syahrir's idea of democracy had one practical problem. The resulting political parties established in the Republic were based on the existing nationalist leadership, that is, leaders or potential leaders

AMIR SJARIFUDDIN (PENDETA-KOMUNIS):
„*Hai rakjatku Indonesia, aku bawa Kebenaran bagi kamu sekalian, seba-
gai jang tertulis dalam Kitab sutji Indjil dan dalam Kitab „Das Kapital", maka marilah turut bersama daku kedalam Keradjaan Tuhan di-
atas bumi Rusia......Amen.........Amen..........*

Figure 4.3 Prime Minister Amir Syarifuddin ('Communist Priest'), addresses the People:
'Oh my people of Indonesia, I bring you all the Truth, as it is written in the Bible,
and in "Das Kapital", let us all bow down to the Kingdom of the Lord over
Russia ... Amen ... Amen.' From Ramelan, *Perdjuangan Republik Indonesia
dalam Karikatur* (Djakarta: Tintamas, 1952).

established political parties as a vehicle to power, and formed or linked up
with militias or factions of the army. The emphasis on leadership ahead of
institutions in Indonesia's current fractious party system can trace its roots
back to this legacy of the Revolution.

Attempts to bring the different militias into the army were fraught, and
became worse when the leadership tried to rationalise the military in 1948.
The re-establishment of an official Communist Party added another player
into this complex mix. The underground Communists, those who had

risked imprisonment under the Dutch and death under the Japanese, found themselves in a difficult position when this occurred, because they had not been able to make contact with other Communists or work out a common political or military approach. When the Communist leader of the Three Regions Revolt was captured by the army late in 1946, he was taken to Yogyakarta and imprisoned there. The army was content to let him go, but in 1947 he found himself facing a tribunal, composed of a representative of the radical new Communist leadership, the young D. N. Aidit, accompanied by one of the old guard who had been imprisoned at the Boven Digul camps and just returned (along with over 1,000 others) from Australia, and a third leader recently returned from the Netherlands. It is likely that these three consulted with Amir about how to create a new party discipline. The committee found the Three Regions leader guilty of divergence from the correct party line, even though he could not possibly have known what this line was since it did not exist in 1946. They had him taken to Parang Tretis beach, south of Yogyakarta, where he was shot.

In 1948 one of the other leaders of the Communist Party from the 1920s, Muso (b. 1897), arrived back in Indonesia from the Soviet Union. After the 1926/27 Communist revolts failed Muso spent decades in exile, returning briefly in 1933 in an attempt to reinvigorate the Party. Muso brought the authority of Stalin to his attempt to assert the unity and strength of the Party. Amir for the first time declared in public that he was a Party member, and the two then announced a United Front.

By the middle of 1948 the Republic's territory in Central Java was severely reduced in size as a result of the Dutch Police Action of the previous year. It was overcrowded with political and military groups. The reduced Republican territory did not even include a good port. Workers had not been paid, and there was talk of lay-offs, leading to strike actions around the oil-rich Cepu region and some of the plantations. The commander of the Republican forces in West Java, Nasution, had brought his Siliwangi Division over from West Java, but that meant another 32,000 people had to be housed and fed in addition to the approximately 6 million refugees already there. Tensions, sometimes linked to ideological differences, arose between different factions in the military. Nasution's Division and its hosts, a left-leaning Division based in Surakarta, did not get on well, for example, particularly after Siliwangi troops gunned down their rival commander.

Many blamed former Prime Minister Amir for the poor state of affairs because he had been responsible for negotiating for a settlement with the Dutch in early 1948. Amir had little experience with the issues of foreign relations that were an essential part of being prime minister, and in particular misjudged the role of the United States, which had set up the agreement that ended that phase of the conflict. The US realised that it could not resolve its other international interests until problems of decolonisation had been sorted out, but its focus was on the developing Cold War in Europe, to which at this stage Asia was a side-show. The main advisers on Asian affairs knew very little about the countries they were dealing with, and the US was reluctant to add substance to its rhetoric of self-determination. Amir felt himself betrayed by the US, who had guaranteed to support a neutral settlement, but had ended up backing the Dutch.

In August 1948 one of the left factions of the military, linked to a loose collection of militias, political groups, unionists and sympathisers, seized control of the city of Madiun, calling on other leftist groups to rally there. Muso, Amir and the other Communist leadership had very little choice but to go to Madiun, since their support base was gathering there. Sukarno and Hatta declared this Madiun Affair as an illegal uprising. In a stirring radio broadcast Sukarno attempted to rally popular supported against the left.

While we are involved in a conflict with the Dutch which requires the absolute solidarity of our people behind the Government … this people's unity is broken by a group of rebels.

My brothers, my people, arise!

The insurgents, who lack the patience to await the people's decision at a general election, want to overthrow our government, to destroy our state!

Let us shoulder to shoulder destroy these rebels.

Muso replied that Sukarno and Hatta were 'the slaves of the Japanese and America'.[29] Hatta ordered Nasution to crush those gathering at Madiun.

Another force in this complicated political mix was the Muslim militias and military units, whose Holy War was as much against the left as the Dutch. The events at Madiun were preceded by conflicts between Muslim and leftist factions in villages throughout Central and East Java, conflicts in which there had been attacks on senior religious leaders, resulting in a total of 240 bodies of Muslim leaders being found dumped down wells in three villages by leftists.

Nasution and the angry Muslim militias moved on the city of Madiun from all sides. The fighting that resulted left more dead than the Battle of Surabaya. The combined anti-Communist forces quickly took Madiun, and Muso was killed in the fighting, along with 8,000 others. The fleeing left-wing military and Communist leadership were harried by their enemies, and Amir was captured, his bible in his hands. A further 4,000 dead were reported in Cepu, the writer Mas Marco's home village near Blora, as the fighting moved across the countryside, and towns such as Ponorogo split into open civil war, leading to perhaps as many as 12,000 deaths. In other leftist centres, notably Blora, corpses were reported piled up outside the towns. Another 14,000 members of the left were imprisoned in Yogyakarta, and 900 in Surakarta.[30]

Pramoedya was at this time a prisoner of the Dutch in Bukitduri Prison, Jakarta, a place with a poor reputation. This first experience of gaol put him in touch with the suffering of most of the other nationalists from the 1930s, and thousands of his comrades from the Revolution. Looking at the events of Madiun and his home town from his cell, he captured the sense of hopelessness ordinary people must have felt living in the midst of this conflict. In his story of Blora, 'Those who have vanished', his semi-fictional family includes members who have joined the Dutch army and the Communists. When the Communists were in power in the region, those who were 'feudal remnants' were in danger of being killed, and when the pro-Dutch brother visited, his car and the family's house were burned. When Nasution's forces swept the Communists out, the purge left the family even more diminished, more fearful. Under each regime people were expected to show due enthusiasm, or be accused of belonging to the enemy. The net effect was that each side made a person into 'a prisoner, an employee or a corpse'.[31] Although Pramoedya ignored the role of Islam and viewed the events as a supporter of the Revolution whose sympathies were with the left, his story was of suffering being shared equally.

THE DIPLOMATIC SOLUTION

For the sake of international support Prime Minister Syahrir had already been playing down his own socialism and that of Sukarno and Hatta, as well as countering the Dutch attack on Sukarno for his collaboration with the Japanese. Syahrir guaranteed that the property of foreign companies would be respected, and when the United Nations was established he presented his case to it with great clarity. From early on in the Revolution, Indonesia had secured a supporter in the diplomatic struggle: Australia. Australia's quixotic foreign minister, H. V. Evatt, had been a major figure in the establishment of the United Nations, and advocated Indonesia's case in that forum. Once India achieved independence, it joined the diplomatic push.

The United States, as the key player in the game of international politics, initially supported the Dutch because of the importance of reconstructing post-war Europe through the Marshall Plan. The Dutch played up to this by using touring art exhibitions and other propaganda to argue that it was natural for the Netherlands to keep Indonesia as a Federation under the Dutch Queen. But diplomatic moves by Syahrir and the other leaders were starting to pay off. The crushing of the left at Madiun was the proof for the US that the Indonesian Revolution was not Communist, as the Dutch had alleged.

After the Madiun Affair, the Dutch made a fatal mistake. By initiating a second police action from 19–31 December 1948, and taking over Republican territory, including their capital of Yogyakarta, they broke earlier treaties which the US had helped negotiate. This second police action was a military victory for the Dutch. However, the Dutch learned a lesson that the US might have heeded before it went into Vietnam or Iraq: that military victory is meaningless when guerrillas are still supported by a significant proportion of the population, and can continue to operate across the countryside. At the same time the Dutch strategy of setting up puppet governments in a set of federal states backfired when political manipulation by the Dutch-backed kings, sultans and rajas alienated many Indonesians from the Dutch cause, and exposed Dutch claims of democratic backing as a sham.

The Dutch pushed the Republican Army out of Yogyakarta, the military paused only to execute Amir Syarifuddin and other key Communist prisoners. But Sukarno, Hatta and Prime Minister Syahrir stayed, to be captured and taken to Sumatra, an act of martyrdom that made bad international press for the Dutch. To compound this image problem, the Republican Army launched an attack on Yogyakarta to demonstrate that they were not defeated.

Guerrilla warfare waged for over six months, and with the political leadership out of the way and the army leadership spread across a wide territory, many of the separate militias and factions came into their own. The so-called Trotskyite struggle leader, Tan Malaka, had been released during the Madiun Affair in order to create division amongst the left, and his groups were strong in West and East Java, even though army officers tracked him down and executed him in February or March 1949.

The final demonstration that the Dutch position was untenable was the resignation of the whole leadership of key states of the Dutch-sponsored Federation, particularly the state of Eastern Indonesia. A ceasefire was declared on 7 May 1949, and hostilities officially ended by 1 August, even though the dying head of the Republican Army, General Sudirman, carried from guerrilla base to guerrilla base on his stretcher, wanted to fight on.

In December 1949 the final victory of the combination of struggle and diplomacy took place, with the Dutch eventually agreeing to hand over sovereignty to Indonesia. The Sultan of Yogyakarta led the acceptance of the Dutch surrender of power, and then Sukarno returned in triumph to Jakarta, where the main square, designed by Dutch town planner Karsten, was filled with ten of thousands of elated, free, Indonesians. The portraits of Dutch Governors General were carted out of the official residence at the north of the square, which now became the Presidential Palace, but the leaders of the Revolution had now to confront a host of problems created by their victory.

The country was not yet unified, the nationalists were still a small minority who had to translate their spirit into the form of a state, based on the myth of common struggle against the Dutch. The legacy of division from the Dutch era, the Japanese occupation and the Revolution was too deep to be overcome by this foundational nationalist myth. It was an imperfect new nation that had been born of the fire of occupation and revolution.

CHAPTER 5

Living in the atomic age

[I]f one night a neighbour of mine had an attack of stomach flu and had to run to the common toilet, he would see a well, our well, still brightly lit by a lamp on the wall; the maid, deeply stooped, washing a seemingly endless pile of clothes. Until eleven o'clock, twelve, one, two, sometimes even three ... Later, at five in the morning, that is two hours later, these creatures behind houses began to emerge to go back to the well: to bathe, wash dishes or clothes, until nine o'clock.

What is the significance of the Revolution for these maids, that Revolution that has claimed thousands of victims from their families? From time to time this question flits through my head. And I can't answer it.[1]

Having achieved sovereignty, Indonesians were faced with the task of building a state and nation, but Pramoedya Ananta Toer, reflecting on the fate of the poor, was right to ask if anything had been done to improve their lives. Colonial rule had created institutional structures that could be converted to Indonesian needs, but had also created massive inequalities and an economic system that drained resources and sent profits overseas. The Japanese period and the Revolution left legacies of dislocation, division and death, and it would take a huge effort to rebuild broken lives and industries lost in scorched earth campaigns. Coming out of the Revolution, some Indonesians like Pramoedya expressed deep bitterness about the effects of the tumult, but others felt a great optimism that, free at last, they could form their own destinies.

Even though he was a dissident in many ways, Pramoedya was still one of the new nationalist elite that felt they spoke with the voice of the whole nation. The achievements of his generation, the generation who came to power in the 1950s and created the new Indonesia, often tend to be forgotten in the light of Indonesia's weak economy and the political upheavals of regional revolts, Islamic rebellion and the almost-civil war and mass killings of 1965–6. Yet the 1950s was the era in which they almost created Indonesia as a strong new nation.

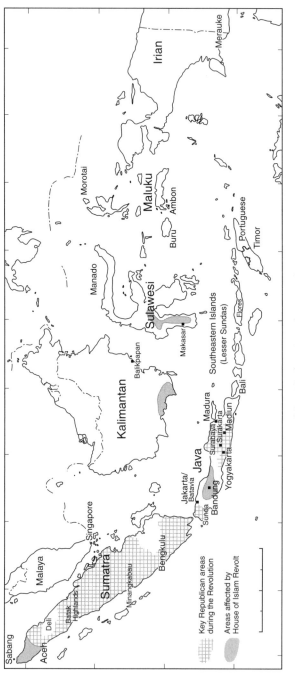

Map 5 Indonesia 1940s to 1960s

Labels on map:

Irian
Merauke
Morotai
Maluku
Ambon
Buru
Manado
Sulawesi
Makasar
Portuguese
Timor
Flores
Southeastern Islands
(Lesser Sundas)
Balikpapan
Kalimantan
Bali
Madura
Surabaya
Surakarta
Madiun
Java
Yogyakarta
Jakarta/
Batavia
Bandung
Sunda
Singapore
Sumatra
Bengkulu
Minangkabau
Malaya
Deli
Batak
Highlands
Aceh
Sabang

Key Republican areas
during the Revolution

Areas affected by
House of Islam Revolt

THE NEW CLASS AND THE NEW STATE

The small group of nationalists who led the Revolution were reassured by their achievements, but they had to convince the rest of the population. Their first task was to take the fragments of state institutions inherited from the Dutch, the Japanese and the Revolution's planning group, and mould them into a functional apparatus of the state.

One of the first points of disagreement was on the nature of the state. The settlement reached on 27 December 1949 was one in which the new Indonesia was a Federation, linking the Republican core to the Dutch-sponsored states. For many Indonesians this was an unacceptable colonial structure, and as a result federalism has for ever more had bad connotations in Indonesian politics. Sukarno in particular favoured centralism over federalism, so on 17 August 1950, the Federal Constitution of the state was scrapped and a unitary Republic declared.

While Hatta, Syahrir and the other main political leaders worked to plan the state, Sukarno used his great talents to build national sentiment. He travelled from one end of Indonesia to the other to address massive public meetings, and each year he gave the speech of speeches, the Independence address of 17 August, that was then published and disseminated throughout the islands. Local governors and aspiring politicians learned from the Great Leader's rhetorical style, and reproduced their own versions in order to muster local solidarity.

Sukarno's great gift was that he could speak directly to the hearts of the people. He made extensive use of his mixed Javanese and Balinese ethnicity to show that he was not just an expansionist Javanese. His periods of exile in Flores and Bengkulu, as well as sojourns in Sumatra during the course of the Revolution, were called upon to show that he understood the daily lives of people no matter where they lived in the archipelago. His language was a blend of European and local Indonesian terms, combining images from the shadow theatre with descriptions of international affairs, intended to give Indonesians the sense that they were simultaneously cosmopolitan participants in a new world and a people firmly rooted in their own traditions. There are still many people today who heard him speak and fondly recall his vividly inspiring words.

Those 70 million people being called upon to be part of the nation were a diverse group. At the core of the citizenship of Indonesia was the new class that had emerged during the Dutch period. The Revolution effectively removed two classes from power: the European ruling class and their uneasy allies in the traditional aristocracy. The Dutch rulers and administrators, with the exception of some of the managers who stayed on to rebuild Dutch enterprises, were gone. The traditional aristocrats who had made up the indigenous civil service had lost most of their power. The Japanese and the Revolution had seen some of them directly deposed and some killed, and the process of subsuming the federal states into the unitary Republic had pushed most of the others out of power. A new civil service was coming in to take its place, one made up of the nationalists who had been on the side of the Republic during the Revolution, and only in local government in the rural areas did the old bureaucratic elite maintain its power.

The majority of the Republic's leadership came from the new class, even though there were still a few kings and aristocrats in power in the Republic, people who had stood up to the Dutch such as Yogyakarta's Sultan Hamengkubuwono IX. The new class was the nationalist class that had received Western education and had rejected government service in favour of professional activities. Many had been journalists or teachers; for others their only occupation had been political-leader-in-prison. Pramoedya Ananta Toer was as much a member of this class as any political leader, but he remained on the fringes of power, critically gauging the direction of the nation.[2]

Having grown up with the nationalist movement, this new class had a common desire to be modern, but its leaders were divided as to how to achieve that end. During the 1950s the leadership worked through the state and the new system of political parties to disseminate the desire for the modern into the rest of Indonesian society, and in so doing they gave meaning to the nation.

Despite the rhetoric of Indonesian Marxists who debated what the role of the 'national bourgeoisie' should be in advancing socialism, there was still not an established bourgeois or middle class in Indonesia. Some of the new rulers had come from entrepreneurial backgrounds, but control over capital still rested either in the hands of the remaining Dutch, or with Chinese Indonesians. The latter were perceived as 'alien' by the majority of Indonesians because of their roles as economic brokers under colonialism, roles that meant that most Indonesians considered the Chinese had been pro-Dutch during the Revolution, which was not necessarily the case.

Was the will of the new class enough then to bring about a new social order? Pramoedya wrote in the mid-1950s of his despair at the grand plans of his leaders: 'the biggest shipyard in Southeast Asia, the biggest monument in Asia, the greatest decline in morals! Everything is the biggest. But there are no bolts, no nuts, no threads, no nipples, no bosses, no pivots and rings on all the machines.' This pessimism about the gap between ideals and reality was reflected in Pramoedya's fiction of the time, particularly a set of short stories, *Tales from Djakarta*. Writing at the time of the break-up of his first marriage, he described the lives of people doomed over generations to remain servants, of the degradation of prostitution, the street sellers, the gangs of toughs, the Chinese and Arab money lenders, and of the small and self-important middle class of the cities. His stories gave vivid reality to the different areas of Jakarta, the market for the poor in the western quarter Tanah Abang, the train station at Gambir on the eastern edge of the main square, the slum quarters where death was a constant element in the life of the poor:

Friend, you've heard the name of my quarter, haven't you? Ginger Flag Garden, five hundred meters in a straight line from the palace. And you also know, don't you? Its gutters are covered in the shit of the residents. To be sure, yesterday, the headman issued an order: 'No more shitting in the gutters.' And what was the first reaction? A neighbour of mine helped his child to shit in someone else's gutter . . .[3]

The massive increase in Jakarta's population since the Japanese occupation had meant that most people could not afford proper housing, so slums sprang up along the canals at the centre of the city. According to one estimate there were 150,000 unemployed in Jakarta in 1956, and another 420,000 labourers living below the poverty level, with tens of thousands of prostitutes, including a type – transvestites or *banci* – supposedly unique to Jakarta, who gathered at night in the markets of Menteng and other areas close to the centre of the city. Jatinegara, once the separate town of Meester Cornelis under the Dutch, now incorporated into the sprawling city, even had its own quarter of beggars.[4] Could a city such as this become a true metropolitan national capital? A sense of the nation was required for such a change to occur.

During the Revolution Sukarno and a number of advisers had laid the basis for an explicit national ideology that could underpin the development of nationalism, which would in turn make Indonesia into a prosperous modern state. The key to this ideology was the doctrine of the Five State Principles, *Pancasila*, first made public in a speech of Sukarno's in the middle of 1945. These Principles in their original form were: Structuring a Free Indonesia in Faithfulness to God Almighty, Consensus or Democracy, Internationalism or Humanitarianism, Social Prosperity, and Nationalism or National Unity.[5]

The Five Principles were connected to the patriotic institutions that had either been created during the development of the nationalist movement or had come into being during the Revolution. Thus the National Anthem, 'Indonesia the Great' and the flag, the Red and White, were already in place as sacred symbols of the nation. Commemorations of national events were centred on Proclamation Day, 17 August, so that flag raisings or government announcements came on the seventeenth of each month, and then a number of other main commemorative days were created, notably National Awakening Day (commemorating the founding of the first official nationalist movement), Kartini Day (for the struggle of women), and Heroes Day (to commemorate the Battle of Surabaya). Heroic songs with a martial flavour were written about events of the Revolution, and works about the struggle were produced by the new generation of artists and writers who had been participants in the Revolution. Artists such as Sudjojono and Hendra Gunawan painted scenes of guerrillas to enshrine the image of the people's fighter. Pramoedya became famous at this time, his novels and short stories about the Revolution contributing to the creation of the popular image of the fight for independence as a struggle of the Indonesian people's will. By connecting such symbols to a central set of state ideals, Sukarno's Five Principles united the sacredness of the nation with religious belief.

FIRST PRINCIPLE: STRUCTURING A FREE INDONESIA IN FAITHFULNESS TO GOD ALMIGHTY

The first principle had been laid down as an alternative to the creation of an Islamic state. There had been many who had pressed for the majority religion to be the basis of the state, but that was inimical to those like sometime prime minister Sutan Syahrir who knew that modern states should be secular, and to key leaders who were steeped in Theosophy as a way of reinforcing and legitimating indigenous spiritualism. These leaders understood how important it was not to exclude minority groups from citizenship. Thus the first principle guaranteed the rights of members of other religions, as long as these religions were recognised by the state.

This last qualification may seem a contradiction in terms, since the status of religions should be obvious, but the indigenous beliefs and practices of various ethnic groups were not recognised under the new Constitution, and despite Sukarno's mother being Balinese, even the Buddhists and the Hindus of Bali had to argue for more than a decade that their religions were not 'currents of belief', but met state-established criteria of a 'world religion', notably having a single God and a holy book. 'Currents of belief' were defined as practices of 'people still without religion' because these were called customary practices of 'backward' peoples rather than developed doctrinal systems. Under Minister of Religion Kiai Haji Wahid Hasyim (1914–53), one of the leaders of the largest Muslim traditionalist party, and son of the party's founder, the religions recognised were Islam, Protestantism and Catholicism. Hasyim had been part of the original committees that formulated the 1945 Constitution. He had to accept that Islam would not be the state religion, despite advocating the opposite. Hasyim personally promoted an open-minded approach to other religions, attempting to create a compromise position between having a state based in Islamic law and one adhering to a broader definition of religion. These were attitudes passed on to his son, the future president of Indonesia Abdurrahman Wahid. The Department of Religion worked to extend the influence of the state, inducing local religious leaders to register marriages and divorces with it.[6]

For some Islamic modernists the first principle was not an acceptable alternative to an Islamic state. S. M. Kartosuwiryo (1907–62) was one such modernist. He had been born at Cepu, the son of an opium official, brought up with a liberal outlook, and given Western education. One of his brothers became a railway union official during the period of activism in the 1920s, but it was his uncle, writer Mas Marco Kartodikromo, who educated Kartosuwiryo in the ways of the nationalist movement, including Marxism. Kartosuwiryo also studied with a modernist religious teacher and became more interested in deepening his religious understanding when he entered medical school in Surabaya in the 1920s, a period in which he became close to the Islamic League chairman. His activist connections and his work in Islamic political groups led to his expulsion from medical school, but this only made him more determined to extend his religious studies. He had been one of the leaders to proclaim the nationalist Youth Oath in 1928, and had joined various Islamic nationalist groups, working as a journalist and editor for the newspaper *The Light of Asia*. He set up his own religious school near Garut, in West Java, where he developed a core group of loyal followers, in the model of Islamic mystic teachers who gather close brotherhoods around them. It was probably at this stage that he acquired two magic swords that were reputed to embody victory and prosperity. During the Japanese period he had been a member of the Islamic Council of Indonesia and received military training in the Hizbullah militia.

When Japan surrendered, Kartosuwiryo was in Jakarta, and made his own proclamation of independence, which he withdrew after Sukarno and Hatta made theirs. Kartosuwiryo was typical of the Islamic modernists in their distrust of secular politicians, and defied the Republic's leadership by staying in West Java and waging his own separate guerrilla struggle, proclaiming an Islamic state known as the House of Islam. Throughout 1949 his forces were engaged in fighting not only with the Dutch, but against the army of the Republic of Indonesia.

As a rebel against the Republic, Kartosuwiryo continued to fight on after the transfer of sovereignty. The House of Islam linked up with like-minded struggles in the Three Regions area of Central Java and in Kalimantan in 1950, in South Sulawesi in 1951 and Aceh in 1953. The House of Islam areas were mostly prosperous rural zones. Those who lived in these areas became more deeply Islamic as a result, because they were drafted into the activities of this proto-state. However, many chose to flee the contested areas, becoming refugees in Jakarta or other large cities. The struggle continued for over a decade, costing over 40,000 lives, and resulting in massive damage to property and the dislocation of millions. It discredited attempts by moderate Islamic leaders within the government to press for a stronger Islamic identity for the Republic, and isolated large areas of territory from the Indonesian state.[7]

Other more local, less pure, versions of Islam sought different ways to come to terms with the new era of independence and the new state. One of these mixed forms of religion was found the northern part of the Mandar coastal region of Sulawesi in 1956. It expected followers to pray seven times a day and make a profession of faith that acknowledged Ali, Muhammad's son-in-law, along with Muhammad. The leader of this movement, Lamusa Dindi Datok Kramat, from Central Sulawesi, proclaimed that God would descend to a village in Mandar. With Him would be the Prophet Muhammad, the President and Vice-President, and the leader of the House of Islam revolt on Sulawesi. Their appearance would signal that Mecca had been relocated to Indonesia, specifically to another nearby village. After being put in prison because his cult was subversive, Lamusa Dindi escaped and wandered the countryside trying to recruit followers by selling magical amulets.[8]

The development of this and other cults in the 1950s replicated the way new beliefs grew in the Dutch period. On Java many practices and beliefs were formalised into new movements during and after the Revolution. The largest of these was Subud, founded originally in the 1930s in Central Java by an aristocrat, but formally registered in 1947 before taking off in the 1950s to develop branches all around the world. Subud is a series of meditation practices that promote inner awareness, and has strong affinities to Islamic systems of mysticism.

Many of the religious belief systems and practices that emerged or re-emerged in the 1950s also had political implications. Religious differences defined provinces, for example South Kalimantan had to be divided in two to defuse the demands of separatists from the ethnic Dayak group who felt they were being overwhelmed by Muslims.[9] The Javanese 'Beauty' movement preached a rejection of Islam and adherence to original Javanese beliefs that made it similar to the Samin movement of the first decades of the twentieth century, but with more emphasis on healing. However the 'Beauty' movement also used contemporary parliamentary procedure as the model for its practices, and its rejection of capitalism was framed in Marxist terms. During the early 1950s this movement was strongly opposed to social groups who advocated modernist Islam, as did the Dayaks who established the 'Pagan Party'. Both religious groups became politically aligned with the peasant base of the Communist Party. This alignment was symptomatic of the potent links between politics and social life, links that deepened over the next decade.[10]

THE SECOND PRINCIPLE: CONSENSUS OR DEMOCRACY

When they were fighting the Revolution, all the nationalists were agreed that freedom was their aim, but beyond that very few people had a clear idea of how a free society would be realised. Most of the nationalists professed opposition to 'feudalism', even though they allowed feudal forms of hierarchy to creep into their political practices. Some were committed to democracy, but were not sure how to give form to the ideal.

The first stage in developing state institutions and political processes to support them involved a contest around democracy. Although there had been attempts to hold lower-level elections in the Republican areas in 1948, none of the political leaders could claim to have been popularly elected, and it was not until 1955 that a national election was staged. Until that time claims about representing the 'sovereignty of the people' and expressing the will of the people were just that, claims without legitimacy or even a clear idea of who 'the people' were.[11]

President Sukarno had already pressed his claim for a one-party state, and it was with this in mind that he came up with the second national principle, defined as 'Consensus or Democracy', later known as 'Consultation and Consensus'. Sukarno wanted a form of democracy that was not just an imitation of what the West had. 'Democracy is jointly formulating truth' was one of his many pronouncements on how his style of 'democracy with leadership' worked. But in 1950 most politicians supported a multiparty democracy based on Western models. Sutan Syahrir and his influential group wanted to protect the people against authoritarianism, which they associated with the forms of Dutch and Japanese rule.

Outside the debates of the political leadership, others were more cynical about democracy, and concerned about the huge gulf between the new class and the majority of Indonesians. Pramoedya's moving account of his visit back to Blora to his father's deathbed, the short story 'It's not a night market', muses about what kind of political system Indonesia had entered into: 'Democracy really is a beautiful system. You are allowed to become President. You are allowed to choose the job you like. You have the same rights as everyone else.' Anti-feudal nationalists like Pramoedya could say 'And it's democracy which makes it so that I don't need to make the gesture of obeisance or bow to the President or ministers or other important people.' But he went on, 'if you don't have money, you will be so paralysed, you won't be able to move. In a democratic country you're allowed to buy whatever you like. But if you don't have money, you're only allowed to look at those goods you'd like to have.' And with his usual irony he added, 'This too is a kind of victory for democracy.'[12]

The political parties that had developed during the Revolution originated in the old anti-colonial groupings, but by the 1950s were significantly reconfigured. The Nationalist Party, the PNI, had grown out of political and educational groups founded by Sukarno and Vice-President Hatta, and was committed to secular nationalism. Its popular base linked the old aristocracy to radical nationalists who had been at the forefront of the Revolution's 'youth' activism. For a while there was Islamic solidarity in an Islamic council originally founded by the Japanese, called *Masyumi*, but traditionalists soon found it too dominated by modernists, and so revived the organisation *Nahdlatul Ulama*, NU, as a political party. *Masyumi* continued to have a strong base amongst the Islamic middle class, particularly in urban areas and in islands outside Java, notably Sulawesi, while NU remained strongly rural and predominantly Javanese. There were other influential religious parties, notably the Catholic Party, but they lacked the numerical strength of the large Muslim parties.

The party that quickly reformed and emerged above a host of smaller parties was the Communist Party, the PKI. It had a new leadership group at the core of its Central Committee, all of whom had been youth activists in the Revolution, led by D. N. Aidit, a young writer. He had been a member of the struggle faction of the Revolution, and imprisoned by the Dutch on one of the Thousand Islands that lie off the coast of Jakarta. His fellow

Central Committee or Politbureau members came from political exile or had participated in major actions during the Revolution. With such impeccable credentials they were both able to resist claims by conservative politicians that the Party should be banned, and to force out the old leadership that had survived the purge of the party by the army in 1948. The reformed Party achieved a strong following amongst landless peasants and urban workers, mainly on Java and some of the plantation and mining areas of Sumatra. Cities such as Surakarta and Surabaya came to be dominated by the PKI, and both at one stage had Communist mayors. The Central Committee gradually moved their Party's orientation from the USSR to Maoist China.

All political parties were committed to socialism, but in a wide variety of forms, and they spent as much time fighting internally as they did fighting with each other. From the end of 1949 until 1957 there were seven different national cabinets, and a provisional People's Assembly where some of the smaller parties had a disproportionately large allocation of seats. Sukarno might have claimed that consensus was an inherent national trait, but the political leadership could not show it.

The main strategy for achieving consensus was to hold a series of elections, the most important of which was the national election of 1955 for the People's Representative Assembly (DPR) and the *Konstituante*, an upper house whose main role was to rewrite the Constitution. This election was the first experience of participatory democracy for most of the 39 million voters. The election did not solve the problem of consensus, since no party received a majority of votes in the Assembly. The Nationalist PNI, with over 22 per cent of votes, was only narrowly ahead of the modernist Muslim *Masyumi*, with 20 per cent. Close to them was the conservative Muslim NU, with 18 per cent, and the PKI with 16 per cent. None of the dozens of other parties and individual candidates was able to gain more than 3 per cent of the vote, and in most cases had only one or two members in the new Assembly. Because of the way electorates were defined, Java had a representation out of proportion to the size of its population. *Masyumi* achieved the largest vote in Sumatra, Kalimantan, Sulawesi and Maluku. The PNI dominated in the Southeastern Islands, which stretch from Bali to Timor. The twenty-eight different parties and groups formed themselves into seventeen factions in the Assembly. Out of 257 members of the Assembly, fifteen were women. This was a high proportion compared to many Western countries, and was in accordance with the government's claim to be ending the gender and racial discrimination of the colonial period.

Splits in politics ran up and down society. Some political leaders spread their influence down into society by gathering groups of followers based on networks of loyalty that came out of traditional social hierarchies or on links established during the Revolution. However, political factions were often grafted onto existing conflicts between social groups. Such conflicts were most noticeable on Java, where whole areas were dominated by one party or another: Blora and a ribbon of districts that went from the north to the south of Central Java were dominated by the PKI; most of the eastern and western extremes of Java by Muslim party followers.[13]

In 1956 a PNI prime minister, the Javanese Ali Sastroamidjojo (1903–75), was able to constitute a new multiparty cabinet. Commentators at the time saw the formation of the cabinet as an example of giving everyone a turn at being minister – not an approach that inspired confidence.[14]

Party politics was not just an issue in Jakarta. During the Revolution the political mobilisation of the population which had begun under Japanese rule turned into intense factionalism. This factionalism drew on pre-existing strong patron–client relationships. In the post-Independence period such patronage networks extended into the bureaucracy and down to the village level. Pramoedya painted a portrait of the typical bureaucrat party official in his short story 'Mastermind', in which a politician rose to power through a combination of opportunism and popularity. In the process of becoming 'a demigod', he had to find work for 'a constant stream of friends and acquaintances. Of course this was all unofficial. But in order to guard his popularity he had to take care of them.'[15] In his novel *Corruption* Pramoedya developed the picture of political power further by showing how patronage networks drew on the prestige of those who had taken part in the national struggle for independence, but had also subverted the resources of the civil service. The parties established or linked up with trade unions, cultural organisations and other kinds of social bodies. At times party loyalties overrode all other considerations. For example, an attempt to stage a general strike in 1955 was undermined by conflict between the Socialist Party-backed unions and the Communist Party-backed unions, with the Communists opposing the strike.

Within the bureaucracy, high-ranking civil servants lacked experience, and there was massive overemployment – more than 500,000 were employed in the civil service. Bureaucratic positions were often a reward for parts played during the Revolution. Under different conditions a well-organised civil service might have been able to make up for the uncertainties of political leadership, but here the bloated bureaucracy became an adjunct of political parties, so that government departments were seen as 'belonging' to one or the other party. While the ideal of service to the nation was still strong amongst many of those who joined, there were huge administrative problems to face. These included the loss of archives during the Revolution, and the problem of how to introduce a uniform territorial system of regencies and villages across the country.[16]

Film director and playwright Usmar Ismail (1921–71) strove to create a film industry that depicted the realities of life in Indonesia at the time. His humorous work *The Exalted Guest* (1955), based on Russian author Nikolay Gogol's famous play *The Inspector General*, gives an insight into the politics of village life at the time. It depicted a remote hill village that was expecting the arrival of an eminent politician, but was presented with a fraud in his place. The village was headed by a committee, whose members belonged to the different political factions, including the 'Women Aware' movement for equality, represented by the village head's wife. Each committee member put factional considerations ahead of consensus. They described their great dreams of development to the false guest, including the hope that their picturesque mountain lake could be a site for tourism, but were brought down to earth when the fraud was revealed. The film was made to convey the message that the best hope for the future was for people to work together to achieve things themselves, rather than pinning hopes on distant political leaders.[17]

Ismail optimistically portrayed villagers learning to cooperate, but in most of the country the splits along factional lines were becoming more and more bitter as the decade wore on. The local party directorates, the new ruling groups of towns and villages, argued their differences more and more fervently. For the poor in rural or urban areas, joining a faction under a local leader linked to national politics was the only way to guarantee access to resources. Strong competition between political groupings meant they had to look after their followers, find them jobs, supplement meagre incomes with rations of rice, cigarettes and coffee as gifts for loyalty, or ensure that a development project was directed to their area.

Sukarno was said to have been displeased with *The Exalted Guest*. It conflicted with the image he wanted to convey. During the 1950s, Sukarno's statements about the People's Assembly and the cabinets undermined their democratic potential. The constitutional framework for politics from 1950 to 1957 took much direct power away from Sukarno, but as the charismatic living embodiment of the spirit of the Revolution, Sukarno inspired a deep devotion among most of the political leadership, among the broader class from which that leadership came, and among the general population. Some of the politicians who knew him best remained suspicious of Sukarno's pro-Japanese past and of the populism that he espoused, but knew his mass appeal was important to carry the vision of the Revolution into the new nation.

THE THIRD PRINCIPLE: INTERNATIONALISM OR HUMANITARIANISM

Pramoedya and other intellectuals recognised Sukarno's unifying power and developed a fierce loyalty to him. Sukarno dealt with grand ideas, he supported and encouraged artists, even if his private art collection showed a tendency towards erotic kitsch. He encouraged Indonesians to think of themselves as cosmopolitan, as enlightened participants in the wider world.

National and regional newspapers, born out of the Revolution, acted as vehicles for its ideals, and carried optimistic messages about the new nation, even while being heavily critical of individual politicians. Newspapers were owned by political parties, but presented a range of common issues: solidarity between new nations, the welfare of the people, and the importance of a unified Indonesia. Indonesia's struggle for independence was discussed in relation to the struggles of other countries, and the detailed coverage of other Asian nations in particular reinforced a sense of commonality. The message of internationalism carried over into comparisons with political, social and economic developments in other Third World countries. Modernisation programmes in China were reported in the Communist newspapers, and when Pakistan declared itself an Islamic state in 1956, Indonesia's Muslim newspapers paid particular attention to its example.[18]

Indonesia's role in world politics was elevated in 1955 as an outcome of the Asia-Africa Conference held in Bandung, West Java. The conference produced the Non-Aligned Movement, creating a separate identity for those countries that did not want to be clients of either the USSR or the USA in the Cold War. All the leaders of Africa, the Middle East and Asia were invited, excepting South Africa, Israel, Taiwan and the two Koreas, but including the African National Congress leadership and China. From this conference came the term 'Third World', originally coined to refer to those countries that did not belong to the First (US-dominated) or Second (Communist) sides of the Cold War, but which acquired its more pejorative meaning of 'underdeveloped' as the non-aligned countries became increasingly impoverished.

Sukarno's speech to the Bandung conference conveyed the conflicting perspectives of the 1950s. He spoke of the twentieth century as 'a period of terrific dynamism', characterised by the splitting of the atom, the major technological advance of the time, but also a period of fear, 'fear of the hydrogen bomb, fear of ideologies . . . ', technological advances needed, he argued, to be matched by social change: 'Man can chain lightning to his command – can he control the society in which he lives?' The conference sought to bring an end to colonialism and war, such as the Indo-China conflict. That, for Sukarno, was the way to link 'freedom, independence and the welfare of man', and success would mean that 'the Light of Understanding has again been lit, the Pillar of Cooperation again erected'.[19] The image of this period as the atomic age was widespread. It captured both the danger and the enormous potential of the times. It could be seen in newspaper advertisements that used the symbol of the atom, as well as in discussions of the Cold War.

The positive sense of Indonesians participating in the modern age comes through in the media images of the time (figure 5.1). New clothes were discussed in the newspapers, not just the trousers, ties and skirts popularised by the 1930s generation of nationalists, but Ray-Ban sunglasses, cowboy hats and tight clothing. People from all over Indonesia travelled down from the hills to the cities to have family photographs taken. Magazines explained the wonders of eating with modern utensils such as spoons and forks, and discussed the kinds of furniture and ornaments people should have in modern houses, such as kitchen tables with chairs and table cloths, wardrobes, wall units with glass doors, imitation flowers and enamelware made by Email, which was opening factories in Indonesia in the 1950s. Ownership of radios was spreading; there were over 377,000 radio licences in 1953, and this was one of many items associated with Western style, which included what was known as 'office-style' housing. All these contributed to the desire for a lifestyle summed up by the popular term 'luxury'. One of the most obvious examples was the building of new ultra-modern apartments and houses for higher-ranking government and multinational company employees in the Jakarta suburb of Kebayoran Baru, one of the few sewered areas of the city.[20]

The newspaper and magazine writers of the time wrote as if they had a duty to teach Indonesians how to be good modern citizens. One newspaper reported with great concern the comments of the mayor of Jakarta that the National Anthem, 'Indonesia the Great', was not being shown sufficient respect: 'on official occasions there are still those who joke around, chatter and move around (walk and even run). This often happens when our President or Vice-President arrives or leaves Ikada Square for international soccer games.' On Bali, a magazine expressed concern that 'sport has only

Figure 5.1 Dutch company Philips radio advertisement from the 1950s newspaper *Duta Masyarakat* (Ambassador of Society). The emphasis on the futuristic quality of the new 'Technology from the Future', and the atomic symbol is in keeping with 1950s ideas of modernity.

spread in the city', and that badminton, tennis, soccer and basketball had not been taken up in the villages 'because they were considered of no practical value, or as foreign (especially for women) or something for the unemployed'.[21] Sport was something that could improve both the physical and mental well-being of the nation, and an activity in which Indonesians, by competing internationally, could participate in the world.

The stronghold of aspirations was the capital. In the 1950s, Jakarta had grown to over 2.5 million people, and was rapidly spreading out from the old East India Company city and the area around the main square. Writers in the city described it to their readers. Pramoedya in the 1957 *Art Almanac* addressed a friend in the country telling him of the changes that the city had undergone. A group of Balinese writers visited the city and wrote an article in the magazine they co-produced, *Devotion*, describing Jakarta to Balinese. The Balinese writers tried to convey the normality of city life to those who held it in wonder. They talked about the small Balinese community in the capital, and their efforts to establish a guest-house for Balinese studying there, not far from the Dutch medical institution that had become the University of Indonesia. One of their goals was also to make connections with other writers who would contribute to their magazine in Bali. They met most of the major contemporary authors, except for Pramoedya, who was in the Netherlands at the time. These articles were part of an effort to link the capital to the rest of the country. As Pramoedya says of the feeling of people outside the capital: 'people aren't 100 percent citizens before they've seen Jakarta with their own eyes.'[22]

In Pramoedya's account of the city he observed that when he first arrived there the main station of Gambir was surrounded by horse-drawn sulkies, but by the 1950s human labour, in the form of the *becak* rickshaw tricycles, had replaced horse power. The *becak* drivers ate raw eggs for energy, but worked themselves to death. 'The total number of such victims is greater than that of the victims of the Revolution. And you want to become a citizen of Jakarta!' By the 1960s one-third of all the cars in Indonesia were in Jakarta.[23]

In Pramoedya's view the capital 'does not yet resemble a city, only a collection of big villages'. There was not yet a city culture, only imported activities, 'dancing, picture theatres, pleasure trips, alcohol and religion, all kinds of religion'. But it was 'the dream of the people from the country'. This had a moral danger, as children growing up in the crowded conditions of the city lost respect for their parents and for long-held social mores. This sense of a 'moral crisis' is evident in newspapers, magazines and fiction of the time, which advocated a moral modernity, as opposed to a decadent

Western form, arguing that 'the people of a modern Indonesia are manifested through their personal growth'.[24] An imagined dialogue between a
Balinese mother and daughter concerning the limits of freedom showed
that the transition to being a modern nation involved a struggle between
traditional gender roles and modern life.

PROGRESSIVE ERA

MOTHER: Child, be careful in this progressive age, so they say.

CHILD: Mother you're so old-fashioned, not wanting to see the
            realities of women's progress. Young women can already
            use motorbikes, hold meetings with men, and are no longer
            timid like the old days. We can economise because dresses
            are above the knee and are sleeveless. In short progressive
            women don't lose out to men.

MOTHER: Child, women and men are always different. Their progress
            is always different too. And why, my child? If a man is too
            progressive it won't ruin him, but suppose a woman is too
            advanced ... her stomach becomes large ... although she
            uses diets to guard her figure and the village head will
            have difficulty with the birth registration. This is the
            difference.[25]

The search for an alternative to Western modernity was a recurring theme in
1950s Indonesian society. Sukarno warned that imperialism was not over,
and stoked up anti-Western feeling. Different organisations found different
ways to guard against the dangers. On the left an organisation called 'The
People's Culture Institute' was formed in 1950 to develop an Indonesian
culture of the people. Most of those associated with the Institute were also
linked to the Communist Party and it became the PKI's cultural vehicle.
Although never a member of the Communist Party, and sometimes critical
of their hardline stance on many issues, Pramoedya was drawn into the
Institute's activities, and became its most prominent member. In the 1950s
the Institute advocated banning the instruments of cultural imperialism such
as Hollywood films. It became embroiled in a debate as to whether the film
The Desert Fox should be banned as 'propaganda for fascism'. In the 1950s,
Indonesia was struggling to establish its own film industry. Most of the forty-
four cinemas of Jakarta and 800 in the other parts of Indonesia showed either
Hollywood films such as *The Robe*, or Indian movies, so this advocacy also
had a nationalist element. The Institute also led campaigns against immoral
Western music, leading to public destruction of records by Elvis Presley and
later the Beatles.[26]

The establishment of the Institute and of other cultural organisations was part of a debate about how culture should contribute to the new free Indonesia. One of the aims of writers who gravitated to the Institute was to draw attention to social problems, but in a way that also opposed feudalism, which they perceived as strongly linked to imperialism. Writers of the time chose social themes about feudal landlords, the suffering of workers who were still exploited as coolies, how to create harmonious family relationships in which women could be liberated from tradition, and about the economic and social hardship caused by rigid adherence to tradition. These were all themes that the early twentieth-century national-ist writers had raised, but in an independent Indonesia there was greater scope to explore them.

One particular controversy for the Institute was how to deal with the *wayang* puppet theatre. For PKI chairman D. N. Aidit, who had been present at the founding of the Institute, the shadow theatre was a feudal tradition which, as a Sumatran, he was quite happy to see abolished. But for Javanese members of the Institute such an idea was anathema. Rather, they argued that the *wayang* should be maintained, but adapted to prole-tarian themes. For Pramoedya, looking back on the period, the *wayang* remained important as a record of historical experience, for its message of survival.

Many political groups supported popular styles of theatre which had evolved through a combination of the pre-war Stambul and earlier forms of traditional theatre, and presented contemporary life in vaudeville manner. Popular culture was an important way to reach the masses and raise awareness of social issues, but competition between cultural groups affiliated to different political parties also contributed to the polarisation that was sweeping the country.[27]

Given the large number of teachers involved in the nationalist move-ment and the new national leadership, it was natural that education should be an important focus. Those who had grown up during the periods of the rise of nationalism and the Revolution shared the deep conviction that literacy was crucial to realising Indonesia's aspirations of becoming a modern nation.

Pramoedya was cynical about the narrow view of education many people held. Many came to Jakarta for education, and stayed in the city afterwards rather than go back to their towns or villages. 'The academic titles obtained every year sit paralysed on placards in the offices, while your region remains barren, wanting leadership. And that leadership still remains suspended high up in the blue sky.' He called for more schools to be built in the

Figure 5.2 Sukarno addresses students in an open-air classroom in Yogyakarta
on the value of education.

villages, for people not to see education as the acquisition of titles and
status, 'I gave a lecture in my town of birth two years ago: mobilise every
pupil to give their service to the people, to study how to be of service,
to turn away from intellectualism that only knows without having the
capability of making use of knowledge.' But funding and facilities for
education were limited (figure 5.2). In the 1950s Jakarta had 280 schools,
but only 180 buildings in which they could be held, which meant that
schools had to be run in morning and afternoon shifts. Paper was still
in short supply, textbooks almost non-existent. In Pramoedya's novel
Corruption, the main misdealings of a civil servant involved him selling
government stationery.

The Communist Party took education seriously, setting up village
schools and people's education groups, and they were probably the most
successful of all political groups in spreading ideas. Through publishing
easy-to-understand analyses of Indonesian society as basic readers the PKI
disseminated its ideology.[28]

Others shared the view that education should be more than just formal
qualifications. The nationalist women's groups of Bali who were educated
in the 1930s, for example, knew that what they had experienced was just the
beginning. For that reason they continued to campaign to eliminate
illiteracy, especially amongst women. They saw education as the first step

towards freedom and equality, something started by 'upper-class' feminists in the early twentieth century, but in which 'the excesses of patriarchy' were still too great to overcome. For that reason, they argued, a second stage of emancipation was needed, one in which women's work opportunities were expanded, in which there was a change in the 'production process', the nature of work and property rights, that would give women equal rights in all aspects of life. From that could come the realisation of full rights and the achievement of prosperity and justice for ordinary women. Although strong feminist views like these are usually identified with the Communist-affiliated Indonesian Women's Movement, they were shared across the political spectrum.[29]

THE FOURTH PRINCIPLE: SOCIAL PROSPERITY

In his article on Jakarta, Pramoedya questioned what economic progress Indonesia had made: 'I know, you people in the regions, the people of the interior, made gods of your leaders, but I'm closer to the realities.' The problem, as he saw it, was that the economy had not fundamentally changed from providing export crops. It was still a colonial economy. 'I know you cry out about the national economy, but the basis of life which is rooted in export trade, is not just typical of an agrarian nation, but of a colonial nation.' Emphasising the dichotomy of modern (urban)-oriented people and 'old fashioned' villagers, Pramoedya added, 'And aren't the farmers of your area still stuck as slaves in the eras of Madjapahit, Sriwidjaja or Maratam?', referring to the medieval kingdoms of Java and Sumatra.

One of the first hurdles for independent Indonesia was to overcome a national debt that would have crushed many countries. When the United States brokered the final settlement of the Revolution, it sacrificed the new nation's interests for its own. The US insisted that the Indonesians accept a deal in which they had to take over Dutch debts of US$1,723 million plus interest. The US wanted to protect the economic rebuilding of Europe established in the Marshall Plan and to create the North Atlantic Treaty Organisation as the basis of their campaign against Communism. Instead of the Dutch compensating the Indonesians for colonial rule, the Indonesians had to compensate the Dutch, based on the fiction that the Indies had been an autonomous entity, not part of the Netherlands.[30]

The Indonesian economy received a sharp, short boost from the Korean War. The price of rubber and other goods rose suddenly. This encouraged the restoration the pre-World War Two industries, particularly in the Outer Islands. Some of the former Dutch plantations remained, but government-owned estates were also important, as were the smaller producers of rubber, copra and other export goods. The 1950s international consumer society, purchasing tyres, margarine and other goods made from such Indonesian products, linked developments in Western society to those in Indonesia. This boost to the economy helped Indonesia to pay off most of the massive debt bequeathed by the Dutch and Americans, and to build up national reserves. The standard of living quickly rose above that of colonial times. Domestic demand for many commodities increased, the first indication that Indonesians were becoming consumers, and thereby active citizens in a developing world. Throughout the 1950s more and more Indonesians moved from subsistence to cash economies. Upland villagers in the jungles of Kalimantan and the hills of Flores moved downriver or closer to the coast to get access to market goods. As they did so social cleavages developed. In the case of Kalimantan those who had integrated into the commercial world generally converted to Islam, and regarded their animist Dayak cousins from upriver as old-fashioned, leading to resentment from the inland Dayaks against the Muslims, something that played into support for the Pagan Party.[31]

The socialists running the economy continued to develop cooperatives as the basis of economic activities. They argued that this was in tune with what they identified as an essential national characteristic, 'mutual help', an idea based on an idealised version of village life. 'Mutual help' was seen as the foundation for the development that would make Indonesians equal to Westerners, the long-term goal of the Revolution.

Indonesia's prosperity could not last, as actions by the United States and Great Britain pushed the price of rubber down in 1953. Other commodity prices fell, and bad weather affected Indonesian agricultural production in 1954 and 1955. All the nation's products declined in value, and rice had to be imported to meet basic needs. Inflation increased and the black market grew as the decade wore on. Particularly damaging to the economy was the massive difference between the official exchange rate for US dollars and the rate that could be realised on the streets, which at its highest was twenty times greater than the official rate. A policy of having different exchange rates for different kinds of international trade transaction compounded the fiscal problems.[32]

Indonesia's need to develop was not matched by the resources needed to do so. Sumatra, Kalimantan and Sulawesi, the islands that supplied so many vital export products, did not have the infrastructure to move these products to market. Out of 7,500 km of roads in South Sumatra province in 1956, only 500 km were macadamised. Bengkalis in Central Sumatra, a vital source of small-holder rubber, was at times totally cut off from nearby cities because of the poor state of its roads.[33]

More and more Indonesians became impatient with the unfulfilled promise of progress. Inflation ate into wages, and most civil servants could not live off their incomes. The initial salary for civil servants had first been established in the latter stages of the Revolution, and had been fixed at Rp 45 per month. General Nasution, describing the government's (probably unrealistic) thinking at the time on how far this wage should go, gave an insight into the lifestyle of a single male wage earner at the time of Independence, in 1948/9 (Table 5.1). This shopping list shows that meat and fish were still more expensive than other items of food, and the extent to which fuel and electricity costs ate into the domestic budget. Six years later a Balinese account of the income and cost of living of a 'goat class' (lower-level) male civil servant supporting a family indicated that wages had risen, but so had the cost of living (Table 5.2). This account shows that religious feasts were a major expense for employees, and confirms that nearly 70 per cent of an income of Rp 181 went on food. As in the colonial period, most people were constantly in debt, but through the creation of cooperatives and the extension of government banking schemes initially introduced by the Dutch, the social damage could be limited.

Rp 181 was worth US$47 at the official 1951 exchange rate, but only US$11 at black-market rates. A well-paid factory worker in Unilever's factory in Jakarta in 1951 could actually make more than a civil servant. He received Rp 11.54 per day (made up of cash, 400–50 g of uncooked rice, free medical treatment, transport by truck for those who had to travel long distances, a weekly cake of soap and cooking oil). In the north Balinese city of Singaraja where the above account of expenditure was published, a labourer earned Rp 1.50 per day, while by 1958 women working in the *batik* industry in Central Java still only earned between Rp 2.50 and Rp 15, depending on whether they were doing the cheaper dyeing work or the more highly paid pattern printing.[34]

In the 1950s the government acknowledged the right of women to equal pay, but did little to enforce it. As socialists, those in government tried to create equality between all levels of income, but wide discrepancies still existed, even though they were not as vast as those under the Dutch. One important difference was that race was no longer important to income. Sukarno and the other political leadership were determined to legislate against the old inequalities and end Indonesia's status as 'a nation of coolies and a coolie amongst nations', a famous phrase of Sukarno's. Workers now had rights and frequently exercised the right to strike.

Table 5.1 *Monthly living costs for a civil servant
in 1948*

Commodity	Rp
Rice	1.10
Sweet potato	0.05
Tempé (bean curd)	.15
Green beans	.06
Meat	.75
Fresh fish	.75
Eggs	.45
Coconuts	.06
Coconut oil	.08
Cane sugar	.13
Salt	.22
Terasi (shrimp paste)	.08
Chillis and shallots etc.	.50
Tea	.19
Coffee	.14
Firewood	1.50
Electricity/kerosene	3.30
Water	1.00
Soap	1.00
Rent including furniture	7.50
Clothes, shoes etc.	2.50
Health care	2.00
Letter writing	.20
Tolls	.50
Sport	1.00
Cigarettes	3.00
Entertainment	1.00
Union membership	1.00
Bicycle/transport	2.50
Savings	2.00
Tax/religious donations	2.50
Other expenditure	2.50

Pramoedya's 1954 novel, *Corruption*, depicted the temptations facing civil servants whose wages were inadequate to feed and educate their families. Adding to the pressure on civil servants were the aspirations of a new consumer society, which translated into the desire for a bungalow in the hills above Jakarta, a car, a piano, and other trappings of the 'luxury' ideal.

Pramoedya's picture of Jakarta as a centre of moral degradation was shared by his contemporaries. One significant area of corruption in Jakarta

Table 5.2 *Monthly living costs for a civil servant in 1954*
(wage: Rp 181 per month)

Costs:	Rp
Union membership (including death benefits and subscription to the union magazine)	3.50
Instalment on cash advance to pay for Galungan (for Balinese) or Lebaran (for Muslims) religious festivals	15.00
Interest to the People's Bank (for a loan of Rp 300)	27.00
Contribution to the office cooperative for e.g. cigarettes, soap etc.	15.00
Cost of rice 40 kg @ Rp 2.40 per kg	96.00
Give to mother to pay for food (kitchen needs)	30.00
Instalment on a pair of trousers	10.00
Total	196.50

was housing, which was in short supply. Bribes, known as 'key money', were paid to move into a house. These were often greater than the cost of the house itself, and when Usmar Ismail produced a film called *Crisis*, exposing this and other related problems, it was popular because it struck at one of the issues that made life difficult for many people.

Corruption existed on all levels. A favourite practice amongst politicians was handing out lucrative import–export licences. Politicians became business partners of licensees. These licences were originally part of an affirmative action for indigenous (i.e. non-Chinese, non-European) businesses, but affirmative action turned into behind-the-scenes kickbacks paid by Chinese businessmen. A popular form of corruption in the military was smuggling, which was excused with the argument that it was necessary to sustain units when the government could not provide adequate resources. Since smuggling drastically depleted government taxation income, it created a vicious circle. Sumatran author Mochtar Lubis's most famous work, *Twilight in Jakarta*, featured a character dragged into corruption through political patronage networks. This was a world in which politics was a tool for enrichment. The competition between political parties was destroying the nation while the queues for rice, salt and petrol grew longer and longer.

Contributing to the social unease of the 1950s was the problem of civil unrest, as political movements combined with widespread local banditry. During 1956 the national economy suffered a set-back when the largest plantation warehouse in South-east Asia, in Aceh, was destroyed by a deliberately lit fire, the work of House of Islam terrorists.[35] Some bandit gangs emerged from political movements, formed either by Dutch right-wingers who could not accept independence, or by guerrilla fighters from the Revolution who wanted to fight on for complete independence. Political groups and criminal gangs lived off the population, levying 'taxation'. Robbery and violence became a lucrative and addictive way of life. Some parts of Indonesia were worse than others: Bali remained dangerous until after 1955, as did the Minangkabau region. Ismail and associated film-makers produced a series of films showing villages in Java and Sumatra that had been taken over by criminal gangs. In one of these, *The Three Fugitives*, the military mobile brigades come to the rescue, sending an officer in disguise to break the power of a gang leader who terrorises villagers.[36]

The sympathetic depiction of the army as the guardians of social order in this film drew on the legacy of the Revolution and the work of its leader General Nasution, in closely linking the army and the state. During what Nasution and others called the 'Second Guerrilla Phase' of the Revolution, when the politicians had seemingly capitulated to the Dutch, the army saw itself as the true guardian of the nation. The memory of this period became an intimate bond between the army and 'the people', and so throughout the 1950s the army presented itself as a people's army 'serving' society. The image projected was of a disciplined force, with efficient lines of command, one that had mastered technology.[37] In this role, the army was the guardian of national unity. Ironically, most of the threats to national unity came from members of the armed forces.

THE FIFTH PRINCIPLE: NATIONALISM OR NATIONAL UNITY

When the Revolution ended, the question remained as to what territory the state should occupy. Sukarno argued about this with his vice-president and ministers. The idea of a 'Greater Indonesia' had been developed by ideologues of the Revolution, in some versions encompassing the countries now known as Malaysia, Brunei and the Philippines. Nationalist writers had used Dutch research on the wide-reaching influence of Sumatran and Javanese kingdoms to argue for continuity between these medieval kingdoms and Indonesia, projecting the modern state backwards 600 years.[38]

'Greater Indonesia' was never going to be acceptable to the British, who were still to give up their colonies in Malaya, Singapore and Borneo. There were arguments, eventually rejected, over whether the little Portuguese colony of East Timor should be incorporated, and Sukarno and Hatta had

Figure 5.3 Volunteers in Jakarta signing up for the campaign to liberate Irian from Dutch control.

a major disagreement over whether West Papua, then known as the Netherlands New Guinea or Irian, should be part of Indonesia, since the Dutch had held on to it. Sukarno won that argument, and it was agreed that the state should go 'from Sabang [an island off Aceh] to Merauke [in Irian]', which then became a key slogan in his speeches. The doctrine of a unitary state, stepchild of General van Heutsz's rule, was set. Sukarno called for a takeover of Irian, and thus made it a focus of nationalist sentiment to recruit civilian and military support. An external enemy, real or imagined, is always a good device around which to rally patriotism, and through Irian, Sukarno could show that he was continuing the struggle against Dutch imperialism as part of a broader Third World conflict with the West.

There were many outside Java who had reason to be disenchanted with the Republic of Indonesia. One of the most immediate reactions came from Ambon, where due to the strong tradition of military service amongst Christian Ambonese, a large segment of the population had been pro-Dutch, and did not want to become part of the Republic of Indonesia. Some of those who grew up in the Dutch barracks went to the Netherlands, but one group declared a separatist Republic of South Maluku under the Dutch crown. This was quickly defeated, but for decades afterwards it lived on as a dream of exiles.

During the early 1950s successive cabinets attempted to demobilise or retire tens of thousands of soldiers. The high point came in 1952 when 80,000 out of the 200,000 in the army were pensioned off. This combined with pressure on the middle class through import tariffs, factionalism in the military, discontent with political leaders, and a strong feeling that the leaders were surrendering revolutionary values to Western pressure to rationalise. The combination led to a near-coup in 1952, and ongoing tensions within the military.[39]

The region of Aceh had played a key role as defender of the Republic during the darkest hours of the Dutch attacks. Autonomy had been promised, but not delivered, which was the main reason why Aceh joined the House of Islam revolt. Slowly legislation was put together to facilitate a process of autonomy, but too slowly for the regions who felt their sacrifices during the Revolution and the wealth they brought to the nation were not being recognised.

By 1956, the sense of crisis was coming to a head, as the Jakarta leadership under Syahrir and the Islamic party leaders became more and more suspicious of Sukarno. Relations between Sukarno and the more conservative Sumatran Hatta were increasingly strained. In 1957 Sukarno was visiting his children's school in Cikini, in central Jakarta, when a hand-grenade was thrown at him. Many Indonesians believed strongly that Sukarno possessed supernatural strength and magic protection, manifested in his collection of ancient daggers and the swagger stick he carried with him. Their beliefs were confirmed when he survived this assassination attempt, one of seven, relatively unscathed.

The attempt had been carried out by Sumatran officers, who joined other officers in northern Sulawesi to create a full-scale rebellion against the central authority. These were more than separatist uprisings: they were attempts to usurp the power of Jakarta. Central politicians from the modernist Islamic party joined in, with support from others who were worried about Sukarno's lust for power and the increasingly corrupt nature of politics. Suspicions that the CIA was behind the revolts were confirmed when a US pilot was shot down in Eastern Indonesia. The US had become increasingly suspicious of Indonesia's stance of non-alignment, and acting on the principle of 'whoever is not my friend is my enemy', sought to undermine any leftist leanings in the government. US companies such as Stanvac and Caltex had their investments in the oilfields of Sumatra to protect. CIA sponsorship of right-wing military officers in the regional revolts came in the form of substantial provision of arms, training and intelligence support, similar to the support for military dictatorships in other parts of the Third World that was US policy during the Cold War.[40]

In response Sukarno formed an alliance with Nasution and his faction of the military and declared a state of war and siege. Two of the main political parties, *Masyumi* and the PSI, were discredited by their connection to revolts and banned. The military became the main vehicle of national unity, a role that has remained. Sukarno went on to declare an end to the Western model of democracy of 'fifty-per cent-plus-one', and the inauguration of a 'Guided Democracy'. By 1962, when the head of the House of Islam revolt was executed by the government for sedition, central power had been enforced over the regions, and the campaign to take Irian from the Dutch had entered a dramatic military phase.

When Jakarta had been finally liberated in 1949 all the Dutch street and place names were changed to names of heroes of the nationalist struggle. Main streets commemorated figures such as the Revolution's hero General Sudirman and the leading nationalist from one of Jakarta's old families, Thamrin, the uncle of Pramoedya's second wife. Van Heutsz Boulevard changed its name to Teuku Umar Street, named after an Acehnese leader of resistance against the Dutch. It was appropriate that this was the street where General Nasution, General van Heutsz's successor, had his Jakarta residence. Nasution, however, was not the one who united military and civilian power: this was left to the Javanese Suharto, whose ability to grasp control in the midst of uncertainty made him the strongest and most centralist of all Indonesia's leaders.

The emergence of the army out of the Revolution, and its role in the power politics of the 1950s, was an important factor in Indonesia's stalling on the path to democracy. Of equal importance was the inability by Sukarno to translate nationalist rhetoric into common purpose. In the absence of strong institutions that would promote commitment to the state, the new leadership of the nation egged each other on to seek self-advancement and personal enrichment. When factional interests outweighed national ones, the result was always going to be bad for Indonesia. Sukarno could have done more to promote democracy, and while he was not economically corrupt, he allowed his own desire for power to undermine the novel and delicate institutional structures Indonesia needed to thrive.

CHAPTER 6

From Old to New Orders

We welcome this social instability because it provides the opportunity for Progress. Progress positively demands an element of instability and even of risk.

Ruslan Abdulgani, later Deputy Head of the Supreme Council of Review and Head of the Committee to Develop the Spirit of the Revolution[1]

In the early 1970s a local leader in a poor suburb of Jakarta, Pak Sumitra, described for an American sociologist how political control was exercised on a local level. He described how Indonesia shifted from a society polarised between Communists and non-Communists, to one where a distant military government was able to pacify and manage the country. The new government's aim was to create the appearance of order and control.

Pak Sumitra was a veteran of the Revolution, like most political leaders of the times. During the struggle in Tegal, coastal Java, he had come across a magical stone that had protected him from harm when all his comrades were being killed. He attributed to this stone his ability to gain a following when he moved to Jakarta to work in the railway yards, where he became a foreman. The community of which he became leader consisted almost entirely of railway workers, many of whom were Communists. This man had an antipathy to Communists because members of his family had been killed by them during the conflict in Madiun in 1948. When, around 1955, he became aware that Communists were taking control of the main railway union in the yards, he gravitated to an alternative union linked to the Socialist Party. He voted for that party in the 1957 regional elections, and became a main union organiser in 1962, using his social networks to sign up hundreds of workers. By this stage the yards were split down the middle into one or the other faction, and each group of workers became increasingly dependent on their unions to supply them with basic benefits. These benefits included a *gamelan* musical ensemble that the Communist union obtained for its members, and extra rice rations. By 1964 rampant inflation and national political division turned verbal sparring between the two unions to open hostilities. The leader and some of his faction were stoned by Communist union members outside a picture theatre.

In a rally on 29 September 1965 the Communists called for his union to be banned, but an abortive coup the next day and the resulting crushing of the Communist Party meant that Sumitra's union triumphed. The Communist leaders were killed or imprisoned, most of them being sent to the remote prison island of Buru, except for one, the leader's estranged younger brother.

With military support, Sumitra took over leadership of the whole neighbourhood. He appropriated all the goods that the Communists had stored for their members, including the *gamelan*. When he held meetings and they were poorly attended, recalcitrants were told that those not present would be suspected of still being Communists. Thereafter everyone attended, and loyally raised funds to build a Muslim prayer room. Religious observance had not been a feature of the neighbourhood up to that point, and Communism was often perceived to be synonymous with atheism, so by the 1970s nearly everybody attended prayers. The union and the neighbourhood organisations were restructured to ensure that only people loyal to Sumitra held office, and he took control of a new neighbourhood 'civil protection unit' whose members, largely unemployed, received about Rp 300 per month plus coffee and cigarettes. They were part of a rule by force that included a network of spies throughout the area to inform him of any signs of dissent or disloyalty to the government, which were considered signs of Communism. Sumitra kept the local administrative head informed of any public works that were needed in the neighbourhood, and was able to tell the military that this 'hot' area was now under control.[2]

CONTINUING THE REVOLUTION

Sumitra's story shows how one group emerged as winners in the politics of the 1960s. Pramoedya was one of those who ended up on the losers' side. In 1957 he was one of the leaders of a group of artists and writers who went to the Presidential Palace to pledge their support for Sukarno's new 'conception' of Guided Democracy and Revolution. Pramoeyda had become a radical, and was later identified as a Communist, even though he never joined the Party. He had turned his attentions to the plight of the poor, convinced that the parliamentary period had done nothing to improve their lot. He was more and more convinced that writers should participate in politics, and follow the greatest of political leaders, Sukarno.[3]

Sukarno's declaration of Guided Democracy was the most dangerous step taken by a political leader in Indonesia's history. It set in motion a chain of events that led to the fall of his own government, the deaths of as many as 1 million people, and the creation of a military, centralised, rule that would last until the end of the twentieth century. Indonesia would not see democracy for another forty years, and its early leaders' hopes of building a just society would be dashed on the rocks of political ambition.

From 1957 to 1965 Sukarno's authoritarian tendencies pushed the country beyond the limits of its economic base, its social framework and its political institutions. In the name of continuing the Revolution, Sukarno nationalised Dutch industry and increased the power of the military. Then, to try to keep the military under control he supported the Communist Party. The crash-through or crash approach led to the greatest disaster in the nation's history.

The 1945 Constitution of the Republic of Indonesia had been a temporary device, pulled together immediately after the Proclamation. The 1949 Federal Constitution did not last long because the national leadership were opposed to federation, and its 1950 replacement provided no formula to create a balance between the political parties. The 1950 Constitution was in the long process of being rewritten by the Indonesian Upper House when, under the state of war and siege that lasted from 1957 to 1962, Sukarno announced a return to the 1945 Constitution as a keystone of Guided Democracy. Thereafter, he and his successor, General Suharto, worked to enshrine the Constitution as sacred and unchallengeable, identical to the Five Principles of the nation. Under this Constitution the president was the centre of power, and the status of the prime minister was reduced. Although in theory the president's powers were limited by a principle of responsibility to the Upper House, Sukarno was often able to outmanoeuvre its membership.

Those, like Pramoedya, who believed in Sukarno's message of national unification, supported his justification for sweeping aside the 1950 Constitution. Guided Democracy was still a form of representative democracy, made necessary because the party system had failed to deliver consensus, and contributed to the regional uprisings that threatened to split the nation. Representation was now through 'functional groups' standing for different elements in society, such as workers, artists, women and the military. Some political parties remained because they approximated functional groups.[4]

The banning of some political parties accompanied a series of measures that rolled back many of the democratic gains of the 1950s. Guided Democracy was announced at the same time as laws aimed at promoting regional autonomy were coming into play. These laws, although too late to quell regional antipathies to Java, would, if implemented, have taken power away from the central bureaucracy, what one observer called the 'mandarinate'. Overturning the local autonomy laws strengthened the Jakarta-based civil service, which was dominated by the Nationalist Party, the PNI, the most fervently Sukarnoist of the political parties. Sukarno's interventions in the appointment of regional governors put in power local loyal Sukarnos.[5]

During the period in which Guided Democracy was institutionalised, the army and ministers around Sukarno were able to act almost arbitrarily. The armed forces developed the basis of what was later to become the doctrine of the 'dual function', by which the military defended the nation, and maintained society by intervening in government. The military set up a new territorial system which involved assuming leading roles in regional administration. It also took over former Dutch enterprises when they were nationalised. General Nasution believed that the military should not actually take over government, but be partners in running the country. He was later to point out that, up until 1962, he could have taken power – other officers and politicians were begging him to – but he did not.[6]

One of the decrees pushed on Sukarno by conservative political groups was to ban the Chinese from being active in the rural economy. This was part of a strategy developed in the 1950s to give so-called indigenous entrepreneurs a head start in business and remove Chinese domination of the economy. The move had particularly harsh effects on Chinese who had long been established in rural areas, such as in West Kalimantan. Many were forced to leave their houses without compensation, and re-establish in the cities. Some Chinese left Indonesia altogether, and like Dutch, Eurasians and other residents threatened by Guided Democracy, moved to Singapore, Australia or other safer places. Those Chinese who remained were also encouraged to change their names to 'Indonesian' ones, usually names that were more Javanese than the Javanese. The echoes of colonial discrimination in this legislation made many, such as Pramoedya, uneasy. When Pramoedya wrote newspaper articles condemning the racist basis of the decree, he was gaoled in Cipinang and Salemba prisons.[7]

By the late 1950s most Indonesians, as with Pramoedya, had been drawn into the political maelstrom. They were exposed to constant political slogans, demonstrations and campaigns, and to sharp divisions in society.

Newspapers and the works of other writers, such as Mochtar Lubis, were censored and banned. Which side you chose in these divisions determined whether you lived or died, went to prison or gained access to the largesse of the winners in the political leadership struggle.

Sukarno wanted to instil a sense of revolutionary will in Indonesians that would overcome all obstacles to development. He stepped up propaganda campaigns emphasising struggle and dynamism. Indonesian life became dominated by acronyms and abbreviations: NASAKOM, was the central revolutionary doctrine that combined Nationalism, Religion and Communism. This doctrine was further refined in the Political Manifesto for the 1945 Constitution, Indonesian Socialism, Guided Democracy, Guided Economy and Indonesian Autonomy – known in short as MANIPOL-USDEK. Often people did not know what the slogans and acronyms meant, but repeated them as mantras of their political groups.

To help the population keep up with the new political language, and facilitate what Sukarno called 'retooling', numerous publications were produced. Chief amongst these was the broadcast and publication of Sukarno's speeches, especially his annual 17 August speech, which each year were given more and more extravagant titles: 'A Year of Decision' (1957); 'A Year of Challenge' (1958); 'The Rediscovery of Our Revolution' (1959); '"An Angel Sweeping Down from the Sky", the Course of Our Revolution' (1960); '*Re-So-Pim*: Revolution-Indonesian Socialism-National Leadership' (1961); 'The Year of Victory' (1962); 'The Ringing Out of the Sound of Revolution' (1963); 'The Year of "*Vivere Pericoloso*"' [Italian for 'Living Dangerously', taken from one of Mussolini's speeches] (1964); and 'Standing on Our Own Two Feet' (1965). Stamps, new printings of currency to cope with massive inflation, and pamphlets were used to spread the message throughout the nation (figure 6.1). The key elements of a dynamic Indonesia were evident in the building of dams and five-star hotels and the holding of international tennis tournaments.[8]

Sukarno gathered around him a group of ideologues who helped him expand his revolutionary language. The Minister for Education and Culture, Priyono (1907–1969), who had studied in Paris and received a PhD at Leiden University in the study of medieval Javanese texts, was chief adviser in the creation of a new set of terms based on the Sanskrit-influenced Old Javanese language. Priyono also planned cultural links with the USSR and China – he sent Pramoedya on a mission to the latter – and established institutions to reinforce national culture that was in tune with the revolutionary sentiment, introducing a new set of 'folk dances'

Figure 6.1 Stamp showing Sukarno's version of modernity, the Ambarrukmo Palace Hotel in Yogyakarta, from a series depicting the leading new hotels of Indonesia built as part of Sukarno's campaign for national pride.

based on the activities of peasants and workers. Along with these invented 'traditions', Priyono's ministry taught ideological songs which people who grew up in the era can still remember.

An important element of Sukarnoism was national history that claimed ancient kingdoms as predecessors for the modern state. To this vision of ancient greatness, Sukarno and his ministers added a pantheon of 'national heroes', beginning with Abdul Muis and other key figures in the early nationalist movement, even the radical Tan Malaka. The largest number of 'heroes' was created in 1964 and 1965, including Kartini as one of the few women, and conservative religious leaders. The variety of heroes was chosen to produce a balance of political and regional interests, included figures from the left and the right, from Islam as well as Communism.[9]

Sukarno saw the need to make a Jakarta that reflected his vision of the nation. He knew that it needed to be more than just one of the regions, it had to be the centre. Accordingly, like Napoleon, he set about expanding boulevards and commissioning monuments. Memorials of the Guided Democracy period include the national Parliament, the national Mosque, and a beach recreation centre, Ancol, in the north of the city. The street leading to the old city and the old Dutch town hall was too narrow, so Sukarno created a main street, with a statue at the centre called

Figure 6.2 1960s stamp showing the monument to the liberation of Irian from Dutch rule – the monument stands on the Buffalo Field to the east of Freedom Square in central Jakarta.

the Welcome Monument, of a young boy and girl throwing their arms out in greeting. Just north of the Welcome Monument was Indonesia's first modern department store, Sarinah, named after the maid in Sukarno's house whom he idealised as the epitome of Indonesian women and his first love. The nearby main square became 'Freedom (*Merdeka*) Square' closely linking it to the Revolution. In the middle of Freedom Square Sukarno commissioned his greatest monument, which he wanted to be Indonesia's 'Eiffel Tower'. This phallic tower, topped by a flame rumoured to be made of solid gold, was known simply as the National Monument, but later was referred to as Sukarno's last erection. A new sports stadium was built to host the Asian Games in 1962 and the Third World version of the Olympics, the Games of the New Emerging Forces or GANEFO, in 1963. Indonesia's first television broadcasts were made in conjunction with these games, but there were only a few television sets in the capital to receive them.[10]

Plans for socialist development reached unrealistic heights. Semaun, the founder of Communism in Indonesia, returned from Moscow as special presidential adviser. He urged the creation of a new city built in the jungle in Central Kalimantan, to be Indonesia's Brasilia or Canberra. Soviet aid would help the project along. In the end there was no government funding, and the Soviets built only a roundabout and a sturdy road about which the locals still brag.

Sukarno's image was everywhere. The cult of personality even included his reputation for sexual prowess. Everyone knew where his mistresses lived – today, taxi driver Ali or retired businessman Pak Marianto can point out their locations as they wait in the capital's traffic jams. When Sukarno was at the height of his anti-American and pro-Communist rhetoric, the CIA made a pornographic film starring a Sukarno look-alike to discredit him. It had the opposite effect, of enhancing his reputation for 'conquest' over the West.

Sukarno's continuing Revolution took him politically further and further to the left, causing American concern. His advocacy of the Third World was articulated as a continuing struggle against imperialism, of which the US and Britain were seen as the chief international agents, evidenced through their support of regional revolts.

By 1962, when the revolts had been quelled by the army, Sukarno's campaign to take over West New Guinea, or 'Victorious Irian', as Sukarno called it, was well underway. The fact that Irian was still in Dutch hands made it an obvious symbol of imperialism impeding Indonesia's national destiny. People all over the country were called to hold rallies and to volunteer to take part in the fighting. This anti-imperialist struggle had already provided the excuse to take over all Dutch assets in Indonesia. The campaign was run under the command of Major-General Suharto (figure 6.3). In just over a year the campaign succeeded, although the United Nations wanted a plebiscite to determine whether Indonesian claims that the Irianese wanted to be integrated were true. In 1965 Indonesia withdrew from the UN.

Sukarno mobilised the population against British imperialism in 1963 by opposing the creation of a new state of Malaysia, which was to combine

Figure 6.3 General Suharto (second from left) as new military commander of the Irian campaign, 1962. Taken in Makasar. Also in the photo from left to right: Lt.-Gen. A. A. Rifai, Governor of Sulawesi, Col. Jusuf, Gen. Gatot and Gen. Yani (at rear).

British colonies on the Malay peninsula with those on the island of Borneo. Sukarno revived ideas of a 'greater Indonesia', shared by some Malays, to argue that much of the Borneo territory was part of Indonesia, and that the new state was a neo-colonial puppet. This second campaign, which he called 'Confrontation', embroiled the military in a messy series of jungle battles against British Commonwealth forces. The weekly, sometimes daily, demonstrations that marked life under Guided Democracy now became anti-British, and the slogan 'gobble up Malaysia' appeared everywhere. British and other Commonwealth businesses were also taken over during 1964 and 1965.

Economic policy became an eight-year plan in which the main aim was to create welfare through projects aimed at improving health, education and the provision of basic necessities. These were to be paid for through other projects for promoting exports and paying off foreign debt. Massive dams were built, and basic infrastructure expanded rapidly. Sukarno, like his predecessors in the period of constitutional democracy, saw that the primary aim of the state was to improve the lives of the people, rather than promote capital. This socialism was deeply offensive to the US. When challenged, Sukarno told the US, 'go to hell with your aid', and proclaimed another slogan, 'Standing on Our Own Two Feet', which meant setting up import substitution schemes and putting resources into state enterprises. Most of these – with one or two exceptions – quickly failed, often because their managers treated the money flowing through them as private income. This creaming-off of state resources, which economists have called, rather generously, 'rent seeking', established a pattern that has continued to the present day. 'Standing on Our Own Two Feet' rapidly meant seeking alternative aid from the USSR and China. By the early 1960s, the military's equipment was mainly Soviet-made.[11]

This aid was not enough to fund all of Sukarno's promises. The policies could have boosted the economy if the government had not ploughed so much state revenue into military adventures. Each year the inflation rate soared to more impossible levels, which in turn put strain on multiple exchange rates against the US dollar, rates that varied according to the nature of transactions. Import tariffs only served as extra sources of income for government officials, they did nothing to improve the situation and all kinds of consumer goods were in extremely short supply. Although US oil companies were allowed to stay in Indonesia through new kinds of contractual arrangements with the army-run national oil company, all other foreign investment had been frightened off by Sukarno. By 1965 foreign reserves were negligible.[12]

For ordinary Indonesians Sukarno's message had a strong effect. The banners and slogans that were painted in public areas, and the constant rallies that everyone had to attend to show support for the Revolution, created great national pride. The patronage system of politics did bring benefits as well. All the new development projects provided work, which was distributed through the parties and their factions in the bureaucracy and local leadership, so that unemployment was just over 7 per cent, although underemployment was and still is a more serious issue than unemployment in Indonesia.

Not everyone was happy. Those who were outside patronage networks, or who found their political parties banned, had no safety net. Slum dwellers in Jakarta were forcibly moved out to rebuild the centre of the city. In the poor inner-city area called Peanut Garden, a set of shanty huts that could be glimpsed from the grand new buildings of the main section of the city, the population increased rapidly when those forced from nearby slum areas moved in. In the deteriorating economic conditions people created new professions in order to survive. For example, as queues for rice, kerosene and other basic necessities grew, slum dwellers were available, for a small fee, to stand in the queue for others too busy to wait. Scavenging and recycling of everything, from sawdust to radios, created a new economy in the inner city, with some of the slum dwellers becoming prosperous enough to be able to buy their own houses at a cost of Rp 6,000 for a 60 square metre home, the equivalent of 200 litres of rice.[13]

Wages could not keep pace with prices. Harbour workers in Jakarta earned Rp 12.74 a day in 1958, equivalent to just over US$1 at prevailing exchange rates. That had jumped to Rp 21 in twelve months, and then up to Rp 48.75 in 1963. But that could not keep pace with inflation, so their US dollar equivalent remained the same. By mid-1965 prices were almost doubling each week and rice jumped from Rp 380 to 450 per kilogram in July of that year. Civil servants on fixed incomes were hardest hit. At least those who were selling goods on the street could adjust their prices accordingly.[14]

Sukarno's revolutionary rhetoric led him to link himself more publicly with the Communist Party. He thought himself able to control them, as he believed he had in the Madiun Affair of 1948. By playing the PKI off against the army, that is installing Communist ministers to balance officers in positions of political and economic power, Sukarno projected himself as national shadow puppet-master.

For the PKI this was their great opportunity. Despite their strength in Java, they were still behind the PNI and the Muslim parties overall in popularity, and their experiences of uprisings in 1926/7 and 1948 had shown them that violent revolution would not enable them to achieve power. Chairman Aidit therefore threw his support behind Sukarno, agreeing that he and other members of the Central Committee should serve as ministers, holding rallies at Senayan Stadium with Sukarno, mobilising the Party to support campaigns such as Irian and 'Confrontation', and increasing the heat of the revolutionary rhetoric.

Pramoedya became a cultural warrior in the politics of the time. As a leading member of the Institute of People's Culture he published a regular column in the leftist newspaper, *Star of the East*, and taught literary history in the independent *Res Publika* University. One of his aims was to challenge the conservative history of the Indonesian nationalist movement and Indonesian literature that others were producing. Through intensive research and teaching he revived interest in early nationalist figures such as Tirto Adhi Suryo and Mas Marco Kartodikromo, attempted to raise the status of their writings from 'dime novels' to that of literature, and to give them recognition as founders of the independence movement.

Some time around the institution of Guided Democracy, Pramoedya's writings shifted towards non-fiction and social criticism. Perhaps his period in gaol had radicalised him, but certainly by the early 1960s he was engaging in battles on paper that put him at odds with old friends and colleagues. His status as a public figure made him fearless. He wrote a scathing attack on Hamka, one of the foremost Muslim authors, which was followed by one of Pramoedya's colleagues accusing Hamka of plagiarism. Such attacks aligned with Sukarno's ideology of opposing enemies of the Revolution and pushing for social progress through strengthening the will of the people.[15]

During the early 1960s the extremism characteristic of party politics pervaded all aspects of life. Pramoedya's strong words against those whom he considered to be reactionaries or counter-revolutionaries were typical of the kinds of statements issued on both sides, although those on the right were in a more difficult position, because even conservative newspapers such as the NU's *Ambassador of Society* had to proclaim their support for Sukarno's Revolution.

The main targets of Pramoedya's attacks became the group of writers who joined together in a declaration against the politicisation of art. The anti-Communist group issued a 'Cultural Manifesto'. Signatories included author Mochtar Lubis, who was gaoled by the Sukarno regime for his criticisms of corruption, and leading film-makers such as Usman Ismail. On the Institute's side, besides Pramoedya, were many other leading writers and Indonesia's foremost painters, S. Sudjojono, Hendra Gunawan and Affandi. Some of the Cultural Manifesto group were worried about the increasingly strident pronouncements from the PKI about censoring certain kinds of art. Others were following a conservative Muslim opposition to Communism. Many of the Cultural Manifesto writers and painters were sponsored by a CIA-backed cultural programme intended to win artists away from the left; they were given scholarships to the US through CIA-funded Asia Society and USAID programmes.

The Manifesto group saw Pramoedya's strong language as part of a general totalitarian push in which many works by established writers such as Lubis were banned. Student demonstrations organised by the PKI terrorised opponents and forced a number of conservative writers out of their employment as academics. One of those on the receiving end of these demonstrations, poet Taufiq Ismail, recalled that 'Every day I read *Star of the East* and felt the terrorism in the campus directed at me, and even to my younger brother, I felt as if I was in a situation where I'd be killed, or kill.'[16]

By 1965 the PKI claimed to have 3.5 million party members, and another 23.5 million affiliates, making it the largest Communist Party in the world outside the Communist countries. There was some inflation in this figure: certainly not all of the members of groups claimed as affiliates – chief amongst them the Institute of People's Culture, the Peasants' Front, the All Indonesia Worker's Federation, the Women's Movement (*Gerwani*) and the People's Youth Movement – would have identified themselves as 'Communists'. In addition, smaller parties that were regarded as 'PKI' by outsiders seem not to have been linked to them that closely. Nevertheless, the PKI and its affiliates were successful in mobilising support across the countryside in ways that other parties were not. Within the core Party membership there was distrust of many of the affiliated groups and allies from the PNI left, who were called 'bourgeois running dogs of capitalism'. Some of the PKI's strongest clashes were with political parties of the left, notably the Proletarian Party. The PKI worked to convince Sukarno to ban this party too.[17]

The PKI's greatest success, but also its greatest disaster, was what came to be called the 'Unilateral Action', a series of land reform campaigns organised to seize land from large land owners. These campaigns continued the land ownership reorganisation processes begun by Dutch officials in the early twentieth century. Across the countryside people were suffering as drought began to hit in 1961. The government's economic policies, including unrealistic production targets, compulsory rice sales and rampant inflation rates well over 200 per cent per annum, increased their privations. Javanese and Balinese villagers like Madé Kantor remember the time as an era of poverty: 'we had to eat cassava'. In Central Java hunger oedema rates increased rapidly, so that by 1963 local officials estimated that 30,000 were malnourished in the area of Gunung Kidul alone. And then there was a mouse plague. A government relief programme distributing flour in the area helped, but corrupt officials took some of the flour, and covered this up by adulterating the remainder with chemicals. Over 1,000 people died of poisoning as a result.

The majority of farmers who owned land had less than half a hectare, not enough to grow food to feed a family, so land reform had general support. Desperate peasants signed up to take over land in the hope of escaping from poor pay as share-croppers and wage labourers. At first 'surplus land' or that belonging to absentee land owners, was taken over, then state or royal lands, but peasants spontaneously took over land owned by the rich. On Java around 300,000 hectares were redistributed from just over 27,000 land owners to nearly 600,000, while on the other islands nearly 400,000 hectares were redistributed to over 250,000 new owners.[18]

In conjunction with the Unilateral Action, the PKI organised cells across the countryside and promoted theatre groups, especially in the popular style called *ludruk*. 'We performed all kinds of stories ... ancient history . . .' One former head of a troupe recalled that their aims were relatively practical and modest, 'to, what's it called, to educate society, containing messages of education to the people . . . Really to reduce the number of people who had gone astray, who did wrong, to reduce that . . . The stories were like this eh, like good actions, how to organise the household and organise a society that, where there'd be elimination of gambling and so on . . .'[19]

The unilateral action had a major impact on Java and Bali in particular, where it deepened the already strong polarisation of society. Those most threatened by the unilateral actions were indeed the large land owners; in many areas these were also Muslim religious leaders or aristocrats. This polarisation was expressed in terms of political allegiances, even though its origins were more complex and went back to other kinds of factionalism typical of any close community. On Bali, those opposed to land reform pushed the PNI to the right, or in some cases split it, while in East Java senior Muslims mobilised support with the NU.

Sukarno struggled to keep control of his 'Five Principles Democracy'. Sometimes criticisms were allowed, sometimes not. The promise of being able to run the country and set policy was held out to the PKI, but then Sukarno's own PNI was brought back to keep the PKI on a leash. Adding to the pressure was protest by many groups against the increasing corruption of the regime, which was particularly bad amongst PNI leaders close to Sukarno. Leading these protests were new student groups sympathetic to the banned 'Cultural Manifesto' group.

The PKI was caught in its own contradictions. It called for a people's militia to be established to balance the power of the army, but wanted to pursue a parliamentary road to power. It advocated radical economic and social equality, but many of its members succumbed to the appeal of a new kind of hierarchy embodied by Sukarno and his ministers. Hersri Setiawan, a cultural activist of the 1950s and 1960s, spent a number of years at the headquarters of the Asia-Africa organisation in Colombo (Sri Lanka). On his return to Indonesia he attended a meeting of political and cultural leaders, but was amazed when PKI chairman Aidit arrived. The chairman came with a cavalcade and entourage, and when he entered the room everyone was expected to stand up. The egalitarianism of revolutionary brotherhood had been replaced by the feudal hierarchies that such progressives were meant to overthrow.

Throughout 1965 rumours of imminent coups circulated. Communists were seen practising military exercises in remote places. Even Western journalists believed a myth originating from the CIA, that shipments of arms were on their way from China, and stories of PKI death-lists spread. Sukarno's lifestyle of excess was catching up with him, and he went to China for medical treatment. The military was weary of the campaign against Malaysia. Irian was a *fait accompli*. Other stories spread that the CIA was active in supporting a council of right-wing generals and helping them draw up death-lists of Communists.

THE DESTRUCTION OF THE PKI

On 30 September 1965 a group of military officers from the airforce and Sukarno's praetorian guard launched what they called an action to defend the Great Leader of the Revolution, proclaiming themselves a 'Movement'. Based at Jakarta's Halim airforce base, they set out to kill seven of the country's generals. Three were shot dead in their houses. Three more were captured and executed at Halim. A seventh, General Nasution, escaped with injuries, but his adjutant was killed in his stead, and Nasution's tiny daughter Ade wounded. By the time she died a week later, the Movement had unravelled.

Sukarno travelled to Halim on 1 October to find out what the group was doing, conferred with them, and then left for the mountains by helicopter. Chairman Aidit also went to the airport, but returned to PKI headquarters in the city and called on his party to remain calm and take no action. The 30th September group did not remove the next most senior military officer after Nasution, Major-General Suharto. Some later claimed this was because Suharto himself had links to the group. Others, including Suharto, said it was an oversight. What really happened remains one of the great mysteries of Indonesian politics. Nasution himself was too distraught to take charge. Suharto, leading one of the military's most elite units, seized control of the centre of the capital, and from there denounced the Movement as a coup. Suharto's faction of the military sprang into action, captured key strategic sites in Jakarta, and launched a propaganda campaign which called the 30th September Movement *Gestapu* (*Gerakan Tigapuluh September*), hoping that the Nazi-like connotations would discredit it. Thereafter the military always referred to the Movement as belonging to the PKI, to create a mental link between the Communist Party and 'the coup'.

By 2 October Suharto's group had a firm grip on power, and on 5 October when the funeral procession was held for the dead generals, the military propaganda campaign against the PKI swept the country. Although there was no evidence that this was a Communist coup, the campaign was successful in convincing both domestic and international audiences that a coup had indeed occurred, and that Suharto was taking appropriate defensive measures. For decades afterwards foreign politicians referred to Suharto as the person who saved his country, while most Indonesians accepted the 'Communist coup' view, and blamed the Communist victims for what followed.

The news of a coup in Jakarta travelled slowly to some regions, and on the more remote islands it was barely relevant to daily life. The news from Jakarta reported the killings of the generals as a series of atrocities. The generals were identified as heroes of the Revolution, attacked in a cowardly manner, their bodies sexually mutilated by crazed members of the Communist-affiliated Women's Movement. In areas of Java, Bali and Sumatra, radio broadcasts and the newspaper reports set off an immediate reaction of anti-Communist outrage, and the lie about the Women's Movement produced vicious attacks on women who were seen as left-wing.[20]

In Sumatra's plantation areas the PKI had organised squatter movements and agitated against foreign companies, so in strongly Muslim areas such as Aceh quick action was taken to wipe out all Communists. Approximately 40,000 were killed around the plantations, one-fifth of all the killings on Sumatra. Elsewhere on Sumatra matters were confused by the aftermath of the 1950s regional revolts, during which many former rebels had been forced to sign up to Communist-affiliated bodies to prove their loyalty to the Republic. From the point of view of most Sumatrans, both the quelling of the earlier revolts and the killings of Communists were part of a 'Javanese occupation' of their island. Certainly from the late 1950s through the 1960s the previously strong role of Sumatrans in leading Indonesia declined.[21]

Army leaders allied to Suharto organised a demonstration in Jakarta in which the PKI headquarters was burned to the ground – after they had removed all documents of interest. There was some confusion within the military as to who should be regarded as Communist and who not, so the ever-helpful CIA created lists of those who should be rounded up. Leading Party members were immediately arrested, some summarily executed, and the airforce in particular was targeted for a purge. The purge rapidly spread to Central Java, to where Chairman Aidit had flown in early October, and where other leftist officers had also supported the Movement through local actions in Yogyakarta, Salatiga and Semarang.

The situation varied throughout the country. In many areas the army guided civilian groups as to who should be targeted or sponsored local militias, but in other places vigilante action preceded the army. In those parts of Central and East Java that had been Communist centres, Muslim groups portraying themselves as victims of aggression called up the events of the 1948 Madiun Affair – even though more Communists had been killed then than Muslims – to justify a wave of slaughter far more horrendous than any previous conflict the island had experienced. The pattern of killings varied from area to area. In some places people were simply shot, in others they were beheaded with Japanese samurai swords, in others such as Kediri in East Java, Communists were lined up by members of the NU's 'youth group' who cut their throats and threw the bodies into the rivers. In this manner 3,500 were killed in five days. The expression 'the rivers ran red with blood' was more than just a metaphor. The waterways were clogged with corpses and people like Sri, who was a child at the time, recall finding human body parts inside fish. Whole quarters of villages were left empty by the executions. The houses of those killed or imprisoned were looted, and frequently turned over to military men.[22]

Amongst those killed were many who had never been Communist Party members, and 'PKI' became a catch-all for anyone of the left, including many in the left of the PNI or smaller parties. In some areas, anti-Chinese racism raised its head and local Chinese were killed on the excuse that Chairman Aidit had brought the party close to China, their shops were looted and houses burned.

In a number of areas Communists regrouped. Bali, like parts of Java, was almost in a state of civil war until military groups came in and tipped the balance in favour of the anti-Communists. The black-shirted PNI youth wing led waves of killings similar to those in Central and East Java. For months militias went from door to door in villages, identifying suspects and taking them away. Members of the Women's Movement or those from Communist families were raped and mutilated, and even children were targets of the death squads. The best way to prove you were not a Communist was to join in the killings, and so many potential suspects were recruited to murder.

There were a few individual acts of heroism. Djelantik, the Balinese prince who had been sent to study in Malang in 1931, was head of Denpasar hospital when the killers arrived. He stood at the door and refused to allow them entry. Very few would have dared to risk being the next victim in this way. Instead the death squads went away peacefully. Djelantik's nephew, however, was one of the victims of the killings. Although he was not a Communist, as an official in a government department dominated by leftists he was considered 'implicated'.[23]

The army also sent students out to the countryside, members of groups who had opposed the PKI in cultural and political debates on campus, and who were encouraged by the army to form into protest groups. The army used them to whip up popular sentiment against the PKI and Sukarno, in effect to de-Sukarnoise the countryside.

In parts of East Java, conflict lasted for years. In Blitar, Sukarno's birthplace, PKI survivors regrouped for guerrilla action before they were crushed in 1967 and 1968. In an area just south of Blora, a *wayang* puppeteer and local mystical teacher, Mbah Suro (b. 1921), became popular for his philosophical advice and his prophecies of a great war that would end all conflict. His followers included many ordinary villagers, some of whom were presumably survivors of the first waves of killing. They built a 'palace' and organised into a small army, carrying magic clubs, protective amulets, and three bren guns. The PKI's modernity was mixed with more ancient ways of thinking here. On 4 March 1967 Mbah Suro and eighty of his followers were shot dead as they waged their war of resistance against the para-commandos.

The military, perhaps exaggerating, later estimated the total number killed during this massive purge as 1 million. Most estimates agree that it was at least half a million, with 80–100,000 killed on Bali alone. Chairman Aidit was killed early on, but many others were gaoled, and for the next ten years people were still being imprisoned as suspects. The Communist Party was banned.[24]

Amongst the first of the high-profile leftists to be arrested was Pramoedya. Most of his manuscripts and books were burned. In Jakarta's Salemba prison he met with leading politicians, and other artists and writers, as well as peasants and soldiers. Many of them did not survive this first period of detention. Pramoedya recalls that the food was so poor and the health conditions so bad that even elite soldiers from Sukarno's guard caught beri-beri within three months. At Salemba and during his initial imprisonment at Tangerang, two to four people died every day. Many more prisoners were beaten to death. Amongst them was Chaerul Saleh, a Menteng 31 nationalist from the early days of the Revolution, leader of anti-Dutch militias in Jakarta, leader of those who had kidnapped Sukarno to force him to declare independence, and a major Proletarian Party figure who had risen to the position of third prime minister under Guided Democracy. His dead body was found in a toilet, beaten black and blue.[25]

From 1966–8, the numbers in prison increased as those who succumbed to torture revealed the names of underground Communists. Overall probably as many as 1,500,000 were imprisoned at one time or another, and even when released they were under house arrest, or had to report regularly to local military headquarters, and were banned from ever receiving government employment. The children of those banned received similar treatment, even if they had not been born when the events of 30 September occurred. Much of a generation of the country's brightest minds, teachers, artists, journalists and natural leaders, was killed or treated like pariahs. Pramoedya was eventually moved for a few months in 1969 to Nusa Kambangan island, Indonesia's Alcatraz, before being shipped off to the remote eastern island of Buru, to the area he called, with his customary irony, 'happy land'.

Sukarno was still the Supreme Commander, president by virtue of the Constitution. If Suharto wanted to be seen as defending the nation from a Communist coup, he could not be seen to be seizing power in his own coup. So for eighteen months after the putting down of the 30th September movement, there was a complicated series of political manoeuvres in which student agitation, stacking of parliament, media propaganda and military threats were used against Sukarno. Conservative politicians, including those who had been leaders of the Sumatran revolt, had some of their power returned, as did members of other parties banned under Guided Democracy. Sukarno transferred much of his authority over the army and parliament to Suharto in a presidential decree of 11 March 1966. Claims emerged many years later that he signed the decree at gunpoint. By 1967 Suharto had effectively had his hold over power legitimated through the Upper House. Even so, in 1968 Suharto was given the title of 'Acting President' only, and he had to organise an election in 1971 to confirm his position. Sukarno died a broken man in 1970 before the election took place.[26]

ESTABLISHING A NEW ORDER

The little town of Blora produced one more remarkable man in addition to Tirto Adhi Suryo and Pramoedya Ananta Toer – Ali Murtopo (1924–84). Despite being a contemporary of Pramoedya's, the two never met. Murtopo's path was a very different one.

Murtopo rose up through the army during the Revolution. He became a para-commando officer in the 1950s, and got to know Suharto during that period when they were both involved in smuggling, ostensibly for the welfare of local peasants and underpaid soldiers. Under Suharto's command, his officers set up businesses through charitable 'foundations', helped in this case by tribute from local Chinese businessmen eager to buy protection. One of these, businessman Bob Hasan, later became a significant player in Jakarta money politics. By the mid-1950s the military was well on the way to becoming an economic force. It was Ali Murtopo who had helped his commander develop new sources of revenue at that time, but Suharto who was punished for criminal activities. He was stripped of responsibilities by General Nasution, who was under pressure from leftist politicians and the army to find a scapegoat.[27]

Under Suharto's command, Murtopo led intelligence work in the Irian campaign, and established his Special Operations group, which played a key role in secret talks that settled confrontation with Malaysia after 1965. One of his factional opponents described him as the consummate intelligence operative, able to bring together and simultaneously play off rival groups for his own purposes, creating tight networks through which to exercise power. Those who followed him were inspired by his daring, which he combined with strong feelings of loyalty to his friends. Suharto made him a 'Special Presidential Assistant' when he came to power, and later Minister for Information.[28]

Of the many officers who became important in the period during and after 1965, Murtopo was probably the most powerful after Suharto. He was the one responsible for extracting elements from Sukarno's ideological brinkmanship that could be used by the new regime. Murtopo recognised that a new device was needed to deflect loyalty from the charismatic Sukarno. The new government was christened the 'New Order' to replace the Revolution based on the personality of the Great Leader. 'Order' was now supposed to come from adherence to the Five Principles, an abstraction of higher value than the president. The Five Principles and the 1945 Constitution became the highest elements of the nation, so that the new regime could claim to be one based on the rule of law.

Most importantly, Murtopo reformulated Sukarno's Guided Democracy into a state based on 'Functional Groups', called *Golkar* after the Indonesian abbreviation of their name (*Golongan Karya*). Civil servants, as one of these 'Functional Groups', had to demonstrate loyalty to *Golkar* rather than to political parties, breaking the nexus of the parties' control over the bureaucracy. The military was another 'Functional Group', which aligned with the military's ideology of having a 'dual function'. The military could therefore extend its control over important state companies and plantations, and get involved in other local enterprises, such as hotels, printing houses, service stations, sugar mills, theatres and transport services. Participation in *Golkar* legitimised those military officers who had been installed as regional governors or put into other state offices during the state of war and siege or the annihilation of Communism. The military had a guaranteed number of seats in the parliament (75 in the Lower House of 460).

Murtopo used the language of conservative socialists to deny that workers existed as a separate class. He claimed that they were a part of a group of 'employed' that included both employers and employees, another Functional Group subsumed into *Golkar*. Thus all unions were united into a single body answerable to the state. The population was no longer there to be mobilised by political parties, rather, the people were the 'floating mass', or the 'ignorant mass', who needed firm guidance so they would not be lured into politics.[29]

Besides formulating key elements of the new regime's ideology, Murtopo manipulated mergers of existing political parties. In the period between 1967 and 1971 the surviving non-Islamic political parties, from the nationalist PNI, to the Catholic Party and the socialist Proletarian Party, were joined into an Indonesian Democatic Party (PDI). Likewise the Islamic parties were brought together into a more neutrally named United Development Party (PPP). These two parties alone were allowed to contest elections with *Golkar*, and they were never allowed to get too large a proportion of the votes. *Golkar*'s guaranteed support from the military, public service and centrally controlled unions made it a highly effective political machine, but Murtopo insisted that it was not to be called a political party like the PDI and PPP.

Merging and purging political parties was not easy. In many areas military supervision of the political process included direct coercion, as former local party leaders were beaten into line or threatened with the fate of the Communists. Ali Murtopo gathered around him a group of criminal thugs, popularly known as his 'zoo', who could be deployed across the country to '*Golkar*-ise' the nation. *Golkar* membership included surviving Communists, for whom demonstrating commitment to the new regime guaranteed that they would be spared. The shaping of the 1971 election involved allowing former Communists to terrorise PNI leaders unwilling to toe the line. The success of the election, where *Golkar* received two-thirds of the vote, surprised even its leaders.[30]

In order to claim legitimacy, Suharto was initially part of a triumvirate with the Central Javanese Sultan Hamengkubuwono IX, who brought with him the weight of Javanese tradition, and Adam Malik, a Sumatran politician who was formerly a member of the youth group which forced Sukarno to proclaim independence, and who represented both non-

Javanese and a liberal, civilian voice in the new government. Malik had been a member of the socialist Proletarian Party, and as one of those at the receiving end of PKI attacks, was firmly anti-Communist.

The US government had closely followed the events of 1965, and approved of the abolition of Communism, by whatever means. While being careful that there should be no direct involvement in the massacres, the US made it clear that it was 'generally sympathetic with and admiring of what [the] Army [was] doing', to quote one US embassy document.[31] Although at first hesitant until they knew who was going to take over and what Suharto was like as a leader, US support for the new regime came once Suharto could demonstrate that he held power legally. Aid programmes were restored. In particular, Indonesia resumed its membership of the international agencies created to manage the world economy, including the World Bank and the International Monetary Fund.

Ali Murtopo's earlier experience in the Irian campaign put him in a good position to oversee the final resolution of Irian's integration into Indonesia. The UN's view was that the people of Irian should have a plebiscite, an 'act of free choice', as to whether they wanted to be Indonesians or not. In 1969 US, Australian and other observers from the United Nations were invited to see this in action. In accordance with New Order principles of democracy, the Irianese were not considered 'advanced' enough to be able to participate in a vote of the whole population, so just over 1,000 'community leaders' were chosen by the Indonesian military, in a fashion eerily reminiscent of the Dutch colonial government's appointment of its People's Council. Foreign observers were not allowed to view the actual voting, but they heard enough stories of intimidation by the army to christen this 'the Act of No Choice'. US advisers involved in the process ensured that a positive report was submitted to the UN. Irian was Indonesia's reward for getting rid of Communism.

Many of the brightest anti-Sukarno student activists were feted by Ali Murtopo, and became key figures in *Golkar*'s politics and in New Order policy-making. A number were coopted into political advisory groups or think tanks. A group of brilliant economists from the University of Indonesia became a special advisory team. They had been trained in the US in neo-liberal economics, and were generally referred to by journalists and critics either as 'the Technocrats' or 'the Berkeley Mafia'. They gave lectures to gatherings of military officers, and established a two-year plan to balance the budget, stabilise prices and provide economic liberalisation.

The economy got worse before it got better. The worst inflation, topping levels of 700 per cent, occurred in 1966 when there was mass starvation in Lombok and other areas. Drought relief programmes were supplemented by foreign aid donations, as gradually the devastation to production caused by the widespread killings eased. A drastic readjustment of the Rupiah in 1966 saw the exchange rate fixed, devaluing the currency by 1,000 per cent. By 1969 inflation was under control and free markets were slowly established in many areas, although not in essential areas such as domestic petroleum, electricity, rice and water. US approval of the anti-Communist actions by the government led to major debt rescheduling, although it took until 1971 for debts to the Soviet Union to be adjusted. Indonesia became the world's second-highest recipient of aid (after India), and all subsequent budget planning was premised on the receipt of significant economic aid.

Once the two-year plan began to take effect, Ali Murtopo announced a more extensive twenty-five-year modernisation strategy, consisting of five five-year plans. Capital was safeguarded for wealthy ethnic Chinese businesses through government guarantees and new partnerships with key members of the government. Foreign capital was welcomed back. Indonesia was to be industrialised through injections of aid and capital, the benefits of which were to be received by the general population as 'trickle down effects'.[32]

After the murder and privation of the mid-1960s, those who were not suspected Communists regarded the initial New Order years as a 'honeymoon' period. During the late 1960s and early 1970s there was a strange mixture of military domination of all aspects of society and the beginning of liberalised youth culture. The military were a strong physical presence, marching through the street, standing armed with machine guns at all public buildings and on public transport. Key 'hot spots' throughout the nation remained under effective martial law, for example the Siliwangi army division controlled a section of Jakarta where they instituted curfews to demonstrate their control.

Students who had been members of the anti-Sukarno movement were also part of an international youth culture, and a new word – 'hippies' – entered the Indonesian language. Drugs such as marijuana and heroin were relatively freely available in big cities. Street gangs and rock music contributed to a wild atmosphere. Many of the gangs in the capital included children of the new ruling group, as the sons of generals and ministers became what were called 'cross boys', young men with access to guns and money. The Jakarta suburb of Kebayoran Baru, particularly its shopping area Blok M, became a fashionable area, albeit a dangerous one during gang fights with sub-machine guns.

International youth culture developed its own local form, as the rock music that had been banned under Sukarno now flourished through circulation of cheap, copied cassette tapes. As well as listening to Carlos Santana and Janis Joplin, young Indonesians formed their own pop groups, such as the Mercys. A new Jakarta art centre was built in Cikini, on the site of the city's former zoo, originally the mansion of a nineteenth-century aristocrat who was, appropriately, Indonesia's first modern artist. The centre was part of government efforts to sponsor local cultural production. In the film industry this helped counter the domination of Hollywood, although despite benefiting from a levy on imported films, local film-makers struggled to find audiences. Only local comedies that dabbled in the erotic, such as the popular *Inem the Sexy Maid*, were commercially successful.[33]

Some of the films of this period struggled to come to terms with the realities of Indonesia, realities that had not changed with the new regime. Despite Jakarta having a popular reformist military governor who had tried to 'close' the city to new migrants, this was where the disparities between the rich and the poor were most apparent. When the children of the rich went to Gambir railway station in the centre of the city they saw others who scavenged cigarette butts to make new cigarettes to sell for a living, and they passed shanties and the muddy black filth of canals that were bathrooms, toilets and sources of water for slum dwellers. A number of film-makers attempted to draw attention to the cause of the poor, and contributed to a growing feeling among the young who had campaigned against Sukarnoist corruption that they should continue their struggle for a more just society.[34]

The same students who had helped the Suharto regime come to power now started to voice opposition to it. Student groups turned their anti-corruption attacks to Suharto's wife, known as Ibu Tien. It had long been rumoured that she had received economic benefits from various state projects, hence, punning on the Dutch word for ten, '*tien*', she became known as 'Madam 10 per cent'.

One of her pet projects was to create a 'Garden of Indonesia in Miniature', a kind of nationalist Disneyland where all the islands would be represented in miniature in a central lake, and examples of each of Indonesia's main cultures would be presented in the form of houses in the distinctive ethnic styles, along with handicrafts of the regions. While this had a laudable aim based on the state motto of promoting 'Unity in Diversity', the main problem for the protesters was that it was a huge waste of state money when basic issues of poverty were not being addressed.

Suharto, a man of simple village origins, as he liked to remind everyone, had a fierce loyalty to his family. Criticisms of his wife stung, and a first round of pressure was applied to student leaders.[35]

A legacy of Sukarno's economic policies that was maintained by Suharto was a close economic relationship with Japan. Sukarno's marriage in 1959 to a Japanese woman who took the name Dewi helped to boost ties to Japanese government and business. Japan agreed to pay war reparations money, some of which was used for high-profile modernisation projects such as the building of the luxury Bali Beach Hotel, and Japanese companies began to set up plants in Indonesia. Suharto's Special Presidential Assistants, especially Murtopo and his allies, furthered these ties, both as a way of getting direct investment and also access to the Japanese-dominated Asia Development Bank's aid funding. But they acted too quickly for those who still remembered the suffering under the Japanese occupation. Prime Minister Tanaka of Japan's visit to Indonesia in 1974 set off a wave of anti-Japanese protests.

The students themselves were inspired by the example of Thailand's students, who in 1973 had brought down a military regime through brave protests. Many of those in Jakarta thought that they could do the same, and targeted the extra-constitutional role of Murtopo and the other Special Presidential Assistants. Throughout Jakarta the protest that took place on 15 January 1974 soon turned into riots, where it was not only Japanese enterprises that were targeted. Coca-Cola was another popular object of disgust at the doings of foreign capital, and again the Chinese became victims of looters and racist attacks. Parts of Jakarta's Chinatown were burned down, and the popular Senen Market and the middle-class shopping area Blok M were attacked. The students from the University of Indonesia who had started the demonstrations were out-manoeuvred by thugs and wild street children, who turned protests into riots and threatened to attack the students in the central suburb of Salemba. Security forces moved in.

The students were caught by surprise. Initially they had received support from the head of the internal security body, General Soemitro, whose power was getting beyond Suharto's control. As it turned out, the riots were manipulated by Ali Murtopo as a way of discrediting Soemitro and his factional allies. The thugs leading the violence were from Ali's 'zoo', the same people who had been used against the political parties. Action was quickly taken by Murtopo's intelligence group to have all the main student leaders arrested, and Soemitro completely lost power. The riots had been a convenient way to put the military on notice that they had to fall into line behind Suharto, or else, and to let the students know that at any point legal and extra-legal force could be used against them. The New Order's claim to represent law and order meant that its enemies were to be ruthlessly suppressed.

The student movement took nearly twenty-five years to recover, and they were certainly in no position to protest at the opening of Madam Suharto's 'Garden of Indonesia in Miniature' in 1975. The honeymoon was definitely over.[36]

Another appeal to US anti-Communism was made as part of Ali Murtopo's biggest campaign. In 1974 Portugal's fascist dictatorship fell, and the new socialist government decided belatedly to carry out a process of decolonisation. In the colony of East Timor, forgotten by Portugal and the rest of the world, locals greeted this decision by establishing a number of political parties, the largest of which was the Front for the Liberation of East Timor, *Fretilin. Fretilin's* declaration of independence was contested by a second more conservative party, the UDT, and a third and much smaller body, *Apodetai,* that advocated integration with Indonesia. Indonesia used *Fretilin's* vaguely Marxist leanings to discredit it in the international media, and the spectre of a civil war was conjured up to induce Australia and the US to support Indonesian actions. Murtopo organised Indonesian 'volunteers' to visit East Timor as a show of goodwill, while secretly building up military forces along the border and working with the *Apodetai* group to prepare the way for a massive invasion and annexation of East Timor.

At least 125,000 East Timorese perished in the civil war, the invasion and the starvation that followed. Six Western journalists were also killed by Indonesian forces, the Indonesians say accidentally, East Timorese witnesses claim deliberately. Sadly, the deaths of the journalists received more attention than those of all the East Timorese, but the campaign to expose their murders rallied support for East Timorese independence at a time when most governments, the US and Australia in particular, would have liked it forgotten.

For the next twenty-five years the Indonesian military used East Timor as its training ground. This was where young officers were 'blooded' into a culture of torture and murder, where they learned to dispose of bodies and to eliminate potential opponents. Many of these officers had been trained in the US, and specifically copied the CIA's programme developed in Vietnam and code-named 'Phoenix', which taught how to target civilian support for guerrilla resistance fighters through assassination and terror.

In 1978, Ali Murtopo had a heart attack which limited his effectiveness. He died of a second attack in 1984. He used to brag to his men that he was the only one who could say 'no' to Suharto. By 1975 Adam Malik and Sultan Hamengkubuwono IX were no longer heeded as co-rulers, their roles were downplayed, the Sultan going into retirement, and Malik taking the back-seat as vice-president in 1978, until his death, also in 1984. Suharto's power was supreme. Once Murtopo was gone Suharto's main advisers were 'yes men' who wanted to make themselves wealthy through access to the state's resources. Having taken control of the milch-cow that was the state, Suharto and his close supporters proceeded to milk it.

Progressive moves in the 1950s to end discrimination, to emancipate the whole population and create broad social welfare were all pushed back between 1957 and 1967. Pramoedya's hero, Sukarno, began a process he could not complete, as upwardly mobile conservative forces, led by the army, took control. The Revolution did not carry everyone along with it, as Sukarno and the PKI had hoped. In the end Sukarno fell victim to his own cult of personality, as internal and external pressures forced Indonesian socialism to collapse.

CHAPTER 7

Terror and development in happy land

When Political Detainee number 641, Pramoedya Ananta Toer, was struggling in 1973 to survive on the harsh and remote island of Buru – 'happy land' – he received a letter, suggesting that he should reform: 'For every person a mistake in judgment is common, but that must of course be followed by its logical consequence, that being: "honesty, courage and the ability to rediscover the true and accepted road."' The indirect Javanese style of the letter belonged to President Suharto, and showed the remarkable combination of threat and solicitation that was the hallmark of Suharto's rule. Pramoedya replied simply that he would 'cherish truth, justice and beauty', that he hoped 'the strong' would 'extend their hand to the weak', and that he would continue to 'strive and pray'. The obliqueness of this response was not just characteristic of the Javanese culture he shared with Suharto, it was also because his guards were supervising his reply.[1]

During his imprisonment on Buru, Pramoeyda wrote his tetralogy *This Earth of Mankind*, retelling the story of the origins of Indonesian nationalism based on the endeavours of Tirto Adhi Suryo. Initially, Pramoedya was not allowed pen and paper, and composed his novels orally, recalling his research in the National Library during the early 1960s. He told fellow prisoners the story so that they might find 'truth, justice and beauty', in order to survive. The tetralogy is a claim that Indonesia had lost sight of its true national identity, and under Suharto was drifting back towards the government of the colonial era. The books, together with his letters and published reminiscences of the time, provide a moving insight into the brutality of a regime based on military force.

CRUSHING THE OPPOSITION

By the mid-1970s, Suharto had become the national puppet-master, using loyal military officers to crush his enemies, and distributing largesse to his family and supporters. For Pramoedya this was the greatest betrayal of

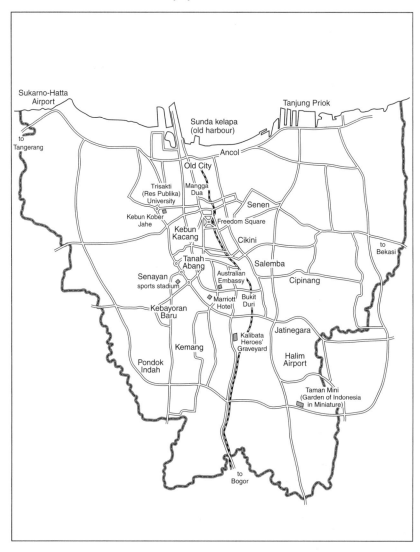

Map 6 Jakarta 1960s–2005

Indonesia's democratic potential, the return to arbitrary use of power that was part of the colonial legacy, part of colonialism's encouragement of feudalism. While there are close links to the Javanese royal systems and to Dutch rule in the New Order period, Suharto's regime was also one that made use of a modern form of domination. Suharto's methods produced two experiences of his rule during an extraordinary period akin to that of Stalin's rule in Russia, where fear and aggrandisement made sure that the regime held control of the nation.[2] This period was punctuated by regular elections with predetermined results, called 'festivals of democracy', and by changes in both the membership of the ruling group and their targets, as first Communism, then Islam, then non-governmental organisations were identified as threats to the nation. Throughout all this the great constant was Suharto, the ultimate politician.

The government was able to maintain the Communist bogey man as the target of its two mainstays of power – terror and development – and in so doing set up a structure that gave the military easy access to power. The terror of the 1965 killings became a warning against any criticism of the government. During the period from 1965 to 1968 people had fled their homes and shed their identities to survive. Some of these exiles never returned home, others did so decades later. The grimness of the killings affected more than family and friends of the victims. Other witnesses still live with life-long trauma. In many villages locals can still point out who were the killers. While some of these killers were well rewarded with public office by the regime, many went mad from the burden of what they did. This was a terror that blighted millions of lives.

The New Order was so successful at creating and spreading its version of 'the coup' that, for most Indonesians, all blame was put upon the Communist Party. Journalists, scholars, artists and officials were employed by the regime to produce accounts and images of 'the coup', giving the Suharto version of what happened, drowning out all other accounts. Publications 'proved' that this was the 'PKI coup', although on close reading they showed nothing of the sort. In 1980 one of Indonesia's leading playwrights made a film called *The Treachery of Gestapu-PKI*. The three-hour film became compulsory viewing on 30 September each year for all school students, supported by school textbooks with plays telling the government's story. Into the late 1980s and early 1990s, periodic campaigns were waged by the government, with names like 'A Clean Environment' and 'Those Considered to be Under the Influence', to weed out 'Communists' from society. People had to carry 'Certificates of Good Conduct' to show they were not 'implicated'. Government statements constantly warned the population of a 'latent danger', a catch-all phrase that could cover any dissenters. Part of the language of threat was a reference to 'organisations without form' that threatened the nation, the spectre of Communism. Sinister suggestions had replaced the slogans of Sukarno's Revolution.

Figure 7.1 500 Rupiah note (value approximately US$2 at time of issue in 1968) showing General Sudirman, hero of the Revolution and founder of the army. The symbol in the upper centre is the badge of the Five Principles.

At the well of Halim airbase known as the Crocodile Hole, where the bodies of the slain generals were dumped, a monument was erected, along with explanatory material and a series of reliefs depicting the official propaganda. This site was the focus of annual ceremonies known as 'Sacred Five Principles Day', through which everyone could give thanks to Suharto and the army for saving them from Communism. Even in the 1990s the government continued to labour the point, establishing a 'Museum of Communist Treachery' that used dioramas to show how Communism had betrayed the nation, and how the armed forces and the people had joined together against it. In official accounts of Indonesia's history no mention was allowed of the killings. Sukarno was removed from public presentations of national history, no mean feat given his omnipresence from 1957 to 1965.[3]

This Orwellian achievement was not, as Pramoedya would have it, part of the colonial legacy, rather it was a distinctive creation of New Order totalitarianism. This totalitarian system was not simply the work of one man, Suharto, rather it was the expression of a group, the military, that had come to power by overtaking the new political class of the Revolution and the 1950s. The military was as much a product of the Cold War as of its own trajectory since the Revolution. The military thrived because membership provided ready access to the crudest forms of power. As a modern institution the military provided upward mobility for young men, while providing a framework for that mobility that was even more hierarchical than the world of the Javanese courts; it was both traditional and modern.

Pramoedya's life on Buru was a microcosm of the way that the regime controlled the nation. After sailing for ten days east to the island – starving, living with daily arbitrary beatings, forced to stay in cells with excrement all over the floor – he and his fellow survivors were dumped in an infertile and uninviting area of swamp with only a few seeds and tools to enable them to clear the jungle, start farms and support themselves. They were meant to bring a Javanese mode of agriculture to the relatively sparsely populated island, to 'develop' it under the eyes of the guards. The beatings continued to be a regular part of life, and even when the prisoners did succeed in producing enough to trade and set up a cooperative, their goods and funds were appropriated by the military commander.

Arrests and trials of those accused of being linked to 'the coup' were still going on in 1977 and 1978, when international pressure to have the Buru prisoners released increased, and Pramoedya was taken back to Jakarta in 1979. In his memoir of over a decade on Buru, he lists 315 fellow prisoners who died on the island. For another decade the government used the image of the Communists to remind the population of who was in control. Members of the PKI and military left remained in prison, many of them on death row. Some of these were executed on various 30 Septembers over a number of years in the 1980s.

By the early 1980s, Pramoedya, under house arrest, was ready to publish his novels, and a fellow ex-political prisoner set up a publishing house for this purpose. One of the quirks of the censorship laws inherited from the Dutch was that works could not be banned until they were in circulation. Consequently, from 1981 to 1988, the four novels of *This Earth of Mankind* were published, sold, and then banned. Initially there were protests about the bans, even Vice-President Adam Malik spoke in Pramoedya's defence in parliament, but by the late 1980s the government's grip was so strong that avenues to express dissent had been closed down. In spite of the bans, Pramoedya's work continued to be widely circulated, the banned novels photocopied and passed around, their prestige enhanced by being forbidden fruit, a kind of political pornography. In 1989 and 1990, a group of students were publicly tried for circulating 'Marxist' literature, including Pramoedya's work, and gaoled.[4]

Periodic anti-Communist campaigns were part of a larger strategy of control. Students and artists were also to be kept under surveillance. In the late 1970s a 'New Art Movement' of young artists from all over the archipelago was proclaimed in Jakarta with a series of paintings and sculptures satirising the New Order vision. One work by the left-wing Jakarta graphic artist, Hardi, depicted himself in military uniform as

'President in 2001'. Such jokes were not appreciated, and Hardi was briefly put into military detention. In order to prevent a repeat of the 1974 protests on university campuses, in 1978 and 1979 a series of security actions were taken under the title of 'Normalisation of Campus'. Troops were brought on to campuses, and student bodies dissolved. Beginning with Jakarta's University of Indonesia, state universities were moved out of the centres of cities, to underdeveloped areas where access points could be controlled by the military and where demonstrations would not spill over into busy public spaces. Academics were strictly monitored by government appointees, who were installed at all levels of the education system. Many of these had little in the way of university qualifications, but were kept in position to report on 'dissent'. Students had to join campus cadet corps, wear military-style uniforms and take part in exercises that would give them 'discipline'. In the 1980s a campaign to teach 'civics' at all levels of the education system produced a new curriculum in which the New Order's watered-down version of the 'Five Principles' of state were to be rote-learned by all students. Everyone had to wear uniforms, especially civil servants, whose outfit was a rayon short-sleeved version of the safari suit.[5]

The period of the 'Normalisation' campaign coincided with a series of other clamp-downs. Operations such as 'Sweep the World' saw the arrest of dissenters and criminals and efforts to seize any weapons in civilian hands. At the same time the government closed a number of major newspapers, including those headed by some of the same people who had opposed Sukarno on the grounds of his authoritarianism. After an initial period of intervention by the Department for Information, then headed by General Ali Murtopo, newspaper editors took the hint and self-censored.

On Pramoeyda's journey to Buru prisoners were subjected to 'saccharine *kroncong* [colonial-era pop music] songs, official announcements, sermons, and advice from nameless authorities who wish for us good luck in the new life that we are headed for'.[6] The whole population was subjected to the same kind of bombardment. The dynamic and highly personalised political slogans that marked the Sukarno years were replaced with a new kind of sermonising, full of dense and uninspiring phrases that crept into all aspects of society. The new language of the New Order was a kind of high Javanese Indonesian, not the language of the street but a formalised and patronising language, typified by the deadly boring speeches of Suharto that droned on about development and were punctuated by earnest pieces of folk wisdom that passed for philosophy.

Readers of 1960s Indonesian newspapers would probably have found newspaper reports of the 1980s unreadable. The short, direct sentences written for readers for whom the language was newly acquired in the post-Independence education boom, had been replaced by long and contorted statements filled with complex constructions and neologisms designed to give the effect of great import without actually saying anything. This New Order style of language was based on a top-down view of society, where 'authorities' told a passive population what it should do. The inflated nature of the language was meant to enhance the speaker's or writer's prestige. Instead of Sukarno's radical slogans, the New Order produced slogans that were almost meaningless, posting banners on public buildings proclaiming such things as the need to 'sportise society, and societise sport'.[7] Pramoedya's Buru novels were a challenge to this kind of language. With his clear, direct style inflected with the speech patterns of common Javanese, he punctured the pretensions of New Order ideology.

Throughout the 1980s, newspaper stories were bland descriptions of the success of development, leavened only by the occasional sensational murder or supernatural story with no political connotations. The only television station was government-owned. TV sets were distributed to every village so that public broadcasts of the government's messages could be viewed as widely as possible. Although initially television advertising was allowed, in 1981 it was removed from the screen because Suharto and his ministers were worried that the 'ignorant masses' would be too easily led by commercial messages. Thereafter programme breaks were punctuated by patriotic music. Most Indonesians now had to interpret politics through inference, knowing that if a minister suddenly disappeared from the headlines he was in disgrace. For example, a new minister of defence announced in 1978 that military officers would no longer be allowed to be involved in business. He was eventually demoted and disappeared from the front pages. In the shade of censorship, rumours grew like toadstools.[8]

The elections held every five years were exercises in controlled aggression. Before these rituals, detailed instructions were given to the relevant local authorities as to how many votes for the government political vehicle *Golkar* their area was to produce. Failure to do so could result in removal from position, success would bring material rewards – prizes such as motorbikes and trips to Singapore. The elections were also ways to draw out potential opposition figures. If local leaders emerged from outside *Golkar*, they were threatened and badgered into supporting the government. Crack military troops were brought into areas that were regarded as particularly troublesome, and thugs transported all over the country by the military burned down the houses of opponents or beat them into line. Only at election rallies were demonstrations allowed to reach emotional levels, as a kind of safety valve. Groups of young men from contending political parties could wage heated battles as part of the election lead-up, and whole towns were decorated in the colour of one or the other party.

This strategy of permitting limited violence was Ali Murtopo's contribution to Indonesian political culture. But the point was always to show that the government had the ultimate monopoly on violence. This was demonstrated in what was called 'The Mysterious Shootings' of the early 1980s. Around that time, the media had run stories raising public fears that crime levels were increasing. In cities on Java members of criminal gangs, readily identifiable because of their abundant tattoos, were found by members of the public, shot dead and left in canals or public streets. While the killers were never named, rumour and inference soon pinpointed off-duty military personnel. The murdered criminals included some of Murtopo's collection of quasi-official thugs. The message of terror was directed both to the public and to gang members who might have needed reminding about who was giving the orders.[9] In subsequent elections and in the political turmoil surrounding the later Suharto years, a 'Five Principles Youth Movement' was deployed, made up of the same thugs.

In government thinking, the New Order represented an 'organic' state, embodied in *Golkar*. The nation was seen as one big family, where there should be no signs of dissent to the benevolent patriarch. Thus the idea of an opposition in the People's Assembly was declared 'un-Indonesian', as were strikes and other elements of conflict that might disturb the goal of social harmony.[10]

The 1977 election, like all others held under Suharto, was a triumph for the government's party-that-was-not-a-party, *Golkar*, but not everything went to plan. The two tame political parties were meant to get some of the vote so that the appearance of democracy could be maintained; however, the vote of one, the Democratic Party or PDI, collapsed markedly. Sukarno's children had been active in this party because it was the successor to the PNI, which had been associated with their father, but because they had been severely restricted from campaigning, voters ignored the PDI in protest. Even though Sukarno had died in 1970, his ghost haunted the political machine of the New Order. Other limited protests occurred in local elections. Even when there was only one candidate for a local election, New Order attention to formality demanded that there be signs of a choice – the candidate's ballot box was placed next to an empty box. If villagers disapproved of the candidate, they placed their votes in the other slot, and the empty box won the election.[11]

The party that showed signs of resurgence in the 1977 election was the combined Muslim Party, the United Democratic Party or PPP. Islamic outrage against Communists had been useful to the New Order in the 1960s, and Islam had also benefited from the purge of Communists, as many people either converted or changed their practices from nominalism or indigenous syncretism to more orthodox Islam. Some strove to demonstrate their faith to escape suspicion of being atheists (and therefore equivalent to Communists); others were genuinely driven towards deep introspection and spiritual fulfilment after the horrors of the killings.

Unfortunately for the New Order, in the early 1970s religious leaders turned their criticism against corruption and the military role in politics. Suharto, under the influence of presidential advisers, embraced Javanese spiritualism, an outlook viewed with suspicion by some Muslim leaders. Political disagreements became heated when in 1973 new marriage laws were forced through parliament. Although these laws met pre-Independence nationalist and feminist agendas in their aims to limit polygamy and abolish child marriage, Muslim leaders feared that they were part of an attempt by the state to control religion. Such control would move them further away from their goal of having Islam as a state religion.

The clash between religious leaders and the regime became particularly marked once it was clear that all political vehicles of Islam were expected to merge into the PPP, and further that this party should have the Five Principles of the nation, not Islam, as its basis. These restrictions were part of a general campaign to reformulate the Five Principles so that they could be used as the political symbol of the New Order. This was done by removing any radical social messages.[12]

Intelligence chief Murtopo manipulated groups dedicated to violence in the name of Islam. Reports emerged that the 1950s House of Islam movement was being revived in Java and Sumatra. In fact, Murtopo encouraged a group of former House of Islam leaders, including the messianic Kartosuwiryo's son, to create a stalking horse. He cultivated them as a group who became known as the '*Jihad* Command', a threat raised in order to justify security crack-downs. Murtopo's use of Islam as an enemy was too clever by half: like the US support for Osama bin Laden and Sadam Hussein in the 1980s, this was a ploy that would backfire with international consequences.[13]

Indonesian Islam has always been heterogeneous, but the New Order magnified differences for their own ends. The 1970s was marked by international waves of Islamic renewal, encouraged particularly by the

Iranian Revolution. The renewal emphasised pan-Islamic solidarity, as did another group opposed to the Iranian version of Islamic Revolution. This second group, a purist network that had developed out of the Muslim Brotherhood in Egypt, eventually spread to Malaysia, from where it reached Indonesian Muslims. This second pan-Islamic movement was opposed to nations and nationalism because they embodied the kind of tribalism the Prophet Muhammad had overthrown in establishing Islam. Both the Iranian Revolution and the Muslim Brotherhood promoted the idea of intellectual youth opposing the state. A small group of Indonesian students in one Central Javanese religious educational community or *pesantren* pursued such ideas with particular vigour. This group, which initially had only about ten members, was led by Abdullah Sungkar, a preacher who had links to the House of Islam Revolt. Sungkar and his followers were attracted to ideals of purity and renewal, and sought to establish networks with like-minded groups, thus linking up with a radical group from an East Jakarta mosque who were involved in quasi-military youth training exercises.

The New Order knew a threat to their power when they saw it. Moderate Islamic leaders voiced suspicions that the '*Jihad* Command' was being used to discredit their religion when in 1981 an 'Islamic Revolutionary Council', supposedly connected to the Command, hijacked an aeroplane of Garuda, Indonesia's national carrier. Throughout the 1980s other actions occurred, some through *agents provocateurs*, including the bombing of a bank belonging to a businessman linked to Suharto, and the ancient Buddhist monument of Borobudur in Central Java.

The major event in the manipulation of Islam took place in the harbour area of Tanjung Priok in Jakarta in 1984. Preceded by strongly worded sermons, defamatory posters, and rumours of unrest, a riot took place outside a mosque. A heavy army presence suddenly materialised, and the rioters found themselves trapped in a confined area, where they were quickly gunned down by the troops. Officially fifty were killed, but more realistic estimates give the number of dead as ten times that.

The Tanjung Priok riot was used by the government as an excuse to crack down on all forms of Islamic radicalism. Outspoken preachers and politicians, along with those who actually did have more hard-line aims, were arrested, tried and gaoled, often on flimsy charges. The wearing of Islamic headscarves was banned in schools. Sungkar's *pesantren* in Surakarta was closed down, and many of the cadres not arrested fled to Lampung in South Sumatra, where they later led another anti-government revolt that was violently put down in 1989, when over 250 died.[14] One of the other senior leaders of the *pesantren*, Abu Bakar Basyir, fled to Malaysia after having been gaoled for three years by Suharto. He was to return at the end of the 1990s with a more extreme challenge to the secular state. This was inspired by Islamic leaders from the Middle East who had joined an armed defence of Islam in Afghanistan and who opposed the corrupting effects of Western secular society. In the 1970s and 1980s the Indonesian government accused those they thought linked to Islamic opposition of belonging to 'the Islamic congregation', a generic term that has since become famous as *Jemaah Islamiyah*, the designation used for the terrorist cell under Abu Bakar Basyir responsible for the October 2002 Bali bombings.[15]

Islam was described by government ministers as the force of the 'extreme right', which like the 'extreme left', Communism, had to be controlled by the government. One result of this control was that Muslims believed that their religion was under threat. They were, as one sociologist put it, a 'majority with a minority mentality'.[16] Innocuous gestures, such as the wearing of headscarves, had become politicised, which meant that those looking for a voice to oppose the government could channel their energies into religion.

Different religious leaders adopted different strategies to survive the crack-down on Islam. The traditionalist Council of Scholars, NU, when told to become part of the PPP, declared that it was going to do what the government wanted and would be apolitical, so it would not need to become part of the government's party. The NU wanted to be involved only in social work, such as campaigns to improve the welfare of the poor. This oblique method of survival was the brainchild of a new generation of intellectuals in the group, led by future president Abdurrahman Wahid, the wily grandson of the NU's founder and son of Wahid Hasyim, Indonesia's first minister of religion in 1945. Despite government attempts to manipulate the organisation through spies and appointees, this natural leader, popularly known as Gus Dur, was elected and remained chairman of the NU from the 1980s throughout the 1990s, a gentle but persistent voice of opposition to the Suharto regime.

One of the by-products of the revival of House of Islam sentiments was that it encouraged local leaders in Aceh to reignite their own ambitions for a separate Muslim state. In 1977 a Free Aceh Movement was proclaimed, without much support. By 1989 the situation had changed. Aceh had undergone a rapid boom thanks to its oil and other natural wealth, but that also meant increased attention from the government in Jakarta. A stronger central government presence coopted the local religious leadership in order to engineer good results for *Golkar* in the 1987 and 1992 elections. But that alienated the religious leadership from the majority of the population, particularly in rural areas. Rural Acehnese felt frozen out of a boom that was going on around them, and believed that a Javanese regime was taking control. As protest grew, so did the heavy-handed tactics of the military. Dissenters mysteriously disappeared, torture and murder were rumoured. Rather than terrify the population into submission, these brutal tactics helped the Free Aceh Movement to recruit followers. By 1992 a full-scale separatist revolt was under way, and would continue to wax and wane into the twenty-first century.[17]

The heavy hand of military terror played a similar role in Irian (West New Guinea) and in East Timor. In Irian the forcible integration involved in the 'Act of No Choice' had to be continually backed up. Any expression of dissent was ruthlessly squashed. A Papuan anthropologist, Arnold Ap, had been involved in preserving and promoting local music and other forms of cultural expression in the 1970s. The military saw this as potential support for separatist aspirations, so they arrested Ap as part of a crackdown on the Free Papua Movement. In 1984, Ap was shot in the back 'attempting to escape'.[18]

While the Free Papua Movement remained a small group fighting on with bows and arrows, the *Fretilin* Movement of East Timor had some modern weaponry from their brief period of government before the 1975 invasion, and were able to capture weapons from the Indonesian military in ambushes. Despite the capture and execution of *Fretilin*'s leader in 1978, they successfully waged a guerrilla struggle throughout the 1980s and 1990s. The fact that they were able to kill some 20,000 Indonesian troops in twenty years of fighting did not lessen the suffering of ordinary East Timorese, like Isabella, a woman in the capital Dili who recalled that 'to live in Dili was not happy. There was a lot of fear. The future was always uncertain. You heard shots, you saw piles of soldiers' bodies in sacks. You just worked, didn't dare think – your life may be very short.'[19] As in Aceh and Irian, constant military use of murder, torture and rape, and the abduction of children, to control the population, increased, rather than diminished, support for those who wanted an independent East Timor. Mr Hong, an ethnic Chinese East Timorese, was typical of those who were not involved in the fighting but got caught up in it. He described his experience of torture, of electric shocks and beatings, to an Australian researcher: 'When they beat me they ask always if this person or that person is Fretilin. But then I really don't know. So they keep beating me. They say I should know and then they beat me.'[20] Such actions were never going to convince East Timorese that they should be part of Indonesia.

The military used the heavily censored reports of what was going on in the outlying provinces to argue that the army was an essential part of the state, because they guarded the nation from separatist disintegration. The police force was a branch of the military, not a separate civil organisation, so they were also a part of what ordinary people saw as state power used to suppress society, the 'order' of the New Order. In the wake of political upheavals in 1974, state security activities were tightened. In particular, the various intelligence agencies were coordinated by a centralised authority that could monitor the population.

BENEFITS OF DEVELOPMENT

While fear can explain the struggles for control on the margins of the Indonesian state, on its own it cannot explain why Suharto was able to stay in power for over thirty years. His regime also provided the population with ritual displays to promote the appearance of inclusiveness, and with unprecedented economic growth that created wealth for some, and the anticipation of wealth for others. It was those ritual displays to which Pramoedya referred when he wrote about the return of feudalism under Suharto.

During the period when Pramoedya's Buru novels were being published and banned, a young playwright, Norbertus Riantiarno, wrote *The Cockroach Opera* for his Comma Theatre. It, too, was banned. *The Cockroach Opera*, modelled on Brecht's *Threepenny Opera*, was a

Figure 7.2 Stamp showing President Suharto as Chief Scout of Indonesia, 1993.

celebration of the under-life of the big city, the prostitutes, transvestites, pimps and gangsters who live on the streets and in the slums, who, like cockroaches, could survive anything. Riantiarno's piece was produced to show an audience of a growing middle class how the underclass lived, whilst satirising the actions of the bureaucratic elite.

Scene (15):
[Foreign aid guest, Indonesian officials, photographers, security guards arrive first to cover up slum shacks]

GUEST:	(in English [the language of prestige]): 'Wonderful. Great. Satisfactory'. Foreign aid that has really been used appropriately ...
FIRST OFFICIAL:	This is nothing yet. On that empty piece of land in front, we're going to build schools, public libraries, houses of worship, and markets for petty traders. Everything for the prosperity of the people.
GUEST:	A noble plan. Once more, amazing ...
SECOND OFFICIAL:	And not only that – art and culture will also be given attention. We will erect facilities for all of that over here. Yes, there. The vitality of the arts, modern as well as traditional, will continue to be subsidised. This is important – and of course, has been the nature of our people since the age of Majapahit and the Javanese kings ... Ancient remains are to be rebuilt, all of them, and even cemeteries revered by their communities will be restored. Our descendants must know in the future that our generation had great respect for ancestral history. A generation with great respect for cemeteries ...
SECOND OFFICIAL:	And monuments. We will erect a monument for each event, the common as well as the heroic. If there are a million heroes, we'll build a million monuments ... The Bleeding Hearts say that rice is more important than monuments. But we and the masses say: monuments are important. Monuments are just like wearing pants. Civilisation.[21]

The play homes in on the twin pillars of support for the New Order, its vision of a compartmentalised Indonesian culture that was subject to government control, and its promise of development. By the end of the New Order, almost every major intersection or public site in Indonesia had been filled with a monument that gave cultural form to development, from the giant statue of Christ that was the regime's gift to the people of East

Timor, to the smaller statues commemorating local military leaders from the Revolution in country towns.

The radical leftism of Sukarno's rule had provided a vision of an ultra-modern Indonesia, in which the PKI and Sukarno's other modernists fought feudalism and imperialism as their enemies. In the years of destruction that followed 1965, the corollary of this radical vision was the assertion of tradition, a return to the feudal.

Suharto chose Javanese culture, the feudal culture in which he had grown up, as the embodiment of the values of his regime. Up until the late 1990s he fostered an image of himself as an adherent of Javanese mysticism. Even in the dying years of his regime, rumours abounded that he had summoned a council of all the greatest shamans, spiritual teachers and mystics to the family's Bali Cliff Hotel to stave up his rule against the economic and political pressures that threatened it.

Madame Tien Suharto's 'Garden of Indonesia in Miniature' project, her family links to the royal house of Surakarta, and rumours spread by flatterers that Suharto had royal ancestry all contributed to this image of Suharto as a Javanese king. Suharto family weddings were choreographed in the style of Javanese royalty, and set the tone for the culture of the ruling elite. The rituals that they encouraged were bowdlerised versions of real Javanese rituals, with any raucous expressions of conflict removed.[22] These rituals emphasised display of wealth: for example, the traditional *batik* cloths of Central Java that were a key part of royal ceremonies were considered too dull, with their browns and deep indigo blues, so in New Order-style they were overlaid with gold paint. Gold paint took on a life of its own, as it spread to interior decoration and public ornaments, its ubiquity synonymous with the nouveau-riche culture of rule.

As non-Javanese politicians and generals were pushed out of the power group, those outside Jakarta felt more and more marginalised. The government's style was to emphasise the power of the centre and the peripheral nature of each of the regions, whereas Sukarno had pandered to regional pride during his very public visits around the country.

The only New Order concession to regions was towards cultural arte-facts, but in a way that emphasised hierarchy. The peoples of Irian were told they were 'still primitive', so the Dani of the highlands were allowed to wear traditional penis gourds, but only over baggy shorts. At the same time the government sponsored programmes to preserve tradition. Selected aspects of cultural performance that were considered to be representative of their regions – without, of course, being at all political in content – were selected for display in Jakarta, in particular in the 'Garden of Indonesia in

Miniature'. Even when such performances were new versions of local arts, they were slotted into the category of representations of ancient heritage.[23] Annual National Day programmes within and outside Indonesia fore-grounded this cultural selection process. As part of a performance entitled 'Unity in Diversity' (the national motto), couples paraded in regional examples of wedding costumes, the acme of traditional dress. The gold paint on the Central Javanese *batiks* was matched by gold threads on textiles from other regions, such as Minangkabau and Sulawesi. On such occasions the embarrassing costumes actually worn by peoples of Irian were replaced by suede jackets and pants with shredded fringing, modelled on what 'Indians' wore in old American western films. Selected traditional dances and music completed the national display.

Yet most of the Indonesians who went to such events were more interested in the stand-up comedy routines based on groups made famous by television, or went to hear pop music. The popular 'Coffee Stall' ensemble exemplified the style of comedy that received the biggest audiences, a modernised form of the clown scenes of local theatre styles. The music style most popular in the 1980s was called *dangdut*, which mixed musical forms from the Middle East and South Asia with elements of Sumatran and urban Javanese musical styles. The lyrics were often risqué, but *dangdut* was adopted as the preferred musical style of modern Islamic gatherings, its popularity a testimony to the fact that as much as the government wanted to control and engineer all aspects of culture into an essential and value-free version of tradition, culture is not a thing to be controlled.

THE DEVELOPMENT STATE

The identification of the state with 'development' as satirised in the *Cockroach Opera* stems from the literal meaning of the word in Indonesian. It means 'building'. Development spread rapidly throughout the late 1970s and 1980s as grand government buildings appeared in each provincial capital, making liberal use of concrete, thanks to the national cement monopoly owned by one of Suharto's cronies. Vast amounts of money from international aid combined with state revenue to create this growth. During the period of the New Order the average annual increase in gross national product was a remarkable 6.7 per cent, which on a per capita basis made Indonesia a leader amongst the fastest-growing economies of the world.[24]

That it took until the late 1970s for development to take hold says something about the nature of the New Order state. Indonesia was one of the major world oil producers, and the international oil crisis of the early 1970s was expected to make the country rich in a short time. The boost from oil revenues did indeed help the government's team of 'technocratic' advisers get the economy under control and start a series of five-year plans, but in 1974 the state oil company was suddenly revealed to be bankrupt.

Lieutenant-General Ibnu Sutowo (1914–2001) had been installed as head of Pertamina, the state-owned oil company, by General Nasution when Dutch assets were nationalised in 1957, despite (or some say because of) involvement in smuggling during the early 1950s. During the emergency cabinets of 1966 he became minister for mining and energy, before being reconfirmed by Suharto as head of Pertamina. Sutowo's younger brother had been Communist mayor of Surabaya, but Pertamina was a vital element in Suharto's establishment of rule, so the family connection that would have ruined others was ignored. Through Pertamina, Suharto, and other members of the power group, had ready access to an ongoing source of funding which meant that they were not accountable. They ran this cash-cow into the ground, using it for both military and personal ends. For example, Ibnu Sutowo paid over US$1 million for his daughter's wedding in 1973, and indulged in lavish displays of hospitality as well as personal signs of status such as gold-plated fittings on his Rolls-Royce.

Sutowo's mismanagement left the company US$15 billion in debt when borrowing restrictions prevented him from rolling-over debts. He was never held responsible for this. All errors and corruption were attributed to deputies, and Sutowo was allowed to quietly retire, later becoming head of the Red Cross in Indonesia. His family remained in the power group, his son taking over the franchise of Hilton Hotels in Indonesia given to Sutowo by one of Suharto's Special Presidential Advisers. Sutowo also sponsored B. J. Habibie, a brilliant, eccentric, engineer whose family would go into business with Suharto's children, and who succeeded Suharto as president in 1999. Ibnu Sutowo's son, Pontjo, became head of the Indonesian Hotels Association, and in 2004 passed management of the Hilton Group to his own son. Pontjo's sister became director of a leading bank that was saved from collapse by government intervention during the economic crisis of 1997. On his death in 2001, Ibnu Sutowo was interred in the National Heroes' Cemetery at Kalibata, in Jakarta.[25] In the early hours of New Year's Day 2005 Sutowo's youngest son was arrested in the bar of the Hilton Hotel, Jakarta. According to witnesses, when the woman with whom he was drinking had her expired credit card returned by a young part-time waiter, the young Sutowo said, 'Don't you know who I am?', and then pulled a gun and shot the waiter dead.

The Sutowo story was typical of the way Indonesia's vast wealth was used during the Suharto years – some deployed for projects to help the poor, but not before huge amounts were raked off for the benefit of the governing group. Alliances with powerful ethnic Chinese-Indonesian businesses helped to confirm the power of the ruling group, and to exaggerate the negative image of ethnic Chinese amongst ordinary Indonesians. Monopolies or near monopolies on such important areas as production of cement and timber licences were given to key Chinese-Indonesian entrepreneurs who acted as agents for the Suharto family or other generals.

By sharing these benefits within the group, Suharto was able to buy loyalty and keep tight control over economic power. This resulted in a mixed economic legacy. While there is no doubting the considerable achievements in improving Indonesia's economic life, the long-term effects of New Order policies have seen Indonesia lose its position in world trade, to the point where its share by the 1990s was almost one-third of the levels under the Dutch. The Suharto government's economic policies were a struggle between the US-trained technocrats who fought for deregulation, and Suharto's own tendency towards economic nationalism, which placed great store in import substitution and control via tariffs, quotas and subsidies. Two devaluations of the Rupiah, in 1978 and 1986, coincided with rises in influence of the technocrats, but support of national industries was important because this helped businesses owned by the ruling family and their cronies. The national budget underreported revenues and over-reported expenditures, as revealed by investigations in 1981, a clear indicator that something untoward was going on.[26]

By the late 1990s, the president had set up his children as heads of conglomerates, including in banking, road tolls, hotel and shopping centre development, and television stations. One son, Tommy, took over the state clove monopoly, buying cheaply in order to sell to the *kretek* cigarette manufacturers at five times the rate paid to farmers, even if one of those manufacturing companies had been taken over by one of Tommy's sisters in 1990.[27] Suharto, Murtopo and the other masterminds of the New Order put great emphasis on Indonesia as corporate state, underpinned by 'family' values. Suharto's version of family values was enrichment for his children, in-laws and grandchildren.

Although some economists have argued that the New Order created local capitalism, in most cases business empires were not established through investment, but by forceful appropriation. If a local business started to expand, one of the Suharto family or their friends would 'offer' to become a 'partner'. Shares were signed over to the family member, but at no cost. Control over banks gave the conglomerates ready sources of capital. When it was time for annual audits, the books would be handed over accompanied by a gun, a message that the accountant should not identify any irregularities. Auditors for the state bank commissioned to examine projects funded by major loans were told not to report any 'bad news'. Economists, Indonesian and foreign, duly endorsed the resulting figures as indicators of the New Order's success.

The agglomeration of money and power made Jakarta the centre of the nation. Until 1965 the organisation of power in Indonesia had been Java versus the Outer Islands, but under the New Order it was Jakarta versus the rest. Even other parts of Java were left out of key decisions and power plays. Major projects were distributed from the centre, and civil servants received their instructions from Jakarta – local initiatives were frowned upon. Reports from below were always positive, and the culture of the bureaucracy became one of 'as long as the boss is happy'.

Centrally controlled projects raised the standard of living unevenly because corruption was so entrenched. A 1970s example from the state oil company, Pertamina, was typical of the general pattern. Pertamina ordered expensive pipes for its pumping stations from a Japanese company, but those responsible for making the payment acquired inferior quality pipes that leaked so badly that it took four times as long to transport the oil as it would have for good quality pipes. At each stage of the transaction chain somebody was getting a percentage, so that the money left over for buying the actual pipes was a small proportion of the recorded total. If accidents occurred, as in 1972 when eighty impoverished people died in an explosion as they scavenged petroleum from one of the leaking pipes, they could be covered up. Such commissions from Jakarta to local contractors occurred in projects funded by World Bank loans, and at the end of the Suharto era, the Bank itself could not deny that between 20 and 30 per cent of all their US$25 billion in loans had disappeared in this manner.[28] Such debts had to be repaid, and as a result Indonesia became one of the world's largest debtor nations.

Becoming a state official meant getting a share of the commissions. At the lower levels of the bureaucracy, the corruption of superiors encouraged petty corruption, such as bribes to process forms, 'cigarette money' for any transaction. People at higher levels offered large gifts to gain connections with the Suharto family and their friends. At lower levels parents would pay the equivalent of thousands of dollars to buy positions for their children in areas of the civil service or the police force that offered access to illicit income. A desirable area into which to buy was the traffic police, whose main activity was collecting bribes. In one of the periodic attempts to stimulate the economy under the government's five-year plans, in 1985 the entire customs service was paid to stay at home while their work was outsourced to a Swiss company so that import and export goods could move freely.[29]

Despite the system of fraud and fakery the New Order put in place, there were genuine successes. Even though the number of qualified medical practitioners in the country remained only in the thousands until the 1980s, remote regions received basic health care in the form of rural nurses and polyclinics. According to official figures passed on to the World Bank, infant mortality rates, which had been at disastrous levels of 200–300 per 1,000 births during Dutch colonial rule, had fallen to 56 per 1,000 by 1995. Allowing for the dubious nature of Indonesian statistics, this was still an achievement of great meaning to people's lives. Underlining this was an increase in basic subsistence and health, as average daily caloric intake increased from 2,035 in 1968 to 2,781 in 1990.[30]

A key part of the health care programme of the New Order was family planning. Initiated in the 1970s as part of the process of regulating marriage, family planning was initially opposed by leaders of various religions, but was pushed through by the government. Each village or urban neighbourhood was given instruction about family size, in a campaign using the slogan 'two is enough'. In this campaign the ideal Indonesian family was depicted as father, mother, son and daughter, wearing conservative Westernised costumes of civil service uniform and school uniforms for the father and children, and sarong and *kebaya* top for the mother. Village heads were expected to establish and monitor family planning programmes, mainly using intra-uterine devices. In their offices, these heads had lists of every family displayed publicly on blackboards, with indicators of what kinds of contraception the families used. Contraception was made available to families only after they had two children, and there was no attention paid to the growing evidence that some of the forms of contraception had dangerous side-effects, including infection and sterility. With its combination of surrealistic formalism and actual success, the Family Planning Programme was typical of New Order projects. It did slow down the rate of population growth. In the 1970s, government officials and outside analysts estimated that left unchecked, the population would rise from 110 million at that time to between 250 and 300 million by 2001. In 2001 the population reached the family planning target of 210 million.[31]

Benevolent paternalism also increased the number of schools and trained teachers, but the teachers were so poorly paid that they usually had to moonlight in private schools or find other employment, meaning that there was no time for lesson development or attention to the educational needs of students. The school curriculum was heavily imbued with the New Order version of history and the message that society should be the passive recipient of government wisdom. Basic education was achieved for the whole population, a miraculous achievement, but the skill level of the workforce was not greatly improved, and throughout the Suharto era Indonesia remained a source of cheap labour for foreign companies, with the lowest wage levels in South-east Asia.[32]

The New Order's rise to power coincided with the most dramatic change in Third World agriculture of the twentieth century, the Green Revolution. With funding from international aid agencies, scientists in the Philippines developed new strains of rice that allowed for more intensive farming. Whereas older varieties of rice could only produce one or at most two crops a year, the new varieties allowed two or three crops on the same plot of land.

The Green Revolution came to Indonesia in the late 1960s, but it was not until the mid-1970s that it began to take over in most rice-growing areas. Farmers complained that the new varieties of rice tasted bland, and indeed they did have lower nutrient content. More important to the structure of rural economies, the new varieties depended on heavy use of fertiliser and insecticides, which locked peasants into government subsidy schemes, and ultimately had devastating effects on the delicate ecologies of the Indonesian islands. Whereas the old varieties had to be harvested by peasant women working collectively and using labour-intensive small knives, the new varieties could be harvested with sickles by fewer people. With the Green Revolution came labour-reducing mechanised threshing and milling processes, irrevocably changing the lives of the peasantry, causing mass unemployment and pushing farmers into a more commercialised world, albeit one mediated by government agencies. Despite droughts at the end of the 1970s and in the early 1980s, Indonesia increased its overall rice production markedly, until it could claim to be a net exporter, rather than an importer, of rice.[33]

In the villages of Indonesia people commonly refer to the period before the 1970s as 'before electricity'. The 1970s saw major improvements in the provision of basic infrastructure throughout most of the islands, including electricity and clean running water. Significant improvements in transport, especially the building of sound roads that linked up with major highways running through each of the islands, broke down the barriers of distance to trade and communication. Conversation between people from different parts of the archipelago was often a comparison between the quality of infrastructure: 'my village road has just been upgraded to three layers of bitumen.' The government always reminded people of its benevolent role in these improvements, with huge signs depicting President Suharto, clad in safari suit, overseeing the planting of rice, proclaiming that he was 'the Father of Development'. Members of the military were sent on regular assignments to villages to help with local projects, as a way of demonstrating unity with the people, and students were sent to live in villages as a form of internship. The effects were sometimes quite different from the intention of these strategies, however. For villagers, the presence of the military was a reminder of control, while for students, experiences of village life engendered a social awareness that had a radical potential.

During the 1980s, Indonesians became more aware that they were Indonesians. They had greater interaction with their fellow citizens and greater mobility. The levels of interaction were uneven, because prosperity was unevenly spread. Jakarta, the source of wealth and power, was the centre of integration, to which people from all over the archipelago moved to study and work. Some of the areas rich in primary products, notably parts of Kalimantan, kept part of the income from those products, although this was not the case in Aceh and Irian, which were poor in terms of standard of living, despite their oil and mineral wealth. As development took on different forms in the 1980s, different regions rose in prosperity. When tourism became a major foreign investment earner, Bali, the centre of tourism, became one of the wealthiest provinces, envied by all the others. When Singapore entered into an agreement to co-develop part of the Riau archipelago, the cost of living in Batam city, the centre of that development, was almost equal to Jakarta's. Indicators such as access to radio and television, and standards of health care, show that areas such as the Southeastern Islands became poorer and poorer in relation to the advantaged areas.

One province that was a success story in this era was East Java, which achieved a balance in the nature of its development between high growth rates and income disparity. Numbers of absolute poor were reduced from two-thirds to one-third of the population by the 1980s. This development was achieved without substantial foreign investment, but instead growth in agriculture went hand-in-hand with growth of areas of manufacturing, from the cigarette industry of the north coast to the production of prawn crackers or *krupuk* in Sidoarjo, just south of Surabaya. The locus of Indonesia's poverty had moved away from Java.[34]

Increased mobility meant more people moving to cities, and throughout the 1980s the distinction between 'country' and 'city' blurred. Some people moved between rural and urban employment. For example Budi, a young man from a rice-farming family in Central Java, worked part of the time on his family rice farm outside Yogyakarta, but the rest of the year pedalled a trishaw or *becak* in the area of the city south of the Sultan's palace, to which growing numbers of tourists were coming. In this and the other tourist area near the railway station, there were always more *becak* drivers than passengers, so Budi would pass his days playing chess with his colleagues until he could strike it lucky and get a tourist who would pay more than the usual fare, and perhaps give him enough to live off for a few days. Budi would have been counted as employed and boosted the government's unemployment statistics, but he was one of the 30 or 40 million underemployed whose occasional income gave them the US$1 a day needed to put them above the official poverty line.

New Order culture favoured sanitised depictions of the remote past to engagement with social issues in the arts, but a few film-makers attempted to come to terms with the gulf between rich and poor. The film *My Sky, My Home*, made in 1989 by brothers Slamet Rahardjo and Eros Djarot, showed the parallel lives of a Jakarta street kid, Gempol, and his friend from a wealthy family, Andri. The film attempted to demonstrate that it is possible to bridge the huge gap in experience between rich and poor through its presentations of their lives, but ultimately this has remained an unbreachable gap in perceptions. Because it called for the gap to be breached, and also because it made veiled criticisms of the government's failure to deliver on its promises of social prosperity, the film was controversial in Indonesia, and Suharto's stepbrother, who owned the major film distribution chain in Indonesia, attempted to have it withdrawn from screening. Street children remain a major problem in Indonesian cities, their lives lived by begging at traffic lights, prostitution or petty theft, their only ambition, according to Topo, a street child of Java, 'To become an old street kid'. One of his colleagues put it in these terms, 'It must be nice to be a neighbourhood kid. You go to school in the morning and when you come home all you have to do is eat. It's not like being a street kid who has to fight for the leftovers.'[35]

During the 1980s, factories were set up in rural areas, as urban sprawl met rice-fields. The area from Bali to Riau became one almost continuous urban corridor, linked up through the infrastructure and the movement of labour to Singapore, Kuala Lumpur, Bangkok and beyond. At the same time, people in cities still largely thought of their suburbs or quarters as transplanted villages. City authorities did their best to establish demarcation lines, as when the mayor of Jakarta attempted to declare the capital a 'closed city' to new migrants, but there was a disparity between the formal definition of the city and the true area of urbanisation. To reinforce the idea of keeping the centre of the city as a separate area, and to control the traffic, successive mayors of Jakarta have tried to expel *becaks* from the streets. But by the 1990s, the official population of the capital fluctuated by 3 million people a day, the number who commuted from outlying towns such as Tangeran, Bekasi and even the former Dutch hill station of Bogor.

Where did all those women go who lost their rural employment as a result of the Green Revolution? They started making clothes. The low skill levels required and surplus labour available helped Indonesia to boost its manufacturing sector in the 1980s. Despite primary school levels of education being provided to all, Indonesia lagged behind many Asian countries in its expenditure on education, and the proportion of those achieving secondary education during the Suharto era actually fell, an indicator that fewer and fewer people were being equipped for anything other than basic labour. Government planners realised that they could not depend on oil and natural gas, particularly after a downturn in the prices of oil and other commodities in 1981. Thus incentives were given to foreign and local investors to build up basic manufacturing. Existing enterprises such as North Java's *kretek* cigarette industry expanded on the back of cheap female labour and mechanisation of production in the 1970s and 1980s, as did the textile and garment industries of Java and Bali. Young women moved away from their villages to board in big factories, or to become outworkers in small rooms set up by sub-contractors. The cheapness of their labour inhibited manufacturers from investing in higher levels of technology.[36]

Sari, in her twenties and working twelve hours a day, six or seven days a week in a garment factory in Central Java for less than minimum wages, was typical of the young women of the new workforce of the Suharto era. Such women had no recognised rights: their fathers – or husbands if they were married – had to provide written permission for them to make any decisions about work. When they were initially hired they were expected to work a few months without income, as an 'apprenticeship'. When they were paid, their salaries were always one to two months in arrears. As she and her friends explained to a foreign researcher, 'everybody's scared ... The Javanese people are like that y'know, always afraid of being fired.'[37] Sari and her friends complained to the Department of Manpower, a body which did nothing. Some of their contemporaries took stronger steps. Marsinah, a twenty-three-year-old factory worker in

East Java, organised her fellow workers in a watch factory, and threatened to publicise the fact that the factory was robbing the international companies to whom they were contracted. When Marsinah was raped, mutilated and murdered by security guards in 1993, her case attracted international attention and brought the spotlight on to the collusion of police, factory owners and local authorities that underpinned the New Order's development success in manufacturing.[38]

The expansion of manufacturing and tourism attracted workers to move to Java and Bali, but the last thing the government needed was more people on these the most densely populated islands on Earth. The answer to overpopulation was a policy called transmigration, an idea which came from Dutch policies. Suharto made transmigration one of his pet projects. Initial government plans were to move out 200,000 people per year, but this was never realistic, and the targets were regularly halved so that officials could report modest success. The scheme was funded by the World Bank, and so was seen as part of development aid.

Families induced to move travelled on rusty ships to remote locations. Major destinations included Sumatra (particularly Lampung and Jambi), Kalimantan and Sulawesi. The journey was often one full of anxiety, since those who travelled were often peasants who had never been out of their own village. As Mangku Lunas, an impoverished Balinese who moved to the eastern island of Sumbawa recalled of the journey, 'Everyone in our group was exhausted, and full of regrets, we felt miserable and couldn't sleep.' They went driven by poverty – 'we felt embarrassed because we were so poor' – knew nothing of where they were going, and found themselves in more and more isolated locations as they moved closer to their destinations. Left in the jungle or on wasteland with only bare necessities, Balinese and Javanese transmigrants struggled to set up wet-rice farming terrace systems. In Lunas's community they suffered through three seasons of crop failure and a major flood, enduring major disease outbreaks that killed a large number of people. Those who persevered were eventually rewarded with prosperity. They could buy horses and cattle, radios, bicycles and carts, and build shrines and temples 'as results of development'.[39]

The government put particular pressure on transmigrants to move to East Timor as a way of Indonesianising the province, in particular of increasing the Muslim population of this largely Christian and pagan region. Since news censorship did not allow transmigrants to get an accurate picture of the state of unrest in East Timor, many were shocked to find that they were pawns in a major conflict, constantly under threat of attack by East Timorese resistance fighters, and heavily resented by the local population whose land had often been appropriated by the government for the programme.

Many transmigrants simply gave up and went home after a few years. A few succeeded and obtained a level of prosperity that would have been impossible if they had remained on their island of origin, and in this they contributed to the integration of Indonesia that was the general effect of the New Order's policies. They remained in their new homes as wealthy citizens who were able to send their children to school in Jakarta or other major centres. The transmigrants were joined by unsponsored internal migrants. Throughout the east of Indonesia, from West Papua to East Timor, the entrepreneurial cultures of South Sulawesi left their mark as members of the Makasar, Bugis and Butonese ethnic groups set up stalls and shops that grew into major enclaves. A popular saying has it that if you climb the most remote mountain in Indonesia you will find at the summit a food stall set up by a Makasar, Bugis or Butonese. The infertile and overcrowded island of Madura was a major source of migration to other parts of Indonesia, particularly to Kalimantan.

The influx of transmigrants to Kalimantan occurred at the same time as forestry was expanded. Logging companies from neighbours such as Malaysia were given huge concessions to turn the giant rainforests into pulp for Japanese paper mills. While world environmental attention was turned to areas such as Brazil, Indonesia's forests disappeared, their removal concealed by official statistics that showed they were being managed efficiently. The real situation was only revealed when forest fires began during annual dry seasons in the areas that had been stripped. Since much of the forest area of Kalimantan is on peat soil, once started the fires took months to be extinguished. As areas larger than the whole of Tasmania burned, huge palls of smoke engulfed neighbouring Singapore and Malaysia. Some of these fires were encouraged by Suharto cronies who set up palm plantations in the cleared areas, to provide cooking oil for international fast food chains.

By the 1990s New Order development had produced a large group of Indonesians who shared in the wealth through patronage from the ruling group, generally spoken of as 'connections'. The ruling class had extended into an upper middle class, generally known as the New Rich, who lived in large white air-conditioned monumental mansions in suburbs such as Pondok Indah on the outskirts of Jakarta. The New Rich travelled everywhere in chauffeur-driven air-conditioned cars, shopped in the shiny new shopping malls of suburbs such as nearby Kemang, the home of growing numbers of well-paid expatriate professionals, or lunched at the splendid five-star hotels in the centre of the city where a cup of coffee would cost the equivalent of two weeks' worth of meals at one of the nearby street stalls of the poor.[40] In the greater Jakarta area there were new self-contained suburbs built for the middle class, such as Lippo-Karawaci, a company town established one hour's hair-raising taxi ride away along the toll-ways owned by Suharto's daughter Tutut. In the centre of Lippo-Karawaci is the largest of the Matahari shopping malls that are part of the Lippo group of companies, and the town's quiet, uncrowded nature is very different from the hectic scenes of broken footpaths, milling street sellers and polluting traffic jams in central Jakarta.

The children of New Order prosperity grew up in families that were aware of the precariousness of their situations. Having lived through the economic and political upheavals of earlier eras, their parents knew that at any time they could be put out in the streets or thrown in gaol. Yet these families were also the audience of Riantiarno's *Cockroach Opera*, and the readers of Pramoedya's illegally circulated novels. Pramoedya, quite rightly, identified the youth of the middle class as the engines of change. Increasing numbers of them went to study in Western universities. As Suharto's grip on power became more monolithic, the growing middle class felt they were prevented from making decisions about their lives. Displays of feudal-style paternalism and sham elections were no longer enough, they wanted real democracy.

By the 1990s the children of the middle class were developing a different style of politics. They could not set up political parties, but their non-governmental organisations (NGOs) became ubiquitous. Some of these organisations protested in the 1980s and early 1990s against the dispossession of peasants whose land was appropriated for dams or other development projects. Others protested against the environmental destruction carried out by the logging companies. Legal aid organisations supported peasant actions against land developments. By the 1990s, NGOs were linking up with growing workers' movements, and it was thanks to such links that Marsinah's murder in 1993 received international attention. Islamic groups also formed their own NGOs, trying to avoid government attempts to control and monitor their activities.

The state intelligence bodies had ambitions of totalitarian control, but had limited resources to carry these out, since many of their agents were more concerned with finding ways to increase their own income through selling drugs or taking bribes than in state security. While NGO activists were monitored, and could be hauled in at any time, the New Order felt complacent enough to let them keep operating. The appearance of order was always maintained, statistics concocted to show that economic growth was on the increase, and reports were sent to keep the boss happy. Suharto's regime was a bubble, but one that took a remarkably long time to burst.

CHAPTER 8

Age of globalisation, age of crisis

The view that history is the story of the lives of those who want to grasp the power of the throne means that in our cultural life we know nothing but power. We have not known humanity as the driving concept in life and in our traditional art and culture. Forgive me if I am mistaken.

Pramoedya Ananta Toer[1]

OPENNESS AND THE FALL OF SUHARTO

The 1980s was an exceptional period in Indonesia's history. The near monopoly on violence by the government meant that it could maintain an image of quiescence that assured it of international support. Western countries built up close relations with Indonesia, particularly with the military, to whom Britain sold arms, the US provided intelligence training and Australia co-sponsored exercises with the Special Forces Command, the elite troops responsible for maintaining control in the rebellious provinces. Inside and outside Indonesia, authoritarianism was seen as the price the country paid for development, a view that served the interests of Western governments keen to support the operations of multinational oil and mineral companies in Indonesia.

There was always some room for dissent in the New Order. Pramoedya and his fellow leftists who were sent from Buru to house arrest could not express themselves in the mass media, but many others could. In the mid-1980s a coalition of discontented military figures, including former head of the armed forces, General Nasution, former prime ministers, conservative regional politicians who had been important in the 1950s, and socialists who had been pushed out of power, organised a 'Petition of 50' which protested against corruption and abuse of power. Despite the fact that some of the signatories were gaoled, the petition provided a rallying point for middle-class activism, as a call for 'democratisation' spread into NGOs.

Dissident artists and writers continued to publish and perform protests. The most famous of these was W. S. Rendra, a poet and playwright. Rendra's poems provided a picture of tourist development prostituting Balinese culture, of the continued suffering of the poor, and of the processes of dispossession underlying development. He depicted multinational firms pushing aside isolated ethnic groups to strip the country of mineral wealth. Artists and NGOs publicised protests and repression that belied the appearance of order the regime wanted to convey. The hand of NGOs was strengthened by support from international agencies. The World Bank, realising that it was almost impossible to work through the corruption of the New Order, began to direct funding to NGOs as alternative social institutions.[2]

In 1989 the Cold War was declared officially over. Communism had fallen in Europe, and it was thought that China, Vietnam and the other Communist countries could not be far behind, as each declared that it would welcome market forces. The United States announced itself as the winner, its power in the world unchallengeable. Perhaps those like Pramoedya who suffered at the hands of the New Order's anti-Communist ideology could appreciate the irony that the end of the Cold War spelled the end of New Order power. The new US-sponsored ideology of free markets and political liberalism did not allow room for old Cold War dictators, and put pressure on the corrupt control of the economy exercised by Suharto, his family and friends.

Coinciding with the end of the Cold War Indonesia's government proclaimed a period of liberalisation of the economy, together with an official policy of social liberalism called 'Openness'. Laws restricting foreign investment, including purchase of land, were changed to allow a freer flow of capital, and suddenly the country was awash with money, as five-star hotels mushroomed in Bali and Jakarta's sky-scrapers trebled in number overnight. The economy was growing at an annual rate of over 7 per cent, inflation was low, and business boomed as Indonesia was hailed by international observers as an emerging 'New Tiger' of Asia.[3] The government could no longer exercise its tight control over the changes, nor claim the credit for prosperity.

Prosperity resulting from the boom manifested itself in signs of a new consumer culture. Shopping malls spread throughout the archipelago. The very poor were excluded from entry by vigilant security men, but the growing middle class and even the respectable working poor were allowed in. On Saturday nights students and the young women who worked in the garment factories could hang about in the mall, listening to Western and Indonesian popular music, or window shopping for the franchised international goods of Ralph Lauren or Body Shop. Indonesians who could not afford expensive foreign goods pooled their money to buy cheap copies so they could maintain the appearance of participating in consumer lifestyles. Young men would save up for a big date to take their girlfriends to McDonald's.[4]

While the new economic liberalism boosted pockets of prosperity in places such as Bali, Batam and Jakarta, it did nothing to narrow the gap between rich and poor. Overall the number of those living below the poverty line dropped markedly to just over 10 million in 1996. Sectors such as manufacturing continued to improve as export earners. The gap between rich and poor became a gap between urban and country dwellers, as rice production flattened out in the mid-1990s, and Indonesia moved further away from its rural roots. Import substitution programmes, designed to bolster local manufacture and lessen reliance on foreign goods, combined with government subsidies of essentials such as rice and petroleum to protect ordinary Indonesians against the more exploitative aspects of the world economy, but by the 1990s the international buzz-word of 'globalisation' was being used by the Indonesia media in general and Western-trained economists in particular who wanted to do away with tariffs and welfare programmes.[5]

One of the most far-reaching changes in government attitude was a U-turn in the handling of Islam. No longer was Islam to be repressed, but rather the government provided support. A new officially approved body, the Association of Indonesian Muslim Intellectuals (ICMI) appeared. ICMI signalled a recognition amongst Suharto strategists that the ruling group was too closed and too alienated from any support base to be able to maintain power. It was designed to appeal to the influential new group currently being identified by foreign and indigenous scholars – 'the middle class' – but in a way that still kept the ruling class in power. The key players included genuine Muslim intellectuals who had come out of the traditional institutions of *pesantren* and Islamic higher education colleges, key liberals involved in the original creation of the New Order – some of whom had been able to remain unsullied in the sinkhole of Suharto corruption – and a representative of the Suharto group's interests, B. J. Habibie.

Habibie, of Javanese and Bugis ethnicity, had known Suharto when the latter was in Sulawesi in 1950. Suharto recognised the far-sighted intelligence of Habibie, who went on to gain a doctorate in engineering in Germany, and then become the first non-German vice-president of Messerschmitt. Suharto encouraged Habibie to come back to Indonesia. Later, when a minister, Habibie sought to bring his national vision of rapid technological development to fruition via a national aircraft corporation. Habibie's idea of a high-tech kickstart to jerk Indonesia out of its poverty was sound, but he never found the right conditions to realise this plan. The levels of technical training and infrastructure, and the constant siphoning of funds for personal purposes, meant that the aeroplanes produced did not meet international quality standards. Like other products of the New Order, they were all appearance, and no substance. Nevertheless, Suharto continued to bestow his personal patronage, grooming Habibie as a likely successor, and at the beginning of 1998 finally making him vice-president.[6]

However briefly, the Association of Muslim Intellectuals did answer the aspirations of many in the Muslim community for a political and social voice. Dissidents found some common ground with those close to government, and felt that they were being heard. Limited access to politics was opened to people such as Dr Amien Rais, a Central Javanese political scientist who combined membership of the Association of Indonesian Muslim Intellectuals with leadership of the modernist Muslim educational body, *Muhammadiyah*, which claimed a membership of 20 million. However uneasy the alliance with Habibie, ICMI served to provide links to a popular base that the increasingly moribund government political body *Golkar* did not.

Muslim traditionalists preferred to participate in the 30 million-strong NU (*Nahdlatul Ulama*) which had opted out of direct politics under Abdurrahman Wahid, Gus Dur. Ever a slippery politician, Gus Dur proclaimed that he would cooperate with the regime. He also sought out links to the NGOs, now growing into a dissident movement of their own in the space offered to them by the 'Openness' policy, and to other religions through a series of inter-faith dialogues.

The talk about 'globalisation' was a two-edged sword during the 1990s. For opponents of the regime such as Gus Dur, it served as a way of showing that the government could not control all aspects of life, and that Indonesia was increasingly under international scrutiny. Whereas once unfavourable international media reports could be blacked out or cut out of imported magazines, the growth of new forms of media meant that controlling information was getting harder and harder. This was dramatically illustrated in 1991, when Indonesian troops massacred East Timorese protesters in Dili. Although hardly the first military massacre in the province, it was the first televised massacre, as a Western journalist was able to smuggle footage of the killings out to world attention. Subsequently copies of this footage were circulated back to Indonesia through videos brought in through NGO networks. Indonesians now had a chance to find out what their government was doing. A few daring student magazines began publishing interviews with Pramoedya about the history and future of Indonesia.

'Openness' was a fleeting policy, lasting from the late 1980s until 1994. In July 1994, the regime demonstrated that 'Openness' was just another form of manipulation by closing down three magazines that had published information on how Habibie had purchased the bulk of the former East German navy. The purchase was made without reference to the Indonesian armed forces, who were becoming increasingly fed up with the group around Suharto, and in any case the cost of refurbishing the rusty East German vessels was going to be greater than the original purchase price – it would probably have been cheaper to build new boats.

Another nail in the coffin of 'Openness' was growing public criticism of the Suharto family. Economic liberalisation had allowed the large conglomerates controlled by the Suharto children and key ethnic Chinese-Indonesians close to Suharto, such as Bob Hasan, to increase their wealth and power. The conglomerates became more and more overt in their actions, demonstrating that they were not just above the law, but that they made the law, throwing farmers off land to build hotels, or seizing other local assets for one or another of the family concerns.

The situation worsened when Madam Tien Suharto died in 1996. This had two effects on popular rumour and imagination. On a symbolic level, observers of Javanese political culture noted that the ideal ruler was the king in the *wayang* theatre who ruled in partnership with his spouse, implying that with his wife gone, Suharto should resign.[7] On a practical level many imagined, probably correctly, that Tien had exercised a restraining hand on her children and grandchildren. Wild stories circulated that she had not died of a heart attack, as the official explanation had it, but had been accidentally shot in an argument between her sons. Such fantastic explanations were a reflection of how the public had grown increasingly cynical about media censorship and manipulation; they were prepared to believe any alternative explanation to that put out by the government.

Two other key events of 1996 weakened the regime, at a time when it was preparing for another 'Festival of Democracy' in 1997. Despite all attempts to smother the memory of Sukarno and to buy off his children, the First President had remained a popular symbol for many Indonesians. He embodied a sense of 'the good old days' for those unhappy with the New Order, and because he was so closely associated with Independence and national pride, his image had grown stronger over the years. The fiftieth anniversary of Independence, in 1995, aroused all these images of the past for Indonesians at all levels of society. Pramoedya's appeals for his fellow

Indonesians to reflect on how much they had lost sight of their nation's origins were now being heard.

Within the Indonesian Democratic Party (PDI) there was a growing movement to connect with its past as the key Sukarnoist party, and so Sukarno's daughter, Megawati, was promoted in the organisation. The regime had been able to control the party twenty years earlier when Megawati's siblings were influential, and sought to do so again by engineering an internal split and then using their hired thugs to launch an attack on Megawati's party headquarters in Jakarta. Indonesians from all over the country followed the events in the media, and volunteers flocked to her side. The victory of force that eventually pushed Megawati out of her headquarters was a pyrrhic one. As a martyr to New Order oppression, she was a symbol to the poor and dispossessed, and her breakaway Indonesian Democratic Party of Struggle (PDI-P) gained a mass following. Having renewed their taste for showy public demonstrations in the period of Openness, students and other members of the middle class found themselves joined by peasants and the urban poor in displays of defiance. People like Sungkono, a scavenger who lived off what he could find in the main garbage tip of Jakarta, switched his allegiance to Megawati's party, after years of being paid by Suharto's *Golkar* to vote for them. The head of his work group recalled: 'The local administration made us fill out ballots in the names of other people. Each scavenger was given five and ordered to cast votes for *Golkar* at various poll stations. Each one was paid, I forget how much. So my 50 workers cast 250 votes for *Golkar*'. Even though it was not in their short-term economic interests, the poor as well as the rich were disillusioned.[8]

The New Order was definitely losing its grip. In 1996 government agents attempted a similar manipulation of violence in East Java to destabilise Gus Dur and undermine his base in the traditional Islamic organisation NU, but this served to galvanise support and to bring Gus Dur into a close alliance with Megawati.[9] An atmosphere of violence and intimidation was perpetuated by *agents provocateurs* whom everybody believed to be linked to either the Suharto group or to military leaders unhappy with the regime. Churches were burned, and there were minor acts of terrorism in selected locations that fed into the link between politics and violence in the popular imagination.

The ultimate symbol of what was going wrong with the New Order was its most extravagant scandal, which began late in 1995. News seeped out that the world's largest gold deposit had been discovered in Busang, Kalimantan. The main foreign company involved, an obscure Canadian firm called Bre-X, ended up in a bidding war with major US companies in which more and more generous offers were made to members of the governing inner circle to see who could buy the most influence. One of the Suharto children was rumoured to have been offered US$1 billion. With all the international agencies publishing accounts of Indonesia's growing prosperity, investors felt assured of returns on their money. In true New Order style, there was of course no gold. The geologist who had signed off on the discovery mysteriously fell out of a helicopter, but the fraud was revealed late in 1996 through the actions of honest public servants and the investigations of the international media. The Suharto children, and friends such as Bob Hasan who had been involved, were not at all concerned that Bre-X and other companies had lost millions on the investment, or that Indonesia's reputation was irreparably tarnished in the eyes of international investors. They had got their commissions. While some economists maintain that a level of corruption is a normal part of the operations of capitalism, the Bre-X scandal showed that the regime's corruption was eating into the base of the economy.[10]

The reluctance of foreign investors to get involved in another Bre-X coincided with the massive flight of capital away from South-east Asia in the Asian financial crisis of early 1997. The New Order boom of the 1990s had been built on huge foreign loans, and when signs emerged that the boom was really a bubble, lenders became nervous. Following a sudden and dramatic fall in the Thai Baht, currency speculators and Indonesian companies rushed to sell off the Rupiah, which crashed to one-fifth of its value against the US dollar. The currency crash coincided with Indonesia's worst drought of the twentieth century. The effects were more drastic than the economic crises of the 1960s or the Great Depression of 1929–31.

Talk of Indonesia's place in a globalising world was replaced by one word that summed up the national experience: 'crisis'. Most industries collapsed, and the number of officially registered poor more than doubled, slipping back to levels not seen since the early 1980s. The effects of the crisis were very uneven. Although sixteen banks were closed, creating serious liquidity issues, the Suharto group and their friends were able to juggle finances between holdings and use state funds to support most of their banks, particularly after the International Monetary Fund agreed to pour US$43 billion into the country in stages. IMF support was provided to lessen the impact on Indonesians, and to protect investors from wealthy countries so that the crisis did not lead to another world depression. Funding was dependent on reforms to Indonesia's financial sector, the end of monopolies and of government subsidies for many areas of the

Figure 8.1 Benny Rachmadi and Muhammad Misrad's image of the height
of elite consumerism just before the fall of Suharto, from Lagak Jakarta, *Krisis* . . .
Oh . . . *Krisis* (Jakarta: Kepustakaan Populer Gramedia, 1998).

economy, albeit with IMF provisions to create social 'safety nets' for the
very poor.[11]

Suharto's age of development and the subsequent age of globalisation
had turned into the 'age of crisis'. Popular cartoonists Benny Rachmadi
and Muhammad Misrad depicted the pre-crisis world of profligate consumption where women brought back shopping trophies from Singapore,
the USA and Paris, and new real estate complexes sold their expensive
condominiums, while fathers bought their sons BMWs for succeeding in
exams (figure 8.1). In this world rich women fed fat bejewelled cats with
imported food before going to aerobics with their personal trainers. These
indulgences were supported by systems of corruption where, by toadying,
employees and civil servants hoped to gain a share of 'commissions'. In one
cartoon a cockroach was shown exclaiming that 'the fundamentals of our
economy are strong', a contemporary catch-phrase of both Indonesian
technocrats and foreign economists. In the cartoons this happy picture
was disturbed by the discovery of the huge cavern of debt just beneath
the surface of the economic indicators. The process of crisis, in this commentary, began with a personified Rupiah becoming weaker and weaker,

spawning a new everyday language of terms such as 'liquidation', 'merger', 'downsizing', 'redundancy notice', 'reformation', 'market forces' and 'speculator'. The causes of the crisis were identified in the popular acronym KKN, 'Collusion, Corruption and Nepotism'. General cynicism was expressed about politicians, shown as distant and anonymous, ignoring the real needs of the people, in what was a 'crisis of trust'.[12]

In the face of this crisis, no matter how much Suharto and those around him tried to engineer mass violence against their enemies, the call for 'Reform' was now heard on all levels of society – students, supporters of Islamic groups, the poor who backed Megawati, even elements of the military from whom a future president would arise. The demonstrations continued, the students' capacity to organise enhanced by the increasing use of mobile phones and the internet. One demonstration, at the affluent private Trisakti University in the main part of Jakarta, resulted in troops killing at least four demonstrators. The violence of government forces had turned from marginal areas to the centre of power, against the children of the middle class. The outrage was overwhelming. Outbreaks of violence occurred again and again: one of the worst was a series of mass sexual assaults on Chinese women by members of the military or thugs supported by backers of the Suharto regime.

A dramatic few weeks climaxed in a day of threatened action by the reformists. The military closed down the whole of Jakarta: a city of 15 million people was turned into a ghost town for one morning. Students risked their lives by occupying the parliament building. The state-run television showed scenes of Suharto in crisis meetings with a wheelchair-bound Gus Dur, who had just suffered a stroke as a result of diabetes.

A new cabinet convened following the 1997 election had included some of the few honest politicians with public support, but when the leading moral authority amongst them, Emil Salim, resigned and joined the students at the parliament building, taking with him the other political leaders with credibility, Suharto finally realised the game was up. He resigned on 21 May 1998, handing power over to Habibie, who was hastily sworn in as Indonesia's third president.

Suharto was brought down by a combination of factors. The end of the Cold War meant that the US was no longer willing to turn a blind eye to the regime's abuses of power, but external pressures for human rights were only a small part of the story. A more important external pressure was that to liberalise the economy and let Indonesians participate in the international consumer society. No matter how much Suharto had been able to deliver on basic needs for Indonesians, that would not have been enough

Figure 8.2 Protest poster by Dodi Irwandi (b. 1974), showing the proclamation of the 'People's Oath', recalling the 1928 nationalist Youth Oath which proclaimed the nation of Indonesia, this time proclaiming freedom for workers and peasants from Suharto's rule, 1999.

to satisfy aspirations for consumer goods and lifestyles that were bolstered by mass media images. Ordinary Indonesians not only saw tourists and Jakarta-based expatriates living luxurious lifestyles, their televisions and newspapers also showed prosperous Indonesians. During the riots around the fall of Suharto, the police were sent out to safeguard McDonald's, while the Timor cars manufactured on behalf of Suharto's son Tommy were favourite mob targets.

People knew Habibie's presidency was only temporary. In government offices throughout the land the photographs of Suharto were thrown out, but some officials did not bother to print photographs of the new president. They simply applied white-out to remove the 'Vice' from existing photographs of Habibie as vice-president.

A novel published just before the fall of Suharto expressed the forces that brought him down. Ayu Utami's first book, *Saman*, had an initial print run of 3,000, but within a year the book had to be reprinted to one hundred times that number, such was its popularity. Ayu, a Catholic West Javanese born in 1968, was the perfect symbol of the new mood of middle-class Indonesia. Raised on the works of Pramoedya, she saw herself as part of a new generation which did not need to give voice to the 'bigger issues' he confronted, but which had to 'speak about issues that are smaller and smaller'. The feminist former fashion model became a journalist in the early 1990s, and led the formation of the Independent Journalism Alliance after the 1994 press bans, risking the imprisonment that was the fate of some of her colleagues in the Alliance.[13] The underground publications put out by the Alliance and similar bodies paved the way for the plethora of grassroots publications that have appeared since 1998.

Utami's award-winning novel illustrated different levels of Indonesian life. The narrator represented the new cosmopolitan Indonesians who had grown up in the Suharto-era prosperity and could live in New York and participate in international discourses of sexual and political freedom. She connected international political awareness to the activism of NGO members depicted in other parts of the novel. They described dark deeds around the plantations of Sumatra. The main characters on Sumatra included a young Christian minister who came face-to-face with poor labourers, descendants of Javanese who had been coolies in the plantations of the 1930s, now once again under threat by authority. This time the threat did not come from foreign colonialism, but from the New Order's alliance of monied interests and military muscle. The narrator's lover was one of a group of Indonesians working on North Sea oil rigs. He represented the outward movement of Indonesian labour that occurred from the late 1980s onwards. Some, like him, lived dangerous offshore lives in the oil and mineral exploration industries, or laboured as crew on the rustbucket 'flag of convenience' ships so crucial in international trade. Others became servants in the Middle East or East Asia, hired because their employers considered that the poverty and low social standing of these young women

would make them compliant. Ayu had moved beyond Pramoedya's vision
of nationalism as a social force whose aspirations for freedom were stifled
by Suharto's neo-colonialism. Instead she showed that the power relations
in Indonesian society were more diffuse, and more directed to an ethos of
individual freedom in the context of global influences.

The globalised mobile labour force of Indonesia demonstrates that
national boundaries no longer contain the pressures for Indonesians to
meet the necessities of life. There has been a long history of migration into
Malaysia, and except for occasional actions against 'illegals' by the
Malaysian government, the borders are more or less porous. Men went
to work in the factories manufacturing heavy goods, and women went into
the garment factories. Indonesians could feel at home in Malaysia. Their
languages were more or less the same, and they blended in. By the mid-
1990s there were nearly 2 million Indonesians working in Malaysia. Many
shared the fate of Mohammed Soh from Lombok, who pawned his family
fields to get to Malaysia, only to find his first year's wages eaten up in
payments to the Chinese middleman who had organised his passage and
job. After three years overseas he returned home to his family, 'I left
Malaysia with 2 million *ringgit*, but arrived with only 200,000. The rest
was taken by the police in Sumatra, and at every port of crossing. My ideals
of a better life haven't materialised, I can't even pay my bills.' A common
scene in major Indonesian airports is of workers returning from overseas
being herded into special customs and immigration rooms to be fleeced by
officials, with the government turning a blind eye.

In the late 1980s this migration extended to the Middle East, where
young women went to work as maids for the oil rich. Cultural connections
counted: the Islamic link eased the minds of the young women and their
families, but when they got to countries such as Saudi Arabia the women
had a sense of foreboding. They had their passports taken away and lost
rights that women take for granted in Indonesia, such as being allowed to
drive cars. Stories came back to Indonesia of abuse by employers, and
worse, such as the fate of women arrested for adultery after they had been
raped. Such stories were swept aside by a government that did not want to
hear bad news.

In the late 1990s, word-of-mouth reports about work conditions and
exploitation in the Middle East meant that women wanted to work closer
to home. Recruitment to Singapore became easier once Singapore and
Indonesia had created a common economic zone around the island of
Batam. Maid shops, featuring photographs of young Indonesians in livery
showing off their house-cleaning skills, appeared in Singaporean shopping

malls. Through the same Chinese business networks that supported work opportunities in Singapore, Indonesians were also hired to work in Taiwan and Hong Kong. Young girls from Flores or Lombok usually found themselves without rights against predatory employers, but driven by poverty, they kept coming, since life at home provided no income and no hope of improvement. In the words of one woman, Atun from Krawang in West Java, 'school doesn't guarantee anything and we don't have money to pay our debts. Even graduating from high school doesn't mean you'll get a job. By working abroad, there's a much better chance of being able to pay our debts and earn some capital.'[14]

By the early years of the twenty-first century young women, following the example of Marsinah, the factory worker who died defying the New Order, were beginning to organise into unions, learning from their Filipina sisters, and taking part in international NGO networks. Slowly, reluctantly, the Indonesian state has had to take notice of its citizens overseas and try to protect their rights, if only because their remittances have become the mainstay of many regional economies. If Indonesia was perhaps briefly in the 1970s and 1980s a nation-state within clear political boundaries, by the end of the twentieth century the state was buckling under international and internal pressures, and the nation was spilling over its borders. Pramoedya's desire for a national liberation seems as nostalgic as Suharto's harking back to aristocratic Javanese tradition.

PRESIDENTS AND OLIGARCHY

While most Indonesians continued to talk about the post-Suharto era as the age of crisis, the new leadership that emerged from the expanding middle class and the fraying ruling class encouraged people to think of themselves in an age of reform. Reform, rather than Revolution, would not scare away international investors and aid agencies, with their 'good governance', 'transparency', 'social capital' and 'empowerment'. Those who replaced Suharto had to speak the same language, but their attempts to reassure an uneasy and frustrated population were always going to be difficult. They were dealing not only with economic collapse, but with political forces prepared to use violence to achieve sectional interests, and with a new kind of local identity politics that was the uneasy obverse of globalisation.

Central politics in Indonesia after Suharto saw three presidents in the space of four years. B. J. Habibie, fearing his rule would only last until the 1999 elections were resolved, sought to distance himself from Suharto by instituting a series of far-reaching policy reforms that saw the fundamental structure of the state altered, an achievement seldom recognised because he was never going to be able to overcome the stigma of his Suharto links. Habibie lifted legislation that discriminated against Chinese, took power away from the military, decentralised government, and provided the East Timorese people with a democratic vote over their future.

Amongst Habibie's reforms were massive changes in the economic structure of the country, most of which had been set out in the International Monetary Fund's stipulations for its bail-out package. The view of economic management that had become the only possible way of seeing the world was a legacy of the post-Cold War consensus created by Britain's Prime Minister, Margaret Thatcher, in alliance with US President Ronald Reagan. In this view, privatisation, the removal of tariffs and radical reduction in the size and power of civil services, amounting to the reduction of the power of the state, were the only possible alternatives. For Indonesia this was both good and bad medicine. While allowing those in power to act against the corrupt monopolies of the Suharto children and cronies, fully implementing such changes would mean massive unemployment and the removal of any protection for the poor who depended on government subsidies for enough rice to eat and kerosene with which to cook.

The IMF policies have been partially implemented with mixed results. The middle class was reduced in size overnight, particularly as savings were wiped out when banks folded. Never having been able to afford imported goods, the poor continued to recycle whatever was to hand, but were nevertheless hard hit between 1997 and 1999. The overall level of poverty increased 100 per cent. After 1999 the worst effects of the crisis were over, but in some areas people had sold assets or gone into debt to tide them over. People found that the real value of wages had declined by up to 40 per cent, meaning that they would never be able to recover to their original pre-crisis standard of living. The falls in social status accompanying such economic changes were profoundly distressing and humiliating for many people, and are part of the real impact that often goes unacknowleged in economic studies.[15]

Other rural people did well, like the clove farmers whose crops had previously been forced into the monopoly held by Tommy Suharto. This monopoly drove many growers out of the industry. The remaining clove farmers initially thrived in 1998 when the monopoly was removed because they were able to receive market value for their output, since they could earn US dollars for exports. Likewise the luxury hotels of Bali had direct access to income outside the devalued Rupiah. However, some of the gains were short-lived. In Kerinci, in the middle of Sumatra, where farmers grew cinnamon, the initial high prices they received in 1997 and 1998 led to overproduction, as everyone rushed to get into the boom, so that by the 2001 harvest the market had been flooded and prices collapsed. This forced thousands to leave the area and travel to Malaysia to find work.[16]

In the years between 1999 and 2001 a tricky visionary was president of Indonesia. Abdurrahman Wahid, a blind East Javanese preacher who had suffered two serious strokes, became president almost by accident. Wahid, Gus Dur, was the compromise candidate in a People's Assembly vote for the position. His style was chaotic, one of informality and contradictory statements. Gus Dur's casual dress made him unpopular with the besuited representatives of the international agencies who provided the money to keep Indonesia afloat at a time of massive economic collapse. His lack of interest in hierarchy shocked those political leaders who had been brought up in the Suharto era when displays of status and wealth were equated with power. His lack of interest in management and his lack of consistency drove even his advisers to distraction. His willingness to embrace other religions, and even to visit Israel, was an affront to hardliners who had hoped that as a Muslim religious leader he would bring an Islamic state. Most of all he offended the military, challenging their control over key resources and their interference in politics, and calling them to account for the years of ruthlessness licensed by Suharto. It is not surprising that Gus Dur lasted less than two years as president, no one trusted him, and his administration lurched from crisis to crisis.

Indonesia was not ready for Gus Dur's push towards democracy. A key factor in bringing him down was his apology to the victims of the 1965 massacres of Communists and political prisoners. His attempt to create a process of national reconciliation upset those in his own party, including family members who had led the killings in East Java, and angered the military. An alliance of Muslim and military politicians forced him out in what amounted to a constitutional coup. He was replaced by Megawati, the daughter of Sukarno.

During his discussions over reconciliation, Gus Dur made a number of visits to Pramoedya, who disagreed that there could be reconciliation while so much of the New Order was still in power. When the pressure was on, however, Pramoedya was one of those who called on Gus Dur not to step down: 'Gus Dur told me about all the criticism and calls for him to resign. But I told him to remain courageous and continue ruling the country.'[17] Although Suharto had fallen in 1998, his shadow loomed over the new period of democracy, and despite disagreements with Gus Dur over tactics, Pramoedya knew that as president Gus Dur could overcome the legacies of Suharto's New Order. Gus Dur's defeat was a sign of how the New Order's culture and institutions were still deeply entrenched in the ruling class of Indonesia.

The coalition of Suharto-regime politicians and military hardliners who brought Gus Dur down backed Megawati Sukarnoputri as replacement president in 2002 because to them she was a safer, more conservative, option. Pramoedya was now a free-ranging political commentator able to travel overseas and enjoy some modest prosperity, finally able to receive income from his work. He summed up just how much Megawati represented continuity with the old government:

During Suharto's New Order regime, Megawati, Sukarno's daughter, served in parliament ... But did she ever say anything about the way her father was treated? Did she ever protest when her fellow countrymen were imprisoned? Never. Did she ever call Suharto to task? Never! But then she's not alone. Even after Suharto resigned, no one would take him to task, no one dared to bring him to trial. Silently, through his New Order protégée, he still holds power in this country.

Megawati came to power on the crest of a wave of youth rebellion. Those kids didn't really think about it; they didn't have any other figurehead, so they adopted her because she was Sukarno's daughter. That's all she is.

Maybe Megawati hasn't read her father's books. I don't see that she has inherited any of his better characteristics. She has no experience. There is no evidence that she can resolve the country's problems ... Her heart goes out to the people, she says, but that's the most they get. The villagers praise her, but that's because of ignorance. They don't know her.[18]

New Order ways of thinking and acting have become so heavily entrenched in the political and economic system that it is now almost impossible to work outside them in national and regional politics. To get into power, Gus Dur had to buy votes, and those in his party took part in the influence peddling and 'extra budgetary' use of state-owned enterprises that were the New Order norm.

Attempts by Gus Dur to reform the corrupt financial and legal systems failed because almost everybody in the government and bureaucracy had been part of the Suharto system. Companies associated with the Suharto family and their cronies could not be dismantled. They had covered their tracks well, and were usually so closely linked to foreign businesses that attacks on them were construed as threats to foreign investment. Suharto suffered a stroke and was considered too ill to be prosecuted, but there were small successes: Tommy, the most venal of the Suharto children, was eventually gaoled, although in the process he ordered the murder of one of the judges who had tried his early cases. Crony Bob Hasan also ended up in prison, but was able to set up his cell in luxurious style. Other Suharto children continued to operate freely, with one of his daughters, Tutut, contesting the 2004 election on a platform of 'Suharto nostalgia'. The low vote she received was ample demonstration of how much the Suharto clique lived in a fantasy of their own popularity.

Pramoedya's judgement of Megawati may seem harsh, but if Gus Dur failed in many of his reform attempts, those around Megawati reversed many of the gains made immediately after Suharto's fall. The leaders of political parties, including Megawati's husband, took part in oligarchic manipulation of finance and business.[19] The good intentions of genuine reformers have been drowned by a political culture in which access to power is synonymous with access to the economy. This culture is Suharto's strongest legacy. The New Order inherited an outlook from the Dutch that taught Indonesians to see the state as something distant, something that they could never own or take part in. The New Order then ran down what few state institutions there were because they impeded the naked use of power that was part of the military outlook of that regime. Suharto left the state an empty shell, unable to address social problems, its personnel mostly unwilling to act beyond self-interest.

VIOLENCE AND THE MULTIDIMENSIONAL CRISIS

In the years following the fall of Suharto, the most immediate impact of political changes in Jakarta for ordinary Indonesians was political violence. As if the tightly controlled violence emanating from the centre of Suharto's regime had erupted like one of the country's many volcanoes, Indonesians were presented with a moving parade of violent events. One of the first was the mysterious killings of healers and sorcerers in East Java. Stories abounded that mysterious 'ninjas' were responsible. However, as with the violence surrounding the fall of Suharto and subsequent events, responsibility was attributed to elements of the military or to thugs authorised and paid by Suharto and his supporters.[20] There was good reason to believe this, since destabilisation of the country would have provided justification both for a return to power by Suharto, and for the military to intervene by means of a coup.

Luckily the military was divided. One of the important reforms just after Suharto fell was to separate the police force from the military. From its inception the police had been one of the branches of the armed forces.

During the Suharto regime the territorial command system of the armed forces served as an instrument of state power as regional commanders intervened in local events, and military governors or deputy governors were the norm in almost every province. This double layer of administrative control reinforced the economic power of the military through its many legal and illegal enterprises. An immediate outcome of the fall of Suharto was the opportunity for regional commanders to become local warlords, but this tendency was curbed by separating the police from the military. In many regions local police mobile brigades, the chief instruments for controlling popular unrest, became the focus of power plays against local army commanders, and in some cases the rivalries turned into open fire-fights, with casualties on both sides. Higher up in the military there was also division, and various generals and colonels attempted to create a more professional army, with calls to go 'back to the barracks' and dismantle the 'dual function' doctrine of the military. Divisions at all levels of the military contributed to local conflicts.

One of Suharto's policies had been that there should be no public discussion of sectarianism, that differences in 'ethnicity, race and religion' were forbidden topics in the media. This policy did indeed keep the lid on potential communal conflict. Where there were outbreaks of violence, for example anti-Chinese riots, media censorship and military control meant that these could be contained. With an end to censorship and strict social engineering in 1998, the pot of difference boiled over. Many saw their inability to discuss these matters as conspiracy by minority groups with the regime. It was the Chinese who were first victims of violence in 1998 and 1999.

Some of the anti-Chinese violence was stoked by Muslim extremist groups, who since the early 1990s had been active in burning the churches of the mainly Christian Chinese. Thus anti-Chinese sentiment blended with wider Christian–Muslim conflicts. The worst of these were not, however, in the cities of Java where Chinese populations were largest, but were in outer provinces where indigenous Christians were the subject of jealousy or competition. Christian evangelical and charismatic groups had been established in Indonesia, but under Suharto the Ministry of Religion circumscribed their activities. The fall of the New Order saw funding of large new churches. Even in Hindu Bali signs were emerging by 1999 of tension between assertive Christian groups and a growing movement towards a Hindu fundamentalism fed by developments in religious politics in India, the home of Hinduism. Hindus in Bali began to organise vigilante groups against 'outsiders'.[21] Christian and Hindu fundamentalisms are dangerous in themselves. When they encounter Islamic fundamentalism, the results are usually fatal.

The worst outbreaks of religious violence were in Ambon, a region with almost equal numbers of Christians and Muslims, and Central Sulawesi, where a similar situation held. Previously harmonious mixed neighbourhoods became war zones, as local grudges spiralled into cycles of revenge, and, inspired by ideas that this was the end of the millennium, as indeed it was, religious leaders of both sides incited their followers to battle to the death. The cycles were magnified by the newly freed media, who were able to report what they liked. As conflicts escalated, both sides used all of the available new and old media, from newspapers to websites and VCDs, to inflame the situation by reporting real and imagined atrocities and calling for them to be avenged.[22]

Such use of the media was instrumental in spreading the conflict. Many of the Christians who were involved in the violence had associations with the Ambonese separatist movement of the 1950s, the Republic of the South Moluccas. Thus it was easy for their enemies to depict the local conflict as one with national implications. Militias were established locally and on other islands, notably Java, and under the name of 'refugee aid', funds were raised for the defence of Islam against forces that were unpatriotic and anti-Muslim. Military transport was often provided to assist militia members to join in the conflicts of Ambon and other regions. The quasi-official groups of thugs that had been a mainstay of New Order manipulation of violence were brought in either by elements in the military or through finance from New Order supporters, to make such situations worse.

The most-publicised violence, this time with definite military instigation, surrounded the independence of East Timor in 1999. The most important Habibie reform was his attempt to solve the problem of conflict there by offering the people of East Timor a referendum for independence. In the lead-up to the referendum, military leaders organised local militias in a clear attempt to continue the Suharto-era manipulation of voting. The people of East Timor were not intimidated, and chose overwhelmingly to be independent. The vote itself brought a reaction from Indonesians who, having been brought up believing that the East Timorese had welcomed them in 1975, could not believe that the East Timorese did not want to remain part of Indonesia. Most Indonesians accepted newspaper stories blaming the United Nations, who supervised the vote, and Australia, who had applied pressure on Habibie to grant independence. Violence led by pro-Indonesian East Timorese militias broke into open conflict and massacres of at least 2,000 people, only settled after Habibie was forced

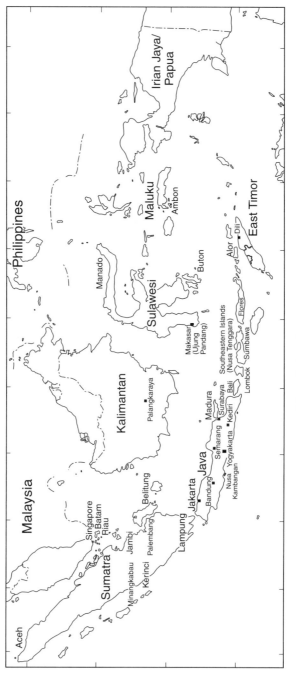

Map 7 Indonesia 1970s–2005s

to invite in Australian-led UN forces. The military appealed to patriotic feeling, saying that the 20,000 who had died from its forces since the invasion of 1975 should not have perished in vain, and predicted that this was the beginning of the break-up of the nation, a shattering of its territorial integrity. The conflict was represented in the media as one of Christian East Timorese against Muslim Indonesians. The militias and the military, in a final act of peevishness before they left, destroyed as much as they could of East Timor's infrastructure. Considering the East Timorese ungrateful for the 'development' the New Order had bestowed on them, many Indonesians felt that the burning of Dili was a just revenge.

The violence in East Timor and Ambon was part of a wider series of conflicts throughout the archipelago. The 1999 elections, in the style of New Order elections, had involved clashes between supporters of political parties. With the removal of the *Golkar* monopoly over access to official violence, the playing field was more equal, as different political parties set up their own militias to guard electoral processes.[23] This was the first indication that violence had become democratised. From 1998 onwards the lack of faith in state institutions such as the police meant that local militias and vigilante groups took over. The media became full of stories of increases in crime, as the economic collapse drove the poor to theft, followed by acts of mob violence. People suspected of theft or other crimes were beaten to death on the streets of Jakarta, Bandung, Denpasar or in the villages of most islands.[24]

Other conflicts revolved around ethnicity, the most horrifying examples of which were attacks led by ethnic Dayaks against internal migrants or transmigrants, particularly Madurese, in provinces on Kalimantan. Appeals to symbols of Dayak identity were manifested in acts of head-hunting against Madurese. Local politicians used such assertions to attempt to gain control of local resources.[25]

The violence of the period of 'reform' added to the sense that it was a period of crisis, increasingly described in the Indonesian media and popular discourse as 'multidimensional'. Violence was an easy tool to use if, like many military and political leaders, one wanted to destabilise the government and assert one's right to control. But any such short-term gains were going to come with long-term costs. By 2001 there were over 1 million people displaced by various conflicts, including Madurese who once sold meat balls on the streets of Palangkaraya, East Timorese who supported militias, or followed them out of fear, and Christian and Muslim Ambonese whose neighbourhoods had been turned to rubble.

Islam has proven a useful tool in local and national power plays. Arguments about the form of a 'reformed' Indonesia have included a return to the argument that Indonesia should be an Islamic state. Some provinces have responded to these calls by instituting Islamic law, and some political parties leaders have made it part of their appeal for votes, although unsuccessfully if the 2004 election was any indicator. However, in its most extreme form politicised Islam is a direct threat to the state, because of its destabilising nature, and because its most extreme exponents follow a millenarian vision of bringing down the Indonesian state and replacing it with a broader regional Islamic union.

While the actions of Muslim militias in Ambon were grabbing the headlines nationally and internationally, a small and relatively unknown group organised through small and secretive cells began to organise a series of bombings in Jakarta in 1999. Since there were so many sources of violence active at the time, and since Gus Dur's reforms attempted to close down the power of the intelligence arms of the military, very little attention was paid by anyone in power to identifying the sources of these bombings. By 2002 Indonesia had a vice-president, Hamzah Haz, trying to make mileage by speaking out in favour of Islamic leaders known to be linked to the violence in Ambon. Haz thought this was a good way to present himself as a defender of the faith, and to appeal to his United Development Party's following, which mainly came from the urban slums. Even when the finger of blame for church-burnings and incitement to violence turned to Abu Bakar Basyir, the Islamic preacher recently returned from exile after fleeing the Suharto regime, Vice-President Haz protected him by arguing that any criticism of Basyir was a criticism of Islam. Like Haz, Basyir maintained that Islam was under threat from an international conspiracy, involving the West, but especially Jews, Chinese, Masons and other stereotyped enemies. These paranoid fantasies had long been fed by the underground publication in Indonesian of works such as the fraudulent *Protocols of the Elders of Zion*, which were now given free voice. In May 2002 Basyir gave sermons exhorting students of his *pesantren* to sign up to fight for the Palestinian cause: 'Don't you dare to fear death. Those of you who die in such a battle will die the death of a holy one on the path of God.' Not all of his pupils wanted to take up such a militant path, as one, Yahya, put it: 'I want to have a job, a house and a nice family ... It's not that I don't want to join the struggle for Islam, but the struggle doesn't mean that you have to fight.' For some it did.[26]

On 12 October 2002 over 200 people, mostly Westerners, the largest number of whom were Australians, were murdered in three coordinated bombings on Bali. Initially bizarre conspiracy theories appeared in the Indonesian media to explain the event – like 9/11, the Bali bombings were said in the Muslim press to have been caused by the Western–Jewish–Chinese–Masonic plot to discredit Islam. Indonesians, who were used to the culture of rumour and violence under Suharto, considered such theories credible. Given that the Hindus of tourism-prosperous Bali were the object of envy by many other Indonesians, such theories might have been allowed to run unchecked if the Bali bombings had not been followed by a bombing in the centre of Jakarta, at the luxury Marriott Hotel in 2003, and then the bombing of the Australian Embassy in Jakarta in 2004, where the victims were all ordinary Indonesians, including a gardener and a passing motor-cycle taxi driver. Although there were few deaths, these demonstrations that militant groups could threaten the heartland of the Indonesian oligarchy and kill innocents brought revulsion from the public and a swift reaction from the Indonesian military and security forces. Even the most reluctant politicians were forced to admit that the evidence was overwhelmingly against a small group of violent agitators led by Basyir. The prosecutions of those linked to Basyir helped to turn public opinion away from extremist uses of Islam in political violence, but they also strengthened the hands of intelligence bodies, the police and the military.

In the complicated politics of Indonesia, however, political leaders have to be seen not to be surrendering to US or Australian pressure in the US-proclaimed 'war against terror'. Thus anti-foreign rhetoric has been a persistent feature of media representations of these bombings and other violent events. It has also been difficult in Indonesian politics to use the label 'Jemaah Islamiyah' for Basyir's group, both because the name means 'Islamic congregation', and this because term has associations with Murtopo's manipulation of images of Islam. Besides, Indonesians who had experienced the upheavals of the fight for independence, the conflicts of the 1950s and 1960s, the threatening atmosphere of the New Order and subsequent struggles were not going to be convinced that suddenly they were in a new 'age of terror'.

Governing a population of 220 million people was always going to be hard. Governing in the face of such upheaval required consummate political skills and a firm power base. Gus Dur had the former, but they rested on unpredictability rather than control, and his attempted reforms took him beyond his power base. Despite all the political upheavals during his presidency, Gus Dur's government improved the economic situation, restoring economic growth to around 5 per cent, with increases in consumer confidence and investment, overcoming the crippling corporate debt he inherited. Although there have been subsequent falls in various economic indicators, the successes created a momentum that has continued after Gus Dur. Even so, the idea of an improving economy meant different things to different people. Sugiyem, a woman from Central Java whose main livelihood came from scavenging newspapers, found that under Megawati the price per kilo of her recycled goods had fallen from Rp 900 to Rp 400 (US9 cents to US4 cents), forcing her out of business.[27]

On the national level Gus Dur attempted to negotiate with the more rebellious provinces, holding talks with Acehnese leaders over whether there should be an East Timor-style referendum, and placating Irianese nationalist sentiments by changing the province's name to Papua. Both of these moves angered firm nationalists, including his vice-president and uneasy former ally, Megawati, but they were steps on the path to quelling regional and separatist violence. Military groups worked to undermine such moves. In the case of Irian, now called Papua, the most prominent of the local leaders was assassinated, and other violence, including the killing of foreign workers, was instigated to threaten the Papuan independence movement and to discredit it in international eyes.[28] That Gus Dur fell so quickly demonstrated that his reputation for mystical power did not equate to miracle working.

After Gus Dur, Megawati managed to muddle through, but only just. In Aceh she allowed the military to run things its way, giving up peace talks in favour of a renewed military campaign against the separatist Free Aceh Movement that led to thousands of deaths, but no clear improvement. Under Megawati, there were attempts to restrain the press, although these have never been as drastic as they were in the days of Suharto. Many of Megawati's policies had this 'two steps forward, one step back' approach.

REGIONAL AUTONOMY

Probably the most far-reaching of the many dramatic changes after Suharto's fall was the policy of decentralisation, called Regional Autonomy. This policy grew from a strong antipathy to the nature of the centralist state run by Suharto. The conflicts in many regions were based on resentment of central control and the drain on resources. In the period up to 2000, there were many movements for independence, not just from the provinces of Aceh and Irian, who had suffered under the New Order, but also from resource-rich regions such as Riau and Kalimantan. Because of historical associations between Dutch colonialism and federalism, making Indonesia a federation was not a popular option, even though a number of new provinces were created in the years after 1998. The solution was to devolve power down to a level below that of the provinces, to the regencies. The legislation was passed hastily under President Habibie, and implemented under President Wahid with almost no preparation time for such a drastic change. But the change had to be quick, for those in power felt that the whole existence of Indonesia was threatened.

Regional Autonomy was based on US models of local government, and its main architects had been trained in, or at least visited, the US.[29] Underlying the US models was opposition to the state, a key part of the ideology perpetuated by international aid agencies as well. However, in the US case, there are strong traditions of local government built around a federal system. From the Dutch period onwards Indonesia has mainly known top-down systems of government. While some areas of Indonesia – Bali and the Minangkabau highlands, for example – do have traditional village or supra-village institutions, these were threatened by New Order policies.[30] The decision to make regencies the main unit of decentralisation harked back directly to the creation of these units of government under the Dutch. These were based on former areas of royal or aristocratic control, as denoted by their Javanese name, *kabupaten*. The temptation for regional leaders to recreate themselves as local lords has been great, and in many regions there has been a strong revival of traditional royal families. Given the 'feudal' style of the New Order, it is ironic that in the post-Suharto era regional autonomy has the potential to promote a return to aristocratic bureaucracy. The same policy, however, could produce other possible results.

In other parts of the country, the local gangsters who were the shock-troops of Suhartoism have emerged as godfathers struggling for control, as in the Sumatran city of Medan which is effectively run by two competing gangs. One, a local branch of the Five Principles Youth Movement, is linked to the local police, while the other, an offshoot of the first gang, has military ties. Both control factions of local business and politics.[31]

Decades of strong centralism left regency-level officials unprepared and unable to conceive of governing in any democratic form. A natural reaction for many of the regency leaders who found themselves in power was to follow the Suharto example, the only model of leadership they really knew. Thus the centralised corruption of the Suharto years rapidly turned to local corruption, as increased local revenues went directly into local leaders' pockets. In resource-rich Kalimantan the depletion of forests increased.

In areas such as Manado where mining provided a major source of income, multinationals suddenly found their mining leases questioned, or were subject to campaigns of intimidation. Locals in Manado, Kalimantan and Sulawesi rushed in to set up their own small mines, using dangerous methods involving arsenic and mercury, which has also stepped up the environmental destruction that developed in the Suharto era. All kinds of local taxes were invented, and the number of local civil servants multiplied a hundred-fold. These increases in taxation and bureaucracy have increased the cost of doing business in Indonesia, and, dangerously, have restricted trade between different parts of the country. For nationalists such as Pramoedya, all this adds up to the potential for the nation to disintegrate.[32]

Many Indonesians consider the increase in corruption as temporary, or at least as a price to be paid for democracy. The negative effects of Regional Autonomy have been balanced by elements pointing to the creation of a better society. New regional heads fighting for clean government have emerged, amongst them a very few women, such as Rustriningsih, regency head of Kebumen in Central Java. Rustriningsih was popularly elected in 1999, aged thirty-two, from Megawati's political party, PDI-P, and carries the aspirations of the poor in matters such as getting roads improved so they can take their goods to market. She is typical of a growing number of younger civil servants struggling to turn around the tide of money politics and bureaucratic inertia.

In Blora, home town of Pramoedya, Tirto Adhi Suryo and Ali Murtopo, local leaders have suddenly found that they are accountable to local populations. Popular protests and media ready to expose cases of corruption have been used to call regency heads to account, and to keep them in line. Voters now have power, and are prepared to use it. Despite initial expectations that Indonesian politics might revert to the 1950s polarisation, where parties were solid political blocs in competition with each other, the voters of Blora, as with other parts of Indonesia, have found that shifting their votes, or threatening to do so, gives them power and can promote democracy.[33]

The national elections of 2004 have demonstrated that post-Suharto Indonesia's combination of optimistic reformism and cynical fatigue has at least leavened the worst aspects of crisis. The violence of previous elections was absent, and for the first time direct election of representatives and of the president gave Indonesians the feeling that participation means more than just joining rallies orchestrated by political parties. The swinging vote of Blora was translated to a national scale.[34] Disillusionment with the major political parties saw their votes fall and the rise of parties advocating

Figure 8.3 Pramoedya Ananta Toer at the height of his early fame at the beginning of the 1960s, before his long imprisonment (photo credit on the back, 'Kempen').

social justice and clean government. Disillusionment with Megawati's unwillingness to act over major national problems saw the rise of a political unknown, retired General Susilo Bambang Yudhoyono, elected president on 20 September 2004. Despite his reputation as a reformer, mediator and peacemaker, the fact that Susilo, popularly known as SBY, was as much a part of the New Order's power structure as any of the other political leaders, means that any optimism will need to be tempered with caution.

His greatest early challenge was the gigantic tsunami that struck Aceh and other parts of Asia around the Indian Ocean rim on Boxing Day, 2004. While Indonesia has been subject to more than its share of political violence in its brief history, the tsunami was a demonstration that the violence of nature is always not far away. Following earthquakes in Flores and Alor, the tsunami resulted in 98,000 deaths on Sumatra alone, and coming in the middle of a military crack-down in Aceh, presented great logistical problems. Sadly, it took a disaster of such magnitude to remind the world that Aceh existed; the impoverished Acehnese will take a generation to recover.

The sense of 'crisis' from 1997 to 2004 has lowered Indonesians' expectations of what government can deliver. The promises of 'Revolution' under Sukarno, or 'development' under Suharto, have not been replaced by any clear sense of national direction for most Indonesians. The older generation, like Pramoedya, still hopes for the fulfilment of the promises of the anti-colonial movement: 'When I was still young, my parents spoke of what Indonesia would be one day – independent, democratic and modern. Obviously all these have not been achieved.'[35] For young women like Atun of Krawang, working in Singapore or Hong Kong as maids, this promise seems even more distant. Pramoedya's hope that the nation-state can deliver prosperity and a just society is struggling to survive against global forces.

Biographies of key figures

SUKARNO (1901–70), son of a Javanese teacher from the lower aristocracy and a Balinese woman. Educated in Surabaya, where he met many of the nationalist leaders, and then Bandung, where he studied engineering. In 1921 he married Utari Cokroaminoto, whom he divorced in favour of Inggit Gunarsih in 1922. His subsequent wives were Fatmawati (m. 1943), Hartini (m. 1953), Kartini Manoppo (m. 1959), Ratna Sari Dewi (m. 1962), Haryati (m. 1963), Yurike Sanger (m. 1964) and Heldy Jafar (m. 1967). Founded the General Study Club in 1925 and the PNI or Indonesian Nationalist Association (later the Indonesian Nationalist Party) in 1927. Arrested in 1929 for his nationalist activities, he was tried and imprisoned until 1931, then rearrested in 1933 and sent into exile to Flores and then in 1938 to Bengkulu. Freed by the Japanese in 1942, he headed a number of bodies established by them, including the committee to prepare for Independence. In June 1945 he declared the Five Principles of the nation of Indonesia, and took part in the drafting of the first Constitution. At the end of the war, Sukarno and Hatta were kidnapped by a group of activists in an attempt to force them to declare independence, which they did on 17 August 1945. Sukarno became president and head of a Republican government. He remained in this position except for the period 1948–9 when he was a prisoner of the Dutch. In November 1949 he became president of the Republic of the United State of Indonesia, and on 17 August 1950 president of the Republic of Indonesia. Subject to seven assassination attempts, he declared martial law and Guided Democracy in 1957. After the 'coup' of 1965 he was subject to military pressure to hand over power to Suharto, which he did provisionally through the Letter of 11 March 1966.

MUHAMMAD HATTA (1902–80), from Minangkabau in Sumatra, studied in the Netherlands, where he became leader of the Indonesian Association in 1922. Arrested in 1927 but tried and acquitted in 1928, he joined Sukarno's PNI on return to Indonesia, and subsequently took part in the Indonesian National Education body or PNI-Baru with Syahrir. Both were arrested and sent into exile to Boven Digul in 1934, and subsequently moved to Banda in 1936. Freed by the Japanese, he became vice-president and part of a duumvirate with Sukarno until the two fell out in 1956. He was also prime minister in 1948 and again in 1949, when he headed the government of the Unitary Republic. Implicated in the regional revolts of the late 1950s, he mainly devoted himself to political commentary.

SUTAN SYAHRIR (1909–66), from Minangkabau, studied in the Netherlands where he was a member of the Indonesian Association. On returning from the Netherlands in 1931 he set up the New PNI. Tried and exiled along with Hatta. Emerged as the leader of a group of anti-fascist intellectuals in Jakarta under the Japanese. Part of the leadership group after Independence, he became prime minister between 1945 and 1947. He led the diplomatic negotiations for Independence. Subsequently led the Socialist Party or PSI during the 1950s, was opposed to Sukarno's authoritarianism, and subsequently was gaoled by Sukarno for alleged association with the regional revolts of the 1950s, and his party banned.

AMIR SYARIFUDDIN (1907–48), a Batak Christian who emerged as a nationalist in the Gerindo or Indonesian People's Movement after its founding in 1937. Funded by the Dutch to establish an anti-Japanese resistance in 1942, he was later arrested by the Japanese. Leading member of various cabinets after 1945, and prime minister 1947–8. Split with Syahrir in 1947 after the formation of the left wing of the Revolution. Declared himself to be a member of the Communist Party and leader of the People's Democratic Front in 1948. Killed by the Republican army after the Madiun Affair.

SYARIFUDDIN PRAWIRANEGARA (1911–89), of Bantenese and Minangkabau descent. Acting president while Sukarno was under arrest by the Dutch, 1948–9, and member of various cabinets. Later (1958–61) head of the rebel United Indonesian Republic government proclaimed as part of the regional revolts. Signatory of the 1980 'Petition of 50' critical of the New Order.

ABDUL HALIM (b. 1911), Minangkabau aristocrat and medical doctor. Non-party prime minister of the Indonesian Republic in 1950. Close to Syahrir, also a member of later cabinets.

MOHAMMAD NATSIR (1908–93), from Minangkabau. Leading Islamic writer of the 1930s who reconciled devotion to religion with nationalism. In 1932 he headed a modernist Islamic education body. Part of the modernist Islamic leadership which emerged after 1945, he led the *Masyumi* Party and the first parliamentary cabinet from 1950–1. Part of the regional revolts of the late 1950s, which led to the banning of *Masyumi* in 1958 and his imprisonment between 1961 and 1966. He played a leading role in international Islamic bodies, including as vice-president of the World Muslim Congress. Signatory of the 1980 'Petition of 50' critical of the New Order.

SUKIMAN WIRYOSANJOYO (1896 or 1898–1974), Javanese leader of the Islamic League Party in the 1920s, and a member of the Indonesian Association while studying in the Netherlands. Subequently a leading figure in Islamic politics, including the Indonesian Islamic Party, which he co-founded in 1933. One of the leading Islamic politicians of the Revolution, and a leader of *Masyumi* in the 1950s, he became prime minister between 1951 and 1952 in coalition with the PNI. Noted for his attempts to suppress the Communist Party in this period.

WILOPO (1908 or 1909–81), Javanese, active in educational and nationalist groups, he emerged under the Japanese as a political leader, and was involved in recruiting forced labour for the Japanese. Leader of the PNI, prime minister 1952–3.

ALI SASTROAMIDJOJO (1903–75), studied in the Netherlands during the colonial period and a member of the Indonesian Association. Led the PNI after Independence, and was prime minister 1953–5. Considered to be part of the left wing of the PNI, he formed another cabinet after the 1955 election (1956–7). Subsequently a minister in Sukarno's Guided Democracy cabinets.

BURHANUDDIN HARAHAP (b. 1917), Sumatran politician from *Masyumi*, prime minister 1955–6. Associated with the regional revolts. Signatory of the 1980 'Petition of 50' critical of the New Order.

RADEN JUANDA KARTAWIJAYA (1911–63), West Javanese aristocrat and *Muhammadiyah* school principal. Non-party prime minister appointed by Sukarno to head the 'Working Cabinets' of 1957 and 1959 until his death. Thereafter cabinet was dominated by Subandrio (1914–2004), Chaerul Saleh (1916–67) and Johannes Leimena (1905–77).

SUHARTO (b. 1921), born in Central Java, he received initial military training under the Dutch before joining a Japanese-sponsored militia. He subsequently emerged as an officer in the Revolution. Suharto rose up through the higher ranks of the military in putting down the House of Islam Revolt in Sulawesi and subsequently leading the military action to take Irian from the Dutch. As one of the only leading generals not targeted by the 30th September Movement in 1965, he was able to take command of Jakarta and lead the crushing of Communist Party. Named acting president in 1968. He consolidated power over the next decade, and remained in firm control until the early 1990s. Married to Siti Hartinah, or Tien (1924–96), from 1947 until her death. In 1998 he was forced to resign, but subsequent attempts to prosecute him have failed due to his ill health.

SULTAN HAMENGKUBUWONO IX (1912–88), studied in the Netherlands, where he was known as 'Sultan Henk'. Recalled by his dying father in 1939, he succeeded him as Sultan in that year. Declared himself a follower of the Revolution in 1945 and made Yogyakarta capital of the Republic in 1946. With strong ties to the army he played a role in many cabinets from 1950 to 1968, and became a co-founder of the New Order after 1965. Made vice-president when the office was restored in 1973.

ADAM MALIK (1917–84), follower of Tan Malaka, a member of the youth group which kidnapped Sukarno in 1945 to force him to declare independence. Founder in 1937 of the Indonesian national newsagency Antara, and active in propaganda activities for the Revolution. He was a leading member of the Proletarian Party in the 1960s, and subsequently became part of the alliance that inaugurated the New Order. Initially ruled in a triumvirate with Suharto and the Sultan of Yogyakarta, where as foreign minister he was responsible for moves to have the new government recognised internationally, and in important debt negotiations. Replaced Hamengkubuwono IX as vice-president in 1978–83.

UMAR WIRAHADIKUSUMA (1924–2003), from West Javanese (Sundanese) aristocracy. Entered the military under the Japanese, later served in the Siliwangi Division under Nasution, had been involved in crushing the Madiun Uprising, the House of Islam Revolt and the regional revolt in Sumatra in late 1958. Leading general at the time of the 1965 coup, during which he allied with Suharto and helped him take power. Vice-president subsequent to Adam Malik (1983–8).

SUDHARMONO (b. 1927), East Javanese lieutenant-general, had been on Suharto's personal staff and was subsequently head of *Golkar*. Vice-president 1988–93.

TRY SUTRISNO (b. 1935), East Javanese general, and military academy graduate. As a teenager he had been involved in the Revolution, joined the military in 1956, and served in the Irian campaign. Involved in suppressing Islamicist groups in the 1980s. A member of Suharto's personal staff, he was made vice-president in 1993 after serving as head of the armed forces.

BACHARUDDIN J. HABIBIE (b. 1936), born in Sulawesi of Bugis and Javanese parentage. Studied engineering in Germany, and subsequently became vice-president of Messerschmidt. Returned to Indonesia where he spearheaded a push for technological development. Made vice-president in 1997; subsequently Suharto named him as his successor in 1998. As president, Habibie managed the transition to democracy, overseeing the first free elections since 1955 and the East Timor independence referendum, both in 1999.

ABDURRAHMAN WAHID (b. 1940), East Javanese religious leader. Grandson of the founder of the *Nahdlatul Ulama*, and son of the first minister of religion. He rose up through the NU in the 1970s, and was elected chairman in the 1980s. The New Order regime attempt to oust him through internal manipulation in the organisation, but he remained in that position until a major stroke in 1998. On his recovery he joined the post-Suharto election campaign, and was subsequently elected president in 1999 by a vote of the People's Consultative Assembly (MPR). He was forced to resign under political pressure in 2001.

MEGAWATI SUKARNOPUTRI (b. 1947), daughter of Sukarno and Fatmawati. Succeeded her siblings as a leader of the Indonesian Democratic Party (PDI). In 1996 became a symbol of resistance to the Suharto regime when the New Order attempted to oust her from the organisation. He break-away group PDI-P received huge popular support, and this translated into a significant party vote in the 1999 election. However, she failed to gain a majority in the MPR election, and was forced to become vice-president to Abdurrahman Wahid in 1999. In 2001 she succeeded Wahid as president, in an uneasy coalition which included as vice-president Hamza Haz, Kalimantan-born leader of the Islamic United Development Party. Megawati lost popularity almost immediately.

SUSILO BAMBANG YUDHOYONO (SBY) (b. 1949), retired general, minister under President Wahid, a role in which he attempted, unsuccessfully, to mediate in conflicts between the president and the army. Restored to his ministerial position under Megawati until a falling-out involving her husband. He and Yusuf Kalla were involved in mediating communal conflicts in Sulawesi. Formed a new political party to contest the 2004 elections, became the first directly elected president of Indonesia in 2004. At the time of his election he made a pilgrimage to the grave of Hatta.

HAJI MUHAMMAD JUSUF KALLA (b. 1942), South Sulawesi businessman, long-time member of *Golkar* who became a minister under Megawati, but fell out with her to join SBY's successful ticket as vice-president for the 2004 election.

OTHER POLITICAL LEADERS

HAJI UMAR SAID COKROAMINOTO (1882–1934), leader of the Islamic Union at its height, from 1911 to 1919. Arrested for perjury in 1921 but acquitted in 1922. Ran a large boarding house in Surabaya where many of the leaders of the nationalist movement gathered. Sukarno, one of his boarders, subsequently married Cokroaminoto's daughter, and was considered his political heir.

SUWARDI SURYANINGRAT alias KI HAJAR DEWANTORO (1889–1959), Javanese prince from the Pakualam House. Member of the Indies Party, exiled to the Netherlands 1913–19 for political activities. Influenced Sukarno. Subsequently founded the Garden of Pupils (*Taman Siswa*) education movement. In 1943 became part of the national political leadership under the Japanese.

SEMAUN (1899–1971), Javanese railway worker and subsequently union leader, who as head of the Semarang branch of the Islamic League established strong left-wing influence. In 1920 founded the Communist Party of the Indies, subsequently the Communist Party of Indonesia, which he led along with Darsono (1897–1968?), Alimin (1889–1964) and Musso (1897–1948). In 1921 he travelled to Moscow, returning to Indonesia in 1922. Exiled in 1923 to Europe after the colonial government crushed a strike by his union, where he remained as a translator and adviser on Indonesia and Islam until his return to Indonesia in 1957. Special adviser to Sukarno and leading figure in the Proletarian Party until his death.

TAN MALAKA (1897–1948), aristocrat from Minangkabau. Early member of the Communist Party and Islamic League, exiled for his involvement in political strikes in 1922. Fell out with the leadership of the Communist Party over the 1926/7 uprisings. Leading member of the Comintern, and involved in founding Communist parties throughout South-east Asia. Returned to Indonesia in 1942 and emerged as an alternative president in the early stages of the Revolution. He represented the 'struggle' position in debates about the direction of the Revolution, and was imprisoned in Yogyakarta by the Republican leadership in 1946. Released to help put down the Madiun Uprising, he led guerrilla groups until his murder by Republican military probably early in 1948. His followers formed the core of the Proletarian Party.

MUHAMMAD H. THAMRIN (1894–1941), leader of the Betawi ethnic group movement, and outspoken member of the People's Council. Leading member of the major political party Parindra (Greater Indonesia Party) after its founding in 1935. Arrested by the Dutch police in 1941 for his links with the Japanese, he died in custody.

SUDIRMAN (1915?–50), *Muhammadiyah* school teacher from Java who trained in Japanese-sponsored military bodies. Elected head of the Republican army at its founding, he led the guerrilla struggle, and opposed the political leadership's negotiated independence. Ill with tuberculosis for the latter stages of the Revolution.

ABDUL HARIS NASUTION (1918–2000), Batak Muslim who trained as an officer under the Dutch. Took over leadership of the West Java-based Siliwangi division in 1946. Led the suppression of the Madiun Uprising, and succeeded Sudirman as head of the army. Suspended from his position after the 17 October 1952 military show of force against Sukarno, he was recalled in 1957 to put down the regional revolts. One of the targets of the 30th September Movement in 1965, he survived but was too grief-striken by the death of his daughter to take control. Later a critic of Suharto and signatory to the dissident 'Petition of 50'.

D. N. AIDIT (1923–65), Sumatran nationalist who trained in the youth hostel at Menteng 31 on the eve of Independence. During the initial stages of the Revolution he was imprisoned by the Dutch on the Thousand Islands but he subsequently emerged as a leader of the Communist Party in Yogyakarta. Led the revival of the Party in 1951, and subsequently became chairman, running the party along with Politbureau members M. H. Lukman (1920–65), Njoto (1925–65) and Sudisman (1920–68).

BENNY MURDANI (1930–2004), Javanese Catholic who joined the military soon after the Revolution. Played a leading role in the Irian campaign and confrontation with Malaysia. Subsequently became a protégé of Ali Murtopo, and under Ali led the invasion of East Timor in 1975. In 1983 he was appointed commander-in-chief of the armed forces, and he played a leading role in security, but later fell out with Suharto over issues of corruption by Suharto's children.

Abbreviations and glossary

ABRI	*Angkatan Bersenjata Republik Indonesia* – Armed Forces of the Republic of Indonesia
AJI	*Aliansi Jurnalisik Independen*
Becak	Tricycle/taxi
Berdikari	**Berdiri diatas Kaki Sendiri** – Standing on Our Own Two Feet campaign for economic autonomy
BKI	*Bijdragen tot de Taal-, Land, en Volkenkunde*
BKR	*Badan Keamanan Rakyat* – People's Security Body
Darul Islam	House of Islam uprising
DPR	*Dewan Perwakilan Rakyat* – the Indonesian People's Representative Assembly
Fretilin	*Frente Revoluciondria do Timor-Leste Independente* – Front for the Liberation of East Timor
GANEFO	Games of the New Emerging Forces
GAPI	**Gabungan Politik Indonesia** – Indonesian Political Federation
Gerindo	**Gerakan Rakyat Indonesia** – Indonesian People's Movement
Gerwani	**Gerakan Wanita Indonesia** – Indonesian Women's Movement
Gestapu	**Gerakan September Tiga Puluh** – Abbreviation given to 30th September Movement by the military under Suharto
Gestok	*Gerakan Satu Oktober* – Abbreviation for the 'coup' of 1965, used by Sukarno to refer to the suppressing of the 30th September Movement by Suharto's forces
Golkar	**Golongan Karya** – 'Functional Groups' in Guided Democracy, that became the state party under Suharto

Gotong Royong	'Mutual help'
Haji	One who has completed the pilgrimage to Mecca
ICMI	*Ikatan Cendekiawan Muslim Indonesia* – Indonesian Muslim Intellectuals Association
IMF	International Monetary Fund
KAMI	*Kesatuan Aksi Mahasiswa Indonesia*
Kampung	'Village' or village-like suburb of a city
KKN	*Kolusi, Korupsi dan Nepotisme* – Collusion, Corruption and Nepotism
Konstituante	Assembly to determine the Constitution
KPM	*Koninklijke Paketvaart Maatschappij* – Dutch Royal Packetship Line
Kromo	'The little man', used to refer to the people
Kroncong	Ensemble influenced by Portuguese and Pacific music styles
LEKRA	**Lembaga Kebudayaan Rakyat Indonesia** – the Institute of People's Culture
Manikebu	**Manifesto Kebudayaan** – the Cultural Manifesto group, as designated by their opponents
MANIPOL-USDEK	**Manifesto Politik-Undang-Undang Dasar** *'45,* **Sosialisme Indonesia, Demokrasi Terpimpin, Ekonomi Terpimpin dan Kepribadian Indonesia** – Sukarno's Political Manifesto-1945 Constitution, Indonesian Socialism, Guided Democracy, Guided Economy and National Identity
Masyumi	*Majelis Syuro Muslimin Indonesia* – Consultative Council of Indonesian Muslims, set up under the Japanese, later a political party
MPR	*Majelis Permusyawaratan Rakyat* – People's Consultative Assembly
Muhammadiyah	Modernist Muslim educational movement
Murba	'Proletarian', a term coined by Tan Malaka and used by the political party he inspired
NASAKOM	*Nasionalisme, Agama, Komunisme* – Sukarno's doctrine of combining Nationalism, Religion and Communism
NICA	Netherlands Indies Civil Administration
NU	*Nahdlatul* or *Nahdlatul Ulama* – Council of Religious Scholars

Pari	*Partai Rakyat Indonesia* – Indonesian People's Party
Parindra	*Partai Indonesia Raya* – Greater Indonesia Party
Partindo	*Partai **Indo**nesia* – Indonesian Party
PDI	*Partai Demokrasi Indonesia* – Indonesian Democratic Party
PDI-P	*Partai Demokrasi Indonesia – Perjuangan*, Indonesian Democratic Party of Struggle, Megawati's breakaway party
Permai	*Persatuan Rakyat Marhaen Indonesia*, Union of the Common People of Indonesia, literally meaning 'Beauty'
Pesantren	Religious boarding institution
PETA	*Pembela Tanah Air* – Defenders of the Fatherland
PI	*Perhimpunan Indonesia* – Indonesian Association of students in the Netherlands
PID	*Politieke Inlichtingendienst* – Political Intelligence Service
PKI	*Partai Komunis Indonesia* – Indonesian Communist Party
PNI	*Perserikatan Nasional Indonesia* later *Partai Nasional Indonesia*, Indonesian National Association/Party. Also *Pendidikan Nasional Indonesia*, Indonesian National Education Movement, in the 1930s known as *PNI-Baru* or the New PNI to differentiate it from the political party
PPP	*Partai Persatuan Pembangunan* – United Development Party
PPPKI	*Permufakatan Perhimpunan-perhimpunan Politik Kebangsaan Indonesia* – Consensus of Indonesian People's Political Organisations
priyayi	'Aristocrat', but applied to civil servants and everyone of higher social class on Java
PSI	*Partai Sosialis Indonesia* – Indonesian Socialist Party
PSII	*Partai Sarekat Islam Indonesia* – Indonesian Islamic League Party
rakyat	'The people'
Repelita	*Rencana Pembangunan Lima Tahun* – Five Year Development Plan

RIMA	*Review of Indonesian and Malaysian Affairs*
RMS	*Republik Maluku Selatan* — Republic of the South Moluccas, the Ambonese-based separatist movement which began in the 1950s
SDI	*Sarekat Dagang Islamiyah* – Islamic Traders League
SI	*Sarekat Islam* – Islamic League
Sarekat Priyayi	Aristocrats'/Civil Servants' Association
Stambul	Popular theatre of the 1930s
Supersemar	**Surat Perintah Sebelas Maret** – Letter of Command of 11 March (1966), a pun on the name of *wayang* figure Semar
TKR	*Tentara Keamanan Rakyat* – People's Security Army
TNI	*Tentara Nasional Indonesia* – National Army of Indonesia

Notes

1 OUR COLONIAL SOIL

1. From the introduction to J. S. Furnivall, *Netherlands India: a Study of Plural Economy* (Cambridge: Cambridge University Press, 1939 [reprinted 1967]).
2. Figures from Furnivall, *Netherlands India*, p. 347; statistics below from Furnivall unless otherwise indicated.
3. J. J. P. de Jong, *De Waaier van het Fortuin. Van Handelscompagnie to Koloniaal Imperium: de Nederlanders in Azië en de Indonesische Archipel 1595–1950* (Den Haag: Sdu, 1998), pp. 335–6; Richard Chauvel, *Nationalists, Soldiers and Separatists: the Ambonese Islands from Colonialism to Revolt 1880–1950* (Leiden: KITLV Press, 1990), pp. 46–52.
4. De Jong, *De Waaier van het Fortuin*, p. 330; A. van der Kraan, *Lombok: Conquest, Colonization and Underdevelopment, 1870–1940* (Singapore/Kuala Lumpur/ Hong Kong: Heinemann/Asian Studies Association of Australia, 1980).
5. De Jong, *De Waaier van het Fortuin*, p. 335; Elsbeth Locher-Scholten, *Sumatran Sultanate and Colonial State: Jambi and the Rise of Dutch Imperialism, 1830–1907* (Ithaca, NY: Cornell University Southeast Asia Program, 2003); Michael Laffan, *Islamic Nationhood and Colonial Indonesia: the Umma below the Winds* (London: RoutledgeCurzon, 2003); Furnivall, *Netherlands India*, p. 236; A. J. S. Reid, *The Contest for North Sumatra: Atjeh, The Netherlands and Britain 1858–1898* (Kuala Lumpur: Oxford University Press, 1969).
6. W. H. van den Doel, 'Military rule in the Netherlands East Indies', in R. Cribb (ed.), *The Late Colonial State in Indonesia: Political and Economic Foundations of the Netherlands Indies 1880–1942* (Leiden: KITLV Press, 1994), p. 67.
7. Elsbeth Locher-Scholten, 'Dutch expansion in the Indonesian archipelago around 1900 and the imperialism debate', *Journal of Southeast Asian Studies* 25, 1 (March 1994), p. 101.
8. Heather Sutherland, *The Making of a Bureaucratic Elite: the Colonial Transformation of the Javanese Priyayi* (Singapore: Heinemann/Asian Studies Association of Australia, Southeast Asia Publications Series 2, 1979), p. 16. C. Fasseur, *De Indologen: Ambtenaran voor de Oost 1825–1950* (Amsterdam: Bert Bakker, 1993).
9. Louis Couperus, *De Stille Kracht* (Utrecht: Veen, 1900, repub. 1983), trans. Alexander Teizeira de Mattos as *The Hidden Force* (Amherst: University of

Massachusetts Press, 1985), pp. 37 and 45. See Sutherland, *The Making of a Bureaucratic Elite*, p. 41; Laffan, *Islamic Nationhood*, p. 45; and Pramoedya Ananta Toer, *Sang Pemula, Disertai Karya-Karya Non-Fiksi (Jurnalistik) dan Fiksa (Cerpen/Novel) R. M. Tirto Adhi Soerjo* (Jakarta: Lentera Dipantara, 2003, orig. edn Jakarta: Hasta Mitra, 1985), p. 33.

10. On the 'whistleblowers' and accompanying controversies, Jan Breman, 'Het beest aan banden? De koloniale geest aan het begin van de twintigste eeuw', *BKI* 144, 1 (1988), 19–43.

11. Elsbeth Locher-Scholten, *Ethiek in Fragmenten: Vijf Studies over Koliniaal Denken en Doen van Nederlanders in de Indonesische Archipel 1877–1942* (Utrecht: HES, 1981), ch. 1; C. Snouck Hurgronje, 'The ideal of association', trans. C. L. M. Penders, in C. L. M. Penders, *Indonesia: Selected Documents on Colonialism and Nationalism 1830–1942* (St Lucia, Queensland: University of Queensland Press, 1977), p. 164.

12. Furnivall, *Netherlands India*, p. 392; the preceding argument from Locher-Scholten, *Ethiek in Fragmenten*, ch. 5.

13. Quotations and income information from Madelon H. Lulofs, *Rubber* (Singapore: Oxford University Press, 1982), pp. 56, 79, 117, 145, 151.

14. On management Jan Breman, *Taming the Coolie Beast: Plantation Society and the Colonial Order in Southeast Asia* (Delhi: Oxford University Press, 1989), esp. pp. 79, 84–8 and 196; the story of Heer O from Ann Laura Stoler, *Capitalism and Confrontation in Sumatra's Plantation Belt, 1870–1979* (New Haven: Yale University Press, 1985), pp. 56–7; also Stoler, *Carnal Knowledge and Imperial Power: Race and the Intimate in Colonial Rule* (Berkeley: University of California Press, 2002), pp. 25–6, 34–45.

15. J. à Campo, 'Steam navigation and state formation', in Cribb (ed.), *The Late Colonial State*, pp. 11–30; Howard W. Dick, *Surabaya, City of Work: Socioeconomic History, 1900–2000* (Athens, OH: Ohio University Center for International Studies, 2002).

16. Furnivall, *Netherlands India*; Anne Booth, *The Indonesian Economy in the Nineteenth and Twentieth Century: a History of Missed Opportunity* (Houndmills, Basingstoke/Canberra: Macmillan/Australian National University, 1998), pp. 45, 38; Howard W. Dick *et al.*, *The Emergence of a National Economy: an Economic History of Indonesia, 1800–2000* (Sydney: Angus & Robertson, 2001), esp. p. 143; Dharma Kumar, 'The taxation of agriculture in British India and Dutch Indonesia', in C. A. Bayly and D. H. A. Kolff (eds.), *Two Colonial Empires: Comparative Essays on the History of India and Indonesia in the Nineteenth Century* (Dordrecht: Nijhoff, 1986), table 3.

17. Furnivall, *Netherlands India*, pp. 261–87; Elsbeth Locher-Scholten, *Women and the Colonial State: Essays on Gender and Modernity in the Netherlands Indies 1900–1942* (Amsterdam: Amsterdam University Press, 2000), ch. 5; Anton Lucas, 'Images of the Indonesian woman during the Japanese occupation 1942–45', in Jean Gelman Taylor (ed.), *Women Creating Indonesia: the First Fifty Years* (Clayton: Monash Asia Institute, 1997), pp. 57–8; Snouck Hurgronje 'The ideal of association', p. 157.

18. Bob Hering, *Soekarno: Founding Father of Indonesia 1901–1945* (Leiden: KITLV Press, 2002), p. 25.
19. The Soetardjo petition of 1936 and the Governor General's recommendations translated in Penders, *Indonesia*, pp. 141–7.
20. Couperus, *De Stille Kracht*, p. 95.
21. Theodore Friend, *The Blue-Eyed Enemy: Japan against the West in Java and Luzon 1942–1945* (Princeton: Princeton University Press, 1988), pp. 34–42, Harry A. Poeze, 'Political intelligence in the Netherlands Indies', in Cribb (ed.), *The Late Colonial State*; Takashi Shiraishi, 'A new regime of order: the origins of modern surveillance politics in Indonesia', in James T. Siegel and Audrey R. Kahin (eds.), *Southeast Asia over Three Generations: Essays Presented to Benedict R. O'G Anderson* (Ithaca, NY: Cornell Southeast Asia Program 2003), pp. 47–74.
22. Huib Akihary, *Architectuur en Stedebouw in Indonesië: 1870–1970* (Zutphen: De Welburg Pers, 1990), esp. pp. 43–52, 64–7, 115–20; Rudolf Mrázek, *Engineers of Happy Land: Technology and Nationalism in a Colony* (Princeton: Princeton University Press, 2002); and J. A. van Doorn, 'A divided society: segmentation and mediation in late-colonial Indonesia', in G. Schutte and H. Sutherland (eds.), *Papers of the Dutch-Indonesian Historical Conference held at Lage Vuursche, The Netherlands 23–27 June 1980* (Leiden: Bureau of Indonesian Studies, 1982), p. 150; Dick, *Surabaya*, p. 196.
23. Liesbeth Hesselink, 'Prostitution: a necessary evil, particularly in the colonies', in Anke Niehof and Elsbeth Locher-Scholten (eds.), *Indonesian Women in Focus: Past and Present Notions*, pp. 205–24 (Dordrecht: Foris, 1987); Peter Boomgaard, 'The development of colonial health care in Java: an exploratory introduction', *BKI* 149, 1 (1993), 77–93; Terence H. Hull, 'Plague in Java', in Norman G. Owen (ed.), *Death and Disease in Southeast Asia: Explorations in Social, Medical and Demographic History* (Singapore: Oxford University Press/ Asian Studies Association of Australia, 1987), pp. 210–34; Hans Gooszen, *A Demographic History of the Indonesian Archipelago, 1880–1942* (Leiden/ Singapore: KITLV/ISEAS, 1999), ch. 5; A. P. de Hartog, 'Towards improving public nutrition: nutritional policy in Indonesia before independence', in A. M. Luyendijk-Elshout *et al.* (eds.), *Dutch Medicine in the Malay Archipelago 1816–1942* (Amsterdam: Rudopi, 1989); Susan Abeyasekere, 'Health as a nationalist issue in colonial Indonesia', in David P. Chandler and Merle Ricklefs (eds.), *Nineteenth and Twentieth Century Indonesia* (Clayton, Vic.: Monash University Centre of Southeast Asian Studies, 1986), p. 5.
24. Van Doorn, 'A divided society'; Locher-Scholten, *Ethiek in Fragmenten*; Stoler, *Carnal Knowledge*; Gerard Termorshuizen, 'In memoriam Rob Nieuwenhuys 30 Juni 1908–7 November 1999', *BKI* 158, 2 (2002), p. 147.
25. Furnivall, *Netherlands India*, pp. 415–25; Locher-Scholten, *Ethiek in Fragmenten*, chs. 3, 4; Leo Haks and Guus Maris, *Lexicon of Foreign Artists who Visualized Indonesia (1600–1950)* (Singapore: Archipelago Press, 1995).
26. Hella S. Haasse, *Heren van de Thee: Roman* (Amsterdam: Querido, 1992), p. 20.

27. Van Doorn, 'A divided society', p. 134; F. Steijlen (comp.), *Memories of 'The East': Abstracts of the Dutch Interviews about the Netherlands East Indies, Indonesia and New Guinea (1930–1962) in the Oral History Project Collection* (Leiden: KITLV Press, 2002), esp. pp. 114–15; Marianne Hulsbosch, 'Pointy shoes and pith helmets: dress and identity construction in Ambon from 1850 to World War II', PhD thesis, University of Wollongong (2004).

28. P. J. Drooglever, *De Vaderlandse Club 1929–1942: Totoks en de Indische Politiek* (Frankeker: Wever, 1980); G. Roger Knight, 'A sugar factory and its swimming pool: incorporation and differentiation in Dutch colonial society in Java', *Ethnic and Racial Studies* 24, 3 (May 2001), 451–71.

29. Van Doorn, 'A divided society', p. 152; Steijlen, *Memories of 'The East'*, p. 73; comparison with apartheid and quotation from the 1927 Logemann Committee of enquiry into legal reform, cited by C. Fasseur, 'Cornerstone and stumbling block: racial classification and the late colonial state in Indonesia', in Cribb (ed.), *The Late Colonial State*, p. 31; W. F. Wertheim, 'Netherlands-Indian colonial racism and Dutch home racism', in Jan Breman (ed.), *Imperial Monkey Business: Racial Supremacy in Social Darwinist Theory and Colonial Practice* (Amsterdam: VU University Press, 1990), pp. 71–88, esp. pp. 72–4.

30. Locher-Scholten, *Women and the Colonial State*, pp. 17, 89–93; Van Doorn, 'A divided society', p. 150.

31. Locher-Scholten, *Women and the Colonial State*, pp. 91–102; Hulsbosch, 'Pointy shoes and pith helmets'; Stoler, *Carnal Knowledge*.

32. Knight, 'A sugar factory and its swimming pool'.

33. Gosse Kerkhof, 'Het Indische zedenschandaal: een koloniaal incident', MA thesis/dokotraal skriptie, Vakgroep Moderne Aziatishe Geschiedenis, Universiteit te Amsterdam (1982).

34. Shirley Fenton Huie, *The Forgotten Ones: Women and Children Under Nippon* (Sydney: Angus & Robertson, 1992), esp. pp. 172, 186.

35. P. S. Gerbrandy, *Indonesia* (London: Hutchinson, 1950), p. 47; Couperus, *De Stille Kracht*, p. 95.

2 CULTURES OF THE COUNTRYSIDE

1. Savitri Scherer, 'From culture to politics: the writings of Pramoedya A. Toer, 1950–1965', PhD thesis, Australian National University (1981); Barbara Hatley, 'Blora revisited', *Indonesia* 30 (Oct. 1980), 1–16.

2. Jan Breman, *Control of Land and Labour in Colonial Java: a Case Study of Agrarian Crisis and Reform in the Region of Cirebon during the First Decades of the 20th Century* (Dordrecht: Foris, 1983); George Larson, *Prelude to Revolution: Palaces and Politics in Surakarta, 1912–1942* (Dordrecht: Foris, 1987).

3. Heather Sutherland, *The Making of a Bureaucratic Elite: the Colonial Transformation of the Javanese Priyayi* (Singapore: Heinemann/Asian Studies

Association of Australia, Southeast Asia Publications 2, 1979), pp. 69, 19; J. S. Furnivall, *Netherlands India: a Study of Plural Economy* (Cambridge: Cambridge University Press, 1939 [reprinted 1967]), pp. 182–7; Sartono Kartodirdjo, *Modern Indonesia: Tradition and Transformation* (Yogyakarta: Gadjah Mada University Press, 1984), p. 159; Christian Heersink, 'The green gold of Selayar. A socio-economic history of an Indonesian coconut island c.1600–1950: perspectives from a periphery', PhD thesis, Vrije Universiteit te Amsterdam (1995), pp. 194–5.

4. Pramoedya Ananta Toer, *Sang Pemula, Disertai Karya-Karya Non-Fiksi (Jurnalistik) dan Fiksa (Cerpen/Novel) R. M. Tirto Adhi Soerjo* (Jakarta: Lentera Dipantara, 2003, orig. edn Jakarta: Hasta Mitra, 1985); Onghokham, 'The inscrutable and the paranoid: an investigation into the sources of the Brotodiningrat Affair', in Ruth T. McVey (ed.), *Southeast Asian Transitions: Approaches through Social History* (New Haven: Yale University Press, 1978), pp. 112–57.

5. Raden Ngabehi Ronggawarsita, *Serat Kala Tidha/A Time of Darkness* (trans. J. Joseph Errington), in A. L. Becker (ed.), *Writing on the Tongue* (Ann Arbor: University of Michigan Press, 1989), pp. 107–10; Larson, *Prelude to Revolution*, p. 83; Savitri Scherer, *Keselarasan dan Kejanggalan: Pemikiran-Pemikiran Priyayi Nasionalis Jawa awal Abad XX* (Jakarta: Penerbit Sinar Harapan, 1985); Takashi Shiraishi, *An Age in Motion: Popular Radicalism in Java, 1912–1926* (Ithaca: Cornell University Press, 1990).

6. C. L. M. Penders, *Indonesia: Selected Documents on Colonialism and Nationalism 1830–1942* (St Lucia, Queensland: University of Queensland Press, 1977), p. 167; see also p. 152; G. McT. Kahin, *Nationalism and Revolution in Indonesia* (Ithaca, NY: Cornell University Press, 1952), p. 31; *Memori Serah Jabatan 1921–1930 (Jawa Tengah)* (Jakarta: Arsip Nasional Republik Indonesia, 1977); Nederlandsch-Indië, *Uitkomsten der in de Maand November 1920 Gehouden Volkstelling*, 2 vols. (Batavia: Buygrok, 1922).

7. Joost Coté (trans.), *On Feminism and Nationalism: Kartini's Letters to Stella Zeehandelaar 1899–1903* (Clayton, Vic.: Monash Asia Institute, 1995), introduction, pp. xi, 1, 3, 71; Joost Coté (trans.), *Letters from Kartini: an Indonesian Feminist, 1900–1904* (Clayton, Vic.: Monash Asia Institute and Hyland House, 1992), esp. pp. xiii, 11–12, appendix 1, 'Give the Javanese education'.

8. Harry J. Benda and Lance Castles, 'The Samin movement', *BKI* 125 (1969), 207–40; G. Sujayanto and Mayong S. Laksono, 'Samin: melawan penjajah dengan Jawa Ngoko', *Intisari* (July 2001, www.indomedia.com/intisari/2001/Juli/warna-samin.htm, accessed 02/03/04).

9. Pramoedya Ananta Toer, 'Blora', cited by Harry Aveling, 'A note on the author', in Pramoedya Ananta Toer, *A Heap of Ashes*, ed. and trans. Harry Aveling, pp. ix–xxii (St Lucia: University of Queensland Press, 1975), p. ix; Pramoedya, *The Mute's Soliloquy*, trans. Willem Samuels (New York: Penguin, 1998), p. 105; Hatley, 'Blora revisited'.

10. M. R. Fernando, 'Dynamics of peasant economy in Java at local levels', in David P. Chandler and M. C. Ricklefs (eds.), *Nineteenth and Twentieth Century*

Indonesia: Essays in Honour of Professor J. D. Legge (Clayton, Vic.: Monash University Centre of Southeast Asian Studies, 1986), pp. 97–121; and M. R. Fernando, 'Javanese peasants and by-employment at the turn of the century', in Ron May and William J. O'Malley (eds.), *Observing Change in Asia: Essays in Honour of J. A. C. Mackie* (Bathurst: Crawfurd House, 1989), pp. 155–69; Breman, *Control of Land and Labour*; Larson, *Prelude to Revolution*; Anton Lucas, *One Soul, One Struggle: Region and Revolution in Indonesia* (St Leonards: Allen & Unwin, Asian Studies Association of Australia Publications 19, 1991), p. 6; Geoffrey Robinson, *The Dark Side of Paradise: Political Violence in Bali* (Ithaca, NY: Cornell University Press, 1995), 54–6; Mary Margaret Steedley, *Hanging without a Rope: Narrative Experience in Colonial and Postcolonial Karoland* (Princeton: Princeton University Press, 1993), p. 108; W. R. Hugenholtz, 'Famine and food supply in Java 1830–1914', in C. A. Bayly and D. H. A. Kolff (eds.), *Two Colonial Empires: Comparative Essays on the History of India and Indonesia in the Nineteenth Century* (Dordrecht: Nijhoff, 1986), pp. 155–88; W. J. O'Malley, 'Variations on a theme: socio-economic developments in four Central Javanese regencies', in May and O'Malley (eds.), *Observing Changes in Asia*, p. 130; Mike Davis, *Late Victorian Holocausts: El Niño Famines and the Making of the Third World* (London: Verso, 2001), pp. 93–4, 196, 253; Furnivall, *Netherlands India*, p. 347; Heersink, 'Green gold of Selayar', p. 178; Hans Gooszen, *A Demographic History of the Indonesian Archipelago, 1880–1942* (Leiden/Singapore: KITLV/ISEAS, 1999), pp. 37–49.

11.   Sartono Kartodirdjo, *Protest Movements in Rural Java: a Study of Agrarian Unrest in the Ninetenth and Early Twentieth Century* (Singapore: Oxford University Press, 1973); Larson, *Prelude to Revolution*, p. 5; R. E. Elson, *Javanese Peasants and the Colonial Sugar Industry: Impact and Change in an East Java Residency 1830–1940* (Kuala Lumpur: Oxford University Press, 1984), p. 187; M. R. Fernando, 'The trumpet shall sound for rich peasants: Kasan Mukim's uprising in Gedangan, East Java, 1904', *Journal of Southeast Asian Studies* 26, 2 (1995), 242–62; Lorraine Aragon, *Fields of the Lord: Animism, Christian Minorities, and State Development in Indonesia* (Honolulu: University of Hawai'i Press, 2000), p. 106; J. Thomas Lindblad, *Between Dayak and Dutch: the Economic History of Southeast Kalimantan, 1880–1942* (Dordrecht: Foris, 1988), p. 135; Steedley, *Hanging without a Rope*, pp. 60–3; Takashi Shiraishi, *Age in Motion*; Bambang Sulistyo, *Pemogokan Buruh: Sebuah Kajian Sejarah* (Yogyakarta: Tiara Wacana, 1995).

12.   Clifford Geertz, *The Religion of Java* (Glencoe, IL: Free Press, 1961); Toby Alice Volkman, *Feasts of Honour: Ritual and Change in the Toraja Highlands* (Urbana: University of Illinois Press, Illinois Studies in Anthropology No. 16, 1985); J. J. Fox, 'Ziarah visits to the tombs of the wali, the founders of Islam on Java', in M. C. Ricklefs (ed.), *Islam in the Indonesian Social Context* (Clayton, Vic.: Monash University Centre of Southeast Asian Studies), pp. 20–38; Lucas, *One Soul, One Struggle*, p. 19; Patricia Spyer, *The Memory of Trade: Modernity's Entanglements on an Eastern Indonesian Island* (Durham and London: Duke University Press, 2000), pp. 135–40.

13. Lucas, *One Soul, One Struggle*, pp. 19–20; B. R. O'G. Anderson, *Java in a Time of Revolution: Occupation and Resistance, 1944–46* (Ithaca, NY: Cornell University Press, 1972), p. 8, n. 16.

14. Furnivall, *Netherlands India*, p. 317; Rudolf Mrázek, *Engineers of Happy Land: Technology and Nationalism in a Colony* (Princeton: Princeton University Press, 2002), p. 11; W. F. Wertheim, 'Conditions on sugar estates in colonial Java: comparisons with Deli', *Journal of Southeast Asian Studies* 24, 2 (1993), 268–79, p. 275.

15. Kahin, *Nationalism and Revolution*, pp. 18–27; Furnivall, *Netherlands India*, esp. p. 359; Anne Booth, *The Indonesian Economy in the Nineteenth and Twentieth Century: a History of Missed Opportunity* (Houndmills, Basingstoke/Canberra: Macmillan/Australian National University, 1998), pp. 105–7 and 'Living standards and the distribution of income in colonial Indonesia: a review of the evidence', *Journal of Southeast Asian Studies* 29, 2 (1988), 310–34; Nico Dros, *Wages 1820–1940*. Volume 13 of Peter Boomgaard (ed.), *Changing Economy in Indonesia: a Selection of Statistical Source Material from the Early 19th century up to 1940* (Amsterdam: Royal Tropical Institute, 1992); Elsbeth Locher-Scholten, *Women and the Colonial State: Essays on Gender and Modernity in the Netherlands Indies 1900–1942* (Amsterdam: Amsterdam University Press, 2000), p. 72; W. F. Wertheim, *Indonesian Society in Transition* (The Hague and Bandung: Van Hoeve, 1959), p. 263, Davis, *Late Victorian Holocausts*, p. 39; 'Ideal caloric intake' (http://www/goaskalice.columbia.edu/0576.html, 24 February 1995, accessed 03/03/04).

16. Furnivall, *Netherlands India*, p. 356; Jan Breman, *Taming the Coolie Beast: Plantation Society and the Colonial Order in Southeast Asia* (Delhi: Oxford University Press, 1989); Ann Laura Stoler, *Capitalism and Confrontation in Sumatra's Plantation Belt, 1870–1979* (New Haven: Yale University Press, 1985); Madelon Székely-Lulofs, *Rubber*, trans. G. J. Renier and Irene Clephane (Singapore: Oxford University Press, 1982, orig. 1931); *Coolie*, trans. G. J. Renier and Irene Clephane (Singapore: Oxford University Press, 1982, orig. 1932), the former, p. 118, is the source of the quotation; G. T. Haneveld, 'From slave hospital to reliable health care: medical work on the plantations of Sumatra's east coast', in A. M. Luyendijk-Elshout *et al.* (eds.), *Dutch Medicine in the Malay Archipelago 1816–1942* (Amsterdam: Rudopi, 1989), pp. 73–87; Erwiza, 'Miners, managers and the state: a socio-political history of the Ombilin coal-mines, West Sumatra, 1892–1996', PhD thesis, University of Amsterdam (1999), esp. p. 51; Gooszen, *Demographic History*, pp. 200–5; William O'Malley, 'The Great Depression', in Colin Wild and Peter Carey (eds.) *Born in Fire: the Indonesian Struggle for Independence* (Athens, OH: Ohio University Press, 1986), p. 66.

17. Gooszen, *Demographic History*, table 2.2; Steedly, *Hanging without a Rope*, ch. 3; Bambang Purwanto, 'From dusun to the market: native rubber cultivation in Southern Sumatra, 1890–1940', PhD thesis, School of Oriental and African Studies, University of London (1992); Howard W. Dick *et al.*, *The Emergence of a National Economy: an Economic History of Indonesia, 1800–2000*

(Sydney: Angus & Robertson, 2001), p. 138; Booth, *Indonesian Economy*, p. 106; O'Malley, 'The Great Depression'; Kahin, *Nationalism and Revolution*, p. 27; Lance Brennan, Les Heathcote and Anton Lucas, 'The causation of famine: a comparative analysis of Lombok and Bengal 1891–1974', *South Asia* 7, 1 (June 1984), 1–26.

18. Pramoedya, *Mute's Soliloquy*, p. 107; Benda and Castles, 'Samin movement', p. 231; Greg Barton, *Gus Dur: the Authorized Biography of Abdurrahman Wahid* (Jakarta, Singapore: Equinox, 2002), pp. 38–40; J. J. Fox and Pradjarto Dirjosanjoto, 'The memories of village *Santri* from Jombang in East Java', in May and O'Malley (eds.), *Observing Change in Asia*, pp. 94–110; Marcel Bonneff, 'Le Kauman de Yogyakarta: des Fonctionnaires religieux convertis au réformisme et a l'esprit d'entreprise', *Archipel* 30 (1985), 175–205.

19. Fox and Drijosanjoto, 'Memories'; Anderson, *Java in a Time of Revolution*, pp. 4–10; K. H. I. Zarkasyi, 'Le *pondok pesantren* en Indonésie', *Archipel* 30 (1985), 163–74, A. J. Day, 'Islam and literature in South East Asia: some premodern, mainly Javanese perceptions', in M. B. Hooker (ed.), *Islam in South East Asia* (Leiden: Brill, 1983), pp. 130–59; Susan Rodgers, *Telling Lives, Telling History: Autobiography and Historical Imagination in Modern Indonesia* (Berkeley: University of California Press, 1995), pp. 208–13; Pramoedya's 'Sunat', cited in C. W. Watson, 'Pramoedya Ananta Toer's short stories: an anti-poststructuralist account', in C. D. Grijns and S. O. Robson (eds.), *Cultural Contact and Textual Interpretation: Papers from the Fourth European Colloquium on Malay and Indonesian Studies held in Leiden in 1983*, pp. 233–46 (Dordrecht: Foris, 1986); Heersink, 'Green gold of Selayar', p. 229.

20. Cited in Mitsuo Nakamura, *The Crescent Arises over the Banyan Tree: a Study of the Muhamadijah Movement in a Central Javanese Town* (Yogyakarta: Gajah Mada University Press, 1993), p. 34.

3 'TO ASSAIL THE COLONIAL MACHINE'

1. Pramoedya Ananta Toer, *Sang Pemula, Disertai Karya-Karya Non-Fiksi (Jurnalistik) dan Fiksa (Cerpen/Novel) R. M. Tirto Adhi Soerjo* (Jakarta: Lentera Dipantara, 2003, orig. edn Jakarta: Hasta Mitra, 1985), p. 24.

2. A. A. M. Djelantik, *The Birthmark: Memoirs of a Balinese Prince* (Singapore: Periplus, 1997), pp. 60–6; Andreas Tarnutzer, *Kota Adat Denpasar (Bali). Stadtentwicklung, Staatliches Handeln und Endogene Institutionen* (Zürich: Geographisches Institut Vol. 12, 1993).

3. Howard W. Dick, *Surabaya, City of Work: Socioeconomic History, 1900–2000* (Athens, OH: Ohio University Center for International Studies, 2002), table 3.1.

4. Pramoedya, *Sang Pemula*; Ahmat B. Adam, *The Vernacular Press and the Emergence of Modern Indonesian Consciousness (1855–1913)* (Ithaca, NY: Cornell University Southeast Asia Program, 1995); Sartono Kartodirdjo, *Modern Indonesia: Tradition and Transformation* (Yogyakarta: Gadjah Mada University Press, 1984), pp. 163–71.

5. William H. Frederick, *Visions and Heat: the Making of the Indonesian Revolution* (Athens, OH: Ohio University Press, 1989), pp. 62–3; Henri Chambert-Loir, 'Muhammad Bakir: a Batavian scribe and author in the nineteenth century', *RIMA* 18, 2 (Summer 1984), 44–72.

6. H. M. J. Maier, 'From heteroglossia to polyglossia: the creation of Malay and Dutch in the Indies', *Indonesia* 56 (Oct. 1993), 37–65; James Sneddon, *The Indonesian Language: Its History and Role in Modern Society* (Sydney: University of New South Wales Press, 2003), esp. pp. 86–106.

7. J. A. van Doorn, 'A divided society: segmentation and mediation in late-colonial Indonesia', in G. Schutte and H. Sutherland (eds.), *Papers of the Dutch-Indonesian Historical Conference held at Lage Vuursche, The Netherlands 23–27 June 1980* (Leiden: Bureau of Indonesian Studies, 1982) pp. 128–71; Frederick, *Visions and Heat*, esp. p. 17; Susan Abeyasekere, *Jakarta: a History* (Kuala Lumpur: Oxford University Press, 1987).

8. Text of *Nyai Ratna* in Pramoedya, *Sang Pemula*, trans. Elizabeth Riharti, Joost Coté and Markus Soema, *RIMA* 32, 2 (Summer 1998), 45–95.

9. Foreword to Mark Hanusz, *Kretek: The Culture and Heritage of Indonesia's Clove Cigarettes* (Jakarta: Equinox, 2000), p. xiv, pp. 32–47.

10. Suzanne April Brenner, *The Domestication of Desire: Women, Wealth, and Modernity in Java* (Princeton: Princeton University Press, 1988).

11. James Rush, *Opium to Java: Revenue Farming and Chinese Enterprise in Colonial Indonesia, 1860–1910* (Ithaca, NY: Cornell University Press, 1990), pp. 248–53; Peter Post, 'The Kwik Hoo Tong trading society of Semarang, Java: a Chinese business network in late colonial Java', *Journal of Southeast Asian Studies* 33, 2 (2002), 279–96; Didi Kwartanada, 'Competition, patriotism and collaboration: the Chinese businessmen of Yogyakarta between the 1930s and 1945', *Journal of Southeast Asian Studies* 33, 2 (2002), 257–77; Dick, *Surabaya*; Abeyasekere, *Jakarta*.

12. Beryl de Zoete and Walter Spies, *Dance and Drama in Bali* (London: Faber and Faber, 1938; repr. Kuala Lumpur: Oxford University Press, 1973), p. 215; Robert Martin Dumas, *'Teater Abdulmuluk' in Zuid-Sumatra: op de Drempel van een Nieuw Tijperk* (Leiden University: Onderzoekschool voor Aziatische, Afrikaanse, en Amerindische Studies, 2000).

13. Abeyasekere, *Jakarta*; Frederick, 'Dreams of freedom, moments of despair: Armijn Pané and the imagining of modern Indonesian culture', in Jim Schiller and Barbara Martin-Schiller (eds.), *Imagining Indonesia: Cultural Politics and Political Culture* (Athens, OH: Ohio University Center for International Studies Monographs in International Studies Southeast Asian Series, Number 97, 1997), pp. 54–89; liner notes to *Keroncong Asli, Gesang*; Pramoedya cited in Rudolf Mrázek, *Engineers of Happy Land: Technology and Nationalism in a Colony* (Princeton: Princeton University Press, 2002), p. 196.

14. Freek Colombijn, 'The politics of Indonesian football', *Archipel* 59 (2000), 171–200; Antariksa, 'The life and happy times of soccer supporters', *Latitudes* 5 (June 2001), 27–33.

15. Abeyasekere, *Jakarta*, p. 113; Salim Said, *Shadows on the Silver Screen: a Social History of Indonesian Film* (Jakarta: Lontar Foundation, 1991), ch. 1; Aiko Kurasawa, 'Propaganda media on Java under the Japanese 1942–1945', *Indonesia* 44 (Oct. 1987), pp. 72, 77, 79, and p. 89; Frederick, 'Dreams of freedom', p. 60; Mrázek, *Engineers of Happy Land*, pp. 174–91.

16. *Three Early Indonesian Short Stories* (trans. and ed. Paul Tickell) (Clayton, Vic.: Monash University Centre of Southeast Asian Studies, 1981); originally attributed to Marco, these stories were written by one of his Semarang collaborators.

17. Anne Booth, 'Living standards and the distribution of income in colonial Indonesia: a review of the evidence', *Journal of Southeast Asian Studies* 29, 2 (1988), 310–34, p. 325; and Nico Dros, *Wages 1820–1940*. Volume 13 of Peter Boomgaard (ed.), *Changing Economy in Indonesia: a Selection of Statistical Source Material from the Early 19th Century up to 1940* (Amsterdam: Royal Tropical Institute, 1992) (but *cf.* Dick, *Surabaya*, table 5.2); John Ingleson, *In Search of Justice: Workers and Unions in Colonial Java, 1908–1926* (Singapore: Oxford University Press, 1986), pp. 15–19; W. F. Wertheim, *Indonesian Society in Transition* (The Hague and Bandung: Van Hoeve, 1959), pp. 266–7; Elsbeth Locher-Scholten, *Women and the Colonial State: Essays on Gender and Modernity in the Netherlands Indies 1900–1942* (Amsterdam: Amsterdam University Press, 2000), p. 91; Ann Stoler and Karen Stessler, ch. 8 of *Carnal Knowledge and Imperial Power: Race and the Intimate in Colonial Rule* (Berkeley: University of California Press, 2002); Ingleson, 'Urban Java during the Depression', *Journal of Southeast Asian Studies* 19 (1988), 292–309, table 1; Dick, *Surabaya*, pp. 189–92, 277–9; Abeyasekere, *Jakarta*, p. 91.

18. Michael Laffan, *Islamic Nationhood and Colonial Indonesia: the Umma below the Winds* (London: RoutledgeCurzon, 2003), pp. 181–9; B. R. O'G. Anderson, *Java in a Time of Revolution: Occupation and Resistance, 1944–46* (Ithaca, NY: Cornell University Press, 1972), p. 436; George McT. Kahin, *Nationalism and Revolution in Indonesia* (Ithaca, NY: Cornell University Press, 1952); Takashi Shiraishi, *An Age in Motion: Popular Radicalism in Java, 1912–1926* (Ithaca: Cornell University Press, 1990), esp. pp. 83–6; Harry A. Poeze, 'Early Indonesian emancipation. Abdul Rivai, Van Heutsz and the *Bintang Hindia*', *BKI* 145, 1 (1989): 87–106; C. L. M. Penders, *Indonesia: Selected Documents on Colonialism and Nationalism 1830–1942* (St Lucia, Queensland: University of Queensland Press, 1977), pp. 232–4; Ingleson, *In Search of Justice*, p. 252.

19. H. M. J. Maier, 'Written in the prison's light: the *Hikajat Kadiroen* by Semaoen' (trans. Ernst van Lennep), *RIMA* 30 (1996), 1–18; trans. Jan Lingard *et al.*, 'The story of Kadiroen', *RIMA* 30 (1996), 19–139.

20. G. W. J. Drewes, 'The struggle between Javanism and Islam as illustrated by the Serat Dermagandul', *BKI* 122 (1965), 309–65; Locher-Scholten, *Women and the Colonial State*, pp. 202–5.

21. Mitsuo Nakamura, *The Crescent Arises over the Banyan Tree: a Study of the Muhamadijah Movement in a Central Javanese Town* (Yogyakarta: Gajah Mada University Press, 1993), pp. 60–2; Frederick, *Visions and Heat*, p. 68

(see also p. 39); *Hikajat Kadiroen*, pp. 113–14; Semaoen, 'An early account of the independence movement', trans. Ruth McVey, *Indonesia* 1 (April 1966), 46–75; Dewi Yuliarti, *Semaoen: Pers Bumiputera dan Radikalisasi Sarekat Islam Semarang* (Semarang: Bendera, 2000), pp. 130–4.

22. Elsbeth Locher-Scholten, 'State violence and the police in colonial Indonesia', in Freek Colombijn and J. Thomas Lindblad (eds.), *Roots of Violence in Indonesia: Contemporary Violence in Historical Perspective* (Leiden: KITLV Press, 2002), pp. 81–104.

23. Trans. C. L. M. Penders, *Indonesia,* pp. 308–11.

24. J. D. Legge, *Sukarno: a Political Biography* (Sydney: Allen & Unwin, 1972); Bob Hering, *Soekarno: Founding Father of Indonesia 1901–1945* (Leiden: KITLV Press, 2002).

25. Pramoedya Ananta Toer, *The Mute's Soliloquy*, trans. Willem Samuels (New York: Penguin, 1998), p. 109.

26. I Nyoman Darma Putra, *Wanita Bali Tempo Doeloe: Perspektif Masa Kini* (Denpasar: Bali Jani, 2003), pp. 21–48, referring to research by Lyn Parker.

27. Syahrir's *Out of Exile* quoted by Maier, 'From heteroglossia to polyglossia', p. 39.

28. Frederick, *Visions and Heat*, p. 27.

29. Interview I Made Darma (b. 1927), by Pujastana 1996; Kwartanada, 'Competition, patriotism and collaboration', pp. 267–70; Hiroshi Shimizu, 'Rise and fall of the *Karayuki-san* in the Netherlands Indies from the late nineteenth century to the 1930s', *RIMA* 26 (Summer 1992), 44–62; Frederick, *Visions and Heat*, pp. 84–5; Peter Post, 'Japan and the integration of the Netherlands East Indies into the world economy, 1868–1942', *RIMA* 27, Special Edition: Island Southeast Asia and the World Economy (Winter/Summer 1993), 134–65; Netherland Government Information Bureau, *A Decade of Japanese Underground Activities in The Netherland East Indies* (London: His Majesty's Stationery Office, 1942); Shigeru Sato, *War, Nationalism and Peasants: Java under the Japanese Occupation, 1942–1945* (St Leonards, NSW: Allen & Unwin, Asian Studies Association of Australian Publications Series 26, 1994); Elly Touwen-Bouwsma, 'The Indonesian nationalists and the Japanese "liberation" of Indonesia: visions and reactions (the Japanese occupation in Southeast Asia)', *Journal of Southeast Asian Studies* 27, 1 (March 1996), 18–32.

4 THE REVOLUTION

1. Quoted by Tantri Yuliandini, 'Photos recount WWII horror', *The Jakarta Post*, 19 February 2004.

2. Pramoedya Ananta Toer, *The Mute's Soliloquy*, trans. Willem Samuels (New York: Penguin, 1998), pp. 157–8, also 'The vanquished' (trans. H. Aveling), in *A Heap of Ashes*, pp. 74–106 (St. Lucia: University of Queensland Press, 1975).

3. Pramoedya, 'The vanquished', p. 50.

4. B. R. O'G. Anderson, *Java in a Time of Revolution: Occupation and Resistance, 1944–46* (Ithaca, NY: Cornell University Press, 1972), pp. 413–14; Bob Hering *Soekarno: Founding Father of Indonesia 1901–1945* (Leiden: KITLV Press, 2002), pp. 13, 223; Jacques Leclerc, 'Afterword: the masked hero', in Anton Lucas (ed.), *Local Opposition and Underground Resistance to the Japanese in Java, 1942–1945* (Clatyon, Vic.: Monash University Papers on Southeast Asia No. 13, 1986), pp. 342–4.

5. Anthony J. Reid and Oki Akira (eds.), *The Japanese Experience in Indonesia: Selected Memoirs of 1942–1945* (Athens, Ohio: Ohio University Monographs, 1986), pp. 43–4, 9–30; *Numbers of POWS and Civilian Internees* (www.beckett73.freeserve.co.uk/baker/prisoners.htm, accessed 04/06/04), with some caution; Elsbeth Locher-Scholten, 'After the "distant war": Dutch public memory of the Second World War in Asia', in Remco Raben (ed.), *Representing the Japanese Occupation of Indonesia: Personal Testimonies and Public Images in Indonesia, Japan and the Netherlands* (Zwolle/Amsterdam: Waanders/Netherlands Institute for War Documentation, 1999), p. 56 and n. 6.

6. Richard Chauvel, *Nationalists, Soldiers and Separatists: the Ambonese Islands from Colonialism to Revolt 1880–1950* (Leiden: KITLV Press, 1990), pp. 173–89.

7. Pramoedya, *Mute's Soliloquy*, pp. 307–8; Sintha Melati, 'In the service of the underground: the struggle against the Japanese in Java' (trans. and annot. David Bouchier), in Lucas (ed.), *Local Opposition and Underground Resistance*, pp. 123–264; Yuki Tanaka, *Hidden Horrors: Japanese War Crimes in World War II* (Boulder: Westview Press, 1998), ch. 3; Suharti quoted in Maria Hartiningsih, 'Indonesia's "comfort women"', *Latitudes* 3 (April 2001), 10–15.

8. Audrey Kahin, *Rebellion to Integration: West Sumatra and the Indonesian Polity* (Amsterdam: Amsterdam University Press, 1999), pp. 95–106; Anton Lucas, 'Images of the Indonesian woman during the Japanese occupation 1942–45', in Jean Taylor (ed.), *Women Creating Indonesia: the First Fifty Years* (Clayton: Monash Asia Institute, 1997), pp. 52–90, p. 74; Yuliandini, 'WWII horror'; A. N. Krisna, 'Asisten perapian kereta api'; 'Jejak getir korban romusha', *Suara Merdeka* 1/03/04; see 'Kisah seorang romusha Jawa', *Suara Independent* 3, 1 (1995); Shigeru Sato, *War, Nationalism and Peasants: Java under the Japanese Occupation, 1942–1945* (St Leonards, NSW: Allen & Unwin, Asian Studies Association of Australia Publications 26, 1994), pp. 154–60, p. 259, n. 8.

9. Theodore Friend, *The Blue-Eyed Enemy: Japan against the West in Java and Luzon 1942–1945* (Princeton: Princeton University Press, 1988), pp. 193–6; Tanaka, *Hidden Horrors*, ch. 5.

10. Quotation from Pramoedya, 'The vanquished'; Elly Touwen-Bouwsma, 'The Indonesian nationalists and the Japanese "liberation" of Indonesia: visions and reactions (the Japanese occupation in Southeast Asia)', *Journal of Southeast Asian Studies* 27, 1 (March 1996), 18–32.

11. Pramoedya, *Mute's Soliloquy*, p. 189; and foreword to Mark Hanusz, *Kretek: the Culture and Heritage of Indonesia's Clove Cigarettes* (Jakarta: Equinox, 2000), p. xiv; Pierre van der Eng, 'Indonesia's economy and standard of living in the 20th century', in Grayson Lloyd and Shannon Smith (eds.), *Indonesia Today:*

Challenges of History (Singapore: Institute of Southeast Asian Studies, Indonesia Assessment Series, Research School of Pacific and Asian Studies, Australian National University, 2001), p. 191.

12. William H. Frederick, *Visions and Heat: the Making of the Indonesian Revolution* (Athens, OH: Ohio University Press, 1989), p. 102; Howard W. Dick *et al.*, *The Emergence of a National Economy: an Economic History of Indonesia, 1800–2000* (Sydney: Angus & Robertson, 2001), pp. 165–7.

13. Pramoedya, *Mute's Soliloquy*, pp. 178–88; Aiko Kurasawa, 'Propaganda media on Java under the Japanese 1942–1945', *Indonesia* 44 (Oct. 1987), 59–116.

14. Lucas, 'Images of the Indonesian woman'.

15. Friend, *Blue-Eyed Enemy*, p. 98.

16. Pramoedya, *Mute's Soliloquy*; Anderson, *Java in a Time of Revolution*.

17. Douglas Miles, *Cutlass and Crescent Moon: a Case Study in Social and Political Change in Outer Indonesia* (University of Sydney: Centre for Asian Studies, 1976), p. 111.

18. Mochter Lubis, *Jalan Tak Ada Ujung* (Jakarta: Yayasan Obor Indonesia, 2002 [originally published 1952]), p. 78; Anthony Reid, *Indonesian National Revolution* (Hawthorn, Vic.: Longman, 1974), chs. 2 and 3; Frederick, *Visions and Heat*; Marguerite Schenkuizen, *Memoirs of an Indo Woman: Twentieth Century Life in the East Indies and Abroad*, ed. and trans. Lizelot Stout van Balgooy (Athens, OH: Ohio University Center for International Studies, 1993), p. 185; Shirley Fenton-Huie, *The Forgotten Ones: Women and Children Under Nippon* (Sydney: Angus & Robertson, 1992); Anthony Reid, 'Indonesia: revolution without socialism', in Robin Jeffrey (ed.), *Asia: the Winning of Independence* (London: Macmillan, 1981), pp. 107–57; Friend, *Blue-Eyed Enemy*.

19. Idrus, 'Surabaja', in H. Aveling (ed. and trans.), *From Surabaja to Armageddon: Indonesian Short Stories* (Singapore: Heinemann, 1976), pp. 1–28; Frederick, 'The appearance of revolution: cloth, uniform and the pemuda style in east Java, 1945–1949', in Henk Schulte Nordholt (ed.), *Outward Appearances: Dressing State and Society in Indonesia* (Leiden: KITLV, 1997), pp. 199–248.

20. My thanks to Bill Frederick, personal comment 22/4/04; see Friend, *Blue-Eyed Enemy*, pp. 228 and 237; Nyoman S. Pendit, *Bali Berjuang* (2nd edn Jakarta: Gunung Agung, 1979 [original edn 1954]); Reid, *National Revolution*, p. 58, n. 25, p. 119, n. 7, p. 120, n. 17, p. 148, n. 25 and n. 37; Pramoedya Ananta Toer, Koesalah Soebagyo Toer and Ediati Kamil, *Kronik Revolusi Indonesia* [Jakarta: Kepustakaan Populer Gramedia, vol. I (1945); vol. II (1946) 1999; vol. III (1947); vol. IV (1948) 2003]; Ann Stoler, *Capitalism and Confrontation in Sumatra's Plantation Belt, 1870–1979* (New Haven: Yale University Press, 1985), p. 103.

21. Ni Cenik, interviewed by Cok Sawitri for the Bali Oral History Project; Robert Cribb, 'Political dimensions of the currency question 1945–1947', *Indonesia* 31 (April 1981), 113–36.

22. Schenkuizen, *Memoirs*, pp. 185–91.

23. Pramoedya, 'Dendam', translated as 'Revenge' by B. R. O'G. Anderson, in A. L. Becker (ed.), *Writing on the Tongue* (Ann Arbor: University of Michigan Press, 1989), pp. 15–34; *Di Tepi Kali Bekasi* (Jakarta: Lentera Dipantara, 2003, original edn Jakarta: Gapura, 1951); William H. Frederick, 'Shadows of an unseen hand: some patterns of violence in the Indonesian Revolution, 1945–1949', in Freek Colombijn and J. Thomas Lindblad (eds.), *Roots of Violence in Indonesia: Contemporary Violence in Historical Perspective* (Leiden: KITLV Press, 2002), pp. 143–73.

24. Reid, *National Revolution*, ch. 4; Robert Cribb, *Gangsters and Revolutionaries: the Jakarta People's Militia and the Indonesian Revolution 1945–1949* (Sydney: Allen & Unwin, 1991); Mary Margaret Steedly, *Hanging without a Rope: Narrative Experience in Colonial and Postcolonial Karoland* (Princeton: Princeton University Press, 1993), pp. 209–11; Stoler, *Capitalism and Confrontation*; Anton Lucas, *One Soul, One Struggle: Region and Revolution in Indonesia* (St Leonards: Allen & Unwin, Asian Studies Association of Australia Publications Series 19, 1991).

25. Pramoedya, *Di Tepi Kali Bekasi*, p. 27; Frederick, 'The appearance of revolution'; Steedly, *Hanging without a Rope*.

26. Interview by Steedley, *Hanging without a Rope*, p. 210.

27. Anderson, *Java in a Time of Revolution*, p. 206.

28. Sutan Syahrir, *Our Struggle*, cited in Anderson, *Java in a Time of Revolution*, p. 191 (emphasis in the original).

29. In Ann Swift, *The Road to Madiun: the Indonesian Communist Uprising of 1948* (Ithaca NY: Cornell Southeast Asia Program. 1989), pp. 97–102; alternative trans. Reid, *National Revolution*, p. 143.

30. David Charles Anderson, 'The military aspects of the Madiun Affair', *Indonesia* 21 (April 1976), 1–53; Leclerc, 'Afterword'; George McT. Kahin, *Nationalism and Revolution in Indonesia* (Ithaca, NY: Cornell University Press, 1952), p. 274; Agus Sunyoto Maksum and A. Zainuddin, *Lubang-Lubang Pembantaian: Petualangan PKI di Madiun* (Jakarta: Grafiti, 1990), pp. 49, 52, 59.

31. Pramoedya, 'The vanquished', p. 104; *Mereka Yang Dilumpahkan* (Jakarta: Hasta Mitra, 1995, rev. edn of 2 vol. original, Jakarta: Balai Pustaka, 1951).

5 LIVING IN THE ATOMIC AGE

1. Pramoedya Ananta Toer, 'Creatures behind houses', in *Tales from Jakarta: Caricatures of Circumstances and their Human Beings*, trans. the Nusantara Translation Group (Jakarta/Singapore: Equinox, 2000), pp. 183–4.

2. Following Herbert Feith, *The Decline of Constitutional Democracy in Indonesia* (Ithaca, NY: Cornell University Press, 1962), pp. 100–3; William Frederick, *Visions and Heat: the Making of the Indonesian Revolution* (Athens, OH: Ohio University Press, 1989), where the class is described as the 'New *Priyayi*'.

3. 'My Kampung', in *Tales from Jakarta*, p. 77 (translation adapted). The name comes from a famous graveyard.

4. Rn, 'Sedikit tentang kota Djakarta', *Harian Rakjat* 23/06 and 25/06/1956.
5. Sukarno, *Lahirnja Pantja-Sila: Bung Karno Menggemblèng Dasar-Dasar Negara*, 2nd edn (Jogjakarta: Goentoer, 1949) (although this is not the order of the Principles).
6. Martin Ramstedt, 'Introduction: negotiating identities – Indonesian "Hindus" between local, national, and global interests', in Martin Ramstedt (ed.), *Hinduism in Indonesia: a Minority Religion between Local, National, and Global Interests* (London: Routledge Curzon, 2004), pp. 1–34; Paul Stange, '"Legitimate" mysticism in Indonesia', *RIMA* 20, 2 (1986), 76–117; Greg Barton, *Gus Dur: the Authorized Biography of Abdurrahman Wahid* (Jakarta, Singapore: Equinox, 2002), pp. 41–51; C. van Dijk, *Rebellion under the Banner of Islam: the Darul Islam in Indonesia* (The Hague: Martinus Nijhoff, 1981), pp. 47–52.
7. 'SM Kartosoewirjo: pemberontak atau Mujahid?' *Suara Hidayatullah* (May 1999, (www.hidayatullah.com/sahid/9905/sejarah.htm), accessed 03/02/04); van Dijk, *Rebellion*; M. C. Ricklefs, *A History of Modern Indonesia* (London: Macmillan, 1981, 2nd edn 1993, 3rd edn 2001), p. 227 (which gives 1905 as his year of birth); Anthony J. S. Reid, *Indonesian National Revolution* (Hawthorn, Vic.: Longman, 1974), pp. 166–7; Feith, *Decline*; Kathryn Robinson, 'Living in the hutan: jungle village life under the Darul Islam', *RIMA* 17 (1983), 208–29; Esther Velthoen, 'Mapping Sulawesi in the 1950s', in Henk Schulte Nordholt and Gusti Asnan (eds.), *Indonesia in Transition: Work in Progress* (Yogyakarta: Pustaka Pelajar, 2003), pp. 103–23; Theodore Friend, *The Blue-Eyed Enemy: Japan against the West in Java and Luzon 1942–1945* (Princeton: Princeton University Press, 1988), p. 239.
8. 'Agama baru di Pasangkaju (Utara Mandar)', *Duta Masjarkat* 15/05/56.
9. Douglas Miles, *Cutlass and Crescent Moon: a Case Study in Social and Political Change in Outer Indonesia* (University of Sydney: Centre for Asian Studies, 1976).
10. Clifford Geertz, *The Interpretation of Cultures: Selected Essays by Clifford Geertz* (New York: Basic Books, 1973), p. 150; Paul Stange, 'The Sumarah movement in Javanese mysticism', PhD thesis, University of Wisconsin, Madison (1980).
11. Feith, *Decline*, pp. 38–45; see James T. Siegel, *Fetish, Recognition, Revolution* (Princeton: Princeton University Press, 1997).
12. Pramoedya Ananta Toer, 'It's not an all night fair' (trans. William Watson), *Indonesia* 15 (1973), 21–80.
13. Donald Hindley, *The Communist Party of Indonesia, 1951–1963* (Berkeley: University of California Press, 1964), maps 1 and 2; J. D. Legge, *Central Authority and Regional Autonomy in Indonesia: a Study in Local Administration 1950–1960* (Ithaca, NY: Cornell University Southeast Asia Program, 1961), appendix.
14. Feith, *Decline*, pp. 425–77; 'Hasil resmi pemilihan umum DPR seluruh Indonesia', *Duta Masjarakat* 28/01/1956.
15. Pramoedya Ananta Toer, 'The mastermind', in *Tales from Jakarta*, p. 217.
16. Feith, *Decline*, pp. 306 and 312; Legge, *Central Authority and Regional Autonomy*.

17. Usmar Ismail (producer/director), *Tamu Agung* (Perfini Films, 1955) (www.arts.monash.edu.au/mai/films/guest.html); Salim Said, *Shadows on the Silver Screen: a Social History of Indonesian Film* (Jakarta: Lontar Foundation, 1991); *cf.* Clifford Geertz, *Peddlers and Princes: Social Change and Economic Modernization in Two Indonesian Towns* (Chicago: University of Chicago Press, 1963), esp. pp. 14–16.

18. *Pikiran Rakjat* 01/09/1952; *Harian Rakjat* 18/12/1954; *Duta Masjarakat* 24/03/1956.

19. Sukarno, Speech at the opening of the Bandung Conference, 18 April 1955 (Modern history sourcebook (www.fordham.edu/halsall/mod/1955sukarno-bandong.html), accessed 05/19/2004).

20. I Nyoman Wijaya, '1950s lifestyles in Denpasar through the eyes of short story writers', in Adrian Vickers and I Nyoman Darma Putra with Michele Ford (eds.), *To Change Bali: Essays in Honour of I Gusti Ngurah Bagus* (Denpasar: Bali Post, 2000), pp. 113–34; and unpublished notes; Feith, *Decline*, p. 315. See further *Bhakti* 15/12/1953; Huib Akihary, *Architectuur en Stedebouw in Indonesië: 1870–1970* (Zutphen: De Welburg Pers, 1990); Susan Abeyasekere, *Jakarta: a History* (Kuala Lumpur: Oxford University Press, 1987), pp. 173–5.

21. 'Hormatilah lagu kebangsaan kita "Indonesia Raja"', *Duta Masjarakat*, 28/01/1956; Ngurah W. S., 'Olah raga hanya meluas di kota sadja', *Bhakti* 29, 15/12/1953; Wijaya unpublished notes.

22. Pramoedya Ananta Toer, 'Djakarta', written in 1955, published in *Almanak Seni* 1957, reproduced on (www.radix.net/~bardsley/prampage.html accessed 27/01/04); *Bhakti* 3, 01/01/1954, pp. 4–7.

23. Pramoedya, 'Djakarta'; Abeyasekere, *Jakarta*, p. 176.

24. *Pikirian Rakjat* 01/09/1952.

25. *Damai* 2, 2, 17/01/1955, p. 10, cited by I Nyoman Darma Putra, *Wanita Bali Tempo Doeloe: Perspektif Masa Kini* (Denpasar: Bali Jani, 2003), p. 70; Feith, *Decline*, p. 223.

26. Keith Foulcher, *Social Commitment in Literature and the Arts: the Indonesian 'Institute of People's Culture' 1950–1965* (Clayton, Vic.: Centre of Southeast Asian Studies, Monash University, 1986), p. 44; see Rn, 'Sedikit tentang kota Djakarta', film advertisements in *Duta Masjarakat*; Feith, *Decline*, p. 315 (for 1951–3).

27. I Nyoman Darma Putra, 'Bali and modern Indonesian literature: the 1950s', in Adrian Vickers and I Nyoman Darma Putra (eds.), *To Change Bali* (Denpasar: Bali Post, 2000), pp. 135–53; Ruth T. McVey, 'The *wayang* controversy in Indonesian communism', in M. Hobart and R. H. Taylor (eds.), *Context, Meaning and Power in Southeast Asia* (Ithaca, NY: Cornell University Southeast Asia Publications, 1986), pp. 21–53; and Pramoedya Ananta Toer, *Nyanyi sunyi* vol. 1, pp. 34–41 (not in the translation).

28. Pramoedya, 'Djakarta'; Ruth T. McVey, 'The *wayang* controversy'; Rn, 'Sedikit tentang kota Djakarta'.

29. Nj. Jasmine Oka, 'Garis baru pagi perjuangan wanita Indonesia', reproduced in Darma Putra, *Wanita Bali*, pp. 181–91; Saskia Wieringa, *Sexual Politics in Indonesia* (Basingstoke: Palgrave Macmillan, 2002).

30. George McT. Kahin, *Nationalism and Revolution in Indonesia* (Ithaca, NY: Cornell University Press, 1952), p. 443.
31. Howard W. Dick *et al.*, *The Emergence of a National Economy: an Economic History of Indonesia, 1800–2000* (Sydney: Angus & Robertson, 2001), p. 192; Miles, *Cutlass and Crescent Moon.*
32. *Duta Masjarakat* 1956; Feith, *Decline*, pp. 556–69; Dick *et al.*, *Emergence*, pp. 153–93.
33. *Duta Masjarakat* 07/01/1956.
34. A. H. Nasution, *Sekitar Perang Kemerdekaan Indonesia* (Bandung: Angkasa, 1977–9), vol. 8, p. 64; Made Arja, 'Seorang pegawai rumah pendjara' (in column 'Suka-Duka'), *Bhakti* 3, 1 (01/01/1954); Geoffrey Robinson, *The Dark Side of Paradise: Political Violence in Bali* (Ithaca, NY: Cornell University Press, 1995), pp. 236–8 (n.b. his rice prices are higher than Arja's); Jan Elliott, 'Bersatoe kita berdiri bertjerai kita djatoeh [United we stand divided we fall]: workers and unions, in Jakarta, 1945–1965', PhD thesis, University of New South Wales (1997), pp. 31, 144, 176–7, 189; Jan Elliott, 'Equality? The influence of legislation and notions of gender on the position of women wage workers in the economy: Indonesia 1950–58', in Jean Gelman Taylor (ed.), *Women Creating Indonesia: the First Fifty Years* (Clayton: Monash Asia Institute, 1997), pp. 127–55.
35. *Duta Masjarakat* 07/01/1956.
36. Nya 'Abbas Akup (director and writer, producer Usmar Ismail), *Tiga Buronan* (Jakarta: Perfini Films, 1957); D. Djajakusuma (producer and director), *Harimau Tjampa* (Jakarta: Perfini Films, 1953) (www.arts.monash.edu.au/mai/films/tiger.html).
37. E.g. Marsidik [?], *Buku Kenangan 1950–1958* (n.p.: Pusat Pendidikan Peralatan Angkatan Darat, n.d.).
38. Anthony J. S. Reid, 'The nationalist quest for an Indonesian past', in Anthony J. S. Reid and David Marr (eds.), *Perceptions of the Past in Southeast Asia* (Singapore: Heinemann, 1979), pp. 281–98.
39. Feith, *Decline*, pp. 246–71; exchange rates and other data, Dick *et al.*, *Emergence*, p. 192; A. Booth, *The Indonesian Economy in the Nineteenth and Twentieth Century: a History of Missed Opportunity* (Basingstoke/Canberra: Macmillan/Australian National University, 1998), pp. 112–21.
40. Audrey Kahin, *Rebellion to Integration: West Sumatra and the Indonesian Polity* (Amsterdam: Amsterdam University Press, 1999); Audrey R. Kahin and George McT. Kahin, *Subversion as Foreign Policy: the Secret Eisenhower and Dulles Debacle in Indonesia* (New York: New Press, 1995).

6 FROM OLD TO NEW ORDERS

1. Cited in Herbert Feith, *The Decline of Constitutional Democracy in Indonesia* (Ithaca, NY: Cornell University Press, 1962), pp. 606–7.
2. Dennis Cohen, 'Poverty and development in Jakarta', PhD thesis, University of Wisconsin, Madison (1975), pp. 131–58.

3. Savitri Scherer, 'From culture to politics: the writings of Pramoedya A. Toer, 1950–1965', PhD thesis, Australian National University (1981), esp. p. 22.
4. Pramoedya Ananta Toer, 'Sukarno', *Time* 154, 7/8 (23–30 August 1999).
5. J. D. Legge, *Central Authority and Regional Autonomy in Indonesia: a Study in Local Administration 1950–1960* (Ithaca, NY: Cornell University Southeast Asia Program, 1961); also comments in Herbert Feith, 'John Legge and Cornell', in David P. Chandler and M. C. Ricklefs (eds.), *Nineteenth and Twentieth Century Indonesia: Essays in Honour of Professor J. D. Legge* (Clayton, Vic.: Monash University Centre of Southeast Asian Studies, 1986), pp. 83–95.
6. David Jenkins, *Suharto and His Generals* (Ithaca, NY: Cornell University Southeast Asia Program, 1984), p. 207.
7. See Charles Coppel, *Indonesian Chinese in Crisis* (Kuala Lumpur: Oxford University Press, 1983); Richard Robison, *Indonesia: the Rise of Capital* (Sydney: Allen & Unwin, 1986), pp. 39–53; Max Lane, unpublished introduction to the translation of Pramoedya's 'Hoakiau di Indonesia'.
8. *Tudjuh Bahan Pokok Indoktrinasi, dengan Tambahan Re-So-Pim, Tahun Kemenangan, Genta Suara Revolusi Indonesia* (Surabaya: Pertjetakan Negara d/h Pers Nasional, n.d.); Sukarno, *Dibawah Bendera Revolusi*, 2 vols. (2nd edn Djakarta: Panitia Penerbit, 1965); *Berdikari* was the 17 August 1965 speech. Thanks to Susanna Rizzo for the Italian link.
9. Klaus Schreiner, 'The making of national heroes: Guided Democracy to New Order, 1959–1992', in Henk Schulte Nordholt (ed.), *Outward Appearances: Dressing State and Society in Indonesia* (Leiden: KITLV), pp. 259–90.
10. See Susan Abeyasekere, *Jakarta: a History* (Kuala Lumpur: Oxford University Press, 1987), pp. 163, 170; Philip Kitley, *Television, Nation, and Culture in Indonesia* (Athens, OH: Ohio University Press, 2000).
11. Anne Booth, *The Indonesian Economy in the Nineteenth and Twentieth Century: a History of Missed Opportunity* (Basingstoke/Canberra: Macmillan/ Australian National University, 1998), p. 177; Robison, *Indonesia*, pp. 74–7.
12. Howard W. Dick *et al.*, *The Emergence of a National Economy: an Economic History of Indonesia, 1800–2000* (Sydney: Angus & Robertson, 2001), p. 192.
13. Lea Jellinek, *The Wheel of Fortune: the History of a Poor Community in Jakarta* (London: Allen & Unwin, 1991), p. 14.
14. Malcolm Caldwell and Ernst Utrecht, *Indonesia: an Alternative History* (Sydney: Alternative Publishing Cooperative, 1979), p. 117; Carol Warren, *Adat and Dinas: Balinese Communities in the Indonesian State* (Kuala Lumpur: Oxford University Press, 1994), p. 328; *Duta Masjarakat*, 9 July 1965 and 27 July 1965, also Cohen, 'Poverty and development', p. 20.
15. Pramudya [sic] Ananta Toer, 'Hamka: pencipta djalan keneraka', *Bintang Timur*, 27 May 1959; Keith Foulcher, *Social Commitment in Literature and the Arts: the Indonesian 'Institute of People's Culture' 1950–1965* (Clayton, Vic.: Centre of Southeast Asian Studies, Monash University, 1986), p. 117.
16. Foulcher, *Social Commitment*; M. Dwi Marianto, *Surealisme Yogyakarta* (Yogyakarta: Merapi, 2001), ch. 3; Taufiq cited by Gunawan Mohamad, 'Dari "Bumi Manusia"', in Adhy Asmara, *Analisa Ringan Kemelut Roman*

Karya Pulau Buru Bumi Manusia Pramoedya Ananta Toer (Yogyakarta: Nurcahaya, 1981), p. 79.

17. Rex Mortimer, *Indonesian Communism under Sukarno* (Ithaca, NY: Cornell University Press, 1974); quotation from my confidential interviews.

18. Figures from Caldwell and Utrecht, *Indonesia*, p. 113; Fadjar Pratikto, *Gerakan Rakyat Kelaparan: Gagalnya Politik Radikalisasi Petani* (Yogyakarta: Media Pressindo, 2000), esp. pp. 123–9; C. van Dijk, *Rebellion under the Banner of Islam: the Darul Islam in Indonesia* (The Hague: Martinus Nijhoff, 1981), p. 379.

19. Interview by André Liem, 'Perjuangan bersenjata PKI di Blitar Selatan dan Operasi Trisula', in John Roosa, Hilma Farid and Ayu Ratih (eds.), *Tahun yang Tak Pernah Berakhir: Memahami Pengalaman Korban 65: Esai-esai Sejarah Lisan* (Jakarta: Lembaga Studi dan Advokasi Masyarakat, 2004), pp. 163–200, p. 169.

20. Saskia Wieringa, *Sexual Politics in Indonesia* (Basingstoke: Palgrave Macmillan, 2002).

21. See Audrey Kahin, *Rebellion to Integration: West Sumatra and the Indonesian Polity* (Amsterdam: Amsterdam University Press, 1999), ch. 10.

22. Robert Cribb (ed.), *The Indonesian Killings 1965–1966: Studies from Java and Bali* (Clayton, Vic.: Monash University Centre of Southeast Asian Studies, 1990); further detail on the coup and killings in Edward C. Keefer (ed.), *Foreign Relations of the United States, 1964–1968* Volume XXVI, *Indonesia; Malaysia-Singapore; Philippines* (Washington: United States Government Printing Office, 2001), pp. 142–339.

23. A. A. M. Djelantik, *The Birthmark: Memoirs of a Balinese Prince* (Singapore: Periplus, 1997), pp. 299–301.

24. Harold Crouch, *The Army and Politics in Indonesia* (Ithaca, NY: Cornell University Press, 1978); Geoffrey Robinson, *The Dark Side of Paradise: Political Violence in Bali* (Ithaca, NY: Cornell University Press, 1995); Hermawan Sulistyo, *Palu Arit di Ladang Tebu: Sejarah Pembantaian Massal yang Terlupakan* (Jakarta: Gramedia, 2000); David Mitchell, 'Communists, mystics and Sukarnoism', *Dissent* 22 (Autumn 1968), 28–32; Cribb (ed.), *Indonesian Killings*.

25. Pramoedya Ananta Toer, *Nyanyi Sunyi*, vol. 1, pp. 125–32 (not all of which is in the translation).

26. Crouch, *The Army and Politics*.

27. R. E. Elson, *Suharto: a Political Biography* (Cambridge: Cambridge University Press, 2001), pp. 60–6, 71–4.

28. Biographical details from Peter Polomka, *Indonesia since Sukarno* (Harmondsworth: Penguin, 1971), pp. 133ff.; additional information David Jenkins, *Suharto and His Generals: Indonesian Military Politics, 1975–1983* (Ithaca, NY: Cornell University Southeast Asia Program, 1984), p. 70; Soemitro, *Pangkopkamtib Jenderal Soemitro dan Peristiwa 15 Januaryi '74*, as told to Heru Cahyono (Jakarta: Sinar Harapan, 1998), pp. 281–307.

29. On the changing role of Functional Groups, David Reeve, *Golkar of Indonesia: an Alternative to the Party System* (Kuala Lumpur: Oxford University Press,

1985); Murtopo quoted in David Bourchier and Vedi R. Hadiz, *Indonesian Politics and Society: a Reader* (London and New York: RoutledgeCurzon, 2003), pp. 34–6, 43–9, 110–12; Jacques Leclerc, 'An ideological problem of Indonesian trade unionism in the sixties: "karyawan" versus "buruh"' [trans. P. A. Wallace], *RIMA* 6, 1 (1972), 76–91; Ken Ward, *The 1971 Elections in Indonesia: an East Javanese Case Study* (Clayton, Vic.: Monash University Papers on Southeast Asia 2, 1974), p. 37.

30. Ward, *The 1971 elections*; confidential informants on Bali; David Bourchier, *Dynamics of Dissent in Indonesia: Sawito and the Phantom Coup* (Ithaca, NY: Cornell University Southeast Asia Program, 1984), p. 13.

31. US embassy cable, cited in Robinson, *Dark Side*, p. 284.

32. Dick *et al.*, *Emergence of a National Economy*, pp. 195–206; Lance Brennan, Les Heathcote and Anton Lucas, 'The causation of famine: a comparative analysis of Lombok and Bengal 1891–1974', *South Asia* 7, 1 (June 1984), 1–26.

33. My thanks to Diane Galung on Jakarta circa 1968; see also Suzan Piper and Sawung Jabo, 'Indonesian music from the 50s to the 80s', *Prisma* 43 (March 1987), 24–37; the 'honeymoon' term was coined by the late Umar Kayam; Salim Said, *Shadows on the Silver Screen: a Social History of Indonesian Film* (Jakarta: Lontar Foundation, 1991), ch. 6.

34. Krishna Sen, *Indonesian Cinema: Framing the New Order* (London and New Jersey: Zed, 2004), pp. 105–30; see Jellinek, *The Wheel of Fortune*.

35. Hamish McDonald, *Suharto's Indonesia* (Melbourne: Pan, 1980); Soemitro, *Pengkopkamtib*, pp. 144–9; John Pemberton, *On the Subject of 'Java'* (Ithaca, NY: Cornell University Press, 1994).

36. Soemitro, *Pengkopkamtib*; Soehario Padmodiwirio, *Memoar Hario Kecik* (Jakarta: Obor, 1996 and 2001), vol. II, pp. 278–9.

7 TERROR AND DEVELOPMENT IN HAPPY LAND

1. Pramoedya Ananta Toer, *The Mute's Soliloquy*, trans. Willem Samuels (New York: Penguin, 1998), p. 63.

2. David Jenkins, *Suharto and His Generals: Indonesian Military Politics, 1975–1983* (Ithaca, NY: Cornell University Southeast Asia Program, 1984), pp. 157–9.

3. Brett Hough, *Contemporary Balinese Dance Spectacles as National Ritual* (Working Paper 74, Clayton, Vic.: Centre of Southeast Asian Studies, Monash University, 1992); Rob Goodfellow, *Api dalam Sekam: the New Order and the Ideology of Anti-Communism* (Clayton, Vic.: Monash University Centre of Southeast Asian Studies Working Paper 95); Klaus Schreiner, '"National ancestors": the ritual construction of nationhood', in Henri Chambert-Loir and A. J. S. Reid (eds.), *The Potent Dead: Ancestors, Saints and Heroes in Contemporary Indonesia* (Crows Nest, NSW: Asian Studies Association of Australia in association with Allen & Unwin, 2002) pp. 183–204; Katharine McGregor, 'Commemoration of 1 October, *Hari*

Kesaktian Pancasila: a post-mortem analysis?', *Asian Studies Review* 26, 1 (March 2002), 39–72.

4. Adhy Asmara, *Analisa Ringan Kemelut Roman Karya Pulau Buru Bumi Manusia Pramoedya Ananta Toer* (Yogyakarta: Nurcahaya, 1981); Ariel Heryanto, 'Discourse and state terrorism: a case study of political trials in New Order Indonesia 1989–1990', PhD thesis, Monash University (1993); the idea of 'political pornography' is from M. Dwi Marianto.

5. Ingo Wandelt, "The New Order interpretation of the Pancasila: its development and structure as reflected in "Pendidikan Moral Pancasila" and "Penataran P-4"', in Wolfgang Marshall (ed.), *Texts from the Islands: Oral and Written Traditions of Indonesia and the Malay World* (Berne: University of Berne, 1994), pp. 317–28.

6. Pramoedya, *Mute's Soliloquy*, p. 18.

7. Cited by Amin Sweeney, *A Full Hearing: Orality and Literacy in the Malay World* (Berkeley: University of California Press, 1987), p. 99; B. R. O'G. Anderson, *Language and Power: Exploring Political Cultures in Indonesia* (Ithaca, NY: Cornell University Press, 1990), Virginia Matheson Hooker, 'New Order language in context', in Matheson Hooker (ed.), *Culture and Society in New Order Indonesia* (Singapore: Oxford University Press, 1993), pp. 272–93; Jennifer Lindsay, 'Kayam's *Kedaulatan Rakyat* column and New Order talking', *RIMA* 37, 2 (2003), 11–26.

8. Philip Kitley, *Television, Nation, and Culture in Indonesia* (Athens, Ohio: Ohio University Press, 2000).

9. John Pemberton, *On the Subject of 'Java'* (Ithaca, NY: Cornell University Press, 1994), pp. 311–14; James T. Siegel, *A New Criminal Type in Jakarta: Counter-Revolution Today* (Durham and London: Duke University Press, 1998).

10. Pemberton, *On the Subject of 'Java'*, pp. 3–7.

11. John Wilkinson, 'Electioneering in Tanahbelig: aspects of social change in an isolated Balinese community', *RIMA* 24 (1991), pp. 39–54.

12. Jenkins, *Suharto and his Generals*, p. 158.

13. See Soemitro, *Pangkopkamtib Jenderal Soemitro dan Peristiwa 15 Januaryi '74*, as told to Heru Cahyono (Jakarta: Sinar Harapan, 1998), p. 71.

14. Abdul Syukur, *Gerakan Usroh di Indonesia: Peristiwa Lampung 1989* (Yogyakarta: Ombak, 2003); TAPOL, *Indonesia: Muslims on Trial* (London: TAPOL, 1987).

15. Julie Southwood and Patrick Flanagan, *Indonesia: Law, Propaganda and Terror* (London: Zed, 1983), p. 93.

16. W. F. Wertheim, 'Indonesian Moslems under Sukarno and Suharto: majority with a minority mentality', in Christine Doran (ed.), *Indonesian Politics: a Reader* (Townsville: Centre for South-east Asian Politics, James Cook University of North Queensland, 1987), pp. 111–32.

17. C. van Dijk, *Rebellion under the Banner of Islam: the Darul Islam in Indonesia* (The Hague: Martinus Nijhoff, 1981), pp. 338–9; Tim Kell, *The Roots of Acehnese Rebellion, 1989–1992* (Ithaca, NY: Cornell Modern Indonesia Project, 1995).

18. Danilyn Rutherford, *Raiding the Land of the Foreigners: the Limits of the Nation on an Indonesian Frontier* (Princeton: Princeton University Press, 2003), pp. 212–13.

19. Pseudonymous interview by Michelle Turner, *Telling East Timor: Personal Testimonies 1942–1992* (Kensington, NSW: University of News South Wales Press, 1992), p. 160.

20. Ibid., p. 161.

21. Mary Zurbuchen, 'Images of culture and national development in Indonesia: the *Cockroach Opera*', *Asian Theatre Journal* 7, 2 (Fall 1990), 127–49.

22. Pemberton, '*Java*'.

23. Philip Yampolsky, 'Forces for change in the regional performing arts of Indonesia', *BKI* 151, 4 (1995), 700–25; Rutherford, *Raiding the Land of the Foreigners*, ch. 7.

24. Howard W. Dick *et al.*, *The Emergence of a National Economy: an Economic History of Indonesia, 1800–2000* (Sydney: Angus & Robertson, 2001), p. 198.

25. Howard W. Dick, *Surabaya, City of Work: Socioeconomic History, 1900–2000* (Athens, Ohio: Ohio University Center for International Studies, 2002), p. 100; Hamish McDonald, *Suharto's Indonesia* (Melbourne: Pan, 1980); Jenkins, *Suharto and his Generals*, pp. 21, 23, 70; Brian May, *The Indonesian Tragedy* (London: Routledge, 1978), pp. 216–18; *Bisnis.com*, 'Shindi, Generasi Ketiga Grup Hilton', 1 June 2004; 'What the elite do when their banks are in trouble', *Inside Indonesia* 52 (October–December 1997); *Kompas* 12/01/2001; George Aditjondro, *Dari Soeharto ke Habibie: Guru Kencing Berdiri, Murid Kencing Berlari. Kedua Puncak Korupsi, Kolusi, dan Nepotisme Rezim Orde Baru* (Jakarta: Masyarakat Indonesia untuk Kemanusiaan, 1998).

26. Ann Booth, *The Indonesian Economy in the Nineteenth and Twentieth Century: a History of Missed Opportunity* (Basingstoke/Canberra: Macmillan/Australian National University, 1998), pp. 187–200 (esp. p. 192), 205–10.

27. Mark Hanusz, *Kretek: the Culture and Heritage of Indonesia's Clove Cigarettes* (Jakarta: Equinox, 2000), pp. 70, 137.

28. May, *Indonesian Tragedy*, p. 217; Theodore Friend, *Indonesian Destinies* (Cambridge, MA and London: The Belknap Press of Harvard University Press, 2003), p. 364; Marcus W. Brauchli, 'Why the World Bank failed to anticipate Indonesia's deep crisis', *Wall Street Journal*, 14 July 1998, reproduced on *Economic Justice Now*, (www.economicjustice.org/resources/media/wsj-indonesia.html, accessed 11/08/2004).

29. Booth, *Indonesian Economy*, p. 196.

30. Cited in Friend, *Indonesian Destinies*, pp. 148–9; Booth, *Indonesian Economy*, p. 30.

31. Anna Lowenhaupt Tsing, *In the Realm of the Diamond Queen: Marginality in an Out-of-the-Way Place* (Princeton: Princeton University Press, 1993), pp. 107–8; McDonald, *Suharto's Indonesia*, pp. 183–5.

32. Barbara Leigh, 'Making the Indonesian state: the role of school texts', *RIMA* 25, 1 (1991), 17–43; Lynette Parker, 'The creation of Indonesian citizens in Balinese primary schools', *RIMA* 26, 1 (1992), 42–70.

33. McDonald, *Suharto's Indonesia*, p. 170.

34. Christine Drake, *National Integration in Indonesia: Patterns and Policies* (Honolulu: University of Hawai'i Press, 1989); Hal Hill (ed.), *Unity and Diversity: Regional Economic Development in Indonesia since 1970* (Singapore: Oxford University Press, 1989); Howard Dick, James J. Fox and Jamie Mackie (eds.), *Balanced Development: East Java in the New Order* (Singapore: Oxford University Press, 1993); Booth, *Indonesian Economy*, p. 131.
35. Quoted in Kirik Ertanto, 'Street children: talk and reality', *Latitudes* 4 (May 2001), 43–6; Laine Berman, 'Surviving the streets of Java: homeless children's narratives of violence', *Discourse and Society* 11, 2 (2000), 149–74.
36. Booth, *Indonesian Economy*, pp. 277–85.
37. Laine Berman, *Speaking through the Silence: Narratives, Social Conventions and Power in Java* (New York: Oxford University Press, 1998), pp. 138–9.
38. 'The Marsinah case: the death of a labor activist causes headaches in Jakarta', *Asiaweek*, 23 March 1994, pp. 28–31.
39. Jero Mangku Lunas, *Geguritan Transmigrasi ka Luñuk*, transcribed and translated by I Gusti Made Sutjaja, typescript, n.d.; I Gusti Made Sutjaja, 'Balinese transmigrants in Lampung: language change and tradition', in A. Vickers (ed.), *Being Modern in Bali: Image and Change* (New Haven: Yale University Southeast Asia Studies Monograph 43, 1997), pp. 212–22.
40. Lizzy van Leeuwen, *Airconditioned Lifestyles: Nieuwe Rijken in Jakarta* (Amsterdam: Het Spinhuis, 1997).

8 AGE OF GLOBALISATION, AGE OF CRISIS

1. Pramoedya Ananta Toer, 17 August Oration, read in 'Orasi Kebudayaan 2002' at Kafe SALSA, Jakarta, 20 August 2002.
2. Richard Robison and Vedi R. Hadiz, *Reorganising Power in Indonesia: the Politics of Oligarchy in an Age of Markets* (London: RoutledgeCurzon, 2004), p. 25.
3. Howard W. Dick *et al.*, *The Emergence of a National Economy: an Economic History of Indonesia, 1800–2000* (Sydney: Angus & Robertson, 2001), p. 231.
4. Solvey Gerke, 'Global lifestyles under local conditions: the new Indonesian middle class', in Chua Beng-Huat (ed.), *Consumption in Asia: Lifestyles and Identities* (London and New York: Routledge, 2000), pp. 135–58; Hans Antlöv, 'The new rich and cultural tensions in rural Indonesia', in Michael Pinches (ed.), *Culture and Privilege in Capitalist Asia* (London and New York: Routledge, 1999), pp. 188–207.
5. Dick *et al.*, *Emergence*, pp. 210–35.
6. Robert R. Hefner, *Civil Islam: Muslims and Democratization in Indonesia* (Princeton: Princeton University Press, 2000); George Aditjondro, *Dari Soeharto ke Habibie: Guru Kencing Berdiri, Murid Kencing Berlari. Kedua Puncak Korupsi, Kolusi, dan Nepotisme Rezim Orde Baru* (Jakarta: Masyarakat Indonesia untuk Kemanusiaan, 1998).
7. Onghokham, 'A pillar of Indonesia's New Order', *The Australian* 01/05/96.

8. Ajar Aedi, 'Kampung garbage', *Latitudes* 23 (December 2002), 52–7.
9. Hefner, *Civil Islam*, pp. 191–2.
10. Denise Leith, *The Politics of Power: Freeport in Indonesia* (Honolulu: University of Hawai'i Press, 2003), pp. 46–53; Jennifer Wells, *Bre-X: the Inside Story of the World's Biggest Mining Scam* (London: Orion Business, 1998); Robison and Hadiz, *Reorganising Power*, p. 10.
11. Dick *et al.*, *Emergence*, pp. 231–40; R. E. Elson, *Suharto: a Political Biography* (Cambridge: Cambridge University Press, 2001), pp. 286–8.
12. Lagak Jakarta, *Krisis ... Oh ... Krisis* (Jakarta: Kepustakaan Populer Gramedia, 1998).
13. Ayu Utami, *Saman* (Jakarta: KPG, 1998); Andre Syahreza, 'Ayu Utami', *Latitudes* 3 (April 2001), 60–2; 'Crest of a wave', *The Star Online*, 17 August 2004 (www.thestar.com.my, accessed 02/09/2004); Ayu Utami *et al.*, *Bredel 1994: Kumpulan Tulisan tentang Pembredelan Tempo, Detik, Editor* (Jakarta: Aliansi Jurnalis Independen, 1994).
14. M. Soh quoted in Abdul Haris, *Memburu Ringgit, Membagi Kemiskinan: Fakta di Balik Migrasi Orang Sasak ke Malaysia* (Yogyakarta: Pustaka Pelajar, 2002), p. 112; Atun quoted in Maria Hartiningsih, 'An old doll in rags', *Latitudes* 12 (January 2002), 42–8; see Michele Ford, 'Beyond the *Femina* fantasy: female industrial and overseas domestic labour in Indonesian discourses of women's work', *RIMA* 37, 2 (2003), 83–113.
15. Hotze Lont and Ben White, 'Critical review of crisis studies, 1998–2002: debates on poverty, employment and solidarity in Indonesia', in Henk Schulte Nordholt and Gusti Asnan (eds.), *Indonesia in Transition: Work in Progress* (Yogyakarta: Pustaka Pelajar, 2003), pp. 125–60.
16. Mark Hanusz, *Kretek: the Culture and Heritage of Indonesia's Clove Cigarettes* (Jakarta: Equinox, 2000), p. 70; Paul Burgers, 'Household livelihood strategies in response to the economic crisis (1997–2001) in Kerinci, West Sumatra', in Schulte Nordholt and Asnan (eds.), *Indonesia in Transition*, pp. 161–79.
17. *The Jakarta Post*, 7 July 2001.
18. Pramoedya Ananta Toer, 'I just don't believe in her', *Time Magazine*, 158, 5 (06/08/2001).
19. Robison and Hadiz, *Reorganising Power*.
20. Caroline Campbell and Linda H. Connor, 'Sorcery, modernity and social transformation in Banyuwangi, East Java', *RIMA* 35, 2 (Summer 2000), 61–98.
21. Linda H. Connor and Adrian Vickers, 'Crisis, citizenship, and cosmopolitanism: living in a local and global risk society in Bali', *Indonesia* 75 (April 2003), 153–80.
22. Patricia Spyer, 'Fire without smoke and other phantoms of Ambon's violence: media effects, agency, and the work of imagination', *Indonesia* 74 (October 2002), 21–36.
23. Philip King, 'Securing the 1999 Indonesian election: Satgas Parpol and the state', BA Honours thesis, Department of History and Politics, University of Wollongong (2000).

24. Connor and Vickers, 'Crisis, citizenship, and cosmopolitanism'.
25. Gerry van Klinken, 'Indonesia's new ethnic elites', in Henk Schulte Nordholt and Irwan Abdullah (eds.), *Indonesia in Search of Transition* (Yogyakarta: Pustaka Pelajar, 2002), pp. 67–105.
26. See Hefner, *Civil Islam*; my thanks also to Raechelle Rubinstein for drawing my attention to translations of *The Protocols* in Indonesia since the early 1980s. The original text was written in nineteenth-century Russia to incite violence against Jews. Basyir cited in Antariksa, 'School for Jihad', *Latitudes* 16 (May 2002), 14–17.
27. Kelly Bird, 'The economy in 2000: still flat on its back?' in Grayson Lloyd and Shannon Smith (eds.), *Indonesia Today: Challenges of History* (Singapore: Institute of Southeast Asian Studies, 2001), pp. 45–66; Mohamad Ikhsan, 'Economic update 2002: struggling to maintain momentum', in Edward Aspinall and Greg Fealy (eds.), *Local Power and Politics in Indonesia: Decentralisation and Democratisation* (Singapore: Institute of Southeast Asian Studies, 2003), pp. 35–57; Sugiyem quoted in Helena E. Rea, 'Struggle for identity: a "village of beggars" tries to shed its past', *Latitudes* 9 (Oct. 2001), 42–5.
28. Edward Aspinall, 'Modernity, history and ethnicity: Indonesian and Achenese nationalism in conflict', *RIMA* 36, 1 (2002), 11–41; Richard Chauvel, 'Papua and Indonesia: where contending nationalisms meet', in Damien Kingsbury and Harry Aveling (eds.), *Autonomy and Disintegration in Indonesia* (London: RoutledgeCurzon, 2003), pp. 115–27; Peter King, *West Papua and Indonesia since Suharto: Independence, Autonomy or Chaos?* (Sydney: University of New South Wales Press, 2004).
29. S. H. Sarundajang, *Arus Balik Kekuasaan Pusat ke Daerah* (Jakarta: Pustaka Sinar Harapan, 1999 [reprinted in 2000 and 2001]); Syabda Guruh LS, *Menyimbang Otonomi vs Federal: Mengembangkan Wacana Federalisme dan Otonomi Luas Menuju Masyarakat Madani Indonesia* (Bandung: Remaja Rosdakarya, 2000); Aspinall and Fealy (eds.), *Local Power and Politics*.
30. Carol Warren, *Adat and Dinas: Balinese Communities in the Indonesian State* (Kuala Lumpur: Oxford University Press, 1994).
31. The editors, 'Current data on the Indonesian military elite', *Indonesia* 75 (April 2003), 31; Vedi Hadiz, 'Power and politics in North Sumatra: the uncompleted reformasi', in Aspinall and Fealy (eds.), *Local Power and Politics*, pp. 119–31.
32. David Ray and Gary Goodpaster, 'Indonesian decentralization: local autonomy, trade barriers and discrimination', in Kingsbury and Aveling (eds.), *Autonomy and Disintegration in Indonesia*, pp. 75–95.
33. Ade Tanesia, 'A *Bupati* named Rustriningsih', *Latitudes* 27 (April 2003), 46–51; Amrih Widodo, 'Local politics: the view from Blora, Central Java', in Aspinall and Fealy (eds.), *Local Power and Politics*, pp. 179–93.

34. Philip Kitley, 'Civil society as a media-engaged audience: a new emphasis for audience research in Indonesia', paper given at the International Conference on Asian Media Research, Singapore, 9–10 September 2004.
35. Yazid Naim, 'Indonesia is just like a beggar', *New Straits Times* (Malaysia), 17/06/2001.

Bibliography

À Campo, J., 'Steam navigation and state formation', in Cribb (ed.), *The Late Colonial State*, pp. 11–30.

'Abbas Akup, Nya (director and writer, producer Usmar Ismail), *Tiga Buronan* (Jakarta: Perfini Films, 1957).

Abeyasekere [Blackburn], Susan, 'Health as a nationalist issue in colonial Indonesia', in Chandler and Ricklefs (eds.), *Nineteenth and Twentieth Century Indonesia*, pp. 1–13.

  Jakarta: a History (Kuala Lumpur: Oxford University Press, 1987).

Adam, Ahmat B., *The Vernacular Press and the Emergence of Modern Indonesian Consciousness (1855–1913)* (Ithaca, NY: Cornell University Southeast Asia Program, 1995).

Aditjondro, George, *Dari Soeharto ke Habibie: Guru Kencing Berdiri, Murid Kencing Berlari. Kedua Puncak Korupsi, Kolusi, dan Nepotisme Rezim Orde Baru* (Jakarta: Masyarakat Indonesia untuk Kemanusiaan, 1998).

Akihary, Huib, *Architectuur en Stedebouw in Indonesië: 1870–1970* (Zutphen: De Welburg Pers, 1990).

Anderson, B. R. O'G., *Java in a Time of Revolution: Occupation and Resistance, 1944–46* (Ithaca, NY: Cornell University Press, 1972).

  Language and Power: Exploring Political Cultures in Indonesia (Ithaca, NY: Cornell University Press, 1990).

Anderson, David Charles, 'The military aspects of the Madiun Affair', *Indonesia* 21 (April 1976), 1–53.

Antlöv, Hans, 'The new rich and cultural tensions in rural Indonesia', in Michael Pinches (ed.), *Culture and Privilege in Capitalist Asia* (London and New York: Routledge, 1999), pp. 188–207.

Aragon, Lorraine V., *Fields of the Lord: Animism, Christian Minorities, and State Development in Indonesia* (Honolulu: University of Hawai'i Press, 2000).

Asmara, Adhy, *Analisa Ringan Kemelut Roman Karya Pulau Buru Bumi Manusia Pramoedya Ananta Toer* (Yogyakarta: Nurcahaya, 1981).

Aspinall, Edward, 'Modernity, history and ethnicity: Indonesian and Achenese nationalism in conflict', *RIMA* 36, 1 (2002), 11–41.

Aspinall, Edward and Fealy, Greg (eds.), *Local Power and Politics in Indonesia: Decentralisation and Democratisation* (Singapore: Institute of Southeast Asian Studies, 2003).

Aveling, Harry, 'A note on the author', in Pramoedya Ananta Toer, *A Heap of Ashes*, ed. and trans. Harry Aveling (St Lucia: University of Queensland Press, 1975), pp. ix–xxii.

Aveling, H. (ed. and trans.) *From Surabaja to Armageddon: Indonesian Short Stories* (Singapore: Heinemann, 1976).

Barton, Greg, *Gus Dur: the Authorized Biography of Abdurrahman Wahid* (Jakarta, Singapore: Equinox, 2002).

Bayly, C. A. and Kolff, D. H. A. (eds.), *Two Colonial Empires: Comparative Essays on the History of India and Indonesia in the Nineteenth Century* (Dordrecht: Nijhoff, 1986).

Becker, A. L. (ed.), *Writing on the Tongue* (Ann Arbor: University of Michigan Press, 1989).

Benda, H. J., *The Crescent and the Rising Sun: Indonesian Islam under the Japanese Occupation* (The Hague: Van Hoeve, 1958).

Benda, H. J. and Castles, Lance, 'The Samin movement', *BKI* 125 (1969), 207–40.

Benda, H. J. and Larkin, John A., *The World of Southeast Asia: Selected Historical Readings* (New York: Harper and Row, 1967).

Berman, Laine, *Speaking through the Silence: Narratives, Social Conventions and Power in Java* (New York: Oxford University Press, 1998).

'Surviving the streets of Java: homeless children's narratives of violence', *Discourse and Society* 11, 2 (2000), 149–74.

Bird, Kelly, 'The economy in 2000: still flat on its back?' in Lloyd and Smith (eds.), *Indonesia Today*, pp. 45–66.

Blackburn, Susan and Bessell, Sharon, 'Marriageable age: political debates on early marriage in twentieth-century Indonesia', *Indonesia* 63 (April 1997), 107–42.

Bonneff, Marcel, 'Le Kauman de Yogyakarta: des fonctionnaires religieux convertis au réformisme et à l'esprit d'entreprise', *Archipel* 30 (1985), 175–205.

Boomgaard, Peter, 'The development of colonial health care in Java: an exploratory introduction', *BKI* 149, 1 (1993), 77–93.

Booth, Anne, 'Living standards and the distribution of income in colonial Indonesia: a review of the evidence', *Journal of Southeast Asian Studies* 29, 2 (1988), 310–34.

The Indonesian Economy in the Nineteenth and Twentieth Century: a History of Missed Opportunity (Basingstoke/Canberra: Macmillan/Australian National University, 1998).

Bourchier, David, *Dynamics of Dissent in Indonesia: Sawito and the Phantom Coup* (Ithaca, NY: Cornell University Southeast Asia Program, 1984).

'Totalitarianism and the "national personality": recent controversy about the philosophical basis of the Indonesian state', in Schiller and Martin-Schiller (eds.), *Imagining Indonesia*, pp. 157–85.

Bourchier, David and Hadiz, Vedi R., *Indonesian Politics and Society: a Reader* (London and New York: RoutledgeCurzon, 2003).

Breman, Jan, *Control of Land and Labour in Colonial Java: a Case Study of Agrarian Crisis and Reform in the Region of Cirebon during the First Decades of the 20th Century* (Dordrecht: Foris, 1983).

'Het beest aan banden? De koloniale geest aan het begin van de twintigste eeuw', *BKI* 144, 1 (1988), 19–43.

Taming the Coolie Beast: Plantation Society and the Colonial Order in Southeast Asia (Delhi: Oxford University Press, 1989).

Brennan, Lance, Heathcote, Les and Lucas, Anton, 'The causation of famine: a comparative analysis of Lombok and Bengal 1891–1974', *South Asia* 7, 1 (June 1984), 1–26.

Brenner, Suzanne April, *The Domestication of Desire: Women, Wealth, and Modernity in Java* (Princeton: Princeton University Press, 1988).

Budiman, Arief (ed.), *State and Civil Society in Indonesia* (Clayton, Vic.: Centre of Southeast Asian Studies, Monash University, 1990).

Burgers, Paul, 'Household livelihood strategies in response to the economic crisis (1997–2001) in Kerinci, West Sumatra', in Schulte Nordholt and Asnan (eds.), *Indonesia in Transition*, pp. 161–79.

Caldwell, Malcolm and Urtecht, Ernst, *Indonesia: an Alternative History* (Sydney: Alternative Publishing Cooperative, 1979).

Campbell, Caroline and Connor, Linda H., 'Sorcery, modernity and social transformation in Banyuwangi, East Java', *RIMA* 35, 2 (Summer 2000), 61–98.

Cederoth, Sven, *The Spell of the Ancestors and the Power of Mekkah: a Sasak Community on Lombok* (Gothenburg: Acta Universitatis Gothoburgensis, 1981).

Chambert-Loir, Henri, 'Mas Marco Kartodikromo (c.1890–1932) ou l'éducation politique', in Denys Lombard and Pierre Bernard Lafont (eds.), *Littératures Contemporaines de l'Asie du Sud-Est* (Paris: l'Asiathèque, 1974), pp. 203–14.

'Muhammad Bakir: a Batavian scribe and author in the nineteenth century', *RIMA* 18, 2 (Summer 1984), 44–72.

Chandler, David P. and Ricklefs, M. C. (eds.), *Nineteenth and Twentieth Century Indonesia: Essays in Honour of Professor J. D. Legge* (Clayton, Vic.: Monash University Centre of Southeast Asian Studies, 1986).

Chauvel, Richard, *Nationalists, Soldiers and Separatists: the Ambonese Islands from Colonialism to Revolt 1880–1950* (Leiden: KITLV Press, 1990).

'Papua and Indonesia: where contending nationalisms meet', in Kingsbury and Aveling (eds.), *Autonomy and Disintegration*, pp. 115–27.

Cohen, Dennis Julius, 'Poverty and development in Jakarta', PhD thesis, University of Wisconsin, Madison (1975).

Colombijn, Freek, 'The politics of Indonesian football', *Archipel* 59 (2000), 171–200.

Colombijn, Freek and Lindblad, J. Thomas (eds.), *Roots of Violence in Indonesia: Contemporary Violence in Historical Perspective* (Leiden: KITLV Press, 2002).

Connor, Linda and Vickers, Adrian, 'Crisis, citizenship, and cosmopolitanism: living in a local and global risk society in Bali', *Indonesia* 75 (April 2003), 153–80.

Coppel, Charles, *Indonesian Chinese in Crisis* (Kuala Lumpur: Oxford University Press, 1983).

Coté, Joost (trans.), *Letters from Kartini: an Indonesian Feminist, 1900–1904* (Clayton, Vic.: Monash Asia Institute and Hyland House, 1992).

On Feminism and Nationalism: Kartini's Letters to Stella Zeehandelaar 1899–1903 (Clayton, Vic.: Monash Asia Institute, 1995).

Couperus, Louis, *De Stille Kracht* (Utrecht: Veen, 1900, republ. 1983), trans. Alexander Teizeira de Mattos as *The Hidden Force* (Amherst: University of Massachusetts Press, 1985).

Cribb, Robert, 'Political dimensions of the currency question 1945–1947', *Indonesia* 31 (April 1981), 113–36.

Gangsters and Revolutionaries: the Jakarta People's Militia and the Indonesian Revolution 1945–1949 (Sydney: Allen & Unwin, 1991).

Historical Atlas of Indonesia (Honolulu: University of Hawai'i Press, 2000).

Cribb, Robert (ed.), *The Indonesian Killings 1965–1966: Studies from Java and Bali* (Clayton, Vic.: Monash University Centre of Southeast Asian Studies, 1990).

The Late Colonial State in Indonesia: Political and Economic Foundations of the Netherlands Indies 1880–1942 (Leiden: KITLV Press, 1994).

Crouch, Harold, *The Army and Politics in Indonesia* (Ithaca, NY: Cornell University Press, 1978).

Danandjaja, James, 'From *hansop* to *safari*: notes from an eyewitness', in Schulte Nordholt (ed.), *Outward appearances*, pp. 249–58.

Darma Putra, I Nyoman, 'Bali and modern Indonesian literature: the 1950s', in Vickers and Darma Putra (eds.), *To Change Bali*, pp. 135–53.

Wanita Bali Tempo Doeloe: Perspektif Masa Kini (Denpasar: Bali Jani, 2003).

Davis, Mike, *Late Victorian Holocausts: El Niño Famines and the Making of the Third World* (London: Verso, 2001).

Day, A. J., 'Islam and literature in South East Asia: some pre-modern, mainly Javanese perceptions', in M. B. Hooker (ed.), *Islam in South East Asia* (Leiden: Brill, 1983), pp. 130–59.

De Jong, J. J. P. *De Waaier van het Fortuin. Van Handelscompagnie to Koloniaal Imperium: de Nederlanders in Azië en de Indonesische Archipel 1595–1950* (The Hague: Sdu, 1998).

Dick, Howard W., *Surabaya, City of Work: Socioeconomic History, 1900–2000* (Athens, OH: Ohio University Center for International Studies, 2002).

Dick, Howard, Fox, James J. and Mackie, Jamie (eds.), *Balanced Development: East Java in the New Order* (Singapore: Oxford University Press, 1993).

Dick, Howard W., Houben, Vincent J. H., Lindblad, J. Thomas and Thee Kian Wie, *The Emergence of a National Economy: an Economic History of Indonesia, 1800–2000* (Sydney: Angus & Robertson, 2001).

Dijk, Cees van, *Rebellion under the Banner of Islam: the Darul Islam in Indonesia* (The Hague: Martinus Nijhoff, 1981).

Djajakusuma, D. (producer and director), *Harimau Tjampa* (Jakarta: Perfini Films, 1953).

Djelantik, A. A. M., *The Birthmark: Memoirs of a Balinese Prince* (Singapore: Periplus, 1997).

Doel, H. W. Van den. 'Military rule in the Netherlands East Indies', in Cribb (ed.), *The Late Colonial State*, pp. 57–78.

Doorn, J. A. van, 'A divided society: segmentation and mediation in late-colonial Indonesia', in G. Schutte and H. Sutherland (eds.), *Papers of the Dutch-Indonesian Historical Conference held at Lage Vuursche, The Netherlands 23–27 June 1980* (Leiden: Bureau of Indonesian Studies, 1982), pp. 128–71.

Drake, Christine, *National Integration in Indonesia: Patterns and Policies* (Honolulu: University of Hawai'i Press, 1989).

Drewes, G. W. J., 'The struggle between Javanism and Islam as illustrated by the Serat Dermagandul', *BKI* 122 (1965), 309–65.

Drooglever, P. J., *De Vaderlandse Club 1929–1942: Totoks en de Indsiche Politiek* (Frankeker: Wever, 1980).

Dros, Nico, *Wages 1820–1940*. Volume 13 of Peter Boomgaard (ed.), *Changing Economy in Indonesia: a Selection of Statistical Source Material from the Early 19th century up to 1940* (Amsterdam: Royal Tropical Institute, 1992).

Dumas, Robert Martin, *'Teater Abdulmuluk' in Zuid-Sumatra: op de Drempel van een Nieuw Tijperk* (Leiden University: Onderzoekschool voor Aziatische, Afrikaanse, en Amerindische Studies, 2000).

Editors, The, 'Current data on the Indonesian military elite', *Indonesia* 75 (April 2003), 9–60.

Elliott, Jan, 'Bersatoe kita berdiri bertjerai kita djatoeh [United we stand divided we fall]: workers and unions in Jakarta, 1945–1965', PhD thesis, University of New South Wales (1997).

'Equality? The influence of legislation and notions of gender on the position of women wage workers in the economy: Indonesia 1950–58', in Taylor (ed.), *Women Creating Indonesia*, pp. 127–55.

Elson, R. E., *Javanese Peasants and the Colonial Sugar Industry: Impact and Change in an East Java Residency 1830–1940* (Kuala Lumpur: Oxford University Press, 1984).

Suharto: a Political Biography (Cambridge: Cambridge University Press, 2001).

Eng, Pierre van der, 'Indonesia's economy and standard of living in the 20th century', in Lloyd and Smith (eds.), *Indonesia Today*, pp. 181–99.

'Bridging a gap: a reconstruction of population patterns in Indonesia, 1930–61', *Asian Studies Review* 26, 4 (December 2002), 487–509.

Erwiza, 'Miners, managers and the state: a socio-political history of the Ombilin coal-mines, West Sumatra, 1892–1996', PhD thesis, University of Amsterdam (1999).

Fasseur, C. *De Indologen: Ambtenaran voor de Oost 1825–1950* (Amsterdam: Bert Bakker, 1993).

'Cornerstone and stumbling block: racial classification and the late colonial state in Indonesia', in Cribb (ed.), *The Late Colonial State in Indonesia*, pp. 31–56.

Feith, Herbert, *The Decline of Constitutional Democracy in Indonesia* (Ithaca, NY: Cornell University Press, 1962).

'John Legge and Cornell', in Chandler and Ricklefs (eds.), *Nineteenth and Twentieth Century Indonesia*, pp. 83–95.

Feith Herbert and Castles, Lance (eds.), *Indonesian Political Thinking 1945–1965* (Ithaca, NY: Cornell University Press, 1970).

Fernando, M. R., 'Dynamics of peasant economy in Java at local levels', in Chandler and Ricklefs (eds.), *Nineteenth and Twentieth Century Indonesia*, pp. 97–121.

'Javanese peasants and by-employment at the turn of the century', in May and O'Malley (eds.), *Observing Change in Asia*, pp. 155–69.

'The trumpet shall sound for rich peasants: Kasan Mukim's uprising in Gedangan, East Java, 1904', *Journal of Southeast Asian Studies* 26, 2 (1995), 242–62.

Ford, Michele, 'Beyond the *Femina* fantasy: female industrial and overseas domestic labour in Indonesian discourses of women's work', *RIMA* 37, 2 (2003), 83–113.

Foulcher, Keith, 'Perceptions of modernity and the sense of the past: Indonesian poetry in the 1920s', *Indonesia* 23 (April 1977), 39–58.

Social Commitment in Literature and the Arts: the Indonesian 'Institute of People's Culture' 1950–1965 (Clayton, Vic.: Centre of Southeast Asian Studies, Monash University, 1986).

'Sumpah Pemuda: the making and meaning of a symbol of Indonesian nationhood', *Asian Studies Review* 24, 3 (2000), 377–410.

Fox, James J., 'Ziarah visits to the tombs of the wali, the founders of Islam on Java', in M. C. Ricklefs (ed.), *Islam in the Indonesian Social Context* (Clayton, Vic.: Annual Lecture Series, Monash University Centre of Southeast Asian Studies), pp. 20–38.

Fox, James J. and Dirjosanjoto, Pradjarto, 'The memories of village *Santri* from Jombang in East Java', in May and O'Malley (eds.), *Observing Change in Asia*, pp. 94–110.

Frederick, William H., 'Rhoma Irama and the Dangdut style: aspects of contemporary Indonesian popular culture', *Indonesia* 34 (Oct. 1982), 103–30.

Visions and Heat: the Making of the Indonesian Revolution (Athens, OH: Ohio University Press, 1989).

'The appearance of revolution: cloth, uniform and the pemuda style in East Java, 1945–1949', in Schulte Nordholt (ed.), *Outward Appearances*, pp. 199–248.

'Dreams of freedom, moments of despair: Armijn Pané and the imagining of modern Indonesian culture', in Schiller and Martin-Schiller (eds.), *Imagining Indonesia*, pp. 54–89.

'Shadows of an unseen hand: some patterns of violence in the Indonesian Revolution, 1945–1949', in Colombijn and Lindblad (eds.), *Roots of Violence in Indonesia*, pp. 143–73.

Friend, Theodore, *The Blue-Eyed Enemy: Japan against the West in Java and Luzon 1942–1945* (Princeton: Princeton University Press, 1988).

Indonesian Destinies (Cambridge, MA and London: The Belknap Press of Harvard University Press, 2003).

Furnivall, J. S. *Netherlands India: a Study of Plural Economy* (Cambridge: Cambridge University Press, 1939 [reprinted 1967]).

Geertz, Clifford, *The Religion of Java* (Glencoe, IL: Free Press, 1961).

 Peddlers and Princes: Social Change and Economic Modernization in Two Indonesian Towns (Chicago: University of Chicago Press, 1963).

 The Interpretation of Cultures: Selected Essays by Clifford Geertz (New York: Basic Books, 1973).

Geertz, Hildred, *Images of Power: Balinese Paintings Made for Gregory Bateson and Margaret Mead* (Honolulu: University of Hawai'i Press, 1994).

Gerbrandy, P. S., *Indonesia* (London: Hutchinson, 1950).

Gerke, Solvey, 'Global lifestyles under local conditions: the new Indonesian middle class', in Chua Beng-Huat (ed.), *Consumption in Asia: Lifestyles and Identities* (London and New York: Routledge, 2000), pp. 135–58.

Goodfellow, Robert, *Api dalam Sekam: the New Order and the Ideology of Anti-Communism* (Clayton, Vic.: Monash University Centre of Southeast Asian Studies Working Papers 95).

Gooszen, Hans, *A Demographic History of the Indonesian Archipelago, 1880–1942* (Leiden/Singapore: KITLV/ISEAS, 1999).

Haasse, Hella S., *Heren van de Thee: Roman* (Amsterdam: Querido, 1992).

Hadiz, Vedi, 'Power and politics in North Sumatra: the uncompleted reformasi', in Aspinall and Fealy (eds.), *Local Power and Politics*, pp. 119–31.

Haks, Leo and Maris, Guus, *Lexicon of Foreign Artists Who Visualized Indonesia (1600–1950)* (Singapore: Archipelago Press, 1995).

Haneveld, G. T., 'From slave hospital to reliable health care: medical work on the plantations of Sumatra's east coast', in Luyendijk-Elshout *et al.* (eds.), *Dutch Medicine in the Malay Archipelago*, pp. 73–87.

Hanusz, Mark, *Kretek: the Culture and Heritage of Indonesia's Clove Cigarettes* (Jakarta: Equinox, 2000).

Haris, Abdul, *Memburu Ringgit, Membagi Kemiskinan: Fakta di Balik Migrasi Orang Sasak ke Malaysia* (Yogyakarta: Pustaka Pelajar, 2002).

Hartog, A. P. de, 'Towards improving public nutrition: nutritional policy in Indonesia before independence', in Luyendijk-Elshout *et al.* (eds.), *Dutch Medicine in the Malay Archipelago*, pp. 105–18.

Hatley, Barbara, 'Blora revisited', *Indonesia* 30 (Oct. 1980), 1–16.

 'Indonesian ritual, Javanese drama – celebrating *Tujuhbelasan*', *Indonesia* 34 (Oct. 1982), 55–64.

Hatta, Mohammad, *Portrait of a Patriot: Selected Writings* (The Hague, Paris: Mouton, 1972).

Heersink, Christiaan, 'The green gold of Selayar. A socio-economic history of an Indonesian coconut island c.1600–1950: perspectives from a periphery', PhD thesis, Vrije Universiteit te Amsterdam (1995).

Hefner, Robert W. 'Islamizing Java? Religion and politics in rural East Java', *Journal of Asian Studies* 46, 3 (1987), 533–54.

 Civil Islam: Muslims and Democratization in Indonesia (Princeton: Princeton University Press, 2000).

Hering, Bob, *Soekarno: Founding Father of Indonesia 1901–1945* (Leiden: KITLV Press, 2002).

Heryanto, Ariel, 'Discourse and state terrorism: a case study of political trials in New Order Indonesia 1989–1990', PhD thesis, Monash University (1993).

Hesselink, Liesbeth, 'Prostitution: a necessary evil, particularly in the colonies; views on prostitution in the Netherlands Indies', in Anke Niehof and Elsbeth Locher-Scholten (eds.), *Indonesian Women in Focus: Past and Present Notions* (Dordrecht: Foris, 1987), pp. 205–24.

Hill, David T., '"The two leading institutions": Taman Ismail Marzuki and *Horison*', in Hooker (ed.), *Culture and Society in New Order Indonesia*, pp. 245–62.

Hill, Hal (ed.), *Unity and Diversity: Regional Economic Development in Indonesia since 1970* (Singapore: Oxford University Press, 1989).

Hindley, Donald, *The Communist Party of Indonesia, 1951–1963* (Berkeley: University of California Press, 1964).

Hooker, Virginia Matheson, 'New Order language in context', in Hooker (ed.), *Culture and Society in New Order Indonesia*, pp. 272–93.

Hooker, Virginia Matheson (ed.), *Culture and Society in New Order Indonesia* (Singapore: Oxford University Press, 1993).

Hough, Brett, *Contemporary Balinese Dance Spectacles as National Ritual* (Working Paper 74, Clayton, Vic.: Centre of Southeast Asian Studies, Monash University, 1992).

Hugenholtz, W. R. 'Famine and food supply in Java 1830–1914', in Bayly and Kolff (eds.), *Two Colonial Empires*, pp. 155–88.

Huie, Shirley Fenton, *The Forgotten Ones: Women and Children under Nippon* (Sydney: Angus & Robertson, 1992).

Hull, Terence H. 'Plague in Java', in Norman G. Owen (ed.), *Death and Disease in Southeast Asia: Explorations in Social, Medical and Demographic History* (Singapore: Oxford University Press/Asian Studies Association of Australia, 1987), pp. 210–34.

Hulsbosch, Marianne, 'Pointy shoes and pith helmets: dress and identity construction in Ambon from 1850 to World War II', PhD thesis, University of Wollongong (2004).

'Ideal Caloric Intake' (http://www/goaskalice.columbia.edu/0576.html), 24 February 1995, accessed 03/03/04.

Idrus, 'Surabaja', in Aveling (ed. and trans.), *From Surabaja to Armageddon*, pp. 1–28.

Ikhsan, Mohamad, 'Economic update 2002: struggling to maintain momentum', in Aspinall and Fealy (eds.), *Local Power and Politics in Indonesia*, pp. 35–57.

Ingleson, John, *Road to Exile: the Indonesian Nationalist Movement 1927–1934* (Singapore: Heinemann, 1979).

'Life and work in colonial cities: harbour workers in Java in the 1910s and 1920s', *Modern Asian Studies* 17 (1983), 455–76.

In Search of Justice: Workers and Unions in Colonial Java, 1908–1926 (Singapore: Oxford University Press, 1986).

'Prostitution in colonial Java', in Chandler and Ricklefs (eds.), *Nineteenth and Twentieth Century Indonesia*, pp. 123–40.

'Urban Java during the Depression', *Journal of Southeast Asian Studies* 19 (1988), 292–309.

Ismail, Usmar (producer and director), *Tamu Agung* (Jakarta: Perfini Films, 1955).

Jellinek, Lea, *The Wheel of Fortune: the History of a Poor Community in Jakarta* (London: Allen & Unwin, 1991).

Jenkins, David, *Suharto and his Generals: Indonesian Military Politics, 1975–1983* (Ithaca. NY: Cornell University Southeast Asia Program, 1984).

Kahin, Audrey, *Rebellion to Integration: West Sumatra and the Indonesian Polity* (Amsterdam: Amsterdam University Press, 1999).

Kahin, Audrey R. (ed.), *Regional Dynamics of the Indonesian Revolution* (Honolulu: University of Hawai'i Press, 1985).

Kahin, Audrey R. and Kahin, George McT., *Subversion as Foreign Policy: the Secret Eisenhower and Dulles Debacle in Indonesia* (New York: New Press, 1995).

Kahin, George McT., *Nationalism and Revolution in Indonesia* (Ithaca, NY: Cornell University Press, 1952).

Kayam, Umar, *Semangat Indonesia: Suatu Jalanan Budaya* (Jakarta: Gramedia, 1984).

Para Priyayi: Sebuah Novel (Jakarta: Grafiti, 1992).

Keefer, Edward C. (ed.), *Foreign Relations of the United States, 1964–1968*, volume XXVI: *Indonesia, Malaysia-Singapore; Philippines* (Washington: United States Government Printing Office, 2001).

Kell, Tim, *The Roots of Acehnese Rebellion, 1989–1992* (Ithaca, NY: Cornell Modern Indonesia Project, 1995).

Kerkhof, Gosse, 'Het Indische zedenschandaal: een koloniaal incident', MA thesis/dokotraal skriptie, Vakgroep Moderne Aziatishe Geschiedenis, Universiteit te Amsterdam (1982).

Keroncong Asli: Gesang (audio recording, Gema Nada Pertiwi, 2002).

King, Philip, 'Securing the 1999 Indonesian election: Satgas Parpol and the state', BA Honours thesis, Department of History and Politics, University of Wollongong (2000).

Kingsbury, Damien and Aveling, Harry (eds.), *Autonomy and Disintegration in Indonesia* (London: RoutledgeCurzon, 2003).

Kitley, Philip, *Television, Nation, and Culture in Indonesia* (Athens, OH: Ohio University Press, 2000).

'Civil society as a media-engaged audience: a new emphasis for audience research in Indonesia', paper given at the International Conference on Asian Media Research, Singapore, 9–10 September 2004.

Klinken, Gerry van, 'Indonesia's new ethnic elites', in Schulte Nordholt and Abdullah (eds.), *Indonesia in Search of Transition*, pp. 67–105.

Knight, G. Roger, 'A sugar factory and its swimming pool: incorporation and differentiation in Dutch colonial society in Java', *Ethnic and Racial Studies* 24, 3 (May 2001), 451–71.

Kraan, Alfons van der, *Lombok: Conquest, Colonization and Underdevelopment, 1870–1940* (Singapore/Kuala Lumpur/Hong Kong: Heinemann/Asian Studies Association of Australia, 1980).

Kumar, Dharma, 'The taxation of agriculture in British India and Dutch Indonesia', in Bayly and Kolff (eds.), *Two Colonial Empires*, pp. 203–25.

Kurasawa, Aiko, 'Propaganda media on Java under the Japanese 1942–1945', *Indonesia* 44 (Oct. 1987), 59–116.

Kwartanada, Didi, 'Competition, patriotism and collaboration: the Chinese businessmen of Yogyakarta between the 1930s and 1945', *Journal of Southeast Asian Studies* 33, 2 (2002), 257–77.

Laffan, Michael, *Islamic Nationhood and Colonial Indonesia: the Umma below the Winds* (London: RoutledgeCurzon, 2003).

Lagak Jakarta, *Krisis . . . Oh . . . Krisis* (Jakarta: Kepustakaan Populer Gramedia, 1998).

Lamster, J. C., *J. B. van Heutsz als Gouveneur Generaal 1904–1909* (Amsterdam: Van Kampen, n.d.).

Lane, Max, 'Introduction to the translation of Pramoedya Ananta Toer's "Hoakiau di Indonesia"', forthcoming.

Lanus, Jero Mangku, *Geguritan Transmigrasi ka Luñuk*, transcribed and trans. I Gusti Made Sutjaja, typescript, n.d.

Larson, George D., *Prelude to Revolution: Palaces and Politics in Surakarta, 1912–1942* (Dordrecht: Foris, 1987).

Leclerc, Jacques, 'An ideological problem of Indonesian trade unionism in the sixties: "karyawan" versus "buruh"' [trans. P. A. Wallace], *RIMA* 6, 1 (1972), 76–91.

'Iconologie politique du timbre-poste Indonésien (1950–1970)', *Archipel* 6 (1973), 145–83.

'Afterword: the masked hero', in Lucas (ed.), *Local Opposition and Underground Resistance*, pp. 325–68.

Leeuwen, Lizzy van, *Airconditioned Lifestyles: Nieuwe Rijken in Jakarta* (Amsterdam: Het Spinhuis, 1997).

Legge, J. D., *Central Authority and Regional Autonomy in Indonesia: a Study in Local Administration 1950–1960* (Ithaca, NY: Cornell University Southeast Asia Program, 1961).

Sukarno: a Political Biography (Sydney: Allen & Unwin, 1972).

Indonesia (New Jersey: Prentice-Hall, 1964, 1977, 1980).

Leigh, Barbara, 'Making the Indonesian state: the role of school texts', *RIMA* 25, 1 (1991), 17–43.

Leith, Denise, *The Politics of Power: Freeport in Indonesia* (Honolulu: University of Hawai'i Press, 2003).

Lev, Daniel S., *The Transition to Guided Democracy: Indonesian Politics, 1957–1959* (Ithaca, NY: Cornell Modern Indonesia Project Monograph Series, 1966).

Liem, André, 'Perjuangan bersenjata PKI di Blitar Selatan dan Operasi Trisula', in John Roosa, Ayu Ratih and Hilmar Farid (eds.), *Tahun yang tak Pernah*

Berakhir: Memahami Pengalaman Korban 65, Esai-esai Sejarah (Jakarta: Lembaga Studi dan Advokasi Masyarakat and Tim Relawan untuk Kemanusiaan, Institut Sejarah Sosial Indonesia, 2004), pp. 163–200.

Lindblad, J. Thomas, *Between Dayak and Dutch: the Economic History of Southeast Kalimantan, 1880–1942* (Dordrecht: Foris, 1988).

'The contribution of foreign trade to colonial state formation in Indonesia, 1900–1930', in Cribb (ed.), *The Late Colonial State in Indonesia*, pp. 93–115.

Lindsay, Jennifer, *Klasik, Kitsch, Kontemporer: Sebuah Studi tentang Seni Pertunjukan Jawa*, trans. Nin Bakdi Sumanto (Yogyakarta: Gadah Mada University Press, 1991).

'Kayam's *Kedaulatan Rakyat* column and New Order talking', *RIMA* 37, 2 (2003), 11–26.

Lloyd, Grayson and Smith, Shannon (eds.), *Indonesia Today: Challenges of History* (Singapore: Institute of Southeast Asian Studies, Indonesia Assessment Series, Research School of Pacific and Asian Studies, Australian National University, 2001).

Locher-Scholten, Elsbeth, *Ethiek in Fragmenten: Vijf Studies over Koliniaal Denken en Doen van Nederlanders in de Indonesische Archipel 1877–1942* (Utrecht: HES, 1981).

'Dutch expansion in the Indonesian archipelago around 1900 and the imperialism debate', *Journal of Southeast Asian Studies* 25, 1 (March 1994), 91–112.

'After the "distant war": Dutch public memory of the Second World War in Asia', in Raben (ed.), *Representing the Japanese Occupation of Indonesia*, pp. 55–70.

Women and the Colonial State: Essays on Gender and Modernity in the Netherlands Indies 1900–1942 (Amsterdam: Amsterdam University Press, 2000).

'State violence and the police in colonial Indonesia', in Colombijn and Lindblad (eds.), *Roots of Violence in Indonesia*, pp. 81–104.

Sumatran Sultanate and Colonial State: Jambi and the Rise of Dutch Imperialism, 1830–1907 (Ithaca, NY: Cornell University Southeast Asia Program, 2003).

Locher-Scholten, Elsbeth and Niehof, A. (eds.), *Indonesian Women in Focus* (Dordrecht: KITLV, 1987).

Lont, Hotze and White, Ben, 'Critical review of crisis studies, 1998–2002: debates on poverty, employment and solidarity in Indonesia', in Schulte Nordholt and Asnan (eds.), *Indonesia in Transition*, pp. 125–60.

Lubis, Mochtar, *Jalan Tak Ada Ujung* (Jakarta: Yayasan Obor Indonesia, 2002 [originally published 1952]).

Sendja di Djakarta, trans. Claire Holt as *Twilight in Djakarta* (New York: Vanguard Press, 1963).

Lucas, Anton, *One Soul, One Struggle: Region and Revolution in Indonesia* (St Leonards: Allen & Unwin, Asian Studies Association of Australia Publications 19, 1991).

'Images of the Indonesian woman during the Japanese occupation 1942–45', in Taylor (ed.), *Women Creating Indonesia*, pp. 52–90.

Lucas, Anton (ed.), *Local Opposition and Underground Resistance to the Japanese in Java, 1942–1945* (Clatyon, Vic.: Monash Papers on Southeast Asia 13, 1986).

Lulofs[-Székely], Madelon H., *Rubber*, trans. G. J. Renier and Irene Clephane (Singapore: Oxford University Press, 1982, orig. 1931).

Coolie, trans. G. J. Renier and Irene Clephane (Singapore: Oxford University Press, 1982, orig. 1932).

Luyendijk-Elshout, A. M. *et al.* (eds.), *Dutch Medicine in the Malay Archipelago 1816–1942: Articles Presented at a Symposium held in Honour of Prof. Dr. D. de Moulin* (Amsterdam: Rudopi, 1989).

McDonald, Hamish, *Suharto's Indonesia* (Melbourne: Pan, 1980).

McGregor, Katharine E., 'Commemoration of 1 October, *Hari Kesaktian Pancasila*: a post-mortem analysis?', *Asian Studies Review* 26, 1 (March 2002), 39–72.

McKinnon, Susan, *From a Shattered Sun: Hierarchy, Gender and Alliance in the Tanimbar Islands* (Madison: University of Wisconsin Press, 1991).

McVey, Ruth T., 'The *wayang* controversy in Indonesian communism', in M. Hobart and R. H. Taylor (eds.), *Context, Meaning and Power in Southeast Asia* (Ithaca, NY: Cornell University Southeast Asia Publications, 1986), pp. 21–53.

'Teaching modernity: the PKI as an educational institution', *Indonesia* 50 (Oct. 1990), 5–27.

Maier, H. M. J., 'From heteroglossia to polyglossia: the creation of Malay and Dutch in the Indies', *Indonesia* 56 (Oct. 1993), 37–65.

'Written in the prison's light: the *Hikajat Kadiroen* by Semaoen' (trans. Ernst van Lennep), *RIMA* 30 (1996), 1–18.

Maksum, Agus Sunyoto and Zainuddin, A. *(Tim Penyusun Jawa Pos), Lubang-Lubang Pembantaian: Petualangan PKI di Madiun* (Jakarta: Grafiti, 1990).

Mangunwijaya, Y. B., *Durga Umayi* (Jakarta: Grafiti, 1991), trans. Ward Keeler as *Durga/Umayi: a Novel* (Seattle: University of Washington Press, 2004).

Marco Kartodikromo, Mas [attribution], *Three Early Indonesian Short Stories* (trans. and ed. Paul Tickell) (Clayton, Vic.: Monash University Centre of Southeast Asian Studies, 1981).

Marianto, M. Dwi, 'Slot in the box: options and perspectives on the subject of *Pemilu* through art', *RIMA* 31, 1 (1997), 213–24.

Surealisme Yogyakarta (Yogyakarta: Merapi, 2001).

Marsidik [?], *Buku Kenangan 1950–1958* (n.p.: Pusat Pendidikan Peralatan Angkatan Darat, n.d.).

May, Brian, *The Indonesian Tragedy* (London: Routledge, 1978).

May, Ron and O'Malley, William J. (eds.), *Observing Change in Asia: Essays in Honour of J. A. C. Mackie* (Bathurst: Crawfurd House, 1989).

Melati, Sintha, 'In the service of the underground: the struggle against the Japanese in Java' (trans. and annot. David Bouchier), in Lucas (ed.), *Local Opposition and Underground Resistance*, pp. 123–264.

Memori Serah Jabatan 1921–1930 (Jawa Tengah) (Jakarta: Arsip Nasional Republik Indonesia, 1977).

Miles, Douglas, *Cutlass and Crescent Moon: a Case Study in Social and Political Change in Outer Indonesia* (University of Sydney: Centre for Asian Studies, 1976).

Mitchell, David, 'Communists, mystics and Sukarnoism', *Dissent* 22 (Autumn 1968), 28–32.

Moeis, Abdoel, *Salah Asuhan* (Djakarta: Balai Pustaka, Perpustakaan Perguruan Kem. P. P. dan K., 1956 [originally published 1928]).

Mortimer, Rex, *Indonesian Communism under Sukarno* (Ithaca, NY: Cornell University Press, 1974).

Mrázek, Rudolf, *Engineers of Happy Land: Technology and Nationalism in a Colony* (Princeton: Princeton University Press, 2002).

Nakamura, Mitsuo, *The Crescent Arises over the Banyan Tree: a Study of the Muhamadijah Movement in a Central Javanese Town* (Yogyakarta: Gajah Mada University Press, 1993).

Nasution, Abdul Haris, *Sekitar Perang Kemerdekaan Indonesia*, 11 vols. (Bandung: Angkasa, 1977–9).

Nederlandsch-Indië, *Uitkomsten der in de Maand November 1920 Gehouden Volkstelling*, 2 vols. (Batavia: Buygrok, 1922).

Netherland Government Information Bureau, *A Decade of Japanese Underground Activities in the Netherland East Indies* (London: His Majesty's Stationery Office, 1942).

Niel, Robert van, *The Emergence of the Modern Indonesian Elite* (The Hague: Van Hoeve, 1970).

Numbers of POWS and Civilian Internees (www.beckett73.freeserve.co.uk/baker/prisoners.htm) (accessed 04/06/04).

O'Malley, W. J., 'Second thoughts on Indonesian nationalism', in J. J. Fox *et al.* (eds.), *Indonesia: Australian Perspectives* (Canberra: ANU Press, 1980), pp. 601–13.

'The Great Depression', in Wild and Carey (eds.), *Born in Fire*, pp. 66–71.

'Variations on a theme: socio-economic developments in four central Javanese regencies', in May and O'Malley (eds.), *Observing Changes in Asia*, pp. 127–39.

Oey Hong Lee (ed.), *Indonesia after the 1971 Elections* (Hull Monographs on South-east Asia 5, London: Oxford University Press, 1974).

Onghokham, 'The inscrutable and the paranoid: an investigation into the sources of the Brotodiningrat Affair', in Ruth T. McVey (ed.), *Southeast Asian Transitions: Approaches through Social History* (New Haven: Yale University Press, 1978), pp. 112–57.

'A pillar of Indonesia's New Order', *The Australian*, 01/05/96.

Padmodiwirio, Soehario, *Memoar Hario Kecik*, 2 vols. (Jakarta: Obor, 1996 and 2001).

Parker, Lynette, 'The creation of Indonesian citizens in Balinese primary schools', *RIMA* 26, 1 (1992), 42–70.

Peacock, James, *Rites of Modernization: Symbolic and Social Aspects of Indonesian Proletarian Drama* (Chicago: Chicago University Press, 1968).

Pemberton, John, *On the Subject of Java* (Ithaca, NY: Cornell University Press, 1994).

Penders, C. L. M., *Indonesia: Selected Documents on Colonialism and Nationalism 1830–1942* (St Lucia, Queensland: University of Queensland Press, 1977).

Pendit, Nyoman S., *Bali Berjuang* (2nd edn, Jakarta: Gunung Agung, 1979 [original edn 1954]).

Picard, Michel, *Bali: Cultural Tourism and Touristic Culture* (Singapore: Archipelago Press, 1996).

Piper, Suzan and Jabo, Sawung, 'Indonesian music from the 50s to the 80s', *Prisma*, 43 (March 1987), 24–37.

Poesponegoro, Marwati Djoened and Notosusanto, Nugroho, *Sejarah Nasional Indonesia*, vol. VI (Jakarta: Balia Pustaka/Departemen Pendidikan dan Kebudayaan, 1984).

Poeze, Harry A., 'Early Indonesian emancipation: Abdul Rivai, Van Heutsz and the *Bintang Hindia*', *BKI* 145, 1 (1989), 87–106.

'Political intelligence in the Netherlands Indies', in Cribb (ed.), *The Late Colonial State in Indonesia*, pp. 229–45.

Polomka, Peter, *Indonesia since Sukarno* (Harmondsworth: Penguin, 1971).

Post, Peter, 'Japan and the integration of the Netherlands East Indies into the world economy, 1868–1942', *RIMA* 27 Special Edition: Island Southeast Asia and the World Economy (Winter/Summer 1993), 134–65.

'The Kwik Hoo Tong trading society of Semarang, Java: a Chinese business network in late colonial Java', *Journal of Southeast Asian Studies* 33, 2 (2002), 279–96.

Pramoedya Ananta Toer, 'Blora' (trans. Harold Merrill), *Indonesia* 53 (April 1992), 51–64.

'Dendam', trans., by B. R. O'G. Anderson as 'Revenge' in Becker (ed.), *Writing on the Tongue*, pp. 15–34.

'Djakarta', *Almanak Seni* 1957 reproduced on (www.radix.net/~bardsley/prampage.html, accessed 27/01/04).

'It's not an all night fair' (trans. William Watson), *Indonesia* 15 (1973), 21–80.

'17 August Oration', dibacakan dalam acara 'Orasi Kebudayaan 2002' di Kafe SALSA, Jakarta, 20 August 2002.

'The vanquished' (trans. H. Aveling), in *A Heap of Ashes*, pp. 74–106 (St. Lucia: University of Queensland Press, 1975).

Anak Semua Bangsa (Jakarta: Hasta Mitra, 1980), trans. M. Lane as *Child of All Nations* (Ringwood, Vic.: Penguin, 1984).

Bumi Manusia (Jakarta: Hasta Mitra, 1980), trans. M. Lane as *This Earth of Mankind* (Ringwood, Vic.: Penguin, 1981).

Di Tepi Kali Bekasi (Jakarta: Lentera Dipantara, 2003, original edn, Jakarta: Gapura, 1951).

Jejak Langkah (Jakarta: Hasta Mitra, 1985), trans. M. Lane as *Footsteps* (Ringwood, Vic.: Penguin, 1990).

Korupsi (Jakarta: Hasta Mitra, 2002, original edn, Bukittinggi-Jakarta: Nusantara, 1954).

Mereka Yang Dilumpuhkan (Jakarta: Hasta Mitra, 1995, rev. edn of original 2 vols., Jakarta: Balai Pustaka, 1951).

The Mute's Soliloquy (trans. Willem Samuels) (New York: Penguin, 1998).

Nyanyi Sunyi Seorang Bisu, 2 vols. (Jakarta: Lentera, 1995 and 1997).

Rumah Kaca (Jakarta: Hasta Mirta, 1988), trans. M. Lane as *House of Glass* (Ringwood, Vic.: Penguin, 1992).

Sang Pemula, Disertai Karya-Karya Non-Fiksi (Jurnalistik) dan Fiksa (Cerpen/ Novel) R. M. Tirto Adhi Soerjo (Jakarta: Lentera Dipantara, 2003, orig. edn, Jakarta: Hasta Mitra, 1985).

Tales from Djakarta: Caricatures of Circumstances and their Human Beings, (trans. the Nusantara Translation Group) (Jakarta/Singapore: Equinox, 2000).

Pramoedya Ananta Toer, Koesalah Soebagyo Toer and Ediati Kamil, *Kronik Revolusi Indonesia* (Jakarta: Kepustakaan Populer Gramedia, vol. I (1945); vol. II (1946) 1999; vol. III (1947); vol. IV (1948) 2003).

Pratiko, Fadjar, *Gerakan Rakyat Kelaparan: Gagalnya Politik Radikalisasi Petani* (Yogyakarta: Media Pressindo, 2000).

Purwanto, Bambang, 'From dusun to the market: native rubber cultivation in Southern Sumatra, 1890–1940', PhD thesis, School of Oriental and African Studies, University of London (1992).

Raben, Remco (ed.), *Representing the Japanese Occupation of Indonesia: Personal Testimonies and Public Images in Indonesian, Japan and the Netherlands* (Zwolle/Amsterdam: Waanders/Netherlands Institute for War Documentation, 1999).

Rahardjo Djarot, Slamet (director) and Djarot, Eros (producer), *Langitku, Rumahku* (Jakarta: Ekapraya Films, 1989).

Ramstedt, Martin, 'Introduction: negotiating identities – Indonesian "Hindus" between local, national, and global interests', in Martin Ramstedt (ed.), *Hinduism in Indonesia: a Minority Religion between Local, National, and Global Interests* (London: RoutledgeCurzon, 2004), pp. 1–34.

Ray, David and Goodpaster, Gary, 'Indonesian decentralization: local autonomy, trade barriers and discrimination', in Kingsbury and Aveling (eds.), *Autonomy and Disintegration in Indonesia*, pp. 75–95.

Reeve, David, *Golkar of Indonesia: an Alternative to the Party System* (Kuala Lumpur: Oxford University Press, 1985).

Reid, Anthony J. S., *The Contest for North Sumatra: Atjeh, The Netherlands and Britain 1858–1898* (Kuala Lumpur: Oxford University Press, 1969).

Indonesian National Revolution (Hawthorn, Vic.: Longman, 1974).

'The nationalist quest for an Indonesian past', in Reid and Marr (eds.), *Perceptions of the Past in Southeast Asia*, pp. 281–98.

'Indonesia: revolution without socialism', in Robin Jeffrey (ed.), *Asia: the Winning of Independence* (London: Macmillan, 1981), pp. 107–57.

Reid, Anthony J. S. and Marr, David (eds.), *Perceptions of the Past in Southeast Asia* (Singapore: Heinemann, 1979).

Reid, Anthony J. S. and Oki Akura (eds.), *The Japanese Experience in Indonesia: Selected Memoirs of 1942–1945* (Athens, OH: Ohio University Monographs, 1986).

Ricklefs, M. C., *A History of Modern Indonesia* (London: Macmillan, 1981, 2nd edn 1993, 3rd edn 2001).

Robinson, Geoffrey, *The Dark Side of Paradise: Political Violence in Bali* (Ithaca, NY: Cornell University Press, 1995).

Robinson, Kathryn, 'Living in the hutan: jungle village life under the Darul Islam', *RIMA* 17 (1983), 208–29.

Stepchildren of Progress: the Political Economy of Development in an Indonesian Mining Town (Albany, NY: State University of New York Press, 1986).

Robison, Richard, *Indonesia: the Rise of Capital* (Sydney: Allen & Unwin, 1986).

Robison, Richard and Hadiz, Vedi R., *Reorganising Power in Indonesia: the Politics of Oligarchy in an Age of Markets* (London: RoutledgeCurzon, 2004).

Rodgers, Susan (ed. and trans.), *Telling Lives, Telling History: Autobiography and Historical Imagination in Modern Indonesia* (Berkeley: University of California Press, 1995).

Ronggawarsita, Raden Ngabehi, *Serat Kala Tidha/A Time of Darkness* (trans. J. Joseph Errington) in Becker (ed.), *Writing on the Tongue*, pp. 107–10.

Roosa, John, Farid, Hilma and Ratih, Ayu, *Tahun Yang Tak Pernah Berakhir: Memahami Pengalaman Korban 65: Esai-esai Sejarah Lisan* (Jakarta: Lembaga Studi dan Advokasi Masyarakat, 2004).

Rubinstein, Raechelle and Connor, Linda (eds.), *Staying Local in the Global Village: Bali in the Twentieth Century* (Honolulu: University of Hawai'i Press, 1999).

Rush, James R., *Opium to Java: Revenue Farming and Chinese Enterprise in Colonial Indonesia, 1860–1910* (Ithaca, NY: Cornell University Press, 1990).

Rutherford, Danilyn, *Raiding the Land of the Foreigners: the Limits of the Nation on an Indonesian Frontier* (Princeton: Princeton University Press, 2003).

Said, Salim, *Shadows on the Silver Screen: a Social History of Indonesian Film* (Jakarta: Lontar Foundation, 1991).

Sartono Kartodirdjo, *Protest Movements in Rural Java: a Study of Agrarian Unrest in the Nineteenth and Early Twentieth Century* (Singapore: Oxford University Press, 1973).

Modern Indonesia: Tradition and Transformation (Yogyakarta: Gadjah Mada University Press, 1984).

Sato, Shigeru, *War, Nationalism and Peasants: Java under the Japanese Occupation, 1942–1945* (St. Leonards, NSW: Allen & Unwin, Asian Studies Association of Australia Publications Series 26, 1994).

Schenkhuizen, Marguérite, *Memoirs of an Indo Woman: Twentieth Century Life in the East Indies and Abroad*, ed. and trans. Lizelot Stout van Balgooy (Athens, OH: Ohio University Center for International Studies, 1993).

Scherer, Savitri Prastiti, 'From culture to politics: the writings of Pramoedya A. Toer, 1950–1965', PhD thesis, Australian National University (1981).

Keselarasan dan Kejanggalan: Pemikiran-Pemikiran Priyayi Nasionalis Jawa awal Abad XX (Jakarta: Penerbit Sinar Harapan, 1985).

Schiller, Jim, *Developing Jepara in New Order Indonesia* (Clayton, Vic.: Monash Asia Institute, 1996).

Schiller, Jim and Martin-Schiller, Barbara (eds.), *Imagining Indonesia: Cultural Politics and Political Culture* (Athens, OH: Ohio University Center for International Studies Monographs in International Studies Southeast Asian Series, 97, 1997).

Schreiner, Klaus, 'The making of national heroes: Guided Democracy to New Order, 1959–1992', in Schulte Nordholt (ed.), *Outward Appearances*, pp. 259–90.

'"National ancestors": the ritual construction of nationhood', in Henri Chambert-Loir and A. J. S. Reid (eds.), *The Potent Dead: Ancestors, Saints and Heroes in Contemporary Indonesia* (Crows Nest, NSW: Asian Studies Association of Australia in association with Allen & Unwin, 2002), pp. 183–204.

Schulte Nordholt, Henk (ed.), *Outward Appearances: Dressing State and Society in Indonesia* (Leiden: KITLV, 1997).

Schulte Nordholt, Henk and Abdullah, Irwan (eds.), *Indonesia in Search of Transition* (Yogyakarta: Pustaka Pelajar, 2002).

Schulte Nordholt, Henk and Asnan, Gusti (eds.), *Indonesia in Transition: Work in Progress* (Yogyakarta: Pustaka Pelajar, 2003).

Semaoen, 'An early account of the independence movement', trans. Ruth McVey, *Indonesia* 1 (April 1966), 46–75.

Hikajat Kadiroen (Semarang: Kantoor PKI, 1922?), trans. Jan Lingard, Marcus Susanto, Ian Campbell and Adrian Vickers as 'The story of Kadiroen', *RIMA* 30 (1996), 19–139.

Sen, Krishna, *Indonesian Cinema: Framing the New Order* (London and New Jersey: Zed, 2004).

Sen, Krishna (ed.), *Histories and Stories: Cinema in New Order Indonesia* (Clayton, Vic.: Monash University Centre of Southeast Asian Studies, 1988).

Shimizu Hiroshi, 'Rise and fall of the *Karayuki-san* in the Netherlands Indies from the late nineteenth century to the 1930s', *RIMA* 26, 2 (Summer 1992), 44–62.

Shiraishi, Takashi, *An Age in Motion: Popular Radicalism in Java, 1912–1926* (Ithaca: Cornell University Press, 1990).

'A new regime of order: the origins of modern surveillance politics in Indonesia', in James T. Siegel and Audrey R. Kahin (eds.), *Southeast Asia over Three Generations: Essays Presented to Benedict R. O'G. Anderson* (Ithaca, NY: Cornell Southeast Asia Program, 2003), pp. 47–74.

Siahaan, Hotman M. *et al.*, *Pers yang Gamang: Sudi Perberitaan Jajak Pendapat Timor Timor* (Surabaya: Lembaga Studi Perubahan Social, 2001).

Siegel, James T., *Fetish, Recognition, Revolution* (Princeton: Princeton University Press, 1997).

A New Criminal Type in Jakarta: Counter-Revolution Today (Durham and London: Duke University Press, 1998).

Sneddon, James, *The Indonesian Language: Its History and Role in Modern Society* (Sydney: University of New South Wales Press, 2003).

Soedarsono, *Wayang Wong: the State Ritual Dance Drama in the Court of Yogyakarta* (Yogyakarta: Gadjah Mada University Press, 1984).

Soemitro, *Pangkopkamtib Jenderal Soemitro dan Peristiwa 15 Januaryi '74*, as told to Heru Cahyono (Jakarta: Sinar Harapan, 1998).

Southwood, Julia and Flanagan, Patrick, *Indonesia: Law, Propaganda and Terror* (London: Zed, 1983).

Spyer, Patricia, *The Memory of Trade: Modernity's Entanglements on an Eastern Indonesian Island* (Durham and London: Duke University Press, 2000).

'Fire without smoke and other phantoms of Ambon's violence: media effects, agency, and the work of imagination', *Indonesia* 74 (October 2002), 21–36.

Stange, Paul, 'The Sumarah movement in Javanese mysticism', PhD thesis, University of Wisconsin, Madison (1980).

'"Legitimate" mysticism in Indonesia', RIMA 20, 2 (1986), 76–117.

Steedly, Mary Margaret, *Hanging without a Rope: Narrative Experience in Colonial and Postcolonial Karoland* (Princeton: Princeton University Press, 1993).

Steijlen, Fridus (compiler), *Memories of 'The East': Abstracts of the Dutch Interviews about the Netherlands East Indies, Indonesia and New Guinea (1930–1962) in the Oral History Project Collection* (Leiden: KITLV Press, 2002).

Stoler, Ann Laura, *Capitalism and Confrontation in Sumatra's Plantation Belt, 1870–1979* (New Haven: Yale University Press, 1985).

Carnal Knowledge and Imperial Power: Race and the Intimate in Colonial Rule (Berkeley: University of California Press, 2002).

Sukarno, *Lahirnja Pantja-Sila: Bung Karno Menggemblèng Dasar-Dasar Negara*, 2nd edn (Yogyakarta: Goentoer, 1949).

Speech at the opening of the Bandung conference, 18 April 1955 Modern history sourcebook (www.fordham.edu/halsall/mod/1955sukarno-bandong.html), accessed 05/19/2004.

An Autobiography; as told to Cindy Adams (Indianapolis: Bobbs-Merrill, 1965).

Dibawah Bendera Revolusi, 2 vols. (2nd edn, Djakarta: Panitia Penerbit, 1965).

Nationalism, Islam and Marxism, trans. Karel H. Warouw and Peter D. Weldon; with an introduction by Ruth T. McVey (Ithaca, NY: Cornell University Southeast Asia Program, 1969).

Sulistyo, Bambang, *Pemogokan Buruh: Sebuah Kajian Sejarah* (Yogyakarta: Tiara Wacana, 1995).

Sulistyo, Hermawan, *Palu Arit di Ladang Tebu: Sejarah Pembantaian Massal yang Terlupakan* (Jakarta: Gramedia, 2000).

Sutherland, Heather, *The Making of a Bureaucratic Elite: the Colonial Transformation of the Javanese Priyayi* (Singapore: Heinemann/Asian Studies Association of Australia, Southeast Asia Publications 2, 1979).

Sutjaja, Gusti Made, 'Balinese transmigrants in Lampung: language change and tradition', in A. Vickers (ed.), *Being Modern in Bali: Image and Change* (New Haven: Yale Southeast Asian Studies Monograph 43, 1996), pp. 212–22.

Sweeney, Amin, *A Full Hearing: Orality and Literacy in the Malay World* (Berkeley: University of California Press, 1987).

Swift, Elizabeth Anne, *The Road to Madiun: the Indonesian Communist Uprising of 1948* (Ithaca, NY: Cornell Southeast Asia Program, 1989).

Syukur, Abdul, *Gerakan Usroh di Indonesia: Peristiwa Lampung 1989* (Yogyakarta: Ombak, 2003).

Tan Malaka, *From Jail to Jail*, ed., trans. and introd. Helen Jarvis, 3 vols. (Athens, OH: Ohio University Center for International Studies, 1991).

Tanaka, Yuki, *Hidden Horrors: Japanese War Crimes in World War II* (Boulder: Westview Press, 1998).

TAPOL, *Indonesia: Muslims on Trial* (London: TAPOL, 1987).

Tarnutzer, Andreas, *Kota Adat Denpasar (Bali). Stadtentwicklung, Staatliches Handeln und Endogene Institutionen* (Zürich: Geographisches Institut Vol. 12, 1993).

Taylor, Jean Gelman (ed.), *Women Creating Indonesia: the First Fifty Years* (Clayton, Vic.: Monash Asia Institute, 1997).

Termorshuizen, Gerard, 'In memoriam Rob Nieuwenhuys 30 Juni 1908–7 November 1999', *BKI* 158, 2 (2002), 147–67.

Tirto Adhi Soerjo, 'The story of Nyai Ratna', trans. Elizabeth Riharti, Joost Coté and Markus Soema, *RIMA* 32, 2 (Summer 1998), 45–95.

Touwen-Bouwsma, Elly, 'The Indonesian nationalists and the Japanese "liberation" of Indonesia: visions and reactions (the Japanese occupation in Southeast Asia)', *Journal of Southeast Asian Studies* 27, 1 (March 1996), 18–32.

Tsing, Anna Lowenhaupt, *In the Realm of the Diamond Queen: Marginality in an Out-of-the-Way Place* (Princeton: Princeton University Press, 1993).

Tudjuh Bahan Pokok Indoktrinasi, dengan Tambahan Re-So-Pim, Tahun Kemenangan, Genta Suara Revolusi Indonesia (Surabaya: Pertjetakan Negara d/h Pers Nasional, n.d.).

Turner, Michele, *Telling East Timor: Personal Testimonies 1942–1992* (Kensington, NSW: University of New South Wales Press, 1992).

Utami, Ayu, *Saman* (Jakarta: Kalam/Kepustakaan Populair Gramedia, 1998).

Utami, Ayu *et al.*, *Bredel 1994: Kumpulan Tulisan tentang Pembredelan Tempo, Detik, Editor* (Jakarta: Aliansi Jurnalis Independen, 1994).

Velthoen, Esther, 'Mapping Sulawesi in the 1950s', in Schulte Nordholt and Asnan (eds.), *Indonesia in Transition*, pp. 103–23.

Vickers Adrian, and Darma Putra, I Nyoman with Ford, Michele (eds.), *To Change Bali: Essays in Honour of I Gusti Ngurah Bagus* (Denpasar: Bali Post, 2000).

Volkman, Toby Alice, *Feasts of Honour: Ritual and Change in the Toraja Highlands* (Urbana: University of Illinois Press, Illinois Studies in Anthropology 16, 1985).

Wandelt, Ingo, 'The New Order interpretation of the Pancasila: its development and structure as reflected in "Pendidikan Moral Pancasila" and "Penataran P-4"', in Wolfgang Marshall (ed.), *Texts from the Islands: Oral and Written Traditions of Indonesia and the Malay World* (Berne: University of Berne, 1994), pp. 317–28.

Ward, Ken, *The 1971 Elections in Indonesia: an East Javanese Case Study* (Clayton, Vic.: Monash Papers on Southeast Asia no. 2, 1974).

Warren, Carol, *Adat and Dinas: Balinese Communities in the Indonesian State* (Kuala Lumpur: Oxford University Press, 1994).

Watson, C. W., 'Pramoedya Ananta Toer's short stories: an anti-poststructuralist account', in C. D. Grijns and S. O. Robson (eds.), *Cultural Contact and Textual Interpretation: Papers from the Fourth European Colloquium on Malay and Indonesian Studies held in Leiden in 1983* (Dordrecht: Foris, 1986), pp. 233–46.

Wells, Jennifer, *Bre-X: the Inside Story of the World's Biggest Mining Scam* (London: Orion Business, 1998).

Wertheim, W. F., *Indonesian Society in Transition* (The Hague and Bandung: Van Hoeve, 1959).

'Indonesian Moslems under Sukarno and Suharto: majority with a minority mentality', in Christine Doran (ed.), *Indonesian Politics: a Reader* (Townsville: Centre for South-east Asian Politics, James Cook University of North Queensland, 1987), pp. 111–32.

'Netherlands–Indian colonial racism and Dutch home racism', in Jan Breman (ed.), *Imperial Monkey Business: Racial Supremacy in Social Darwinist Theory and Colonial Practice* (Amsterdam: VU University Press, 1990), pp. 71–88.

'Conditions on sugar estates in colonial Java: comparisons with Deli', *Journal of Southeast Asian Studies* 24, 2 (1993), 268–79.

Widodo, Amrih, 'Local politics: the view from Blora, Central Java', in Aspinall and Fealy (eds.), *Local Power and Politics*, pp. 179–93.

Wieringa, Saskia, *Sexual Politics in Indonesia* (Basingstoke: Palgrave Macmillan, 2002).

Wijaya, I Nyoman, '1950s lifestyles in Denpasar through the eyes of short story writers', in Vickers and Darma Putra (eds.), *To Change Bali*, pp. 113–34.

Wild, Colin and Carey, Peter (eds.), *Born in Fire: the Indonesian Struggle for Independence* (Athens, OH: Ohio University Press, 1986).

Wilkinson, John, 'Electioneering in Tanahbelig: aspects of social change in an isolated Balinese community', *RIMA* 24 (1991), 39–54.

Wright, Astri, *Soul, Spirit and Mountain: Preoccupations of Contemporary Indonesian Painters* (Kuala Lumpur: Oxford University Press, 1994).

Yampolsky, Philip, 'Forces for change in the regional performing arts of Indonesia', *BKI* 151, 4 (1995), 700–25.

Yuliarti, Dewi, *Semaoen: Pers Bumiputera dan Radikalisasi Sarekat Islam Semarang* (Semarang: Bendera, 2000).

Zarkasyi, K. H. Imam, 'Le *pondok pesantren* en Indonésie', *Archipel* 30 (1985), 163–74.

Zoete, Beryl de and Spies, Walter, *Dance and Drama in Bali* (London: Faber and Faber, 1938; repr. Kuala Lumpur: Oxford University Press, 1973).

Zurbuchen, Mary, 'Images of culture and national development in Indonesia: the *Cockroach Opera*', *Asian Theatre Journal* 7, 2 (Fall 1990), 127–49.

NEWSPAPERS, MAGAZINES AND ONLINE JOURNALS

AsiaWeek
The Australian
Bali Post (formerly *Suara Indonesia, Suara Rakjat* and *Suluh Marhaen*)
Bhakti
Bintang Timur
Bisnis.com
Damai
Detik
Duta Masjarakat
Forum Keadilan
Harian Rakjat
Inside Indonesia
Intisari
The Jakarta Post
Kompas
Latitudes
New Straits Times
Pikiran Rakjat
Sinar Harapan
The Star Online
Suara Hidayatullah
Suara Independen
Suara Merdeka
Sydney Morning Herald
Time Magazine
Wall Street Journal

Index